INJUSTICE

Clive Stafford Smith is a lawyer specialising in defending people accused of the most serious crimes, and is the founder and Director of UK legal charity Reprieve. Based in the US for twenty-six years, he now works from the UK where he continues to defend prisoners on Death Row, and challenges the continued incarceration of those held in secret prisons around the world. To date he has secured the release of 65 prisoners from Guantánamo Bay and still acts for fifteen more. His book *Bad Men* (shortlisted for the 2008 Orwell Prize) described this campaign. Alongside many other awards, in 2000 he received an OBE for 'humanitarian services'.

www.reprieve.org.uk

D1111247

ALSO BY CLIVE STAFFORD SMITH

Bad Men

CLIVE STAFFORD SMITH

Injustice

Life and Death in the
Courtrooms of America

VINTAGE BOOKS
London

Published by Vintage 2013

2 4 6 8 10 9 7 5 3 1

Copyright © Clive Stafford Smith 2013

Clive Stafford Smith has asserted his right under the
Copyright, Designs and Patents Act 1988 to be identified as the
author of this work.

First published in Great Britain by Harvill Secker in 2012

Vintage
Random House, 20 Vauxhall Bridge Road,
London SW1V 2SA

www.vintage-classics.info

Addresses for companies within The Random House Group
Limited can be found at: www.randomhouse.co.uk/offices.htm

The Random House Group Limited Reg. No. 954009

A CIP catalogue record for this book
is available from the British Library

ISBN 9780099572190

The Random House Group Limited supports the Forest
Stewardship Council® (FSC®), the leading international
forest-certification organisation. Our books carrying the FSC
label are printed on FSC®-certified paper. FSC is the only
forest-certification scheme supported by the leading
environmental organisations, including Greenpeace.
Our paper procurement policy can be found at
www.randomhouse.co.uk/environment

Printed and bound by CPI Group (UK) Ltd, Croydon, CR0 4YY

This book is dedicated to Marita Maharaj. Marita's own dedication to her husband, through more than a quarter century of his incarceration, remains the inspiration to us all.

The concept of justice as a lady with a blindfold and a pair of scales someone else may lay a decisive finger on without her noticing has often struck me as questionable. It presupposes a readiness in those among whom she dispenses her gifts to keep their hands to themselves. You must agree that would be a perfect world, and in such a world she would be a redundant figure. Keep the figure, by all means, as a symbol of what might be achieved. Keep the illusion of detachment. Cultivate its manner. But admit it cannot be a controlling force without compromising itself.

Paul Scott, *The Day of the Scorpion* (1973)

Our justice system makes two promises to its citizens: a fundamentally fair trial and an accurate result. If either of those two promises is not met, the criminal justice system itself falls into disrepute.

Pascal Calogero, former Chief Justice,
Louisiana Supreme Court (2012)

Contents

1

The Case

The courtroom is modern, confined and ugly. Faux-oak panelling along the walls, synthetic ceiling tiles. Judge Howard Gross nods from his elevated bench. The prosecutor is a clean-cut all-American, close-cropped dark hair, long thin face, sincerely sincere. He walks towards the podium, and towards the jury. The twelve men and women are sitting attentively in their places.

'May it please the court,' he begins. 'Counsel for the defence.' He nods at Eric Hendon, the portly African American lawyer representing the man on trial. 'And ladies and gentlemen of the jury.' He turns back towards the twelve who will decide the case. 'This case is about hate. This case is about vengeance of the highest order. This case is about stalking and lying in wait to murder a victim. This case is about the manipulation of witnesses and the fabrication of an alibi.

'The victims in this case are Derrick Moo Young, a Jamaican businessman, father of four, who died in a hail of gunfire in Room 1215 at the DuPont Plaza Hotel in downtown Miami, on October 16th, 1986. And his son, his eldest son Duane Moo Young, twenty-three years old, was executed to eliminate him as a witness, by the defendant, Krishna Maharaj.' He turns and points at the man sitting beside Hendon. Krishna Maharaj is in his forties, heavyset himself, with thick black hair sprouting upwards from his brown face. The defendant frowns back at the prosecutor.

'Before I talk about what the evidence will reveal to you in this case, I would like to tell you about the types of evidence you will hear. You will hear from witnesses; you will hear scientific evidence regarding fingerprints, ballistics evidence, business records, and the statements that this defendant made to the police. All of that points to this defendant – nobody else – as the killer of Derrick Moo Young and Duane Moo Young.

'Well, as with all brutal, evil acts, there is a beginning. And the beginning was not on October 16th. In the beginning, Derrick Moo Young and the defendant, Krishna Maharaj, were business partners in KDM, which was a corporation that dealt primarily with export and import. They were more than business partners; they were friends. But the business broke up and the friendship came to an end in April.

'The disputes began with the break-up of the business. Suits and countersuits were filed in Broward County Circuit Court, in Fort Lauderdale, and the defendant then initiated the war that culminated in the murder of Derrick Moo Young and his eldest son, Duane.

'The war began, interestingly enough, in the newspaper known as the *Caribbean Echo*. You will hear from the editor of that newspaper, Eslee Carberry. You will hear that in April the defendant – not satisfied with the progress of his civil suit against Derrick Moo Young – paid for a newspaper article in the *Echo* exposing Derrick Moo Young as a swindler. And you will see that newspaper article.

'And Mr Carberry published that article, but refused to publish follow-up articles from Krishna Maharaj, presenting his side of the story. Because Derrick Moo Young came to Eslee Carberry and said, "Hey, there's another side to this story. Let me show you some documents concerning this guy Maharaj."

'Sure enough, starting in June of 1986, the paper began to publish … relentlessly … articles exposing Krishna Maharaj as a swindler, as a forger, as a manipulator. And things began to get very, very dirty.

'What did the defendant do? Well, the defendant offered to buy the *Caribbean Echo*, but Mr Carberry refused to sell it to him. He offered other articles against Derrick Moo Young, but Carberry refused to publish them.

'So what did Krishna Maharaj do next? He started his own newspaper and began to hire the people from the *Caribbean Echo*, lure them away with money and other promises of wealth that they would receive with his paper. And he vowed to destroy the *Caribbean Echo* and to destroy Derrick Moo Young. Well, he did hire those people away, but Eslee Carberry continued publishing his articles, exposing Krishna Maharaj as a money-launderer from Trinidad, a scamster, a fraudster.

'One of the people the defendant hired away from the *Echo* was a person by the name of Tino Geddes. Mr Tino Geddes will testify in this case. Mr Tino Geddes was taken into the defendant's confidence and shortly, when the articles from the *Echo* got intensive, Mr Geddes was recruited to assist the defendant in a plan. A plan that consumed Krishna Maharaj's every waking moment, from July to the murder … the hail of bullets at the DuPont Plaza. And that plan was the elimination, the murder, of Derrick Moo Young and Eslee Carberry, the editor of the *Caribbean Echo*.

'This hatred, which consumed his life, became an obsession and led to what I would call – and the evidence will show – almost comical attempts, that failed, to murder these people.

'The evidence will show that the defendant purchased crossbows, Chinese throwing stars, camouflage gear, weapons of various sizes and sorts, including a nine-millimetre pistol. The pistol will be very important in the case because it is a murder weapon.

'You are going to hear that this equipment was purchased by the defendant for one reason only. Mr Geddes will tell you it was purchased to murder Derrick Moo Young.

'What are the comical types of failed attempts to murder these people? Well, you are going to hear from Mr Geddes that they waited for Mr Carberry late at night on a lonely road, hoping to catch him. But, as fate would have it, they got hungry and went and got a sandwich, and they missed Mr Carberry and didn't get a chance to murder him up at West Palm Beach.

'You will hear about a Ryder Rental truck in late July. Lying in wait out on US Route 27 in camouflage gear with a crossbow, waiting to take out Derrick Moo Young when he happened along the road. They were expecting him. He never showed up. You will hear some of the most bizarre plans that came from the mind of this defendant, obsessed as he was with the murder of Derrick Moo Young.

'This is when Mr Neville Butler comes into the picture. He is a Trinidadian national who worked under the pen name of "Crossley West" at the *Caribbean Echo*. And, as with the other people at the *Echo*, the defendant lured him away from the *Echo* to work for his own newspaper, and destroy the *Echo*.

'It was a combination of several things – the defendant's promise of money, promises of a better job and, Butler himself will tell you, his own ambition, his evil greed for money, caused him to try to move away from the *Echo* to the *Caribbean Times*.

'But the defendant had one condition before Butler could work for the *Times* – one condition. And that condition, in October, was: "You've got to set up a meeting between me and Derrick Moo Young and Mr Carberry."

'Mr Butler said, "Why, you know Moo Young will never meet you under any conditions."

'He said, "Yes, that is why I need you to set it up, to have somebody used as bait to get him to this location, so I could meet you here."

'Butler says, "Why me?"

' "Well," the defendant says, "well, your name has come up as being involved in this extortion attempt down in Trinidad, and I want to clear up your name. What we are going to do is get Derrick Moo Young in there, and have him" – meaning Derrick Moo Young – "write out a confession that he has been the one extorting the money, and we may rough him up a little bit, tie him up. But nobody is going to get killed or really hurt."

'Butler – naïve Butler – agrees, and that sets off the chain of events which led to the murders, including the murder planned for months of Derrick Moo Young.

'Well, the plan takes root with Mr Butler. Butler knows two people from the Bahamas, Prince Ellis and Eddie Dames. They are unwittingly used in this case. Mr Dames is an air-traffic controller, now the manager of the airport in Nassau. And Prince Ellis, he is a caterer and runs Lucky Five Catering Service in Nassau. As a matter of fact, they had been making plans during this period of time to open a night-club, a business in Nassau, which they needed equipment for. And the defendant asked Butler if he knew anybody who could possibly lure the Moo Youngs.

' "I know these two people are coming over here, and they need restaurant things …"

'The defendant said, "Good. It is a great idea, play them up really big. The Moo Youngs will bite on that."

'Butler agrees.

'Phone calls. You will see the evidence of phone calls going between Butler and the Moo Youngs and the defendant, minutes apart, a couple of days before the murder. The Moo Youngs knew that Mr Dames was coming to Miami. Butler hooks them up, saying the Moo Youngs are big importers-exporters. Says Dames and Ellis need large amounts of restaurant equipment, and they also need music equipment.

'They arrive in Miami. Mr Dames arrives in Miami on October 15th, which is a Wednesday. Thursday is the murder, October 16th.

'What the evidence is going to show is that the defendant registered at the DuPont Plaza in Room 1215. Is he registered under the name of Krishna Maharaj? Of course not! He called himself Eddie Dames. And it is him saying this to the people at the DuPont Plaza. You will hear those people testify.

'What does he also do? He says, "Well, there is – I want a room – the penthouse suite upstairs, and it is going to be paid for in cash." That kind of thing is what happened.

'Mr Butler comes in shortly afterwards – the guy gives $110 in cash for the two days that they are going to be there. And Eddie Dames is registered at the room.

'Is this plan going to fail like every other one that has failed? Tragically, no. And that is the reason you folks are here, because Mr Carberry is alive, because they couldn't set up the meeting with Mr Carberry. But Derrick Moo Young is dead and his son, who wasn't expected to be there, just went along with his dad that day – he is dead because he was with his father.

'What happens on the 16th? Well, as planned, they all show up at the DuPont Plaza. Outside, early in the morning. Maharaj is waiting outside and Neville Butler shows up. The maid cleans the room.

'And they go up to the room, make a phone call to Mr Moo Young, confirm that the meeting is on.

'Mr Moo Young, along with his son – who is unexpected, but that doesn't phase the defendant; he doesn't even act surprised that somebody else came along, because as you will picture from all the other evidence, that has always been the game-plan – if somebody else comes along, they have to die too.

'So Butler calls the people up to the room. They come in the room expecting to meet Eddie Dames, the man who wants to import and export. Who do they find? They see him – the defendant. He comes out of the bathroom with a glove on his right hand and a nine-millimetre pistol in his right hand, and a pillow – which will be important also – in his left hand.

'He began shooting at the victim, shooting at Derrick Moo Young – taken totally by surprise by this – to show him he means business. First, he shoots him in the knee, right there in the room. In the knee-cap. Shows him that he means business. You will see pictures of the room, and you will see that the room had been rearranged by the defendant. Fingerprint evidence will also tell you that.

'Pay very close attention to that. And you will see legal pads, which were there for Derrick Moo Young to write a confession to supposedly stealing the defendant's money. And you will see two heating elements, which were used … the heating cords – they were used … they were bought the morning of the 16th by the defendant at the hotel to tie up Derrick Moo Young and anyone else who came along with him. Neville Butler … Butler … Neville Butler knew they were going to use the two cords to tie them up. As a matter of fact, Derrick and Duane Moo Young were tied up at various points during the shooting.

'Well, instead of writing a confession, Mr Moo Young bravely made an attempt to save his own life. He charges the defendant, dives, and is mortally wounded by a hail of gunfire. You will hear evidence that he was shot six times in the chest and through his body. And you will hear the testimony by the medical examiner that he didn't die immediately. And that is important, because somehow he is able to crawl while the defendant is interrogating his son concerning monies, and getting a confession. He is able to crawl and throw himself out into the hallway.

'You will hear testimony that nobody in that entire hotel heard gunfire, and that was due to a few reasons. You will hear that the hotel was very sparsely populated on October 16th. As a matter of fact, three rooms were occupied only, and during the time of the murder, nobody was there. Also, on the eleventh floor below, there was an entire reconstruction going on – remodelling. The normal noises, with hammers banging and moving furniture, that kind of stuff. Then there is the well-constructed nature of the DuPont, being that it is an older hotel and doesn't have paper-thin walls or floors. It is well built, and the noise doesn't travel through there, and nobody really heard any gunfire.

'There was no silencer used by the defendant. He told Mr Geddes about the possible attempt at the DuPont. Mr Geddes asked, "What about the gunfire? What are the people going to hear at the hotel?"

'The defendant says, "Don't worry. This hotel is well built. The walls are soundproof." And that shows you why he thought there would be no problem.

'As a matter of fact, he was right. He is right that nobody heard the gunfire. Nobody heard it. But the blood of Derrick Moo Young out in the hallway is the thing that alerted the people that something was going on.

'You will hear testimony from the security people and the house-people of the hotel, how they responded. And somebody saw the blood, and they brought somebody else up, and they noticed that the door had a pin out, which means that somebody double-locked the door from the inside – live people. Because the only way you can double-lock that room is to have somebody that is alive inside.

'They even have a conversation with the defendant: the security guard from the outside. And he asked if everything was okay in the room. And the defendant responded that everything was okay. They went back downstairs, left the door unlocked – excuse me, unguarded. For five minutes or so. And came back up and the pin was back out – excuse me, back in – which means that they had left. They opened the door and discovered the bodies.

'In that five-minute period of time, the defendant was able to flee, along with Neville Butler.

'Before we get to that, the people who walked up there did not see a "Do Not Disturb" sign initially on the door – a typical "Do Not Disturb" sign. When they came back the second time it was there. Whose fingerprints were on the "Do Not Disturb" sign? Right there – the defendant.

'Whose blood is right next to the defendant's prints on the "Do Not Disturb" sign? The blood of Derrick Moo Young, trying to get away outside. The blood-spattered area. The scene is crucial.

'There is going to be an eyewitness, Neville Butler, who will tell you what happened in the room. But the physical evidence from the scene is also very important. And I am asking you: please pay close attention to that testimony.

'You will hear testimony about that, as I told you – of the finger-prints in places that only the killer would have left them. Listen carefully to that testimony.

'Also there will be a gun scientist's testimony, a ballistics expert, and there were nine-millimetre casings that were fired over projectiles, and only one gun was used, and the gun was never recovered. But if you listen closely to the testimony of the gun expert, as well as the other evidence in the case, it is the gun expert – he can say it was a nine-millimetre semi-automatic pistol. You will hear that the nine-millimetre pistol was sold to this defendant by another person, and you will see the person who sold it.

'As a matter of fact, you will hear testimony from a trooper that stopped the defendant for a traffic … minor traffic infractions back on July 25th, 1986. What did that trooper find on the defendant? It wasn't important then, but for this trial it is crucial that he found the nine-millimetre pistol, silver in colour. The same gun that Neville Butler says; the same gun that matches the scientific evidence; the murder weapon.

'What else did the trooper find in the car? Camouflage equipment, Chinese throwing stars, crossbows – found all of these things.

'Well, the murder happens. What happened then? The defendant flees the room, leaves his fingerprints, his left-hand fingerprints, his left – remember, the glove is on his right hand – his left-hand fingerprints in all the crucial places; some right-handed fingerprints and things when he first arrived in the room with a soda can, reading a newspaper. Fingerprints were there in over ten places; ten places that fingerprints were found. But this is crucial about the left-handed fingerprints, remember that.

'He went downstairs with Neville Butler, and they wait out in the car for three hours while medical emergency people are arriving, the bodies are found. The body of Derrick Moo Young is found – and his son Duane was taken out upstairs. Mr Butler will tell you the defendant couldn't leave any witnesses, and took Duane upstairs and shot him right in the head, murdered him.

'The bodies are found, and they waited downstairs. Mr Butler is telling the defendant that they are waiting there because they have to find out what Eddie Dames knows.

'What does Dames know? He is going to be coming back – he was told to leave by Neville Butler; he went to a music store and he doesn't come back to the hotel until one o'clock. Eddie Dames is in the dark and he was just used as the bait. But they have to wait for him.

'Waiting for him they discussed – the defendant admits to Butler the concerns that he has about the police officer who sold him the gun. You will hear from the lieutenant from the Miramar Police

Department that he sold the defendant the gun, the nine-millimetre. The defendant is concerned about that, and concerned about how to get rid of the gun. And he talked about throwing the gun in the river and doing that kind of stuff.

'Also, primarily waiting for Eddie Dames – Eddie Dames, they miss him, and he gets in and asks for messages for his room. And you can imagine the number of police that grabbed him saying, "What do you mean? Why are you asking for messages for your room, 1215?"

'He said, "That is my room, and to see if there were any messages."

' "Well, I have to talk to you at the police station."

'On his way to the police station Neville Butler sees him from the car. He was getting out of the car and he goes and speaks to Eddie Dames. One thing leads to another, and Eddie Dames and Neville Butler get away from the defendant. The defendant had told Butler, "From now on we are going to stay together. You can trust me, and I am going to promise that I am going to take care of you. I am going to buy a car for you. We have to get our stories straight."

'Butler gets away and flees from the defendant.

'Neville Butler goes to the police that afternoon and tells the police what happened in the room. He says, "By the way, Maharaj wants to meet. He wants me to meet him at the Denny's Diner by the airport." So Neville Butler went to the Denny's and talked with Detective John Buhrmaster, who is the lead homicide investigator in this case, and they go in there. Well, at Denny's, Neville Butler sees the defendant, and the defendant sees him, and Buhrmaster arrests the defendant.

'The defendant goes to the police station and agrees to talk to the police. You will hear that he had a conversation with the police. Sure, he wanted to talk about his case. And what does he tell the police? He tells the police that never has he been inside the DuPont Plaza Hotel on October 16th and, what's more, in his life he had never been on the twelfth floor. Nobody said that he had ever been on the twelfth floor. Unfortunately, Detective Buhrmaster didn't have the results of the fingerprints at that time, and didn't confront him with that evidence. He got that a few days later.

'So the defendant also says, "I have never owned any handguns." You are going to hear evidence that the handgun was sold to him by a police officer.

'Also he says, "By the way, I couldn't have done it, because I was with Tino Geddes at the Kenyaan Press in Fort Lauderdale", which is a printery for the paper. In the morning, through lunchtime. The murder had occurred around lunchtime. He said, "I wasn't up there. I was at the printery with Tino Geddes." Well, that is bunk. Tino Geddes never saw the defendant that day until six o'clock at the airport. Never saw him.

'Geddes will come in here and tell you that when he met him at the airport – when Geddes met the defendant at the airport that night – about his own involvement before in this conspiracy, he agreed that he would lie for him initially. And he did initially give a statement to the defence attorney in the case, like, "I was with him that morning."

'As a matter of fact, Geddes will tell you that, at the defendant's request, he fabricated – actually fabricated – an alibi, manipulating innocent people to be mistaken and say they were with the defendant that morning. They actually did that. Well, Geddes isn't going to lie any more. He is not going to lie for him – the defendant – any more. He is going to come in here and tell you like it is, set the record straight.

'The fingerprints, the ballistics evidence, the trooper who stopped that man, the police officer who sold him the gun – overwhelming evidence. The motive is overwhelming.

'The State of Florida is asking you to do some thinking in this case. Please pay very close attention to the witnesses, observe their demeanours, assess for yourselves whether they are telling you the truth.

'I am going to ask you at the closing of the case to dispense justice, because justice cries out for conviction in this case, which is one of first-degree murder, in two counts. Brutal first-degree murder. The most coldly, mechanically planned type of first-degree murder.

'The blood of Derrick Moo Young and Duane Moo Young is still on his hands. I am going to ask you folks to do the right thing and listen to the evidence, do your duties. And I am confident that you will return a verdict that speaks the truth, that the defendant is guilty of two counts of first-degree murder, kidnapping and terrorising these two people before they died.

'Thank you for your time.'[1]

*

With this, Assistant State Attorney John Kastrenakes takes his seat. The prosecution presentation runs very close to the script that he promised, fleshed out in various details. The jury learns that Krishna Maharaj's anger with the Moo Youngs raged white-hot. Eslee Carberry testifies about the series of articles that he had published in the *Caribbean Echo*. These provide reason enough for Krishna to be furious at both Carberry – the publisher – and Derrick Moo Young, whom he believes to be behind them.

The Maharaj family – Krishna's brothers, Ramesh and Robin, as well as Krishna himself – are accused in the *Echo* of being part of a scam described as 'irregular, illegal and possibly fraudulent', getting money out of Trinidad and into the US. This story runs twice, with the second headline shouting: '$1.5 Million Shared by Three'. If this is true, Krishna could face charges himself in Port of Spain.

'Numerous persons,' Carberry writes, 'seem anxious to clarify many financial dealings involving Krishna Maharaj.' What is this about? The jury is left to speculate: has Krishna been defrauding people other than Derrick Moo Young out of money?

Again, according to the *Caribbean Echo*, Krishna Maharaj holds himself up as the owner of a rival weekly publication, the *Caribbean Times*, aimed at the same South Florida community. But this newspaper is not even his, Carberry says, but is rightfully registered to Derrick Moo Young. Is this another scam conducted by Krishna, stealing Derrick's business?

The scandals escalate, falling over each other with every edition of the *Echo*. Next there is a story about a threat to kill Carberry himself, made in a crowded restaurant. 'I could have killed you a long time ago!' an unhinged Krishna Maharaj shouts at the editor. 'I *will* kill you!' Week after week, Carberry publishes Derrick Moo Young's stories about Krishna Maharaj. Little wonder, as Prosecutor Kastrenakes says, that the defendant has become obsessed with revenge against both men.

As Carberry's evidence is presented, Krishna Maharaj sits impassively beside his lawyer. He does not seem concerned. His face is stolid. When the judge sends the jury out on a break, he turns towards the audience where his wife Marita sits in the front row. Portuguese, her skin is almost as tanned as her husband's, but she is pale, worried. His face breaks into a rare smile, and he encourages her: do not worry.

The defence lawyer, Eric Hendon, in his dark polyester suit, sweats in the air conditioning. He makes a few points on cross-examination as Carberry's venom washes over Maharaj, but he only puts small dents in the prosecution theory. Carberry admits that perhaps the defendant did not threaten to kill him – just to destroy his paper, the *Echo*. But Hendon generally allows the stories to stand. The jury must be getting a fairly damning picture of his client.

And it gets worse. Just as Kastrenakes predicted, another journalist, Tino Geddes, takes the stand. He relates to the jury a bizarre series of plots by Krishna Maharaj to kill both Carberry and Derrick Moo Young. With respect to the murder itself, Geddes describes how Maharaj asked him to cobble together an alibi. He found this easy to do, as the day before the murders – Wednesday, October 15th – they really were all together. Some time had gone by, and it was simple enough to get the others to think the meetings were on the Thursday. But he later felt guilty and refused to continue the charade. His testimony has done Maharaj's case a lot of damage – falsifying an alibi is a clear sign of guilt.

Much of the witnesses' testimony seems to be corroborated by the scientific evidence. There is the gun. Some months earlier Krishna Maharaj bought a nine-millimetre Smith & Wesson pistol from a police officer, who testifies. No murder weapon was ever found on Maharaj or at his house – perhaps, as Neville Butler predicts in his testimony, he threw it into one of the many waterways in South Florida.

The state ballistics expert, Thomas Quirk, testifies that the gun used to commit the crime was a nine-millimetre semi-automatic with six right-hand twists in the barrel. He is slightly less certain in his opinion than Kastrenakes had promised in the opening statement. Quirk says he can narrow down the murder weapon to one of six types of weapon – Browning, Leyte, Llama, Sig-Sauer, Smith & Wesson or Star, all nine-millimetre pistols. He reviewed standard bullets fired out of each type of gun; while he cannot be sure, he thinks a Smith & Wesson is the most likely of the six. The jury has already heard that Krishna Maharaj owned an S&W like this. This is not conclusive, as there would still be more than 270,000 such pistols at large in the US, but where is the gun that the defendant bought? If he would produce it, they could do tests to see whether it fired the fatal bullets. But if he refuses to say where it is, surely that is further evidence of guilt?

Ivan Almeida is the prosecution fingerprint expert. He testifies that there are twenty-one prints in the room that were matched to Krishna Maharaj. As Kastrenakes promised, there are two left-handed prints on the 'Do Not Disturb' sign. Kastrenakes made a big deal, in opening, about the difference between the right- and left-handed prints that were found at the scene. This supposedly corroborates Neville Butler's story that Krishna wore a glove on his right hand only. To be sure, there are lots of left-handed prints. But there are right-handed prints on a soda can and a Miami newspaper. A right palm print on the *USA Today* paper. And both left- and right-handed prints on the outside of the door to the room. Butler's prints are in the room as well, but – as Kastrenakes assured the jury in opening – this is to be expected. Butler freely admits to being there. Regardless of whether Maharaj had a glove on during the actual crime, there can be no quarrel with the fact that the defendant has been in the room.

The fingerprint testimony links into the testimony of the lead homicide officer on the case, Detective John Buhrmaster. He mirrors Kastrenakes: dark hair, similar narrow, smooth face, roughly the same age. He arrested Krishna Maharaj at the Denny's Diner and began to question him at 1.23 in the morning.

'Did you have any discussion with the defendant concerning guns?' Kastrenakes asks him to tell the jury.

'Yes, I did,' replies the detective.

'What kind of conversation did you have with the defendant concerning his ownership of guns?'

'When I asked him if he owned any, he told me that the only guns he owned were two shotguns, and they were at his house now.'

'Did you have any conversation with the defendant as to whether or not he owned any handguns?' Kastrenakes presses on, since this is not quite the answer he was looking for.

'Yes, sir, I asked him if he owned any handguns and he indicated that no, he has never owned any.' From what is already known, it makes Maharaj sound even more guilty – he is trying to cover up the fact that he had a gun of precisely the type used in the murders. And Maharaj also told the detective that he had never been in Room 1215. While Buhrmaster has plenty more to say, these are the key points. With twenty-one of his fingerprints in the room, Krishna Maharaj is clearly lying again – and why would he tell these falsehoods if he had nothing to hide?

Hendon sallies into a few areas in his cross-examination, but makes little headway. There was a Colombian, Jaime Vallejo Mejia, registered in the room across the hall. He asks where Mejia was during the murders. Buhrmaster says that he saw no reason to disbelieve Mejia, who said he was at his office, which was also in the hotel.

'He said he was on the sixth floor, and I believed him,' the policeman says dismissively, making it clear that this is a defence smokescreen.

The Colombian has an import-export business. Hendon asks what this business of his deals in.

'I don't recall,' says Buhrmaster. He sees no relevance in Hendon's suggestion that he should have searched the man's room, or taken his fingerprints. Hendon starts to look as if he is thrashing around in the waterpolo pool, trying to obscure the view of the goal.

As the other expert witnesses appear, Hendon is able to point out that Kastrenakes slightly overstated his case on the blood evidence. David Rhodes, a Miami-Dade County police officer working as a serologist, testifies that the blood on the 'Do Not Disturb' sign was insufficient to match to anyone. But the point is a minor one, as few could doubt that it belonged to Derrick Moo Young. There is no evidence that anyone else bled anywhere near the sign.

A few more holes are filled in, and then the prosecution rests. Everyone turns towards Eric Hendon.

I was not at the trial. Later, as I read through the transcript, it is easy to imagine the suspense in the room. I have been in that position many times. It is time to hear from the defence. What will Eric Hendon put forward to disprove the prosecution case? There are the alibi witnesses discussed by Tino Geddes: will they come forward, or was it true that the alibi was fabricated? Krishna Maharaj has some explaining to do – will he testify first or last, for surely he must take the stand? This will be the highest drama of the case, as the prosecutors try to attack the defendant and tear his testimony apart.

Then there have been hints of other suspects. How will Hendon prove this? And what of the scientific evidence? What experts will the defence present to call the ballistics proof into question, or try to explain what really happened in Room 1215?

But everyone is in for a surprise.

'The defence rests,' Hendon intones.

The defence rests, without calling a single witness … It seems extraordinary. Can Hendon really present no witnesses at all, not try to rebut anything the prosecution said?

The written page of the trial record does not reveal the reaction of those in the courtroom. Later I would review this moment with Ron Petrillo, an investigator who did some work on the case for Hendon. He described the scene.

'Eric stands up to begin the defence portion of the trial, and he simply says, "The defence rests." The prosecutors' jaws drop, their mouths fall open … I think they are going to fall off their chairs. Maharaj is holding my arm so tight I thought he was going to draw blood.'[2]

There is a sense of anticlimax in the courtroom, enhanced because it is the end of the day. The jurors are sent home with instructions that the next morning they should bring suitcases packed. They might be out deliberating for several days, and during that time they will not be allowed to separate and will have to spend the nights in a local motel.

The next morning is Wednesday, October 21st, one year and five days after the murders. The lawyers make their closing arguments. It is all very similar to their opening statements. Judge Solomon reads a lengthy recitation of the law, taking a little over an hour. Unusually, Solomon was not the judge who initially presided over the trial. That was Judge Howard Gross, but on the third day he had not appeared on the bench and had been replaced by his colleague, for reasons that had not been explained to the jury.

Then comes the moment – 10.23 a.m. – when the jury is sent out to consider its verdict.

Waiting on the jury verdict is agony for everyone. What is Krishna Maharaj meant to do, in the holding cell behind the courtroom, alone? Marita, his wife, is alone in the courtroom, not allowed near her husband. He seems so sure of acquittal, but she cannot be so certain, despite her faith in him – her Kris couldn't have committed this murder! But the prosecutors seem confident as well, and there has been no real response from the defence. Members of the Moo Young family are sitting in the audience, behind the prosecution, and they are tense as well, wanting justice for Derrick and Duane. Eric Hendon leafs nervously through papers at his table and goes out to make some telephone calls. The prosecutors go back to their office, as they can return within minutes of the judge's call.

This can go on for hours, for days … waiting for the jury to decide.

But this time it doesn't. The jurors' discussion is brief, interrupted as they eat the sandwiches that are brought in for their lunch. They return at eight minutes past two. They have a verdict.

The twelve jurors and an alternate file back into the courtroom, taking up the same seats they have occupied throughout the trial. They do not look at anyone. To guess the outcome of a jury's deliberation is like reading tea leaves, but a quick verdict is rarely good news for the defence. It tends to take more time for twelve jurors to agree to acquit someone than it does to convict.

The tension rises as the verdict sheet is passed to Judge Solomon, who looks at it impassively, conscious that every eye in the courtroom is on him. He then hands it to the clerk to be read out.

'As to Count One, the murder of Derrick Moo Young. Guilty.

'As to Count Two, the murder of Duane Moo Young. Guilty.

'As to Count Three, the armed kidnapping of Derrick Moo Young. Guilty.

'As to Count Four, the armed kidnapping of Duane Moo Young. Guilty.

'As to Count Five, the unlawful possession of a firearm. Guilty.'

They are unanimous. Krishna Maharaj is guilty beyond a reasonable doubt on all charges.

The lawyers and the defendant have been standing as the verdict is read, but Maharaj has slumped down, falling to the floor. He has fainted.

The judge has allowed both sides two weeks to get ready for the penalty phase. The jury will now make a recommendation as to whether Krishna Maharaj will live or die. Technically, the jury's vote will not be binding on Judge Solomon, who will make the final decision. But their conclusion will be entitled to significant weight, and few elected judges in Florida will override a jury's death sentence, reducing it to life. More will elevate a life sentence to death.

The prosecutors make their case for execution by calling the pathologist, Dr Charles Wetli. Wetli conducted the autopsies on both Derrick and Duane Moo Young. Derrick could have been conscious after being shot – and may have suffered for several minutes. With

Duane, the doctor agrees, the shooting could be described as 'execution-style'.

When the prosecution rests, all eyes turn again towards Hendon, wondering whether he will present any evidence. The case he makes to spare Krishna Maharaj's life is brief, but at least there are some witnesses. They are impressive people. Hendon turns to the bailiff and asks him to summon Mervyn Dymally, a US Congressman from California. Dymally is friends with Maharaj, and believes him to be a gentleman. Next, a judge and a surgeon, both from Trinidad, praise the defendant's generosity. Levi England had been the defendant's attorney in the civil litigation against the Moo Youngs, and he testifies that Maharaj was going to win his suit for the money they had allegedly stolen from him – so why, Eric Hendon wants the jury to wonder, would he need to kill them?

And here is Maharaj himself, finally taking the witness stand to insist on his innocence and express his belief that he will ultimately be vindicated. He describes how he made his money, and how he owned racehorses in Britain. 'I had a firm of accountants, who advised me to buy horses because it was a tax write-off.'

He first met Derrick Moo Young in 1965. Fifteen years later they went into business together, buying property in South Florida, with Krishna putting up the money and Derrick renting out the houses. Later Derrick started embezzling the funds. 'But I say, praise God,' the man on trial testifies, 'what he took from me I could afford. It wasn't important; money was not that important to me, never has been.'

None of the articles in Carberry's paper bothered him, he says. He certainly did not kill the Moo Youngs. 'As true as Jesus Christ was crucified on Friday, I had nothing to do with the murders.' The jurors must have been wondering whether Jesus really did die on a Friday. Hendon is not guiding his client at all, leaving him to speak as he chooses, not asking him questions.

'Ladies and gentlemen of the jury, I have been convicted, I know, for Derrick and Duane Moo Young's deaths. I had, as I said, absolutely nothing to do with it,' Maharaj asserts. It is a bit late now. The jurors found him guilty. 'I feel very badly that those people were killed, but I do not know anything about it. All my life I have been helping my fellow man, regardless of the race, the colour, creed, religion. That has been my life since I was nineteen. It's not how much money I give to charity, but in 1963 I donated ten thousand dollars to build a church in the eastern region of Nigeria. I donated every year five thousand pounds to the Cox fund, programme for famine relief.

'I will not go into the first part of the trial because it is not important now, but all along I believe that the police know in their hearts I have nothing to do with it. I am hoping that time will tell that I was innocent of these murders.

'When you spend 384 days as I have spent in jail, every day I expected at the trial to be released and found not guilty. I was found guilty. I know I fainted. I apologise for fainting, but the reason why I fainted was because I was shocked that I could have been found guilty of it, and I am hoping and praying that with the grace of God I'll be able to be vindicated as soon as possible.

'You know I'm in ...' He hesitates, perhaps wondering where he should go with this. 'In 1967 I donated thirty thousand dollars to the British Cameroon for the polio. In 1968 I donated fifty thousand dollars to the cancer research. I have donated, it's in black and white, I have donated several thousand dollars. Money has never been a goal. I helped Derrick Moo Young. I didn't hurt him and I did not kill him, and the people who are responsible for it will eventually be brought to justice.

'I hope. I can't help it.'

At last Krishna Maharaj shows some emotion. But he has rambled. He finally draws to a close, croaking, a whisper, as he almost loses his voice. He is telling the jury they are wrong, and it is unlikely to go down well.

Judge Solomon offers him a glass of cold water.

'Any cross-examination?' the judge asks the Assistant State Attorney, John Kastrenakes.

'Yes,' comes the slightly fevered reply. 'Take a minute, Judge?'

'Thank you,' says Maharaj. 'I'm ready, sir.'

'Since October 16th of last year,' Kastrenakes begins, 'until November 6th this year, I wanted to ask you one question. One question.'

'Yes, sir.'

'What did you do with the murder weapon? That's the only question that's left – the only one. What did you do with it?'

'Well, can I answer your question Mr ...' Maharaj seems to have forgotten the name of the man who is seeking his execution. 'Ladies and gentlemen of the jury, Detective Buhrmaster, when he arrested me that night, told me that he had found the murder weapon – the gun. He said that the fingerprints … that the fingerprints of that gun would have been matched with mine. I have his identical words written on a yellow piece of paper I just handed to Mr Hendon, when I was arrested … But the jury was never told.'

'Did you hear my question?' Kastrenakes demands, since Maharaj clearly has not answered it. 'What did you do with your Model 39 Smith & Wesson semi-automatic pistol? Where is it today?'

'Right. I told Detective Buhrmaster …' the defendant begins again. 'Are you going to let me answer your question, please, sir? I told Detective Buhrmaster, that particular night I bought a gun from Detective Bernie Buzzo of the Miramar police station, Miramar police, and the last time I saw that gun was when it was – when I was stopped by the state trooper … Hold on!' He holds up his hand as the prosecutor gets set to interrupt again. 'The state did not believe me. Mr Hendon's private investigator spent thirty-two hours, sir, on the turnpike. We supplied, we supplied the state – we supplied you all, sir, with respect – with the address and the name of the state trooper who stopped me. I told—'

'You are telling us that the trooper stole—'

'Counsel, Counsel!' interrupts Judge Solomon.

'That the trooper stole the murder weapon?' Kastrenakes says.

'I never said that,' Maharaj replies.

'Your Honour,' intervenes Eric Hendon. 'I am going to object. My client said nothing—'

'Hold it!' Judge Solomon is holding his hand up now. 'Sustained. Sustained.'

'I never said that,' Maharaj continues anyway.

'Mr Maharaj, don't answer it until I tell you to,' Judge Solomon admonishes him. He turns back to the prosecutor. 'The court does not believe at this time that we should go into matters that would have come out on cross-examination at trial. A decision has been made by this jury as to guilt or innocence.'

Kastrenakes asks to be heard with the jury out of the room. He argues strenuously that, since Krishna Maharaj has asserted his innocence, he should be allowed to cross-examine the defendant on all facets of the case. Hendon says that they cannot retry the case. The debate oscillates back and forth for several minutes, with tempers flaring. For a while Judge Solomon sticks to his ruling. Then he caves in. Kastrenakes can ask the questions, and even call Detective

Buhrmaster to disagree with what Krishna Maharaj says.

Maharaj explains that the gun was supposedly put back in the boot of his rental car by the troopers who had stopped him on the turnpike three months before the murder, but it was missing when he got home that evening. He says it was with the twelve Army & Navy surplus jackets, the six pairs of boots and the twelve machetes. 'And there were nothing like no Chinese throwing gear. I have forty-nine per cent in a farm in Costa Rica that grows tropical plants. I went to get those machetes and so forth for the Costa Rican farm.'

Now it is Kastrenakes' turn to object, saying that the defendant is telling more of the story than the question called for. Judge Solomon overrules him.

The prosecutor now goes through Krishna Maharaj's career as a salesman, and tries to get him to agree that he has been a good salesman. He could sell anything to anybody.

'October 16th – you remember that day?'

'Yes, sir, I do.'

'You told Detective Buhrmaster you were never in Room 1215.'

'I did not say that to Detective Buhrmaster. I said to Detective Buhrmaster I was in Room 1215 earlier on.' Maharaj explains how Neville Butler had set up a business meeting with Eddie Dames, rescheduled from the previous day, to discuss selling the *Caribbean Times* newspaper in the Bahamas. Maharaj waited in the room for an hour before giving up and leaving.

'Was Detective Buhrmaster being truthful when he said to this jury that you told him on the night of the murder you'd never been in 1215?'

'No.' Maharaj is emphatic, saying that the lead homicide detective committed perjury. In a capital trial that is an offence that could carry many years in prison. 'He was not being truthful when he said that, because I told him I was there on Wednesday. I told him I was there on Thursday. I am probably the only one in this court who told the truth from the very beginning to Detective Buhrmaster.'

'All right,' Judge Solomon interrupts. Perhaps he has some sympathy for the man on trial and thinks he is digging his own grave even deeper. He turns to Kastrenakes. 'Go on to the next question.'

'Nobody else in this case told the truth except for you?' The prosecutor cannot resist shaking the bone, despite the judge's order.

'I didn't say nobody else. I said probably one of the few who told the truth, sir.'

'Go on to the next question,' Judge Solomon repeats.

'Who else did not tell the truth in this case?'

'Mr Butler certainly didn't tell the truth.'

'Who else?'

'Mr Butler, Mr Geddes …'

'Mr Carberry?'

'Mr Carberry, well, I don't think he knows the difference. With all due respect to him.'

'With all due respect to him.' Kastrenakes' sarcasm is heavy.

The prosecutor goes on. Where was Krishna Maharaj on the day of the murder, after he allegedly left the DuPont Plaza at ten that morning? The man on the witness stand enters into a long and rambling account of everything that happened that day, throwing in various things that he had told Detective Buhrmaster, and which the policeman ignored.

Finally the judge interrupts him. 'Counsel. Counsel for the State. I don't know how to bring an end to this. You are going to have to help me, State.' He sends the jury out and finally tells the prosecutor he can go no further.

But Krishna Maharaj is not through talking. 'I didn't finish the last question he asked me.'

The judge has heard enough.

The man on trial has one other thing that he wants Hendon to do: offer into evidence the fact that he has taken a lie-detector test and passed, asserting his innocence.

'Who passed the polygraph?' asks Judge Solomon, confused.

'Krishna Maharaj took a polygraph and passed,' says Hendon. It is true. George Slattery, a very respected local expert, has administered a test. Maharaj insisted that he was innocent. Slattery found that he was telling the truth.

'And Mr Butler took a polygraph and passed,' responds Paul Ridge, the lead prosecutor.

So what does this prove? That Butler is telling the truth as well? Recognising that the tests are not accepted as reliable, Judge Solomon excludes any evidence about polygraphs. He thinks it will merely confuse the jury.

*

It is time for the prosecution to argue that Krishna Maharaj should die.

Paul Ridge concludes the case for execution. Ridge is the senior of the two prosecutors from the State Attorney's Office. He does not have much time, as the judge allows each side only half an hour to wrangle over life or death.

'May it please the court and Counsel,' he begins, with the time-honoured language, bowing slightly at the judge and nodding towards Eric Hendon. 'Good afternoon ... or good evening, ladies and gentlemen.

'Today the defendant sits before you a murderer, a man who has killed two human beings. Yet he's had the opportunity to come before you and present evidence in mitigation on his part, evidence in mitigation to convince you that his life should be spared, that he should not be punished with the imposition of the death penalty for the deeds he has committed.

'You are about to go back in a few moments and make a decision. I would submit to you that, under the law and under the facts of this case, this decision is not a tough one.

'We started out approximately a month ago in front of a different judge, in a different courtroom, but the one unifying thread throughout this trial has been you, the ladies and gentlemen of this jury, and it is now that the court is going to ask you to make a recommendation. You are the people that make this system work. You are the unifying thread, people from all walks of life – clerks, people from the military, pilots, realtors, construction workers, manufacturers – living in different parts of Miami.

'Does this man deserve life for what he did, or does he deserve the death penalty? And that is a recommendation that you must make to this court. The court will remind you today, as it has already, that the final decision as to what punishment shall be imposed rests solely with the judge of this court. Remember, ladies and gentlemen, it is only a recommendation.

'You may say to yourself: if I vote that the defendant is guilty of first-degree murder, I may be responsible for placing a man in Florida's electric chair. That is not a matter to be taken lightly, but it is also not your responsibility. You are not putting the defendant in the electric chair. You did not put this defendant in the chair here in the courtroom, either. The only person in this courtroom who put the defendant in the chair in which he now sits is the defendant himself. It was his actions, and his actions alone, that brought him to the chair in which he sits today.

'He was the one motivated by hatred, who lured Derrick Moo Young and his son to the DuPont Plaza on October 16th. He was the one who took justice into his own hands on that day, and decided he was going to be the prosecutor, he was going to be the jury, and he was going to be the judge.

'I would submit to you that under the law in this particular case, and under the facts of this particular case, as much as you may not want to do it to another human being, the law and the facts compel the imposition of the death penalty.

'It is simply that clear.

'Even though you, as jurors, may not like the law, even though you may not believe that it should be the law, nevertheless you all stood up, you all raised your hands, you all took an oath to follow the law, and you must do that now, when you go back to deliberate on this case.

'You must recommend that the appropriate sentence be imposed. When you stop and you take a look at what has transpired in this courtroom over the past month – the facts that you have heard, the evidence that you have heard, and the law that you are about to hear – there can be only one recommendation as to what is the appropriate sentence under the law.

'You will hear from His Honour, Judge Solomon, that there are several mitigating factors that you are to weigh against the aggravating factors. You heard a Congressman come all the way from California or Washington DC to testify on this defendant's behalf. A politician, who admittedly had received campaign contributions from the defendant, came here and testified that the defendant in his opinion was truthful and honest.

'But you, the ladies and gentlemen of the jury, know better. You know the defendant is not truthful. You know he is not honest. You also know he is a violent person, because you convicted him. The only thing Congressman Dymally has demonstrated to you today is what a poor judge of character he is.

'You also heard from Levi England, the defendant's attorney in his civil matters against the Moo Youngs, a man employed by the defendant, a man who has been paid by the defendant, a man who is still paid by the defendant.

'Krishna Maharaj was candid enough to tell you in his testimony that money doesn't mean much to him. What *did* mean much to Krishna Maharaj was this hatred generated by the court battles, by the articles, by Derrick Moo Young ... And it was this hatred that compelled him, that drove him to lure Derrick to the DuPont Plaza.

'If you look at the testimony of the people you heard today, you look at all the advantages that Krishna Maharaj has had throughout his life, this is not a person who is deprived, who didn't have the benefit of a good education, who didn't have the benefit of growing up in a comfortable environment. This is a defendant who at every step along the way of his life has exercised free will. He's had money. He's had status. He's been a successful businessman.

'Look at the people that this defendant had come before you to testify on his behalf: a Congressman ... a *Congressman*; a judge from Trinidad; a neurosurgeon; an attorney. This man has had the benefits of everything that society has to offer. And what does he do? He has no excuse. He has no excuse for what he's done. He is simply a man motivated by hatred for Derrick Moo Young.

'These mitigating factors should be considered in light of the aggravating factors in this case. You'll hear five of them, the aggravating factors.

'Number one, you can consider that the defendant has been convicted at the same time for other capital felonies, and also other violent crimes. In other words, what that means is that, under the law, you as jurors can consider the number of murders that the defendant committed or the number ... number of violent crimes. And I would submit to you that an individual who is committing other violent crimes, and not one but two first-degree murders, within the space of minutes, certainly deserves special consideration, deserves a greater punishment.

'The great punishment in this case is the death penalty.

'Number two, you will also consider that the defendant committed the first-degree murder in the commission of a felony. The felony in this case – the felony that you have found by your vote – is kidnapping. So the law allows you to consider as an aggravating circumstance the fact that he was actually committing another felony when he killed Derrick and Duane Moo Young, a second aggravating factor.

'And I'd like you to focus when you go back, in addition to that, on three other ones, and these are as follows. Three, preventing a lawful arrest. The defendant prevented or attempted to prevent his own arrest. Four, that the homicide, the murder, was especially wicked, evil, atrocious and cruel. And five that, in addition to that, the murder was cold, calculated and premeditated.

'What is it about these murders that sets them apart? You know from the testimony that the defendant had been planning the death of Derrick Moo Young for months. I'm not going to go into that. I'm sure you all remember that. The coldness, the calculating nature, the extended premeditation … certainly is deserving in this case … certainly is deserving of the death penalty in this case.

'This defendant – no compassion, no compassion whatsoever. Yet he's going to ask you for compassion. A man who to this day walks in front of you, and insults you, and tells you, as the members of this jury, that you have convicted an innocent man. The audacity of that individual! The sheer audacity of that individual. He's going to ask you for compassion.

'He showed no compassion to Derrick Moo Young, and Duane Moo Young, and he deserves none from you.

'He put that gun to the back of Derrick Moo Young and he killed him. And then what did he do? He turned his attention to the surviving witness. A boy who has just seen his father murdered in front of him, helpless to do anything for him … helpless … is taken upstairs into the second room to be executed.

'That's exactly what the defendant did in this case – executed him. He forced that boy to watch the murder and execution of his own father, and then he took him upstairs.

'What must have been going through Duane Moo Young's mind at that time we can only imagine. But I think you, as the members of this jury, certainly understand and know that Duane Moo Young knew he was going to die.

'If that is not wicked, if that is not atrocious, if that is not cruel, then nothing is.

'So when you go back to vote, when you go back to make your recommendation, think about that stairway, and Duane Moo Young's walk up that stairway, and being told to kneel down and put his hands behind his back and seeing that gun put in his face.

'Because you know it was right in his face.

'Think about what he thought about. And how he felt. And whether you think that is wicked, atrocious and cruel; and whether that is deserving of the death penalty. When you vote in this case – a young man aware of his own death, he looked death right in the face and he saw the trigger pulled.

'The type of man who would do that deserves but one sentence. I ask you to follow the law, ladies and gentlemen.

'Follow the law, and recommend to this court that it impose the sentence of death for the murders of Derrick Moo Young and Duane Moo Young.

'Thank you.'

And Paul Ridge walks slowly back over to his chair.

Judge Solomon sends the jury out for ten minutes while Eric Hendon, the defence counsel, prepares for his own summation. Hendon is brief. He does not beg for compassion. He tells the jury that they are wrong. That Krishna Maharaj is innocent. They have 'disregarded' the evidence, he says. They have 'paid no attention' to the facts. They need to give the man the chance to prove his innocence.

It's a risky strategy when there has just been a full trial on culpability, where the defence offered nothing. That was Krishna Maharaj's chance, and Hendon did not present any evidence of innocence. Even at the penalty phase, all he gave the jury were his client's self-serving assertions, and the opinion of a few friends that he is an honest man. It's a risky strategy, telling a group of people they are wrong to have decided beyond a reasonable doubt that the man is guilty. Telling them this with only a few whispers – no evidence, mere hints of evidence that might have been. Telling people who have struggled all their lives to make a living that money was no object to Krishna Maharaj, so why would he kill Derrick Moo Young? Telling them, in short, that they are fools.

Judge Solomon reads pages of jury instructions, incomprehensible to most lawyers, deadly dull to any juror.

It is 5.32 in the afternoon. The clerk of court records when everything happens, by the minute. The jury is sent out to deliberate. In the courtroom, there is nothing for anyone to do. The slightest effort to show an interest in anything else seems to undervalue the significance of what is going on in the jury room, so close by. Yet, again, this could last for many hours, even days.

Once more Krishna Maharaj is not allowed to stay with his wife. He must go back to the holding cell, where he waits alone. Marita waits alone. She is still in shock that he has been found guilty. Now she must contemplate whether her husband will be strapped into an electric chair, as the prosecution proposes, and tortured to death. She is shaking.

6.20. There is an announcement.

'Got a question from the jury,' Judge Solomon says. There is a word in the instructions that has apparently confused them. 'As to the definition of the word "contemporaneously". I couldn't find it in *Black's Law Dictionary*, but we have "contemporaneously" in *Webster's Dictionary*: "originating, existing or happening during the same period of time".'

'Fine,' says Paul Ridge.

'Yes,' says Eric Hendon.

'Acceptable,' says John Kastrenakes.

Only twenty-seven minutes pass. It seems an age. Yet it seems nothing.

There is another announcement. The jurors have a verdict. Again it is fast. But at the penalty phase speed doesn't necessarily relate to the outcome: sometimes with the death penalty the jurors can decide quite quickly that they do not want to do it. Sometimes they have already reached some kind of compromise at the first part of the trial. Krishna Maharaj, and Marita his wife, don't know what to expect. They have never been in a capital trial before. They are both numb … separated, and numb.

This is a first for the Moo Youngs as well. They've never had a father or a brother murdered.

The jury files back into the courtroom. In most states it takes a unanimous verdict to impose a death sentence. Not so in Florida. The vote can be split any number of ways. It takes a majority to recommend death. An even division (six-to-six) means life.

Again the tension rises as the verdict sheet is passed to Judge Solomon.

'All right,' says the judge. 'I have the advisory sentence … As to Derrick Moo Young, the jury advises and recommends the court that it impose a sentence of life imprisonment on Krishna Maharaj, without the possibility of parole for twenty-five years.'

The spectators have been warned to show no emotion, but there is a gasp, hardly more than an exhalation of breath, although it cuts loudly across the tension. Krishna Maharaj has been spared.

'The majority of the jury,' the judge continues, 'by a vote of six-to- six. The jury foreman, Mr Udell, has signed it. I'm going to date it today's date. Today is the fifth.'

'The sixth, Judge,' intones the clerk.

'The sixth.' Judge Solomon pauses while he corrects what he originally wrote.

'As to the advisory sentence for the capital crime of first-degree murder as to Duane Moo Young,' he continues. Momentarily some in the courtroom had forgotten that there were two counts of capital murder – one for the father Derrick, one for the son Duane. 'The majority of the jury, by a vote of seven-to-five, advise and recommend to the court that it impose the death penalty upon Krishna Maharaj.'

Judge Solomon places no emphasis on the word *death*, but it resonates across the courtroom. It seems as if there is a vacuum for a moment, as if the floor underneath everyone is falling. Then there is a movement, one prosecutor perhaps clenching his fist. Victorious.

'Signed by Mr Udell,' the judge repeats. 'Dated today.'

A momentary pause. The judge faces the bailiff.

'The defendant will be sentenced on November 20th at eleven o'clock in the morning. Take the defendant out of here, please.'

Formal sentencing will be later, but there seems little doubt what will happen. Krishna Maharaj turns towards his wife, as the court security staff come to escort him to the cells. He shuffles out, a guard on either side.

The judge turns back to the jurors. 'I've got certificates of appreciation for everybody here. Please, when you come out one by one, take it from me and turn in your little red badge to Mr Shapiro. We thank you again for your attendance and your being good American citizens.'

The prosecutors turn to congratulate each other and shake hands. It has been a job well done. The Moo Youngs seem satisfied.

On the other side of the courtroom Marita Maharaj is crying.

2

The Execution

None of the jurors who recommended sentencing Kris Maharaj to death had ever watched an execution. That privilege is reserved for a select group: the prisoner's lawyer, perhaps a family member, relatives of the victim, the prosecutor, a handful of official witnesses and sometimes a journalist fortunate enough to have won a lottery held by the prison. Over the years I have watched six of my clients die: two in the electric chair, two in the gas chamber and two on the lethal injection gurney.

It always happens at night, in darkness. I have never been able to decide whether it matters how they do it, since the prisoner ends up dead anyway. In one sense the gurney is most surreal, since the scene is meant to emulate a clinical setting, yet the prisoner is strapped down in the shape of a cross, his arms set wide to give room for the needle. Sometimes the prison staff take ten minutes, twenty minutes, three-quarters of an hour probing the prisoner's arm, trying to find a vein.

The gas chamber is ghastly, with its overtones of Auschwitz. But if I am forced to choose, I would probably say I hate the electric chair the most.

All six executions have been terrible experiences to watch, let alone for the person being killed, but the one that intrudes on my night-mares most is the death of Nicky Ingram, an Englishman sentenced to death in Georgia for shooting a man, J.C. Sawyer, north of Atlanta. I was his lawyer for several years, but I also came to feel that I was his friend.

It was early one morning, not long after I took on Kris Maharaj's appeal. I drove down to the Georgia Diagnostic and Classification Center, the euphemistic name they give Death Row. The previous evening we had come awfully close to a killing. Federal Judge Horace Ward had stayed Nicky's electrocution just forty minutes before the switch was due to be thrown. Perhaps I should have been prepared for what I was about to experience, but the battle to stop the State of Georgia from killing Nicky had been going on for a fortnight without pause and I was operating on adrenaline reserves, no longer thinking very far ahead.

When Nicky came out for our meeting, with a grim smile of satisfaction that he was still here to greet me for another day, a shocking baldness had replaced yesterday's hair. A couple of days' growth of wispy stubble on his chin stood out, contrasting with the rest of his head, which was razor-smooth. Silently he indicated the skin on his right shin that they had prepared for contact with the other electrode.

'There's some sick motherfuckers back there,' Nicky said, nodding in the direction of the chamber. His eyes were shining, with fear. He needed to share with someone; he described to me the electric buzz as his hair had fallen to the floor the night before when the guards shaved him, ready to die.

'They all made me feel like an animal,' he went on. 'It was like I was a sheep going to slaughter.'

It was not the time to point out that no animal would ever be put in an electric chair.[1]

'Man … you know … I actually laughed …' Nicky paused between words, trying to get them out, and there was a tinge of hysteria in his voice. '… at what the bastards made me wear.'

I sat, quietly sympathetic, as he demanded angrily why they probed his anus before taking him towards the execution chamber. He described the nappy they put on him so that the witnesses would not notice him soil himself as the electricity loosened his sphincter.

I encouraged him. Judge Ward was a decent man, I said. I explained how I thought he would do the right thing by us, that we would win the appeal. I had to add, though, that there was a chance the state would appeal, to try to lift the stay of execution. But we'd been working overnight to prepare for that, and we'd counter anything the state filed that morning.

I left Nicky just before his mother was due to arrive. I went to the office of Warden Zant. Zant was an unpleasant little man, with unfriendly eyes. He was sitting behind a very large desk. I pointed out that Nicky's mother should not have to walk in on his baldness. I asked him to give Nicky a cap of some sort, to soften the blow. He said he would consider it. I replied that there was not much time for pondering. Any minute, keen not to miss a moment of this unexpected extra day, Nicky's mother would be coming through the metal detector a few yards down the hallway. Zant repeated that he would consider my request. He asked me whether there was anything else he could do for me: a peremptory way of telling me to get out of his office.

I left, and drove as fast as I dared – tired beyond all sense of safety – back to Atlanta.

I discovered that the prosecution had already asked the federal appeals court to allow the State of Georgia to kill Nicky that night. My friends back at the office had filed our reply while I was at the prison. Now we had to wait on the three judges' decision. I needed distraction, so I worked on documents for the US Supreme Court, pessimistically, just in case they would be needed later in the day.

It was early afternoon when the appellate judges decided to lift the stay of execution. They said Nicky should die, and Judge Ward had been wrong to have given him any further consideration. The Assistant Attorney General called to tell me they had reset the execution date for seven o'clock that evening.

The Supreme Court in Washington: our last resort. Nine justices, their evening interrupted once again by a motion to stay an execution date – one of a hundred coming to their desks each year. I was hopeful. We had several good issues, carefully framed in the past week for just this moment, to catch the attention of the highest court. It was seven years since I had last lost a client, and I felt I knew more now about the strategic chess game that can put the executioner in check. But I also knew myself. I always convince myself that we will win. Of course. How else can one hope to convince anyone else – the judges who make the final decision? That self-knowledge was enough to dent my confidence.

The papers were filed, page upon page faxed up to the Clerk of Court in far-away Washington. Now I had to drive the forty miles back to the prison, to fulfil my final duty to Nicky, though I still hoped I would not have to. Something made me tune into the car radio. A nephew of the murder victim was speaking.

'I will be happy when they flick that switch,' he said. 'We are not vindictive people. We are Christian people. We think he should die.'

Other people were calling into the local radio show. They were more graphic.

'We should use an electric pew to dispatch a dozen Death Row inmates at one go,' offered one.

'Barry from Evergreen' had strong views on what should happen to the young man whose death might soon take place in front of me.

'We should put him in the chair,' Barry said, his lips smacking over the airwaves as he savoured his fifteen seconds of fame. 'Then we should just jack up the voltage bit by little bit till he gets the vibration going.'

'Yeah, that'd be great,' the announcer agreed, chortling gregariously. 'We could put it on TV and do it for a week. We could have a lottery on what night they were gonna finally fry him for good.'

I listened, hypnotised, until I could stand it no more. I clicked the radio off. Then the silence pressed down on the roof of the car, and the green light on the speedometer oscillated between too slow and too fast. For Nicky's sake, I needed to be there for the appointed hour; his life was seeping away, the sand slipping through a timer that might soon end in agony.

I arrived at the gas-station diner, a hundred yards from the prison gates. Allies were grouped at the tables there, ready for the vigil. I called the office and learned that the Supreme Court had issued a temporary stay, so that they might consider Nicky's 'case' more closely. The execution could not take place before nine o'clock. My optimism crept back in.

I had to go into the prison, though. As I arrived at the gate, I stopped briefly to share a word with the people holding a vigil, waiting in one of the cordoned areas. I told them the news about the Supreme Court. I encouraged them to believe, partly so that I could hear my own words of encouragement.

The prison was already back in execution mode. They'd had a dress rehearsal last night. There was anticipation, tinged with an expectation that they might be disappointed again. But, whatever the outcome, they had to follow the script. When there are rules, it is easier to avoid thinking about what is happening, and perhaps easier to avoid questioning it. The prison's public-relations officer was counting on the condemned man to stick to the script as well, with his final meal, his final prayer and his final remorseful statement. If he did, Nicky would receive a good review; if he let them down, he would spoil the experience for everybody.

The charade had begun some days before. The British media had descended on Georgia. It had been a slow week back in the UK, and the story was soon top of the bill. In the US journalists began to write about why there was a story in the UK. They scrambled for new angles. One hack interviewed some celebrity chefs, discussing what they would choose for their last meal.

'I'd start off with a plate of Jabugo ham, super-extra-fatty,' said Peter Pastan, chef at Obelisk, on P Street in Washington DC. 'Then an *ovoli*-mushroom salad … then some *agnolotti* stuffed with *fonduta* with fresh white truffles on top … Then roast suckling pig – cooked over wood – and some small porcini mushrooms cooked in the pan-drippings under the pig, and a bowl of some stewed fresh cannellini beans on the side. Then I'd have a big chunk of Parmigiano cheese – it'd have to be from a *vacche rosse* cow. For dessert, I'd do a bottle of dessert wine, a 1995 Recioto della Valpolicella by Romano Dal Forno. It's made with dried grapes, so it has a lot of sweetness and a lot of alcohol.'[2]

Inmate Ingram had been unwilling to enter into the spirit of the event. He did not want a meal just before his execution.

'He didn't think he would be hungry,' Vicki Gavalas, the prison spokesperson, told the assembled media, during one of her briefings on the countdown to Nicky's death. Her peeved face emphasised Nicky's failure to appreciate their offer. The prison authorities had been annoyed that he would not respond to their questions, and had asked me to check what Nicky wanted for his final dinner. Why eat, he demanded of me, moments before you die?

'They're sick,' he said. 'If I had to eat, I'd choke on it. And they want to kill me before I could digest it.' All he wanted was a pack of cigarettes, but we had run into a bureaucratic impasse. Earlier that year the institution had imposed a smoking ban on all Death Row prisoners, to avoid the dangers of lung cancer. I had put his request to the warden – the arguments being rather obvious – and prevailed on him to allow Nicky a couple of smokes before his time finally came.

Now, the earliest Nicky's 'moment' could be was nine o'clock. We were back in real time. I was meant to be in the waiting room by eight. The guards at the gate were officiously unconcerned with their own deadline, taking time to process me through security. To their left, the media waited in their own enclave, marked out in yellow. My car was waved into the blue zone, and a prison official shielded me from the more aggressive journalists who wanted an interview, even at this moment. It was already eight twenty when I was driven alone in a white prison van along the long and familiar driveway towards the inner gate.

It was lonely as I arrived at the brightly lit white prison buildings. Now there was nobody else from our side around. Just me.

By eight thirty-two – with so little time, I constantly turned to my watch – I was past the metal detector, standing alone in the visitation area. How often I had been there, waiting to chat with Nicky, over the years. Only this morning I had waited, exultant and exhausted, to discuss the stay of execution that Judge Ward had entered the evening before.

Now the yellow walls closed in on the empty blue plastic chairs around me, uncomfortably bright in the neon lighting. The two large visitor rooms ran off in darkness, one on either side of the electric gate that led to the prison wings. Back on Death Row, 120 other men sat silently in their cells, each huddled with his own thoughts of the electric chair. In front of me, to the left, was the pay telephone I had used on some of my visits, when important news needed to get back to Atlanta before I could drive there. Now, unless five of the nine justices on the Supreme Court came through for us, all I had to look forward to was a phone conversation with Nicky before watching him die.

The prison let me call through to him. The Supreme Court had not ruled, and Nicky still felt they might rule in his favour. By now, I was afraid that I knew differently. On my most recent call to Washington the court clerk had asked me whether we had any other pleadings to file. This was a kindly person's attempt to speak death in shorthand, to give me a warning. If we were going to win, we would not need to present the court with anything else. But I would not be the one to close the final door to hope – not yet. Hope was the only currency Nicky had left. Hope was life, as the second hand swept around the clock face.

I hate the telephone at the best of times. I held the receiver miser-ably, lost, searching for what I should say to someone who was about to be killed. But Nicky was – generously – worried about what effect this would have on me.

'Give 'em hell, Clive, for all those other people,' he said.

Should I give his mum a message?

'Just tell her I love her.'

At 8.46 they made me hang up on him. They cut in suddenly. All I could say was 'Bye'. Still no formal word from the Supreme Court. I got on another line to my colleagues in Atlanta, who were still able to talk to Nicky. I reminded them not to tell him until the last minute. They asked me how I was doing. I changed the subject.

Alone again. I looked at my watch as if somehow the time would be different from the clock that hovered over the waiting area. They would be shaving Nicky again now, in case some insulation had grown on his skull since the night before.

I wondered who I might call, to accelerate time, decelerate time, or take time out of the picture. I wasn't allowed a mobile phone in the prison, and I didn't have my address book. I could not remember the numbers of my friends. How could I have been so thoughtless? Disturbing my self-pity, a guard came walking along the corridor. I glanced at him. He looked as if he might be one of the round-bellied rednecks calling into the radio programmes. I avoided his eye for as long as I could. This was one of Nicky's killers. Maybe this man had even been one of the ones who tormented Nicky when they shaved him yesterday evening.

'I knew Nick five years ago, when I worked his tier,' he said in a low voice, as he came level to me. I started, looking up at his eyes. He stopped, briefly, nervous that someone might notice. 'Never gave us a moment's trouble. You could take half of those guys back there' – he jerked his thumb towards Death Row – 'and let them out tonight, and you'd never hear from them again. Don't get me wrong. There are some real psychos back there, but Nick's not one of 'em.'

He paused and regarded me sadly.

'You get to see the human side of them back there,' he said. 'Nick's not like the press and all them people make out.'

All I could do was smile at him. A part of a smile. Part-shame at my own misjudgement, part-gratitude at a fellow human being reaching out. Fortunately he did not seem to require me to speak. I would have cried.

When he left I felt even more alone than before. Men in guards' uniforms wanted to stop the killing machine, yet it was beyond our power now. I called the office and learned that the Supreme Court had ruled. Nicky had lost. They had just told him, and he had been forced to put down the phone for the final preparations.

I remembered a couple of numbers and tried calling two close friends, people I might speak to from such a terrible place. But both calls rang through to answering machines. I gave up before the final beep. I thought briefly about calling my mother in England, but it was two in the morning there, and I decided that it would upset her more than her friendly voice was worth to me. At least the deciding took up some time.

The guard who came to tell me that the time had arrived was also kind. He was going to drive my van, he said. The victim's representatives were in one white prison van. The media – volunteers who had won the voyeurs' lottery – would ride in another, notepads on knees and foreheads pressed to the window glass.

I was alone in my van, isolated with my silent guard. Now I was glad to be by myself, away from people who *wanted* to be present while Nicky died. I sat behind the metal mesh that normally protected the driver from my clients, as the small cavalcade moved off along the perimeter fence. It was five minutes before nine as we passed through the rear entrance gate.

'BUCKLE UP FOR SAFETY'S SAKE' instructed a sign.

It was the first time I had ever visited the rear of the prison. Halogen floodlights left the prison walls in silhouette, the low ramparts of this fortress. The square generator above the execution chamber looked like a crenellation. The prison could not rely on public electricity, for fear some dissident terrorist might sever the lines immediately before the killing time. So there was an independent generator for the chair, tested each week with a hum that shook the soul of every man in the four wings of Death Row.

I was the last one they led into the witness room. I heard someone shout an order. 'Save that seat for the defence attorney.'

As I took my plastic chair, the black curtains were drawn open, revealing the window to the execution chamber. The electric chair dominated centre stage. It was on a platform in the middle of a white-washed room, an exit door cut out stage left, at the back, and the deadly eye of the executioner's window set in smoked glass behind the shoulder of the appalling wood-and-leather apparatus.

I was two rows back. In front of me was the head of Tom Charron. The once-telegenic, ambitious District Attorney had argued, twelve years ago, for Nicky's death sentence. I noticed how his greying hair was all gone at the back, and thinning elsewhere. In the years since his venomous closing argument had persuaded a jury to send Nicky to Death Row, his own goals had been overtaken by personal scandal. He had little left now but to relive his glory days by attending this – *his* – execution.

The room had been air conditioned before everyone arrived. Now that the witnesses had all filed in, thirty-five sweating people were turning the room back to humid. I worried that Charron would turn round. I disliked him. As much to avoid looking him in the eye as anything, I looked backwards. The journalists were looking about, a mixture of the furtive and the absorbed. I wondered what trivia they would find newsworthy in the anticipatory silence.

Everyone's attention swang back to the front as the door behind the chair opened. The media craned forwards in their seats as Nicky was brought in. He was rigid, tense. He seemed so small. Once again I was startled by his shaved head. He was surrounded by massive guards, who pushed him firmly into his seat.

There seemed to be an expectation among the spectators that Nicky would writhe as they bound him down.

He made no effort to struggle, they wrote in their later reports. I think I would, even though it would be useless. The heavyweight guards had volunteered for their role. Even so, they hurried nervously as they buckled him up. Each guard had one strap to cinch, nobody being more responsible than his neighbour. I saw Nicky wince as they pulled the leather tighter.

Ingram ignored a wave from his lawyer, they later wrote. Nicky and I had not talked much about this moment. My job had been to give hope, not discuss the better ways of dying. But in one of the brief macabre conversations we did have about his fate, he told me to wave. He said I would know he could see me if he acknowledged it with a finger. His finger did not move. Perhaps Nicky was cut off from the people staring at him through the window. Perhaps it was a one-way glass. Certainly, barely any sound carried to us, except when the tinny microphone was turned on. The insulation – a preventive against the sounds of agony – was so complete that it was like watching a gruesome silent film.

Ingram refused his final prayer. Nicky shook his head urgently when the prison chaplain stepped forward. *He must have been an atheist*, they wrote. The chaplain retired, backwards, into the corner. I could feel the frowns around me. The rules said Nicky was meant to have a final prayer, to comport with the state's notion of salvation. *Nothing can save you from us, but perhaps something or someone else in front of you there will be more forgiving.*

Warden Walter Zant, that small and hostile man, read out the warrant of execution: '*It is considered, ordered and adjudged that within a time period set by law the defendant Nicholas Lee Ingram, sentenced to death by a jury of his peers for the crime of murder, shall be executed by the Department of Corrections by passing electricity through his body until he is dead, all in accordance with the law of Georgia.*'

Zant's voice was cold, his delivery directed at the man tightly bound into the chair. It was as if he, Zant, was God's chosen messenger of death.

'*Do you have any final statement?*' Zant demanded.

Now, before us, as the warden's thin voice asked him for words that might salvage his worthless life, Nicky turned his head, his dark eyes full of fear, but still defiant. Instead of speaking, Nicky spat at Walter Zant. Behind Zant, the prison chaplain flinched.

Angry to the last, Ingram spat at the warden.[3]

In truth, Nicky had told me two days ago what he wanted to do. I immediately tried to dissuade him, but I recognised what my concern was: I was worried about his epitaph. Nicky wasn't. He predicted that he would be incapable of speaking so close to death. He said that the best he would be able to manage was to express his contempt for their ritual. I would have to give his final statement, he had told me, a tremor in his voice. We had passed quickly on to my thinly sustained hopes about his appeals.

Momentarily thrown off-script by this disobedience, the guards hurried forward now, reaching to buckle up the chin strap and pull Nicky's mouth tight shut. One guard slipped the metal cap over his head, the damp sponge inside to conduct the electricity better, and began to tighten the wing nut on the electrode. Another knelt in false apology at Nicky's right knee. As my client had shown me just that morning, the right leg had been shaved to allow good contact for the lower electrode.

Ingram stared the audience coldly in the eye, they wrote. All that was left for him was to stare directly forward into some unknown future, and hope that it might be no worse than the past.

But the moment was short-lived. The guard in charge of the skull electrode pulled the dark leather mask down to cover Nicky's face for ever – the visor that had absorbed the final, heaving breaths of so many condemned men.

Nicky was now unable to look his executioner in the eye, or watch for the signal that would soon be given. Instead, this leather flap covered up the grimace that must come with that first shock of electricity. Again, it was to protect us – the witnesses – and surely not for the man before us, who was now waiting in primordial darkness.

This left Nicky as a black-and-white silhouette that I can forever summon when I close my eyes, an unerasable negative: Nicky's small, skinny body clamped into the dark oak chair, unable to move a muscle, no matter what the agony.

And now we had to wait. The guards had filed out of the chamber. The loud sound of nothing reminded me of the heat of that late-spring southern afternoon, the silence of nature sometimes so oppressive. I slumped forward, my head in my hands, palms damp. I could not look at Nicky any more. He could not see me, and my presence could not help him now.

There was no obvious signal. But even though there was barely any sound, the congregation of witnesses started at the vibration of the first electric surge. No insulation could totally eliminate it, as 2,000 volts tore into Nicky's body with the angry hum of a high-tension power line. But the sanitising screen protected the witnesses from any other noise, and even smell, as Nicky began to roast to death.

For a moment, everyone in the witness room was frozen. Then the journalists began their feverish jottings. Mostly I felt, rather than saw, the commotion, since aside from involuntary snatches, I could not bring myself to look up. I stared at the second hand on my watch instead, willing it all to be over. Just as I did not know what to say to Nicky in his last moments of life, I did not know what a person was meant to think when attending his death. My emotions surged from despair to a physical sense of nausea, to disgust and back to despair, against the monotone of the generator.

I gripped my head. If death was as instantaneous as the State of Georgia said it should be, why send electricity through Nicky for two minutes? If it was true that he would die in an instant, why carry on killing him? I studied the hair on my arm through those extra 119 seconds, as the journalists scratched and scribbled around me.

Ingram died a painless death, the journalists wrote later. After the first two minutes, the generator calmed for a moment and the audience stirred. Then the electricity attacked Nicky again, buzzing at a different frequency. After several seconds, it stepped back up to 2,000 volts again.[4] It astounded me that people could be so naïve. If it was all so easy, why the gag to silence Nicky? Why the straps to hold him still? Why the mask to cover his face?

When it was all over I emerged into the April night. I wanted only to get away from that place, but before I could go I had to attend the ritual press conference. It was my job to say those final words that Nicky could not mouth in the execution chamber.

'Nicky wasn't very good at speaking,' I told the assembled media, as he had instructed me. 'He asked me to make a brief statement for him. He asked me to say he wasn't the one getting hurt, but that his family and the family of the Sawyers were, once again, and he's sorry for that. He told me that, as for himself, he hoped for something better now, because what had happened in this life had been so sad.'[5]

Nicky Ingram and Krishna Maharaj had two things in common: first, their British passports; and second, if Kris didn't get his sentence overturned, their fate.

3

The Mission

By the time I took on Krishna Maharaj's appeal, I was a death-penalty veteran – I had already spent nine years losing Nicky Ingram's appeal. I had been a (very) young lawyer at the Southern Center for Human Rights when I agreed to represent Nicky, partly because a friend asked me to, but also due to the fact that Nicky and I had both been born in Cambridge. I thought for a long time that we were born on the same maternity ward at Addenbrooke's, but my mother corrected me. I came along in 1959, the year they broke ground for the new hospital; by the time Nicky arrived in 1964, they had moved to the new facility.

We were, nevertheless, proximate in our introduction to the world, though our lives had taken very different paths. By the age of three Nicky had been transported across the Atlantic by his parents, an English mother and the American serviceman who had swept her off her feet. My grandmother would not have approved: she remembered the Second World War and constantly reminded all those around her that the American GIs were overpaid, oversexed and over here.

The romance faltered when Nicky's parents reached Georgia, and they split up. Nicky's life followed the typical path of a future Death Row prisoner: no stability at home, smoking before I would have learned about swear words, escalating misbehaviour at school, and drugs between classes. Still a teenager when he was implicated in the murder of J.C. Sawyer, Nicky had barely had time to establish a proper rap sheet, though the police suspected him of the odd burglary.

My own experience was rather different. In 1942 the world that my family inhabited changed when my grandfather was bequeathed Cheveley Park Stud, near Newmarket, by the man who had employed him to manage it. Thoroughbred racehorses had been reared there for a thousand years. In our early lives my brother, sister and I lived in a post-and-rail paddock of privilege. Even then it seemed dimly unfair to me that we should be able to roam the 360 acres of the stud, when other children had no such advantage. But it was a glorious inequality: I can still smell the leather seats of the clapped-out van my parents bought me for my fourth birthday; the Super 8 cine-film shows the thrill on my face as I was led out to see it for the first time in my little red shorts. I frantically twisted the steering wheel from side to side, convinced that I was driving a million miles an hour.

I would climb up the wooden steps of the clocktower, halfway along the rank of creosoted horseboxes with their Christmas-red half-doors, sitting for hours watching the simple mechanism counting off the minutes; or I would build castles with my best friend Anthony among the bales of hay – until the stud groom, Bill Cowell, chased us off, gesticulating wrathfully, fearful that we would be crushed in any collapse. Around the tennis court I fell in love with spring's progress from snowdrop to crocus, to daffodil, to tulip – acres of them, shaded by the new beech leaves. Anthony and I would make notched arrows from willow branches and – Robin Hood in the woodlands – would terrorise rabbits down Gypsy Walk.

After boarding at a prep school from the age of eight, I moved on to Radley College, a public school outside Oxford. This was deemed close to the apex of the educational pyramid, and in many ways it was. The houses were called 'socials', and the F Social dormitory was one hundred yards long: seventy-two cubicles containing seventy-two very cold youths on a winter morning. A younger boy – called a 'Stig' in the bizarre language of the public school – would toll a bell as he walked down the middle of the aisle, and we would be turfed out for a sodden morning run in the dawn mist, followed by a cold dip in the cast-iron baths.

I whined to a teacher about this. It was to prepare us to run the Empire, he reprimanded. The news that Britain's global hegemony had ended had not yet passed through the school gates. I told him that Gibraltar did not need me. My grandmother came for a tour of the place where I slept, with its solitary cast-iron pipe running the length of the building, a pointless nod at central heating.

'Ooh, they do spoil the boys these days!' she expostulated, sincerely. That morning ice had been frozen in the glass beside my bed, I told her, equally sincerely. Meanwhile, wondering why parents would pay so much for hypothermia, I tramped off daily to the frigid science labs for chemistry and physics. There was, back then, a clear hierarchy that supposedly divided the brainy thoroughbred from the brawny shire horse. Those who were considered the most intelligent (or, at least, those best at taking exams) were streamed into mathematics and the sciences, perhaps with a smattering of Classics on the side, regardless of personal enthusiasm. For me, the first casualty was Latin: I could not abide it. The language struck me as utterly pointless. It was so dead that nobody could even tell me how the words were really pronounced.

Gradually I came to see science in the same light. I had really only chosen my studies out of a kind of hereditary duty: my older brother Mark had done physics, chemistry, maths and further maths, and I followed in his footsteps. The difference was that he was an excellent scientist and passionate about it. I was neither. I could fake it well enough to get by at A-level, but by then I had reached the zenith of my ability, leaving any curiosity far behind. For me, the route ahead seemed signposted to a lifetime of mediocrity.

The end of the road came for me when the physics S-level exam was set to coincide with our cricket match against the Young Australians. Though only ever a shire horse myself when it came to cricket, it was my passion; I had little natural talent, but whenever I was spared the early-morning run I skipped gleefully down to the gym in darkness to lift weights, in an effort to battle my way into the first eleven. I had finally made it, and now I was to be denied the chance to bowl in the biggest game of my life, by an exam that I considered as pointless as Latin. I sat at the desk, my mind far away, and for the first time in my life I knew I had failed a test. I just did not care; in a way I was answering a question that was not on the exam. I was not, I instantly decided, going to follow the course plotted by my well-intentioned teachers.

My obsession with the death penalty had long been brewing. It went back to prep school. Britain had yet to join the European market, and there was little pressure for a change of attitude. The French were

Frogs; the Germans were Boche. Colonel Horden, teaching history, had the class reading about the Hundred Years War. We were English boys, so slaughtering the French seemed appropriate. Then Joan of Arc intervened, upsetting the natural order. Worse still, there was a pencil drawing in our history book of Joan being burned at the stake by some vengeful men with longbows on their shoulders. She looked like my sister Mary. I began to wonder. Five years later, when asked to write an essay on the death penalty, I discovered what I thought was history was actually still happening: the Americans were killing each other in the name of justice.

So it was that in 1978, when I was just nineteen, I threw in the chance of a place at Cambridge University and scooted off for America. My plans were typically nebulous and naïve, but I had grandiosely decided that I was going to put an end to America's tryst with capital punishment. I began by marching into a London interview with the Morehead Foundation, which doled out scholarships to the University of North Carolina (UNC), available then only to the graduates of ten top public schools. The programme advertised itself as an inverse Rhodes Scholarship, bringing British students to America. While the rivalry was hardly like that of Oxbridge, UNC sported light blue as its colour, in contrast to the dark blue of Duke University ten miles down the road. The Morehead people made me an extraordinarily generous four-year award to study whatever I wanted at UNC.

Next I went to tell a professor at Clare College, Cambridge that I was forgoing a place in natural sciences. The scene remains vivid for me: he wore a tweed jacket and the room smelled of a mixture of leather-bound books and pipe tobacco. He admonished me that Cambridge was the best university in the world, and that I would for ever regret my decision. I left his study with a light heart, confident (as only a teenager can be) that he was wrong.

At UNC I took courses in anything from journalism to African American studies. In the summer holidays I was supposed to follow a programme laid out by the Morehead Foundation. The first year was organised with an Outward Bound programme, intended to toughen scholars up with a month of living rough. I had been to public school, so I figured I didn't need that and went on holiday instead. The second summer was meant to introduce us to the virtues of law enforcement; two months as an intern with the Los Angeles Sheriff's

Department convinced me that, with cops like that, we did not truly need a criminal class.

For instance, they taught me how to cheat on a polygraph – the so-called lie detector. A sergeant put me through a sample test. The way it works is this: you are hooked up to the monitor, with various sensors that are meant to detect your emotional state. At the beginning the examiner asks some anodyne questions, based on true answers that you have already provided, in order to set the baseline for the test – in my case, 'Is your mother's name Jean?' and 'Are we in the month of July?'

The sergeant advised me that when he asked these calibrating questions, I should concentrate on the wildest sexual fantasies possible. Then, with each subsequent real question, he told me to think the same lascivious thoughts and answer yes or no, regardless of the truth. That way, he said, the physiological response that had been set for a true answer would be replicated for the subsequent lies. I am a very bad liar, and it was not easy to summon up images of sex when being questioned about my mother, but I followed the sergeant's instructions and beat the test.[1]

The sergeant told me how he used the machine. Ideally, the witness would be a believer in the technology, and would feel the tentacle wires latching onto his skin, pulsing into his soul. But the key to the lie detector, he said, is the policeman asking the questions. He would size up both the suspect and his story, make his enquiries, peer ominously at the jagged graphs that spat out of the instrument and then pronounce his own verdict: as the truth-diviner, he simply identified those aspects of the story that he did not believe. As likely as not, the witness would begin squirming and the story would start to change.

Ultimately, the sergeant told me, out came the truth. Or at least – I wondered as I listened – the truth as the sergeant deemed it to be?

One evening a Los Angeles deputy sheriff, originally from Scotland, berated me for opposing capital punishment, and told me I was as bad as some commie-pinko chap he'd heard of called Millard Farmer, whose fly-by-night law office was located in Atlanta. He said I should buzz off there to work. I swigged my beer and swore that was precisely what I would do.

So for my third summer I asked if I could substitute my own project for the Morehead plan: instead of a stint absorbing the scheduled lessons of private enterprise, I took off to Georgia to volunteer with Millard's small anti-death-penalty office, called Team Defense Project Inc. Millard may never have known it, but he rapidly became my mentor and hero. He came from a wealthy West Georgia family, but had thrown it all up. Already most of the way to middle age, he had taken a law degree at a local college and begun to spend his inheritance defending those who had no hope. These were the early days of a rejuvenated death penalty – it was 1980, and the Supreme Court had only revalidated capital punishment five years earlier. There was still hope that the next case would see its demise. But Millard watched the political tide and knew this was not going to happen. So he rented a small office and leapt into the trenches to begin decades of lawfare on behalf of the most hated people in his society.

I wanted to be Millard, but I soon realised that I never could be. He scuffed about his office in a tie-dyed T-shirt and faded denims; he spoke as if he were constantly moving half a dozen marbles around in his mouth; and he would embark on long anecdotes about Blue, his old hunting dog, that would hold the jury rapt until he finally got to the point forty minutes later. Because I was only twenty, and of little use around the office, I was dispatched to Reidsville, the capital of Tattnall County, to spend the summer visiting the prisoners on Death Row in Georgia State Prison. Each morning I would drive over to the prison. I'd go early, but the steam was already rising off the tarmac. I'd turn off between the red clay of the drainage ditches, past the welcoming sign: 'Georgia State Prison: Leading the Nation in Corrections'. There was the central tower, with the electric chair way up at the top of it. To the right of the entrance was the visitation room.

The prison staff were uniformly friendly, always wanting to chat about England and comment on the way I spoke. Tediously, I would say that I did not have an accent, since it was my damned language. This would evoke howls of laughter, as if it had just been voted the most original retort of the week. That summer my opposition to the death penalty slipped down from my brain and into my heart. The first morning I had considered the drive to Reidsville an adventure, without pause for thought of the months ahead. I had only begun to worry as I entered the prison. What would we talk about? What could I – a privileged kid from a public school – say that was of interest to someone stuck on Death Row? But it was immediately clear that any human contact is a blessing when you are in prison.

When I headed back to university at the end of the summer vacation, I found I had tired of the termtime traditions I had previously loved – even the late Thursday nights with my darts team, the Cavern Cavemen. So I begged off classes for my last semester and asked my English teacher to sponsor me to write the blockbuster that I felt sure would waft a new Age of Enlightenment into America, a book that would prove the pointlessness of the death penalty.

I had conceived a plan with Millard whereby I would take three months to write the biography of one of the men on Death Row, Jack Potts. Underneath my megalomania lay a project that was considerably more useful – visiting the client every day so that he would not drop his appeals (which Jack did periodically, creating endless work for Millard). I would also be garnering material about his life that could be used in the effort to get him a new trial. I would spend each morning with Jack, and the afternoon with another Team Defense client, five days a week.

It was easy to find the time to write the book, *Life on Death Row*, as I had only my blue portable typewriter for company each evening in my frigid one-room bedsit. I diligently transcribed Jack's version of his life, and then drove across Georgia each weekend, when the prison was closed to legal visitors, cross-referencing each chapter with someone else – his brother, his girlfriend, his chaplain or his lawyer. There were two very different histories: one of how Jack would have liked his life to be, and one perhaps closer to reality. When I finished the book it was obvious that it could never be published while Jack's appeals were still pending. So it went into the desk drawer alongside my grandiose dream of a Pulitzer.

I had now been in the US for three years, and the criminal 'justice' system had me intrigued, but horrified. Here, dozens of men – some younger than me, all of them uneducated – were dependent on Millard Farmer for legal assistance. Once they were on Death Row, and had lost their first appeal, the prisoners had no right to a lawyer unless someone volunteered to represent them for free. Millard and his tiny team were the only lawyers doing capital defence in Georgia, trying to stamp out the flames of one execution before dashing to the next.

Back then, thirty years ago, it was fashionable even for defence lawyers to believe that everyone on Death Row was guilty. At all the conferences and seminars legal experts would stress that a 'victory' in a capital case was to work out a plea agreement whereby the client would serve life. It was a comfortable mythology. I don't think we could deal with the possibility that we might be responsible for an innocent person being killed when our representation failed. In reality, nobody had the time to figure out who was guilty and who was innocent. Nobody conducted a meaningful factual investigation, for the simple reason that there were no funds for investigators, or even the lawyers – all work had to be done voluntarily, as there was no legal aid at all once the case was in its post-conviction challenges.

Millard and his crew thought only in terms of stopping the electric chair from toasting another prisoner. In the late Seventies and early Eighties it was relatively easy to find a legal issue that would stop the execution. The appellate courts had always been more interested in legal minutiae than in basic questions of fact. If a lawyer could speed-read a transcript and spot a legal error, that was a far more efficient way to silence the executioner than retrying an entire capital case. The cost was the wholly random nature of the process whereby some prisoners would fall through the cracks to their deaths, regardless of guilt or innocence, because there was no technical legal issue that could win a new trial.

I decided to go to law school. It would be a three-year investment, but then I could be of more use to society than the manuscript of my book. True to form, I chose Columbia Law School without knowing much about it, solely because it was in New York and that seemed like a fun place to spend three years if I had to toil over a degree. The day I arrived all the students were in suits. As Millard's sartorial acolyte, I was taken aback – surely I'd not have to dress up every day?

I had walked in on the second-year students and their interviews for summer jobs. Corporate law firms were wooing them with promises of huge salaries and beach barbecues on Long Island. There were 313 members of my class. The Placement Dean – the man in charge of finding these students a prestigious job at the end of it all – was a coiffed Brit by the name of Howard Maltbie. I told him early on that I needed to figure out how to get back to Georgia to defend Death Row prisoners. There was no money, I pointed out, and there were no jobs, so we'd need to create one. He looked at me blankly and pushed across the desk a sheaf of papers listing the Wall Street opportunities. He suggested that a few years of learning how to take depositions would flesh out my résumé for the job of my dreams.

Once, early that first semester, I followed his suggestion and went to one of the corporate law-firm receptions designed to lure first-year students. It was on Central Park South, with a promise of free drinks. I stood with a young associate of the firm, admiring the glorious view of the Park from the fiftieth floor. The associate, a recent hire, was required to be there to extol the virtues of the partnership. Instead he raised his own passing thought: what would it be like to throw oneself off a building that was so high?

It was my first and last encounter with the world of commercial law.

Obviously corporate lawyers do not commit suicide *en masse* within a year of taking the job. However, graduates described a frenetic life on Wall Street, billing long hours to massive businesses that were squabbling over millions or billions of dollars. If you opted out, you had no chance of becoming a partner; if you opted in, you would not have any spare time to spend all the money you were earning.Regardless of your choice, you were representing faceless companies, and the closest you would come to a human client was the suit who came to lunch from their internal legal division. Our civil-procedure professor was a loud, balding Dutchman called Hans Smit, and he described to the class with accented glee how the top New York restaurants put up their prices each year because, if they were not among the most expensive, no lawyer would deign to take a client to lunch there.

I was saddened. All the brilliant people around me were being encouraged into a life of conspicuous consumption, where they could not even find the time to enjoy what they consumed. But finding an alternative was not easy. The university was no help. The first summer vacation came and I could not find a way to get back to Georgia, so I went home to work in the ready-mix concrete company run by my cousins in Fordham, near Ely. I had done one stint there before, after my A-levels, and it had been an experience that stayed with me. I had hated it: each morning I dreaded getting up; each afternoon I would come close to tears at the tedium. The men with whom I went to the gravel pits at six o'clock each dreary morning were loyal to the family company, and exceptionally kind to me. They teased me, and pitched in to sort out each catastrophe that I would precipitate. Once I backed a tipper lorry into the pit and it took a crane to get it out;

another time I brought the entire operation to a halt because I was too busy reading poetry to pay attention to the conveyor belt.

I had a reason for repeating my earlier experience at the company. I could not afford to volunteer for Team Defense again, without any kind of grant to fund it. So I needed to remind myself of the converse of my dream: what those born without a silver spoon had to do for fifty years, from the age of fifteen to sixty-five. I wanted to be reminded that if these men carried their lunch boxes to work every winter's morning for less than one pound an hour, then I should accept the same pay to do labour that I loved. And it did give me plenty of time to make my plans.

One obstacle was the student loan that Columbia wished to foist on me. The pernicious idea (later adopted by consecutive British governments) was that a law degree was a ticket to a fortune. Thus a student graduating with $100,000 of debt – a mortgage, with no house to show for it – would be able to pay it off from his inflated Wall Street salary. This made it effectively impossible for anyone to do legal work for the poor, since they could not plausibly hope to repay such a sum. Despite my grants, I would graduate owing roughly $25,000. So I set about establishing a loan-forgiveness programme. My pitch was that so few of my colleagues would take up the university on it that the cost would be limited, compared to the prestige associated with encouraging public-interest law.

Unknown to me, my mother had been watching from afar and was not going to allow a child of hers to be in debt, no matter what the consequences. The stud where I grew up had been forced into bankruptcy when my father's grandiose plans got far ahead of our ability to pay the interest on various bank loans. My parents divorced, and my mother found herself returning to secretarial work. Still, somehow, at my graduation she managed to pay my loans off in full.

The second challenge was to find the job I wanted to do seven days a week for the next several decades. I approached Team Defense, and was devastated when Millard turned me down. I did not want to be paid, but even free help comes with overheads, which they could not afford. So I threw myself at the feet of the other capital-defence office that had opened in Atlanta, the Southern Prisoners' Defense Committee (SPDC). Steve Bright, whom I had never met, talked to me for ten minutes on the phone and then told me to come on down.

The financial woes of the SPDC were often more dire than those of Team Defense, but Steve never let that slow him down. He even promised to find $1,000 to supplement the $3,500 that I had put together myself. So that first year I put in close to 4,000 hours, and it came to a little over a dollar an hour – less even than my wage at the family sand-and-gravel company. To me, though, it was a fortune because I had a job I loved.

It was at the SPDC that I took on Nicky Ingram's ill-starred case. I made contact with the British Consulate to find political support for him and, in 1994, it was a consular officer who asked whether I could help another British citizen, Krishna Maharaj, who had just lost his second appeal in the state court.

I had watched Nicky's execution. I would do as Nicky had admonished: I'd give 'em hell, for Kris.

4

The Defendant

My first meeting with Kris came in 1994 when he had been on Death Row for several years. He had already lost his first appeal to the Florida Supreme Court.[1] 'We conclude that the evidence is sufficient to sustain each of the convictions for which Maharaj was found guilty,' the Supreme Court had opined confidently at his first appeal. 'We affirm the convictions and sentences, including the sentence of death for the murder of Duane Moo Young.'[2]

This did not bode well for Kris' chances. His first appeal was by far the best opportunity to have a case reversed, either for a new sentencing hearing or a full trial. Over the years I have won about half of what are called 'direct' appeals – the initial review straight from the trial court to the state Supreme Court. After this it is a game of hangman, in which the gallows and most of the body have already been drawn and the prisoner is no closer to a solution. A procession of courts may follow, but success is an ever more distant prospect. From the state Supreme Court the prisoner can petition the United States Supreme Court, but the chances of prevailing are roughly one in 1,000.[3] From there it is into state habeas corpus, heard back in the original trial court, but that is often before the same judge who sentenced the defendant to death.[4] The odds get a little better when the prisoner gets to federal district court, though the clock will be ticking away towards execution by then.

*

When I met Kris, I was obviously curious about the person they wanted to execute. When I was led to the visitation room, I found a man who looked far older than his age on file – fifty-four. Those few years in prison had aged him by twenty; pictures from the trial portrayed him with a thick wave of dark black hair. Now, what little hair remained was grey, and as he stood to greet me, he shuffled, stooped by age.[5] He was still fairly thick around the waist, but the dark skin of his face seemed pallid, as if someone had dusted him with talcum powder. He wore ankle shackles and a prison jumpsuit.

Generally, when I first meet a prisoner I never ask him whether he did the crime. He does not know me, and does not trust me. His opening gambit in our relationship is not likely to be an admission to murder. It is as if you went to a cocktail party and expected people to introduce themselves by describing the worst act they ever committed: it would certainly make such evenings more interesting, but they would result in few long-lasting friendships. The prisoner probably wants me to like him; he is human after all. So if I ask him whether he 'did it', he will doubtless lie, if he did. And later on, when we have established a relationship and I really need to know what happened, he will be loath to admit that he began with a falsehood. So it is best to steer clear of such topics on a first date.

I asked Kris how they were treating him in the prison. He launched into a description of his day.

'Around five a.m. I awake, brush my teeth, use the toilet, have a sink bath, then make a cup of instant coffee and wait for breakfast,' Kris explained. The American guards had told me that he sounded very proper and British, but his voice maintained the music of Trinidad, though it was forty years since he had last lived there.

'At six, a guard passes breakfast through the feeding hole on a plastic tray. It is something like scrambled eggs, grits, two slices of bread, two slabs butter, two packets jelly and half a pint of milk.

'The eggs are made from powder,' Kris added.

'At seven, I take my medications,' he continued. Now his voice takes on an edge of complaint. The prison records showed that Kris was a sick man. The good health that had carried him into prison has been worn away by diabetes, high blood pressure, high cholesterol and the residual daily pain from a broken arm.[6] He described in angry detail how he slipped one day in the shower, the metal shackles preventing him from protecting himself as he fell. He knew his arm was broken, but the prison refused to believe him for days. When he finally got to hospital it was going gangrenous, and the civilian doctor told him if they had delayed any longer he would have lost it. His eyes softened briefly as he recalled the doctor's kindness.

'She saved my life,' he said without elaboration.

'After my medications, I listen to the news, and kneel down to say my prayers. At seven-thirty, I start walking up and down my cell, from the back wall to the bars at the front. Some days are faster than others, according to the level of pain in my spine, which I also injured falling in the shower.

'At ten, after walking, I do thirty minutes of leg-raises, lying on my back on the bed – to try and keep the strength in my right leg. At ten-thirty, I take a sink bath and clean the cell.' This was a reminder that even such gentle exercise would work up a sweat. Kris could not take a shower when he wanted to, so he had to swab himself down at the stainless-steel toilet-sink combination in the corner of the cell. The Department of Corrections was keen to remind taxpayers that prisoners were not benefiting from air conditioning as they waited to die.[7]

'I read until lunch. Lunch is served at midday, on a plastic tray. It's something like shredded cold turkey, baked beans, two slices of bread, fruit cocktail. I eat lunch and listen to the news on the radio. At one, I start walking for two hours. At three-thirty, I have a sink bath.' This time Kris added an explanation. 'It's extremely hot in the cell – over a hundred degrees.

'At five, dinner is served on a plastic tray. Normally something like hamburger casserole, green beans, squash, two slices of bread, canned pear slices.' He was only allowed a spoon with which to eat. A knife or fork – even plastic ones – could be a weapon.

'I am reliably informed that the cost of all three meals per day per prisoner is less than one dollar fifty,' Kris reported formally, as if he were assessing a business proposition. Then the bitterness seeped back in. 'Our animals in England are fed better.

'At six, I listen to the local news, then the world news.' Each time the news came on, the world was passing Kris by: far away even for local South Florida stories, but quite remote when the American broadcaster told him about news from England.

'At seven, if it is shower day, I get a shower; I am allowed three a week. I am handcuffed and taken for an eight-minute shower by two guards, and then handcuffed and brought back to my cell. At seven-thirty, I read any mail I've received and write some letters. At ten-thirty, the guards come to collect the letters I've written. At eleven, I brush my teeth, say my prayers and go to bed.

'The only time I leave this cell is either for a shower on shower days, to see the doctor, my attorneys whenever they call, or my wife on her regular visits,' he concluded. 'With these exceptions, I am in this cell twenty-four hours a day, seven days a week.'

I asked him to explain why he refused to go out on recreation. It would not be much, but it would mean a few hours each week in a small area outside. Kris would have none of it. For one thing, it was even hotter there, with no shade from the Florida sun. But more significant was his fear. Kris was the first prisoner I had ever met on Death Row who was afraid of those around him. He was worried that someone might pull out a home-made shank and stab him, so he never went out to 'the yard', as it was called – in reality a small square, fenced in with wire. I pressed him out of curiosity, and nothing had ever happened to him to put flesh on his concerns. His apprehension stemmed from what he had been told about prisoners long ago, when he had been free – before he found that he was one himself.

I talked to Kris about legal strategy – where we would go next, how we might get back for a hearing in the original trial court, and so forth – but he was unusual among the many prisoners I had met in that he insisted on moving directly on to the facts of the crime. I tried to avoid this, but he was insistent.

'I didn't do it,' he said. 'You know that, I suppose.'

I nodded agreeably. 'I understand,' I said. 'So who did, do you reckon?'

'I don't know,' he said. 'I wasn't there.'

After only one visit, I already had many questions. The evidence against him seemed strong, but I was witnessing the troubling hallmarks of someone who might not be guilty. Not only was he personally convincing, but his warders seemed to think he was one of the good guys.

I had chatted with various prison guards while waiting to go in to see Kris and while being escorted out again. Normally prison staff are reticent when it comes to discussing the prisoners in their care. They are warned not to get too close to the people in their custody – men they are ultimately going to kill. But they took a different attitude with Kris. The moment I mentioned who I was here to see, everyone had a kind word for him.

'I've always believed in the death penalty,' Sergeant Guthrie said. He has been in the Department of Corrections since 1977. His father was a policeman; he had been around law enforcement his entire life.[8] 'There are certain things that shouldn't be done – there are some crimes committed in ways that are so different to the way that ordinary people think. Between 1978 and 1992 I had something to do with every execution in Florida.[9]

'Some of the time I was working in the clothing room we'd measure the Death Row prisoners for their uniforms before execution,' he went on. 'I actually witnessed two executions by electric chair – I reckon everyone who's executed since then has been in the category of person I'd consider appropriate to execute.'

But Guthrie explained how he was struck by Kris the first time he met him. 'I opened the cell door, Kris stepped out immediately and across the hall as the rules require, and he said "Thank you." It was such an unusual thing for a prisoner to do. I asked other members of staff about him and I heard that it was just his way.' Guthrie then veered into a long discourse on how Kris was different, explaining how good his hygiene was, how he kept his cell clean and tidy, how he didn't let the misbehaviour of his neighbours rub off on him. 'Other than being behind bars, I don't think he behaves any different than he would if he was outside.

'There's been only one time I've ever had to have words with Kris,' Guthrie said, seeming to search for something negative to say. 'It was when I'd just started running the Visiting Park. Visitors are allowed a kiss and a hug on entry and again on leaving. His wife Marita was here, and one day Kris tried to have two kisses on leaving. I took it up with Kris, he apologised and said it would not happen again. Kris was polite and respectful on this occasion.'

He paused, perhaps considering how this sounded. 'It was a very minor infringement,' he conceded. 'Not a deliberate infringement. He kissed her, they were talking and he kissed her again.

'Kris has always maintained his innocence; he has never changed his behaviour,' Guthrie said, doubt vibrating in his voice. 'It leaves you to wonder.'

*

I had not reached any kind of concrete opinion on whether Kris was guilty or innocent at that point. Far from it. I had only just begun my own investigation into his case. But I was horribly aware of how – if he were innocent – everything could have gone very wrong. I asked myself why Kris Maharaj, an astute businessman, did so little to marshal his defence when he found himself charged with capital murder? I already knew what the answer might be. An innocent prisoner is often worse than useless as a client. Indeed, the first rule of criminal law is that an innocent prisoner is predisposed to being convicted. Consider his position: very often, this will be his first serious encounter with the criminal justice system, so he may have little idea what is really going on. I have been involved in many capital cases, yet I continue to make basic errors. The innocent prisoner is going to make beginner's mistakes from the start of his case to the end.[10]

The majority of people have a rather touching faith in the justice system, perhaps because it's strangely alien to us, and it's so positively advertised – both by its very name, and in endless television programmes where it almost invariably comes out all right in the end. If he is anything like the rest of us, the innocent person is likely to believe that the system works and will have little doubt that he will be acquitted. That's understandable: he is 100 per cent certain that he did not commit the crime, so how can any sensible person (let alone twelve of them on the same jury) be convinced, beyond a reasonable doubt, that he is guilty?

If he is paying for his defence – as Kris did in the early days, before the weight of the bills bankrupted him – he is likely not to want to spend too much, as it is a waste of money. No matter how intelligent he may be, he will see little need for investigation, because the ultimate fact is so clear: he did not do it. When asked to pay large sums for defence experts to refute evidence presented by the prosecution, he may demur.

If he has no money – and this is much more likely in a world where capital punishment means that those without the capital get the punishment – he will have a court-appointed lawyer. Yet the prisoner may not fight for limited public funds to prove that which seems so obvious, if that will delay the trial. He is (reasonably enough) impatient, and he won't allow the time for a proper investigation.

Sometimes the innocent person can provide the lawyer with critical evidence. He may have an alibi. Yet a provable alibi has various preconditions: the time of the crime must be precisely known (it often is not); he must know where he was; and, by the time of his arrest, the relevant period may be days or weeks earlier. How many of us could actually prove our whereabouts for the whole of yesterday, let alone a random day last month?

He must also be able to convince the jury the alibi is true – not just through what the prosecution will tout as his own inherently suspect testimony, but through witnesses or physical proof. And he must have a lawyer with the commitment to present it. Some lawyers share a prejudice that an alibi is dangerous. In theory, alibi evidence only needs to raise a doubt of guilt in the minds of the jury, but the moment the defendant pits his version of where he was against the prosecution's, the jury has a tendency to put him to the same burden of proof. In other words, the defendant may need to prove his innocent whereabouts beyond a reasonable doubt, and if he does not, that shows he's probably guilty.

Successful alibis are rare in contested trials. If there is a solid one, the case is unlikely to go to trial. This underlines the problem that the innocent person faces: he is generally of little assistance to his lawyer, since he does not know what happened. He did not commit the crime.

'So who did it?' you ask.

'I don't know,' he answers. 'I wasn't there.'

Just what Kris Maharaj said to me.

This all made me feel unwell. I don't like representing people who I suspect may be innocent. It's partly the pressure: when you screw up and someone who had nothing to do with the crime gets executed, that is as bad as it gets. Many cases are about why, not *whether*: it is easy to condemn the terrible acts of others, but there is always an explanation. It may not be an excuse, but it tells us why this happened.

Innocent defendants represent the first step in the justice system where everything begins to go badly awry. That is not because innocent people get mixed up in the process – that is a given. Unfortunately, the system does not take account of the ways in which innocent people undermine all of the procedures that we have carefully set in place to try to make our justice less fallible.

*

When Kris Maharaj was convicted, he fainted; was this a guilty person turned thespian, or simple shock? I needed to know who this man was, accused of this horrid double-murder. And so I started digging.

Krishna Nanan Maharaj was born on January 26th, 1939 just south of Port of Spain, before Trinidad gained independence – hence his British nationality and passport. His family were middle-class by local standards. Kris always had ambition. He was young when he quarrelled with his father and left home to seek his fortune in Britain, arriving in Peckham in 1960. He found a job driving a lorry, saving money so that he could establish his own company. Persuading his bank manager to lend him £1,500, he began exporting beef to Nigeria, and then moved into supplying shipping lines with food. But he found his niche importing exotic fruits from the Caribbean and Africa. Even bananas were exotic back then, but Kris was one of the first to bring mangoes and plantains into the country.

It did not take him very long to become wealthy, but he told the truth to the jury when he said that the money did not motivate him.

'All my life, money has never been important to me,' he told me on that first prison visit, half-apologetic about his former riches. 'Whenever I needed, God gave me ten times more than I could have spent and a hundred times more than I deserved.'

It was the struggle that he loved. One of the few moments when his eyes lit up during a prison visit occurred when I prompted him to tell me about making his first million. Business could be ugly, he said. His competitors had planned to call a strike to prevent his plantains and bananas from leaving Africa. Kris was generous, and was generally liked, so a friendly docker warned him of the plot. Kris decided to hoist them with their own petard; he paid the dockers extra to put his fruit on board before anyone else's and then go on strike – without loading any other ships. His fruit reached Liverpool days before his rivals', and he was paid top prices.

His flamboyance escalated along with his bank account. He pulled up in one of his lorries and bought his first Rolls-Royce with cash. He went on to own twenty-four of the cars in succession, never fewer than four at any one time. He personalised the registration plate on one of his Corniches, KNM1. This caught the eye of an Arab sheikh who had the same initials.

'Name your price,' the man said.

Kris politely told him that money was not an object.

To begin with, Kris dabbled in racehorses because his accountant told him that it would save him taxes. But he rapidly came to love the turf. Just twelve years before he would find himself facing the electric chair, Kris was the second-biggest racehorse owner in Britain, with at least 100 thoroughbreds to his name. In the late Sixties he bought two thoroughbreds from my father. I found it an eerie link. My father had driven our stud into bankruptcy when I was twelve, and here was a man who had been similarly absorbed in the Sport of Queens, now sitting in front of me in a uniform for the condemned.

Kris' string of racehorses eventually brought him to the pinnacle, for the Caribbean boy made good – Kris was only thirty-five, but King Levenstall beat the Queen's horse at Royal Ascot. It was the Queen Alexandra Stakes in 1974, one of the longest endurance tests of the year, then over two miles and six furlongs. It had been run for more than a century, named after the Queen Consort to King Edward VII, and was traditionally the final race of the June meeting. Kris still puffed his chest out involuntarily when the subject came up.

While he frittered money on horses and cars, he stayed close to his roots. Even though he could well afford it, he shunned the idea of a home in the London neighbourhoods of Knightsbridge or Mayfair, preferring a property adjacent to his company warehouses in Peckham, south of the river. He shared his good fortune with many people. The case presented at the penalty phase of his trial had been woefully thin. Hendon appeared to misunderstand the purpose of mitigation: it is not a character parade designed to convince the jury to accept the prisoner's word as true. It is a life story, intended to show them the humanity of the person whom they will sentence, with all a human being's diverse frailties. Mitigation should elicit empathy from the jurors, whereas Hendon's parade of a surgeon, a judge and a Congressman would have alienated them. Hendon had not portrayed Kris as a person at all, just as a sequence of acquisitions and name-dropping. The prosecutors had then reflected most of the evidence back onto Kris, to militate in favour of the more severe punishment: there was simply no excuse for a rich, fortunate person to carry out the crime that the jurors had decided, beyond a reasonable doubt, he had committed.

In order to understand who Kris was, it was important to interview the people who knew him. John Currant, who became a famous flat-jockey with more than 700 winners around the world, told me that his career would not have been possible without Kris' support. Some owners of thoroughbreds think they own the jockey as well. Not Kris, who bought Currant a car so that he could get to race meets to ride for other owners.

'Kris was a gentleman,' said Currant. 'Kris bought a training yard at Lambourn, and set Ken Payne up as the yard trainer.' Typical of his Midas touch, the yard cost him £60,000 in 1971 as part of his accountant's scheme to lower his taxes. He was offered £140,000 for it one year later – a profit of 130 per cent. Kris agreed the sale price and informed Ken of his decision to sell, but assured Ken that he would buy a new yard and pay for the costs of moving.

'Ken initially agreed to this,' Currant recalled. 'It was a very generous offer from Kris, as he had no obligation to set Ken up in another yard. Kris also offered to pay Ken some money out of the profits of the sale of the Lambourn yard.' Currant frowned at the memory.

'At the eleventh hour Ken insisted that Kris should pay him an additional twenty thousand pounds, or he would remain in the yard.' This would effectively have scuppered the deal Kris had struck. 'Essentially, Ken was trying to extort money from Kris, and it was a quite outrageous way to behave. Kris called Ken's bluff, although Ken's behaviour nearly caused the deal to fall through. Despite this, Kris continued to finance Ken, and remained a loyal and good patron.'

Currant described how Kris laughed off Ken Payne's behaviour. 'Kris acted with dignity, good manners and integrity throughout the whole episode.'[11]

Mick McManus was another witness who unhesitatingly came forward. I doubt I have watched a professional wrestling bout in my life, but I still remembered his name from television when I was a child. Mick was the Dulwich Destroyer, and his rather bizarre hallmark cry was 'Not the ears, not the ears'.[12] When I came to meet him, he was an improbably wizened man compared to his large persona on the small screen. Given my knee-jerk prejudices about his sport, it was a pleasant surprise to discover his charm. He had first met Kris at a fund-raising dinner for the Lord's Taverners, which tries to help children with special needs to get involved in cricket.[13] Kris had become a donor and, being seated at the same table, the two men figured out that they lived close to each other in south London. They became friends. Both keen on horses, they used to meet once a month, either to go racing or simply to share a drink at the pub.

'Kris was very friendly and tried to do favours for people, without requesting or expecting the favour to be repaid,' Mick told me. He described an occasion when an acquaintance of his spoke to Kris about his business difficulties. Kris offered him advice, gave him money on an interest-free loan and invested in his business.

And so it went on. In a capital case, you're lucky if you can find half a dozen witnesses worth presenting to a jury, no matter how long you look. The team at the small charity where I was working[14] lined up forty-six people from Kris' past life, ready to fill in the picture of who he really was.[15]

Enjoying the good times alongside Kris was a young bank worker, Marita. They married five months after they met at a party in Oxford. Marita had not faced the same struggle as her husband; her Portuguese background was privileged, as her father and uncle had been senior government officials before the revolution in 1974 that overthrew Portugal's military dictatorship. Marita worked in London for the Banco do Brasil. She chattered away in a number of languages. She was glamorous, probably the best-dressed banker of her day, and very much in love with her husband.

Kris had attained the fabled status of millionaire, and his life was sometimes complicated. There were powerful interests who were unhappy at the upstart from Trinidad, muttering in their London clubs that they should clip his wings. The large-scale banana importers – Fyffes Group, Geest Industries and Jamaica Producers – were keen to squeeze Kris out. A word with the British authorities and Kris was denied a licence to bring in the fruit he needed, if he was to expand. He would not give in, and he took them to court, challenging the monopoly. Kris loves to tell his tale of battling against the British Government. Bananas' big three were granted 90 per cent of the import licences, while 120 smaller businesses had to divide up the final 10 per cent.

When they met to try and resolve the issue, Lord Cockfield, Minister for Imports, sneered at Kris' temerity.

'It's Co-field!' he exclaimed haughtily, correcting Kris' pronunciation of his name. 'And you can't win against the British Government.'

The interests of the major corporations were represented by serried ranks of pinstriped government lawyers. The case dragged on, costing Kris £180,000 in legal fees, an enormous sum for the time. The interference with his right to do business, as well as the litigation, put a huge financial strain on him, but on March 4th, 1983 the small-town boy scored a victory over the Establishment. In what had come to be called the Green Bananas Trade Battle, Mr Justice Hodgson ruled that Lord Cockfield had violated the law in denying Chris International Foods, of King's Grove, Peckham, a licence.[16]

'Cock-field,' Kris smiled at the disappointed minister, 'why don't you appeal it?'

'This is a victory for the small importer,' Kris told the *Daily Telegraph*.[17] His import quota rose more than a hundredfold, from 220 tons a year to 26,000.

When he finished telling me this story, Kris turned to another victory that he had over the Nigerian Government in the London courts, and then perorated on the British justice system. 'It may not be perfect,' he conceded, 'but it's the best in the world.'

He could not know then that the high opinion he had developed for the judicial process would contribute to his later downfall in the United States – where he would trust the court implicitly to reach the correct judgement, no matter what the seeming strength of the evidence against him.

Meanwhile the Seventies had been difficult for most people in Britain. Inflation ran at more than 10 per cent for the entire decade, peaking at 24 per cent in 1975. The three-day week was a lot of fun for those of us still at school, but businesses suffered. Britain had joined the European Economic Community in 1973, and voted to remain a member in the 1975 referendum. Kris had won his first legal battle with the fruit importers, but the war continued and he was severely outgunned. Europe promised regulations that would favour the small businessman, but it would be some years before these were in place. Kris decided to wait before expanding any further. Meanwhile he thought he would invest in property in Florida, which was a magnet for British tourism and business.[18]

Kris' wealth and success had attracted all kinds of people in London – some real friends, others simply hangers-on. When he started investigating the best investment opportunities, Kris was contacted by a Jamaican he had met two decades before, who was now living in Florida. Derrick Moo Young had visited England in the 1960s, and the two men had briefly discussed doing some business together then. Now, Derrick proposed that he assist Kris in Florida, essentially acting as Kris' manager. Kris would buy the property and rent it out;

Derrick would ensure that the rent was collected, and would generally tend to the buildings. It seemed a good match, as Kris initially planned to be in England for much of the year. Kris set up a business, KDM International, taking the initials of Kris, Derrick and Marita. Since they were business partners, both he and Derrick had access to the bank accounts.

Kris and Marita visited Florida and liked what they saw. For a couple from Trinidad and Portugal, the climate was a pleasant change from dank London. They bought a large house on South West 193rd Lane, in a suburb of Fort Lauderdale. Derrick recommended the address; the Moo Young family lived adjacent to them on the same street. Kris settled down for an interlude in the sunshine, while he waited for the new European rules to make business easier for him back in London. But his relationship with Derrick rapidly ran into stormy weather.

By rights, by the time I met Kris in 1994, he should have been losing faith in the legal system, since each step of the process simply reconfirmed his plight. But he remained upbeat. He was upset at his deteriorating health, but expected each turn in the legal road to bring relief. When he was first arrested he had worried about his business enterprises, but they had long since folded. He was embarrassed that I was working free for him – for charity. He suggested that as soon as he got out he would make another million, and set things right.

His real concern was his wife.

I stayed with Marita when I visited South Florida, as it saved on hotel bills and reassured her that work on Kris' case was being done. She was keeping up appearances, partly for me, mainly for Kris. She had long since been forced to sell their home and move somewhere much smaller with their dog Lucky, an ageing German Shepherd. 'Having him has saved my life,' she said, grateful just for the companionship. 'But he's getting old and I don't know if he'll still be around when …' She trailed off.

Lucky died, and Marita lost even her little bungalow. She had to live frugally, her rent paid by a benefactor who remembered Kris' generosity from decades past. Kris was relieved, but ashamed not to be able to provide for her. Most things, except for Marita's memories, had gradually gone to the pawnbroker. Her possessions shrank to just pictures of Kris in happier times and a glass cabinet with a few family heirlooms. There was a picture of a very striking Marita from an earlier era; now she was more like a diminutive grandmother pottering around her kitchen.

She was hanging on, albeit by the fingernails, which she still elegantly maintained. 'I got married to Kris for life; I married him because I loved him. And I will be here as long as he needs me … as long as it takes to get him out of this,' she repeated each time I visited.

With each appeal filed so far, Marita had started to pack for England. 'Believe it or not, I started boxing everything up … ready for when Kris comes home—' Her tentative, nervous laughter faded. 'I laugh, yes, but this is not a joke. We have been through hell … I just want us to go home, to London, to live out the rest of our days quietly.'[19]

I kept thinking of Marita's hope as I tried to pull together Kris' next appeal, looking over the transcript of the trial once more. I had the witnesses' pre-trial statements, their depositions and their trial testimony. Now that I was further into the case it made for an increasingly depressing read. Kris' lawyer, Eric Hendon, had been a wallflower. There was plenty that he could have done with respect to most of those who testified against Kris, but there was something particularly shady about the prosecution's main witness, Neville Butler. He was the one who said he watched Kris firing the fatal shots in the DuPont Plaza. If he was telling the truth, then Kris was guilty. If my encroaching doubts were to prove valid, Butler had to be lying. But why? And for whom?

5

The Witness

In most criminal trials, a large portion of the evidence comes from regular witnesses: lay people who happened to see something. One issue that leads – obviously – to a miscarriage of justice is the use of evidence that is simply unreliable. Classically there is hearsay, where he-said / she-said gossip from the street corner is offered as evidence. And there is the police informant, who may make up a story because he is hoping for a benefit.

Proponents of the free admission of evidence argue that everything should be thrown into the hopper, and honesty will filter out. They make grandiloquent statements about the adversarial system. Historically traced to trial by combat, the idea is that two equally matched sides will do battle and the Champion Truth will ultimately win the day.[1] Unfortunately, the reality is more like a medieval trial by ordeal, where the prisoner was hurled into a pond: if he floated, he was guilty, but if he sank, he was innocent (albeit dead by drowning).

Lawyers naturally reassure us that lies will be effectively exposed by lawyers. 'Cross-examination is the greatest legal engine ever invented for the discovery of truth,' said the famed legal scholar John Henry Wigmore.[2] 'You can do anything with a bayonet except sit on it. A lawyer can do anything with cross-examination if he is skilful enough not to impale his own cause upon it.'[3]

Unfortunately, we lawyers vastly overrate ourselves. It is possible to skewer a witness, and leave him twisting in front of the jury. If we are forthright, though, we should admit that it is easiest to do this with people who are lacking education, experience and confidence, even if they are being truthful. The average person is more afraid of speaking in public than he is of death, and has probably never been in a courtroom before, so he is mortally intimidated before you even start.[4] He has been made still more nervous (and therefore shifty-looking) by years of watching witnesses being battered on television. And he is being asked to recall something that happened a year ago, that he could not possibly remember without checking back on a witness statement that was written by the police. When asked for details beyond the police-preferred version, he will either honestly admit that he does not know – 'I see, so your, ah, "memory" is entirely limited to what the police wrote down?' – or he will despairingly make a guess that is proven false by other evidence.

Rarely, however, do biased and mendacious 'professional' witnesses crumble in the face of an aggressive lawyer, throwing up their arms and confessing to their sins. It is difficult to move a committed liar. I have caught sociopathic witnesses in phenomenal falsehoods, yet been unable to get them to admit their duplicity. One example was Carl 'Sick Quick' Holley, who had negotiated his way out of several death sentences to testify against one of my favourite clients, Clarence 'Smitty' Smith. Holley and Smitty had been in the Outlaws Motorcycle Club together, and Holley was accusing Smitty of a few homicides. His best confection involved a murder Smitty was meant to have committed on the Skyway Bridge in Tampa, using a fellow biker called Junkyard as the getaway driver. Unbeknownst to the rather naïve FBI agent, who had forgiven Holley up to a dozen murders and put him in the Federal Witness Protection Program for this testimony, Junkyard was the name of the Outlaws' late and lamented dog, with a gravestone behind the clubhouse.

I confronted Holley with this, and showed him a photo of the grave. It had no effect. I showed him a photograph of my Golden Retriever Melpomene, his paw on the steering wheel, and solicited his advice: should I keep the car keys in a place that could not be opened without opposable thumbs? The jurors tittered, but Holley simply smirked. He never cracked, and calmly continued to insist that Smitty was the killer.[5]

*

No tale told by any witness should be accepted without demur. Inevitably, he may become a partisan member of the team that calls him to testify and, when attacked by the other side, may become defensive and entrenched. All this is predictable. What is less immediately apparent is how the process of trial preparation actually shapes the story that the witness ultimately tells. Working out the distance between the witness' current story and the truth is like an archaeological dig at a Roman villa: here, in a corner of the long-hidden mosaic, is one clue to how the edifice originally appeared; here, another. The juror is like a tourist who has never been to a Roman site before, impressed at the reconstruction that has been put together with modern materials. Unfortunately, the tourist may have little idea how the edifice looked before it was covered by the detritus of the ensuing centuries.

So it was with Neville Butler.

Neville Butler, a jobbing journalist with Eslee Carberry's *Caribbean Echo* who had just started part-time with Kris' *Caribbean Times*, was the 'eyewitness' to the crime for which Kris Maharaj went to Death Row.[6] If Butler was telling the truth, then Krishna Maharaj was in Room 1215 of the DuPont Plaza Hotel at noon on October 16th, 1986, killing Derrick and Duane Moo Young. No doubt about it. Butler said he watched while Maharaj killed the two men.

According to the story Butler originally told Detective Buhrmaster on the night of the murders, he had a scheduled business meeting with Derrick Moo Young at the DuPont Plaza, in a room that he had rented for Eddie Dames. To his great surprise, and wholly unheralded, Kris Maharaj showed up in Room 1215 before Derrick and sat down for a chat. A few minutes later Derrick and his son Duane called from the hotel lobby; Butler vaguely noticed that Maharaj stepped into the bathroom, out of sight, as they came in the door. Once they were in the suite, Maharaj emerged with a gun, which he pointed variously at all three of them. Maharaj was demanding large sums of money from Derrick, and handed Butler two immersion heaters (quite common in the 1980s – a length of electric cord with a heating element for boiling water for tea or coffee). He ordered Butler to tie Derrick and Duane up. Butler complied, in fear for his life, but left the knots very loose. An argument ensued, ending when Maharaj shot Derrick once in the knee and then, when the older

Moo Young lunged at him, several more times in the torso. Maharaj then shot the son.

At this point Maharaj instructed Butler to come with him. They went down in the lift to Kris' car, Butler at gunpoint, whereupon they waited for two or three hours while ambulances and the homicide police arrived. Eventually they left, parting until that evening, when Butler led the police to where Kris was having dinner at a Denny's Diner.

If all this were true, then Kris was guilty on two counts of capital murder, as well as the forcible kidnapping of Butler.

Kris' story – to his lawyer and, too late at the penalty phase, to the jury – was very different. Butler had told him that a man called Eddie Dames was interested in distributing the *Caribbean Times*, Kris' paper. Dames was coming from the Bahamas. They were to meet at the DuPont Plaza Hotel on the morning of October 15th. Kris went to the hotel, but Dames had rescheduled for the next day, so Kris simply left; and on the 16th he waited and read the paper. There was no coffee maker, so he bought two immersion heaters to make drinks for himself, Butler and (if he ever showed up) Dames. After sitting around in Room 1215 for more than an hour, Kris departed, rather irritated.

He drove back to Fort Lauderdale where half a dozen witnesses would confirm he spent the rest of the morning, before lunching at Tarks restaurant. Kris' story accounted for all the physical evidence, such as the fingerprints in the room. Butler's testimony became – starkly – the only direct 'proof' that the various items at the scene were incriminating.[7]

At this stage in the case all I had in front of me was the transcript of the trial. But even on the surface, Butler's tale was implausible: would the killer really show up on the off-chance of a meeting, expecting both Butler and Dames to be there, and then just indulge in idle chatter until Derrick turned up? If Maharaj had carefully planned a murder, why would he bring two immersion heaters with eighteen-inch electrical cords to tie up at least three people (Derrick, Butler and Dames), instead of some rope or handcuffs? Also, it made no sense that Kris would wait outside the hotel for hours after a double-homicide while the police investigated it – what could this hope to achieve? And if Butler was a kidnap victim, why would Maharaj let him live – a witness to a double-homicide? Butler would have died in the room.

Yet Butler stuck with the story for five months, in his initial sworn interview with Buhrmaster, through a number of meetings with the prosecutors, as well as in his first sworn deposition. But then the testimony changed quite radically. Butler said his conscience had pricked him and he was coming forward voluntarily to set the record straight.

Now he had a new story: Kris Maharaj confronted Butler, saying that his name had surfaced as part of an extortion plot against various people in Trinidad. Maharaj wanted a meeting with the true extortionists (the Moo Youngs) to get them to sign cheques reimbursing the money, while allowing Butler to clear his name. Butler had to set it up because the Moo Youngs would not agree to a meeting if they knew it was with Maharaj. He was to pretend that it would provide the Moo Youngs with an opportunity to do business with Eddie Dames.

This still made no sense. With this 'plan' – assuming that Derrick brought his cheque book – what chance was there that a bank would certify a cheque for hundreds of thousands of dollars, when the prosecutors told the jury that his annual income was no more than $24,000? And why would Butler commit the crime of kidnapping (worth life in prison in Florida) with Kris Maharaj, a man he barely knew? According to his own statement, he had only just started working part-time for Kris' new paper, the *Caribbean Times*.

As tends to happen when any of us lies, the story began to break down the moment Butler painted in the details, under oath in a pre-trial deposition. 'He told me he believed I may have been involved in this extortion based on articles that were in the *Echo* and he knew I had been contributing to the articles,' Butler explained.[8] If this was true, why had Kris hired Butler to work on the *Caribbean Times*? Indeed, by the time the trial came round some months later, Butler had forgotten he had said this. Now, he said, he did not actually have anything to clear up.[9] But this did not fit with the prosecution theory, as he would then have no motive to be involved.

'He convinced you that your name was being used in Trinidad in connection with this extortion?' prompted Kastrenakes, attempting to clean up Butler's confused babble.

'Yes,' Butler belatedly agreed.[10] Maharaj's plan, he then insisted, was to get a confession from the person behind the extortion – Eslee Carberry.[11] The witness had gone off-script. Carberry was the man who ran the *Caribbean Echo*. A moment before, the theory had been that they were going to meet Derrick Moo Young to coerce him into admitting what he was doing.

'What did he say that the benefit would be to you of setting up this meeting with Derrick Moo Young?' demanded Kastrenakes. The prosecutor was in his director role, prompting his lead actor. Butler had just said the meeting was to be with Carberry; Kastrenakes neatly substituted the name Derrick, to get the story back on track.[12]

'Very simply,' Butler continued, as if oblivious to the name change. 'He said he would have my name cleared. I would get a statement from him, and once we sit down and talk, it would all be clarified and he would see to it that my name would be cleared and not be associated with this sort of thing.'[13]

This basic issue – Butler's motive for having anything to do with the crime – was all very confusing, even under the revised version he had provided to the prosecution. A second patent problem with Butler's story was the location of the murder: a room in a very public hotel that had been registered to the elusive Eddie Dames. Not only was Kris committing a crime with someone he barely knew – Butler – but he was doing it in the room of a man he had never met, who might turn up at any moment to claim his key.

'What is Mr Dames' occupation?' queried Kastrenakes.

'He is a flight controller and he also had a business in Nassau, a restaurant, discothèque business,' replied Butler.[14]

The jury may have had some early queries around the preliminary part of Butler's testimony, but Judge Howard 'Mousey' Gross interrupted the prosecutor in mid-flow.

'Excuse me, sir,' growled the judge to a member of the audience. 'Let me have that beeper, please. There's a sign outside that you cannot bring those into my courtroom. That is the direct purpose of that, and give that beeper to my bailiff, and you have now lost the beeper. You no longer own that beeper. It will be turned over to the county.'

The miscreant, blushing, passed the offending item across the bar to a suited official.

'Please put that in my office, Casey,' the judge said to the bailiff. He turned back to Assistant State Attorney John Kastrenakes. 'Continue on, sorry.'[15]

*

Just as he interrupted the flow of the trial, Judge Gross' intervention cut into my thoughts for a moment, and I paused from reading the trial transcript to ponder the alternatives. I could not understand why Dames needed to come into the plan at all. If you were going to set up a meeting with someone whom Derrick Moo Young would never actually meet, why use a real name? This would merely create another witness to your conspiracy. Why not just reserve the room in the name of a fake person? And what was Butler's real relationship to Dames? He told the jury that they were close friends, but the prosecution did not call Dames at trial, although his testimony would seem to have been important. Then I remembered that Detective Buhrmaster had spoken with Shaula Nagel, Derrick's daughter. She told him that a man called Dames had repeatedly called her father before the murders, but Derrick had ignored the calls because he did not know who Dames was.[16] How, then, could Butler's testimony be true? These calls meant that Dames was the one trying to set up a meeting with the Moo Youngs, not Butler, and not Kris Maharaj.

On the surface, it all seemed very improbable, yet the jury had bought Butler's story beyond a reasonable doubt and had sentenced Kris Maharaj to death. Indeed, as I read the transcript, Butler's story at trial hung together relatively well, particularly because it went without serious challenge from Eric Hendon, Kris' lawyer. As I reviewed the various documents in the case, a pattern began to emerge, and gradually I came to see how a silk purse had been manufactured out of the sow's ear of Butler's evidence.

Butler was the key prosecution witness. The two Assistant State Attorneys, Paul Ridge and John Kastrenakes, knew they had to use him if they wanted the case to go to trial. They realised that if they gave up on him, a murderer might walk free. They recognised that Butler's evidence presented them with problems, but they were conscientious, and they understood that their job was to put the case together as best they could. So each time they came up against evidence that jarred with Butler's story, they tried to re-engineer his testimony to make it work.

For example, Arlene Rivero, a sales representative for the DuPont Plaza Hotel, was an independent witness and there was no indication that she was biased, so the prosecutors were keen to call her.[17] Rivero had given a sworn statement to Detective Buhrmaster saying she was 100 per cent certain that Kris Maharaj was the person who had reserved Room 1215 for Eddie Dames, around 9 a.m. on October 15th, the day before the murders.[18] This was crucial evidence, as it had Maharaj playing an integral role in the conspiracy.

At trial, Rivero's evidence was not as solid as it had been in her original statement to the police.

'I have already forgotten about it,' she said in an Hispanic accent and a scramble of tenses. She blamed her uncertainty on the two-month delay between the crime and the police asking her to make an identification.[19]

'Were you positive about the identification?' the prosecutor asked her, trying to shore up her memory.

'I want to say positive, but it looked familiar to me, so that is why I identified it,' she replied as helpfully as she could.[20] She had to admit, though, that she had been shown only one picture of the person who might have booked the room – and that was Kris Maharaj.[21]

Her testimony was not as strong as the prosecution might have hoped, but it was still vital – and it was equally important that she not be at cross-purposes with their star witness. But in his early statements, Butler repeatedly asserted that he booked the room himself on the morning of October 15th rather than Kris.[22] The prosecutors noticed this, and they resolved it: Kris must have reserved Room 1215, and Butler must have then paid for it. But when he was under oath at his second deposition, Butler forgot his lines.

'Well, I went to pay for it,' Butler was explaining. 'I said I want a reservation for Eddie Dames, and the lady promptly pulled out a card and said all right, whatever it was, and fifty-five dollars a day I think it was, and she pulled out the card, had me fill out something and she said Room 1215.'[23]

Paul Ridge interrupted.

'My proffer,' the senior prosecutor said, simply butting in and testifying for his witness, 'was that he did not make the reservation, but he signed in and paid for it on the day before the shooting.'[24] Thanks to careful work by the prosecutors, a gaping inconsistency was well on the way to becoming a *fact* that was corroborated by an independent eyewitness.[25]

The prosecution then moved on to 'corroborate' Butler's testimony on a related point. He had handed over two $100 bills as payment for the room, naming the corporate discount,[26] which matched the relevant form from the hotel.[27] Yet Butler had originally insisted that he paid a higher rate.[28] This was another potent indicator of what was going on in the prosecution camp: each mistake their star witness made was corrected,[29] so that the independent physical evidence now *proved* that he was telling the truth.

Unfortunately the subtleties were passing by Kris' lawyer, Eric Hendon, like ships in the night. As I continued my analysis, I became increasingly depressed at what he had missed.

'Do you remember receiving a phone call from the defendant at approximately 7.19 in the morning?' asked Kastrenakes. 7.19? Why did the prosecutor say something so precise? Butler was testifying a year after it all happened, and obviously would not remember the minute of the call. Once more, this seemed designed to 'corroborate' his testimony, since the telephone records showed a call at precisely nineteen minutes past the hour.[30]

'Yes,' said Butler, carefully. 'I believe I received his call.'[31] This timing fitted with Kris' story too. He said he expected to meet Dames at the hotel at 8 a.m. – it was a forty-minute drive from his home near Fort Lauderdale, so he would have been leaving just then. It did not fit, though, with the timing of the murders, which happened at noon. Why would a killer go to the scene, hang about in the room so that any cleaning staff could see him, waiting for a rendezvous scheduled four hours later?

Prosecutor Kastrenakes moved to other independent evidence to buttress his witness. At some point Butler said he called Derrick Moo Young to make sure that he was coming.

'You had indicated … you had called the Moo Youngs,' Kastrenakes asked. 'Did you write the numbers down?'

'Yes, I at that time I couldn't remember the number … all the numbers … so I wrote a number down,' Butler began. If he did not know the number, I wondered, who had given it to him to write it down on a *USA Today* newspaper that was provided free by the hotel? 'Because I remember I wanted to call him to assure him that Dames was there, for me to put Dames on the phone and he would know – to let him know that Dames was here. And we were waiting to …'

Butler had started to ramble into areas that perhaps Kastrenakes did not wish to visit. What was this about putting Dames on the telephone with Derrick Moo Young? That would imply that Dames was in the hotel at 9.47 a.m., the time the call was made. This was after Kris said he had already left to go about his business, irritated at Dames' second no-show in as many days.

'Was there another number that you called Mr Moo Young at?' Kastrenakes interrupted, keen to move along. Kastrenakes must have known about Derrick's daughter's statement: Dames had constantly been calling her father in the week before the murder. Hendon had missed this.

'Yes.'

'What was the number that you called?' Kastrenakes wanted the jury to think that only Butler had called Derrick Moo Young, and the mention of Dames was a slip of the tongue. If Dames had been on the phone as well, it would suggest that he was involved in the conspiracy.

'The one I remember was, I think, 434-5074, I think that is the other number,' Butler testified opaquely. If he did not remember Derrick's number at the time, how could he possibly remember it at trial, a year on? There was only one explanation: he had been carefully prepped:[32] now his memory matched the telephone records, thereby 'corroborating' his evidence.

Not every amendment to the story came from the prosecutors. When the play needed drama, Butler would overegg it himself. According to him, Kris Maharaj went into the bathroom to the left of the main entrance to the suite just before Derrick and Duane came in around 11.30 a.m. Butler greeted them.

'Did Mr Derrick Moo Young make any comments to you concerning Eddie Dames?' Kastrenakes asked.

'Yes, he did,' Butler replied, describing the Moo Youngs' entrance. 'He said, "Where's Dames?" Immediately after, he said, "Where's Dames?" … Immediately after that … he recognised me then. He said, "You are the fellow Carberry or was that from—" He said, "Where's Dames?" I told him to have a seat.'[33]

'Tell the ladies and gentlemen of the jury *exactly* what happened next,' Kastrenakes said, the stress on the word making it clear that this was the *precise* truth.

'As he repeated, "Where's Eddie Dames?"' said Butler. 'I think I mentioned to him, "Well, Dames is not here and I think you need to sort something out about extortion." Before I was able to get the word out, Maharaj came out of the closet and said, "You know, you have to deal with me…" He had in his right hand a gun, and in his left hand there was a small pillow or cushion. I think I remember crying out to him, "Krishna, what is this? What is this?" Because I was surprised as Moo Young was to see a gun and I think I did cry out, "What is this?" '[34]

Butler's feigned surprise at Maharaj wielding a gun was new to the tale, and it was hardly credible. Surely he would have expected a weapon to be involved. Even if the plan really was to make Derrick sign a cheque in compensation, they could hardly do this by artful persuasion alone. Indeed, Butler's story about the gun provides another insight into how the prosecution adapted to the facts. On the night of the crime Detective Buhrmaster had asked for a description of the murder weapon.

'Can you tell me what colour the gun was?' Buhrmaster had asked.

'It was white,' Butler replied.

'Meaning shiny colour?' Buhrmaster asked. He was obviously confused. A white gun would be quite unique, something like the flamboyant Colt revolver brandished by General George S. Patton as his tanks swept through Europe in 1944.[35]

'No,' Butler insisted. 'One colour, white.'[36] He was specific and emphatic. He had allegedly spent three or four hours with the gun early that day – much of the time with it pointing at him.[37] Surely his description would be rock-solid.

Not so. Under the prosecution theory, the murder weapon needed to be a nine-millimetre Smith & Wesson – later they would present evidence that Kris Maharaj had bought such a handgun off a police officer. It was silver, and the officer described it as 'shiny'. There was nothing white about it. So by the time of trial the description had to change.

'Please describe the gun, as you saw it, to the jury?' Kastrenakes now asked Butler, in front of the jury.

'It was a flat gun, sort of flat in his hand,' said Butler.[38]

'Was it dark or a light colour?'

'It appeared to be a light colour,' said Butler.

'How would you call the colour as it appeared to you?'

'Whitish or silver, it was a light colour, off-bone, white, could have been silver.' Butler fudged as best he could.[39] The murder weapon just underwent a transmutation. This was hugely significant, as Kris had only ever owned one handgun. If Kris was telling the truth when he said he did not take part in the murder and did not wave a gun around, Butler would not know what colour his Smith & Wesson really was. His mistake, saying it was white, would be strong evidence that he was confecting the whole story. Yet now he had redrawn his description to match the gun Kris had bought the year before: a yawning discrepancy in his testimony was now physical 'corroboration' that he was being candid. Once more, Kris' lawyer failed to confront Butler with the change at trial.[40]

According to Butler, Maharaj argued with Derrick for several minutes over money.[41] Then Maharaj shot Derrick in the knee, apparently to show that he meant business. As it became increasingly apparent that he might not get out of this alive, Derrick made a desperate lunge at his assailant, whereupon Maharaj allegedly pumped several more shots into him. As Maharaj turned to question the son, Duane, he failed to notice Derrick crawling to the door and throwing himself out into the corridor towards the room opposite. When he saw what was happening, he dragged the older man back in, administering the *coup de grâce*, a bullet to the head.

Another common-sense issue was the noise this would make. BOOM! BOOM! BOOM! BOOM! BOOM! The heavy-calibre handgun was firing repeatedly, first in an enclosed space, before a final shot to Derrick's head in the public hallway. Yet, it later transpired, none of the hotel staff heard anything. This was hard for anyone to believe, even – when pressed – Butler himself.[42] In his original story to Detective Buhrmaster, Butler had insisted that there was no silencer on the gun.[43] The detective seemed to find this story improbable, and probed the issue. Butler retreated, saying that Maharaj brought a pillow with him to the room in a brown bag to muffle the shots.[44] The prosecutors specifically queried whether this could be proven. On a copy of Butler's first statement I noticed that one of them wrote, 'Is that a hotel pillow?'[45] It did not take much of an investigation to figure this out. There were photographs of the room, and the pillow was in the evidence locker; one glance showed that it matched the other cushions on the hotel sofa.

Faced with more physical evidence that Butler might be lying, the prosecutors worked out a way to clear it up. Prior to his deposition by the defence, they decided that there must have been two pillows – one brought in and later taken away.[46] At trial, rather than presenting this tenuous theory, the prosecution used another tactic – they avoided the issue altogether. Kastrenakes pointedly did not ask Butler about any cushion, and Kris' lawyer did not notice.[47]

With respect to the shooting, there was another aspect of Butler's story that I found particularly difficult to believe. In my mind I dubbed it 'Michael Jackson's glove', after the singer's predilection for wearing only one. Butler said that Maharaj had a glove only on his right hand when he fired the gun.[48] Once again, this did not pass the common-sense test. Only golfers buy a single glove, and Kris did not play the game; even Detective Buhrmaster expressed incredulity when Butler first said this is what happened. I wondered what made Butler latch onto this story: had he worried that the police would inevitably do a gunshot-residue test on Kris, and discover no evidence on the swabs that he had fired a gun? If so, Butler was giving them too much credit, as they never did the examination.

When the fingerprint report came in, the prosecution might have viewed it as physical proof of Butler's dishonesty. After all, there were six fingerprints identified as coming from Kris Maharaj's right hand – so he could not have been wearing a glove, at least not all the time. Instead, the prosecution constructed a complicated story for the jury that 'corroborated' Michael Jackson's glove. All the right-handed prints could have been left by Maharaj while he was waiting in the room, they suggested, and before he put on a glove to commit the murder – on a soda can, a newspaper, and so forth. So this physical evidence now supported Butler's previously implausible story.[49]

With Derrick's inert body lying on the carpet, according to Butler, it was time for Duane to die. Room 1215 was a suite on two levels, with the bedroom up a set of stairs, round a corner at the top.

'I remember just before Kris took Duane upstairs, I was pleading with him to let the boy go,' Butler testified. 'I said, "Leave him alone." Even before, I said to him, "It's not too late, you might be able to get the father to the hospital; the boy has nothing to do with this, leave him alone, leave him alone …" He kept talking, "What did your father do with it?"' Presumably Maharaj was talking about the money. 'And finally the kid said to him, "I don't know. I think my sister would know. He doesn't trust me. I think my sister knows about it." He finally said – the last thing he said was to Duane, "All right, why didn't you tell me that before, you are a good boy. I wouldn't kill you." Then I heard a shot.'

BOOM!

'The last words you heard from him were, "I wouldn't kill you"?'
Kastrenakes underlined.

'Yes.'[50]

Duane, a young man just twenty-three years old, was dead, with one
execution-style bullet through the head. It was a point of high drama
in the trial. And suddenly Butler's testimony was interrupted. Eric
Hendon had been quietly seated throughout the performance to
date; but now he was on his feet asking for a sidebar with the judge.

'Your Honour,' the defence lawyer began, 'for the record, I would like
to note that during Mr Kastrenakes' direct examination of Mr Butler,
one of the victims' family members who is in the court stormed out
of the court and commenced screaming or wailing in the hall.' Finally
Hendon was preserving Kris Maharaj's legal rights. If the victims'
family – or any spectator – made an emotional outburst in court, that
could provoke a later reversal. The appellate courts might decide that
it had prejudiced the jury.

'Let the record reflect that defence counsel is incorrect,' said Judge
Gross with some sarcasm, protecting the case from the years of antic-
ipated appeals. 'The victim walked out of the courtroom, did not
scream, did not wail, did not utter a word, and that was the end of it
and that took precisely four seconds.'[51]

He frowned at Hendon, daring a contradiction. None came.
Hendon was cowed by the aggressive judge.

The interruption, as I read the transcript of the appeal, gave me another
moment to reflect. All this while, as Kris Maharaj was supposed to
be marching Duane up to his death, Butler said he was standing at
the bottom of the stairs.[52] Had Hendon bothered to visit the crime
scene, this would have told him at least three things: that Butler could
not have seen what was going on upstairs[53] and therefore could not
describe it; that Kris Maharaj would not have been able to see him;
and that Butler was within two feet of the door to the hallway, and
escape.

'I was sure I was going to get shot,' Butler told the jury, dramatically.
'I was sure my turn was next.'[54] But he made no effort to flee,[55] to
simply open the door and run down the hall. He described how
Maharaj was gone for at least ten seconds.[56] In that time Usain Bolt

could have run more than 100 metres ... Butler was no Bolt, but if he was scared for his life, he could certainly have made it to the lift, or – afraid that it would not come in time – to either of two sets of emergency stairs. Instead, Kris allegedly came downstairs from the bedroom, his brown holdall with him, and they walked out of Room 1215 together.[57] 'I saw the gun in his hands, and I think he took it in his hands as we were walking out of the room going to the elevator.'[58]

One question must still have been reverberating in the mind of any inquiring juror: if Butler and Maharaj were now riding down in the lift together, why was Butler still alive? If Maharaj had committed two murders – one when the situation perhaps got out of control, and the second in very cold blood – then it is difficult to understand why he would not shoot Butler too. Here is a man who had no real connection to Maharaj, who claimed he had vociferously opposed shooting either of the Moo Youngs, and was now the only witness to a crime that would certainly put Kris Maharaj away for life, and quite possibly death. Once again, Hendon never confronted Butler with this at trial.[59]

According to Butler, the two of them were now out of the DuPont Plaza. Most killers – relieved to have escaped the scene of a double-murder – would have been on the next plane to a country with no extradition treaty. But Butler told the jury that he and Maharaj sat in the car in front of the hotel for three hours, with the engine running and the air conditioning on.[60] Police cars were screeching to a halt around them, blue lights flashing. Why were they waiting? Butler suggested that it was to meet the elusive Eddie Dames. But Kris Maharaj did not know Dames, and Dames did not know him, and there was no apparent reason why Maharaj would want to hang around to make his acquaintance. Presumably the only person Dames could finger to the police would have been Butler – which was all the more reason for the killer to give Butler a pair of cement shoes and drop him in the Everglades swamp for an alligator's dinner.

Butler's tale was almost complete at this point. He described how Dames appeared outside the hotel, whereupon Butler leapt out of Maharaj's car and drove off in Dames' rental. Maharaj followed, but they lost him on Biscayne Boulevard. Butler then told the jury about a telephone conversation that he had with Maharaj later in the day.

'Maharaj said, "I want you to meet me at the Denny's." I said,

"Which Denny's?" "The Denny's at the airport." I further said to him, I said, "You know, the police know that I was there and they are looking for me." He said, "It doesn't matter. I want to see you so we can get all our stories." '

'He wanted to get your story straight together?' Kastrenakes clarified.

'Yes.'[61]

Here, the prosecutor had omitted another worrying segment of Butler's story – a long, and potentially crucial, amount of time had passed. This call supposedly took place that evening: seven or eight hours after the Moo Youngs died in the DuPont Plaza. What had happened in the meantime? Butler wasn't saying, but now his story came to an end. He led the police to the Denny's Diner, where Detective Buhrmaster arrested Kris Maharaj for two counts of first-degree murder.

It seemed to me, reading all this, that Butler had simply jiggled along, like a marionette on the end of a string. Each time he said something that was provably false, the prosecutor not only ignored the possibility that it might prove Kris Maharaj to be innocent, but refashioned Butler's testimony so that the physical evidence, or an independent witness, 'corroborated' Butler rather than impeaching him. Yet who exactly was manipulating whom?

In almost every case I have ever had, the main prosecution witness, if he is wrapped up in the crime, has got some kind of sweetheart deal from the state. Even assuming that Butler was telling the truth at trial, he was now admitting that he had conspired with Kris Maharaj to bring the Moo Youngs to the room where they were to be held (kidnapped) until they signed a cheque (extortion) turning over money. And because Butler was wrapped up in a felony that ultimately resulted in death, under Florida law he was guilty of murder at least as an accomplice – notwithstanding his protestation that he never intended the Moo Youngs harm. Thus, at the very least, he faced life in prison. He had also admitted to committing perjury in his earlier statements. Yet he never spent a single night in jail.

All an effective defence lawyer would have had to do was start asking Butler what lengths he would go to in order to avoid life in prison: Would he lie? (Of course.) Would he sell his own mother? (Probably.) Prosecutors don't like to watch that kind of butchering of their witness. John Kastrenakes tried to pull the sting out of the expected cross-examination.

'Has anybody from the State Attorney's office or the police department promised you anything to make you say anything of that nature?' the prosecutor asked.

'Nobody promised me anything,' Butler insisted.

'Have you been promised any immunity whatsoever for your own involvement in this case?'

'Absolutely none.'[62]

Butler knew very well that he needed to toe the prosecution line or he would face decades in prison. For the prosecutors to pretend that there was no deal – overt or covert – was a charade. Indeed, the proof of the pudding was there before me: I was reading the transcript six years after the trial, and Butler had remained at liberty the whole time. That is a mighty incentive for a witness to 'cooperate'; it is a power that no defence lawyer has at his disposal to secure helpful evidence. The prosecutors may have thought that they benefited from Butler's testimony, but who was getting the better deal? Whose strings were really being pulled? Neville Butler's or those of the prosecution?

I doubted the prosecutors even considered the alternative. If Kris was telling the truth, they were rewarding Butler twice: once, by not prosecuting him for his complicity in two murders, and a second time for taking no action as he committed perjury against an innocent man.

It was now up to Eric Hendon, as Kris Maharaj's attorney, to rake Butler over the coals and propose some alternative theory.[63] If cross-examination is meant to be the 'greatest legal engine ever invented for the discovery of the truth', then Eric Hendon was the Little Engine that Couldn't. Butler had answered prosecutor Kastrenakes' questions for more than three hours; Hendon began his own interrogation as lunchtime approached. Before he had made any headway in breaking down Butler's story, he stopped short and turned to the judge.

'Your Honour,' he said, 'I have several other legal pads full of information with reference to my cross-examination of Mr Butler and I must have left those matters at my desk at home.'

Hendon was permitted the lunch break to collect his papers and give more thought to his theory. As they had their sandwiches, the jurors must have been wondering what he would present. Logic dictated that Butler had to be lying for Kris to be innocent. Who else had a motive to kill the Moo Youngs? Kris had told Hendon that he thought they had something to do with drugs, though he could point to nothing more than rumour. Still, there was something very dodgy about the man staying in the room across the hall from the murder scene: Jaime Vallejo Mejia, an 'import-export' businessman from Colombia.

And who was this chap Eddie Dames? The fact that the murder room was booked in his name was hugely suspicious, as was the evidence that he had been calling Derrick from the Bahamas. Dames was an air-traffic controller in Nassau. If Hendon simply read the newspapers, he must have known that this was a classic job in the drug trade. The aircraft that ferry cocaine have to avoid detection. What better ally than the man whose radar keeps track of each flight?

Hendon also needed to explain why Kris was lured into the room that morning. If he was not guilty, there had to be an explanation, and the jury would be waiting to hear it. Perhaps someone planned to frame him? Or was he meant to end up dead as well? Did they mean to shoot him, kill Derrick Moo Young, and try to make it look like a murder-suicide – the furious British businessman kills his mortal enemy, and then takes his own life in horror at his act … ?

When he returned from lunch, Hendon proposed none of these ideas. Instead, he suggested something much less believable. Hendon's theory involved Carberry and his tabloid paper, the *Caribbean Echo*. Butler had worked for Carberry for some months before his recent move to Kris' paper. Perhaps there was a dastardly plot between them to kill the Moo Youngs to provide a scoop for Carberry's paper?

'As a matter of fact, knowing Carberry's zest for sensationalism, you and he devised this particular plot, which would provide the best sensation type of news that could have been put together and put in Mr Carberry's paper.' Hendon confronted his witness, his voice rising with his accusation. 'Isn't that correct?'

Butler must have blinked at him. What on earth was Hendon trying to say? That he and Carberry committed a double capital murder in order to sell a few more copies of the *Caribbean Echo*?

'That's very incorrect,' Butler said, emphatically.[64] This was one of the few things that Butler said with which we can all agree. Hendon had seriously let his client down. The prosecutors must have felt rather smug as they listened. What they feared would be a tough battle was turning out to be a walkover.

Butler's testimony is an example of one of the fatal flaws in the American justice system, where prosecutors, with their innate biases (perhaps not apparent even to themselves), refashion the evidence to fit their view of the truth – doing it in such a way that the jurors barely glimpse it. English barristers may suggest that the only solution is to keep those who present the evidence as far away from the witness as possible. But this merely passes the buck along the trial production line, and is anyway not an easy balance to strike. From the very start, the police interview a witness to prepare the prosecution case, and this is a process that will reflect police predispositions, no matter how careful they may be. A witness must be 'prepared' if he or she is to have any chance of telling an honest story and not being twisted by the cross-examining lawyer. The truth is not something that magically bubbles to the surface in the boiling cauldron of the courtroom.

Preparing witnesses takes place every day in the American courtroom. In the US it is not only considered permissible, but a lawyer might be deemed ineffective for failing to do it.[65] Yet it is rarely discussed, perhaps because there is a rather nebulous line between effective adversarial lawyering[66] and what amounts to suborning perjury.[67] I cannot find any cases where a lawyer has been sanctioned for 'preparing' his witness overzealously.[68] One of the few that comes close involves President Bill Clinton, who was held in contempt for committing perjury concerning Monica Lewinsky in a deposition that he gave under oath.[69] Notably, though, the lawyers who vigorously prepared him (and other witnesses) for this deposition[70] were not punished – although even at the time they must have known that their client was on shaky ground. More to the point, once he subsequently made inconsistent statements in the grand jury, to Congress and in the media, they should have known to correct his earlier testimony.[71] They did not, yet nothing happened to them.

Butler's evidence had undergone a methodical metamorphosis. At every step he edged closer to the story the prosecution wanted to tell, and the truth became less likely to emerge. There is a good argument that the prosecutors' work fell within normal US practice; far from being punished for their work with Butler and other witnesses, Paul Ridge and John Kastrenakes celebrated with their peers when the jury came back with a guilty verdict and a death sentence. They had taken a difficult case and put it together with great care. Ridge would later go into a lucrative private practice, and Kastrenakes would enjoy a dream shared by most state prosecutors – moving to a federal prosecutor's office, followed by elevation to the bench as a judge.

Meanwhile there were a few more shocks in store, as I found other documents relating to Butler – materials that had not been shown to the jury. First, there was a lie-detector test administered to Kris. From the moment he was arrested, Kris demanded to take one. I am sceptical about these truth-telling machines, though advocates optimistically claim 100 per cent accuracy.[72] In my experience, a polygraph's ability to obtain the truth depends on the credulity and biases of those involved.

Kris was a lie-detector acolyte: because he believed that the machine really could see into his soul, that meant he was very likely to tell the truth. Eric Hendon had set up the test with a respected Florida examiner, George Slattery, and Kris insisted that he was innocent. In late January 1987, Slattery determined that Kris had passed, with no ambiguity.[73] Hendon turned over the report to the prosecutors: the machine said they had the wrong man in prison.

It was impossible for both Kris and Neville Butler to be telling the truth, so it was in everyone's interest to work out whether Butler was lying. A few days later, on February 9th, 1987, John Kastrenakes wrote to Hendon saying that he wanted Butler to take a polygraph, but the prosecution did not have funds for it – so would the defendant pay?[74] This showed some gall: the state was holding Kris for capital murder, but wanted him to foot the prosecution bill. It would have been no more than $1,000 or so, but Kris refused. Whether that was a wise decision, only time would tell. Eventually the prosecution came up with some state funding. A little over a month later, following a brief discussion in court, Kastrenakes sent a letter to Hendon regarding Butler's polygraph: 'As I indicated to you previously,' the prosecutor wrote, 'he passed with regard to the questions asked of him as to your client being the shooter in this matter as well as he not being armed or participating in the shootings of the Moo Youngs.'[75] But Kastrenakes said Butler had changed his story somewhat, and Hendon should schedule him for a second deposition.

The carefully worded letter rang an alarm bell for me. The letter did not simply say that Butler had passed – rather, it identified areas in which he had given the right answers. However, as I continued through the transcript, my suspicions faded: the prosecutors said specifically that Butler passed his test.[76] Hendon did depose Butler for a second time, and while Butler admitted that he had not told the truth about everything in his first deposition, he insisted that he had voluntarily come clean.

'How are we sure you are telling us the truth now?' demanded Hendon.

'Objection!' exclaimed Paul Ridge, the lead prosecutor. 'You want to know how we know he is being truthful? Because he took a polygraph examination … I think it is worthless to ask a question like that.'[77]

Then, of course, there was the incident that had taken place at trial. Hendon tried to get Kris Maharaj's polygraph result before the jury, before they imposed the sentence.

'Who passed the polygraph?' Judge Solomon demanded.

'Krishna Maharaj took a polygraph and passed,' replied Hendon.

'And Mr Butler took a polygraph and passed,' countered Ridge.[78] That was clear enough.

Because Judge Solomon could not figure out how to dissect that baby, he excluded both polygraph results from the trial.

Now, in front of me, I had a document that the jury never saw – and neither did Kris Maharaj nor Eric Hendon. Any investigation in a capital case must be exhaustive; a single piece of paper may be the key that unlocks the case. This is not as simple a proposition as it may seem. There is an extraordinary rule in Florida, duplicated in most American states, that the defendant in a criminal case can have access to the prosecution and police file only *after he is convicted*.[79] In Florida the Freedom of Information law is called the Sunshine Law. However, at the time of trial, access to the evidence may be limited by the rules of discovery; there being no sunshine, this is often a time of darkness. In some states I have tried capital cases where all we received from the prosecution was a witness list, with no indication of what anyone might say. None of this makes any sense: surely there would have to be a compelling reason to deny the accused anything related to his case; keeping information from him turns the process into a lottery.

Florida is one of the better jurisdictions, allowing the defence the right to depose each witness under oath before trial. Additionally, the prosecution is obliged to reveal any evidence they plan to use at trial, along with anything 'exculpatory' – although the definition of that term is hotly debated. There are two dangers: first, that the prosecution will not comply with its discovery obligations; and second, that the defence lawyer will come to rely too heavily on the prosecutors, and fail to conduct an independent investigation. One way to test how honest the state has been at trial is to file a Sunshine request after the trial and go and peruse the prosecution file. I generally don't hold out much hope of finding useful information, as in some states inconvenient documents have a bad habit of disappearing. But I had made an appointment with the Office of the State Attorney. When I turned up, a secretary took me into an office where boxes of materials had been laid out on the table.

As I sat leafing through the files, I soon came across an original letter from someone called Dudley Dickson, a polygraph expert from Tampa. He had written to prosecutor John Kastrenakes about a test that he had administered on Neville Butler.[80] I flipped to the expert's conclusion on page three. 'Based on the subject's polygraph responses,' Dickson concluded, 'it is the examiner's opinion he was untruthful and was withholding and falsifying information as indicated above.'[81]

I was taken aback by this discovery. Until that moment I had assumed – as Hendon did at trial – that Paul Ridge told the truth to the judge during the trial and that Butler had passed his test. He had not. Various things were immediately apparent. Certainly Butler had not voluntarily come forward to change his story, as he testified six times under oath at trial. Only under an aggressive interrogation by Dudley Dickson did he back off the version that he originally gave to Detective Buhrmaster and that he had repeated several times in the ensuing five months. By the end of an afternoon hooked up to the polygraph machine he told quite a different tale, much closer to what had emerged at trial.

Dickson obviously thought certain areas of Butler's story were incredible, including the notion that he and Kris had waited for three hours outside the murder scene, with flashing police lights all around. It was as if Vladimir and Estragon knew they were wanted for murder, but decided to wait for Godot on a bench outside the police station. Dickson tried to force Butler into telling the truth, by officially labelling him a liar on that question in the test.

Notwithstanding the fact that Butler failed on various questions – all of which were 'facts' that he subsequently repeated as truth to the jury – Dudley Dickson passed him with respect to central aspects of his examination. I compared these to similar queries put to Kris Maharaj by Slattery.

'On or about October 16, 1986, did you actually see Kris Maharaj shoot Derrick Moo Young?' asked Dudley Dickson.

'Yes,' replied Neville Butler.[82] Dickson called this a pass.

'Regarding the shooting deaths of Derrick and Duane Moo Young,' asked George Slattery. 'Did you kill them?'

'No,' replied Kris Maharaj. Slattery called this a pass.[83]

There was an irreconcilable conflict. They could not both be telling the truth – Kris saying he was innocent, and Butler saying he was guilty. I later came across a copy of Butler's first statement, where each fact had been annotated by one of the prosecutors[84] as 'TRUE', 'FALSE' or 'UNCLEAR'.[85] For a moment I wondered how the prosecutor came to such objective clarity, but then I noticed that he had simply cross-referenced the statement against the lie-detector report. Apparently the polygrapher, Dudley Dickson, was to be the ultimate arbiter of veracity of the central government witness. With every question where Dickson passed Butler, that had now been validated for the prosecutors, and they viewed their task in clear focus: they just had to prove Dickson right. If that meant reshaping Butler's testimony, then that must be the right thing to do. Butler had to tell the truth, and they knew what the truth was.

'Krishna Maharaj …' begins the British television reporter Nick Glenn some years later when he is interviewing Butler. 'Krishna Maharaj, since the trial, says he was denied justice and was innocent of justice.'

'I think this is the most ridiculous statement I have heard in all my years!' Butler exclaims. 'And that's the only way I can put it … kill one man and execute, as far as I'm concerned, the other son, and you're talking about denying justice.'

'He says he's innocent of the charges.'

'Absolutely positively bull.'

'Do you think justice was served?'

'Yeah. No ifs, ands or buts about it,' Butler concludes.[86]

6

The Prosecutor

In theory, the prosecutor is a bulwark between the innocent defendant and the electric chair. According to the United States Supreme Court, the prosecution is 'the representative not of an ordinary party to a controversy, but of a sovereignty whose obligation to govern impartially is as compelling as its obligation to govern at all; and whose interest, therefore, in a criminal prosecution is not that it shall win a case, but that justice shall be done'.[1]

It's a nice idea, but if we took it seriously, we would not design the prosecutor's office as we do. We have already seen the two prosecutors at work on the problems presented to them by Neville Butler – I do not suggest that they were corrupt, or trying to convict an innocent person. Rather, they were striving very hard for justice, as they saw it. The question we must answer is how two men, who were meant to protect someone from a wrongful conviction, could be so single-minded when it came to rehearsing Butler's story and ironing out the flaws that would surely have given the jury a reasonable doubt.

'John, what was the real fascination of this case for you?' a British television reporter asks Kastrenakes years later.

'Breaking, or having Mr Butler tell the truth of exactly what his role was in the case,' Kastrenakes replies.[2]

'You said you broke Neville Butler,' the journalist queries. 'Why use the word broke?'

'That's a term of art,' Kastrenakes corrects himself. 'What, in fact, he did was he changed his testimony to a truthful version of what really happened.'[3]

'Why did he change his version of events?'

'Well,' begins Kastrenakes. 'We, over the course of several months, Paul Ridge and I were able to obtain telephone records, the evidence of other people, that showed that he, in fact, was in touch constantly with Krishna Maharaj, and that as he would call the Moo Youngs to arrange for this meeting, the next phone call would be made to Krishna Maharaj. So it didn't take a rocket scientist to figure out that his role was much more than he had let on to be. We had confronted that with him and we offered him a chance to take a polygraph examination, because we doubted that aspect of his testimony. And, in fact, he flunked the polygraph examination and, over the course of several hours, admitted all these other things that he eventually testified to.'[4]

'Was he offered a deal?'

'He was never offered a deal. He was never offered ... er ... by Paul Ridge or myself ... er ... immunity from prosecution,' Kastrenakes offers cautiously. 'But ... er ... he testified under the fear of being prosecuted for being involved and for perjury ... er ... in his initial sworn statements.'[5]

'A general question about the judicial system here, it's expensive, it's lengthy, what are the general worries you perceive?'

'I think that in a – in a country such as ours and such as yours,' Kastrenakes begins, referring to Britain, 'where the philosophy is that it's better to let 900 people ... 999 guilty people go free than to convict one innocent man, and that the burden is on the government to prove an accused citizen's guilt beyond and to the exclusion of every reasonable doubt, that it's necessarily going to be long, and it's necessarily going to be expensive and it should be tough on the government to prove a person's guilt ...'[6]

'I've always felt that being up front, telling the defence every bit of the evidence that you have, is always the right way to go,' Kastrenakes continues. 'Because ... er ... if you try to hide something, if you try to ... er ... create your own web of deceit, then things come around to haunt you in the end. And certainly ... there was never one bit of deceit by us. The deceit that was spun in this case was ... was spun by Krishna Maharaj, not by the prosecutors.'[7]

I used to think that some prosecutors were wicked, that they intentionally hid material that could be used to destroy their case. But I have long since concluded that the answer is much more dangerous: it never occurred to either John Kastrenakes or Paul Ridge that they were covering up evidence that could help prove that Kris was innocent – for the simple reason that neither believed Kris was innocent, so how could such evidence exist?[8]

The ineptitude of Kris' lawyer – Eric Hendon – also passed by the prosecutors. They probably never noticed that Hendon was doing such a mediocre job: because they believed so firmly that Kris Maharaj was guilty, they would have decided that Hendon simply had nothing to work with.[9] However, their job could have been so much harder if Hendon had prepared effectively, and presented an adequate defence.

I do not mean to speak of Paul Ridge and John Kastrenakes as if they were Siamese twins, indistinguishable in their attitudes. Ridge was older, the senior prosecutor at trial, but he struck me as the less doctrinaire of the two. He left the prosecutor's office sometime after Kris went to Death Row and moved into private practice. Whether it was in his nature, or a product of his later experience, he was more ready to edge towards an admission – for example, he admitted that he should not have told the judge that Butler's failed polygraph was a pass.

Kastrenakes was, in my experience, a better example of the problem of the prosecutor predisposition. He looked the part: dark-haired and clean-cut. His career has followed the archetypal trajectory from a junior state prosecutor to a capital-trials prosecutor, a transfer to a federal prosecution office before a run for judge in Dade County, Miami. Everything about John Kastrenakes reflected his belief in the system.[10]

'Now Krishna Maharaj still claims he's been denied justice and he still claims he's innocent to the charges for which he was convicted,' continues the journalist in his interview with Kastrenakes.

'So do ninety-nine per cent of criminals in America who are imprisoned for their crimes … say that they did not commit a crime,' he replies. 'Er … it's the rare, it's the unique case where you find a prisoner either on Death Row or incarcerated for a crime they committed that owns up to their commission of the crime and say that they did the crime that they are charged with. I dare say that there is not a single person on Florida's Death Row who will come forward to anybody and say I committed the crime that I am being convicted of and sentenced to death for.'[11]

Kastrenakes is entirely wrong about this. It is hardly surprising; he has never represented a prisoner on Death Row, so he would not know. Most of the people I represent who did commit the offence are forthright with me about what happened, and rather scathing about the small group who claim innocence but who appear to be guilty. On the other hand, convicts tend to be very protective of those they believe to be innocent. But Kastrenakes' certainty is understandable: it is simply his mindset, compounded by the natural disinclination that anyone would have to believe he put the wrong person in prison.

'So you have no doubts?' the journalist asks.

'I have no doubts about Krishna Maharaj's guilt, involvement in the murders of a …' he starts, '… or a father and a son, a child who … er … he got the death penalty for killing a boy who had no grudge with Krishna Maharaj, called him uncle, looked up to him as a family member.'[12]

The stumbling choice of words shows Kastrenakes' self-justification. I have sometimes wondered whether it is fair for me to call my clients 'kids' when they are fifteen or sixteen – but I don't like the term 'juvenile', which dehumanises the person on trial. But Duane Moo Young was twenty-three. He was neither a 'kid' nor a 'boy'. Kastrenakes chose the word 'boy' to make the crime seem worse.

'That's what he got the death penalty for,' Kastrenakes says of Kris. 'And that's what he deserves the death penalty for.'[13]

But would he, John Kastrenakes, ever consider the possibility that he might have made a mistake? 'Could it be said that the system is intrinsically flawed, that there have been hundreds of cases of miscarriage of justice this century in capital cases?'

'I … I have no comment on that,' Kastrenakes stutters. 'Because I … I have not been privy to the facts or information in those kinds of cases.'[14]

'What does it mean to you to win a capital case of this kind?' the reporter asks.

'Personally?' Kastrenakes demands. 'I was – I was very satisfied that, in fact, that I … the jury came to the same conclusion that I did about the evidence in the case and that it was overwhelming. That he deserved the death penalty for the crime that he committed and … er … there was the satisfaction that I had done, I hadn't fumbled the ball, I hadn't blown the kick, you know, as to … er … so to speak, and that I'd done the best possible job that I could in presenting the case…'[15]

*

It is not difficult to see where one major flaw is in the Darwinian design of the American prosecutor.[16] There are more than 2,300 local prosecutors' offices in the US handling over 2.3 million felony cases each year.[17] While a minority of state prosecutors' offices have experimented with different practices, all but Connecticut, New Jersey and the District of Columbia 'share one common trait: the job of chief prosecutor, or district attorney, is … an elected position'.[18] Politics, then, enter into every decision that these prosecutors make.[19]

'The political pressure on prosecutors,' writes one commentator, 'has been said to lead to a subtle shift away from the prosecutor's goal of "doing justice" and an increased focus on conviction rates.'[20] The understatement makes me chuckle: there has been no subtlety in the move. It is a very rare prosecutor who runs for election on a platform of 'doing justice',[21] whereas candidates regularly boast about how they will convict more criminals[22] or send more prisoners to Death Row.[23]

It is one matter for this to be the television face of a district attorney who must run for election, but what of the assistants, the staff who more often prosecute the cases? One might hope that they come, youthful out of law school, urgently seeking to do justice. Unfortunately, as a general matter,[24] this is not the nature of the beast.

American prosecutors are chosen (or self-select) from a very specific pool of societal and political attitudes. We will see, when we come to the police, a rigorous effort to identify a particular psychological profile and hire a defined type of person. Similarly, logic would suggest (and practice confirms) that those who choose to be prosecutors believe it is fair and just that people who commit crimes should go to prison for long terms, and that the system generally gets such judgements right. Prosecutors tend to share a perception 'that the police only arrest guilty people in the first place [which] reinforces the belief that the right person was charged and later convicted'.[25] Indeed, more than half of prosecutors in one survey thought the presumption of innocence was tosh, since the issue of guilt had been determined by the police and prosecutorial screening procedures before trial.[26] No matter what focus prosecutors initially bring to the job, there is plenty of evidence that they gradually learn to emphasise convictions as the primary goal, as compared to some amorphous and liberal notion of 'justice'.[27]

In my own experience, the prevailing ethos in the US is remarkable: many prosecutors believe that *all* people who make it as far as trial are guilty.[28] I once called a prosecutor as a witness in a pre-trial hearing and asked him whether he ever had doubts about the guilt of those he was seeking to send to prison. If I were asked how many guilty people I have defended, I would have to respond that there have been a substantial number,[29] but I have also defended many who I am convinced did not commit the crime.

'How many innocent people, or people you think maybe might have been innocent, do you think you've ever prosecuted?' I put this question to Roger Jordan, who was prosecuting Clarence 'Smitty' Smith at the time. I thought Smitty was innocent of the capital murder for which he was on trial. The jury later agreed. Before Jordan replied, I expected a pause, some reflection. His response was instantaneous and emphatic.

'None. Never.'

In retrospect, I suppose this was inevitable, for a number of reasons. First, had he said anything else, I would have made him identify the cases where he had qualms, and I would then have set about investigating their convictions. If the prosecutor has any doubt at all, that has to mean the defendant is very probably innocent. Second, had he prosecuted someone where he harboured a reasonable doubt, he would be admitting to an ethical violation. But I do not believe that Jordan responded for such strategic or self-serving reasons: he said it because he believed it. He subscribed to the creed that, in this facet of their endeavours, human beings were essentially flawless. It is a belief system that is shared by a remarkable number of his peers.

As a matter of human nature, it is probably inevitable that those who spend their lives sending people to prison become increasingly converted to this notion of prosecutorial infallibility. It would be difficult to drive to work every day pondering how many innocent people you might deprive of liberty today. There is a second self-selection procedure, whereby those who continue to harbour doubts move on from the prosecutor's office quite rapidly. The remainder confirm each other's biases around the coffee machine until the wagons are fully circled.

*

There are various very human elements to this process. John Kastrenakes and Paul Ridge spent a lot of time with their star witness, Neville Butler, and no doubt came to see him as a human being, despite his frailties, and appreciated his effort to work with them. In contrast, they never had anything to do with Krishna Maharaj except when he stared at them – doubtless with some hostility – across the courtroom. The lawyer seeking to condemn the defendant never actually talks to him, unless it is to cross-examine him and try to 'break' him. This is another rather unusual aspect of the judicial system: most participants, including the prosecutors, judge and jurors, are asked to reach a decision about the person on trial without ever having met him.

Perhaps there are some company managers who hire employees based on a written résumé of their experiences, without any personal interview. I suspect their success rate is rather low. A depressingly large proportion of those I have hired after a lengthy interview have not worked out (my judgement has been lacking); overwhelmingly, the best decisions I have made have come when the applicants have worked with us as volunteers for several months and we have come to know them. While other people may be better than me at interviews, there are few who would assess someone solely on the say-so of others, particularly when those giving the reference – as Neville Butler did for Kris Maharaj – have their own hidden agendas.

So a system might be more likely to work if the participants all knew each other better. I have sometimes made attempts to bring prosecutors and defendants together. The first person I represented at trial – in 1985, when I was a year out of law school and should not have been allowed into a courtroom in any role but as a spectator – was John Pope. John was a rather hapless forty-two-year-old armed robber who had held up a pharmacy to feed his drug habit. The pharmacist grabbed the gun, the assistant hit John over the head with a broomstick, and during the struggle the gun went off, killing the pharmacist. John was deeply remorseful for what had happened. He was facing capital punishment in a small Georgia town west of Atlanta.

I spent a lot of time with my first client, and it was clear to me that he never meant to kill anyone. It occurred to me that the prosecutor, Bill Foster, might be rather more understanding if he got to know John himself. Bill was a very potent adversary – an experienced lawyer who was respected by jurors, and connected with them. He was also very likeable, and I knew he would get along with John. So I told Bill that he could sit down with John (without me there) and ask him whatever he liked. I told him frankly that, if he did this, I was fairly confident that he would end his campaign to send John to the electric chair. But I said that if it did not change his mind, then he would be free to use anything that John said at the upcoming trial. It was a calculated risk, but we did not have a lot to lose.

Bill would have none of it. He didn't want to talk to John. It was apparent to me that he feared what it would do to his resolve.[30]

Thus does the prosecutor avoid undermining his worldview.[31] Since that time I have tried to get prosecutors to do that same thing, from time to time, without success.[32]

The first three flaws in the prosecutorial design are, then, the mindset of those who take on the job; the reinforcing nature of the prosecutorial club; and the way the system discourages any contact with the person on trial. These factors conspire to make it very unlikely that a prosecutor will accept that he has sent an innocent person to prison. Few people are very good at admitting their mistakes; fewer still when those mistakes are more serious. Meanwhile, the more entrenched the position becomes, the less chance there is of an honest retreat.

If the average American prosecutor enters the fray with his prejudices firmly intact,[33] what legal framework is in place to press the government lawyer in the direction of doing justice? Bizarrely, lawyers have come up with a regime that achieves precisely the opposite, totally insulating the prosecutor from any chance of being held responsible for his actions. The case of Shareef Cousin provides a case-study in how the prosecutor is encouraged by the legal system to perpetuate his mistakes.

Shareef was a sixteen-year-old who had been sentenced to death for a murder in New Orleans, after Michael Gerardi had taken Connie Babin to the Port of Call restaurant in the French Quarter. As the white couple emerged from the restaurant at the end of the evening, three young African American men confronted them and demanded money. A gun went off, and Gerardi fell to the ground, fatally wounded. The prosecutor was Roger Jordan, just as in the earlier case of 'Smitty' Smith. Roger was a couple of years younger than me, the same height – well over six feet – but in other ways we differed. He was good-looking in a classic, American-blond way. He had spent almost his entire career as a prosecutor. The brief stint that he had in a private law practice (defending criminals who could afford to pay) had convinced him to get back on the right side, so he returned to the Orleans Parish District Attorney's office, then run by Harry Connick Senior.

The older Connick was a colourful career prosecutor in New Orleans. His son was the famous balladeer Harry Connick Junior, and Harry Senior had parlayed this into his own Tuesday gig every week in a local bar, where he would shake his hips on-stage, crooning some Fifties songs. His office, meanwhile, had a repertoire of prosecutorial misconduct, all of it built on the notion that New Orleans jurors, who were predominantly African American, let off far too many guilty criminals.

The star eyewitness against Shareef Cousin was Connie Babin. She had been on a first date with Gerardi that evening. Detective Anthony Small, who led the investigation on the case, told his colleagues early in the investigation that he had 'some problems'. One 'problem' that Jordan and Small faced was Shareef's alibi: they didn't come any better. At the precise time of the murder Shareef insisted that he had been some distance away playing basketball. Ironically it was an official programme intended to keep young people off the streets, expending their energies on sport rather than crime. One of the parents at the game came forward with a timed and dated videotape that showed Shareef taking shots with an orange ball at the very moment when someone else was shooting Gerardi outside the restaurant. But the prosecutor, Roger Jordan, was from the same school as Kastrenakes and Ridge, and he meticulously challenged the accuracy of the time shown on the tape. The timing of the video was only as reliable as the setting of the camera, and that – he contended – could only be shown to be true or false by the memories of the witnesses who verified when the game took place. Jordan twisted up several alibi witnesses on their timing, and the defence evidence began to look fallible.

This brought into play another rule that governs the criminal trial process: a picture may paint a thousand words, a videotape a million, but with many juries the testimony of a weeping white woman who says that her boyfriend has been shot down in front of her counts for far more than either. Connie Babin insisted that she was 100 per cent certain that the young man on trial had killed Michael Gerardi. Shareef was convicted and sentenced to death.[34]

Our office, the LCAC, took Shareef's appeal on when he was sent to Death Row. Our investigation revealed that Detective Small and Roger Jordan had obscured a second big 'problem': Connie Babin had made various earlier statements that cast great doubt on the vehement identification she made in court.[35] 'Ms Babin stated she did not get a good look at the perpetrators and probably could not identify them,' wrote the first officer to interview her at the scene of the murder. 'Ms Babin was visibly shaken up.'

'It was dark and I did not have my contacts nor my glasses so I'm coming at this at a disadvantage,' Babin had told the next person who interviewed her that night, Detective Pete Bowen. Some days later, in the calm setting of her own home, she had repeated her uncertainty on tape to Detective Small. 'I saw a movement, my … left eye perfo- rated vision,' she said hesitantly, unable to see the assailant and strug- gling to identify the word 'peripheral'. 'And I knew it was a move- ment.'

In other words, all she really saw was a blur. If this had been known to Shareef's trial lawyers, there could have been no conviction for truancy, let alone a death sentence for murder. The prosecutor had elected to keep these statements from the jury. Indeed, Jordan had made various similar decisions. He failed to turn over information that Babin had identified as one of the perpetrators another person who had no links to Shareef.[36] We tracked down a local birdwatcher who had actually witnessed the crime through his binoculars, writing down a licence plate that might lead to the real killers – Jordan had known this, but kept it to himself. And there was a separate, anony- mous Crime Stopper tip, where someone had called in identifying the same people as the birdwatcher.[37] None of this was disclosed to the defence.[38]

The prosecutor's conviction that the police had the right killer led him even further astray. When we located the various statements indicating that Babin had bad eyesight, the prosecution provided us with her Driver's License Physical Exam. This reflected that her right eye was 20/20 and her left was 20/40, with her full vision being 20/20 *without* corrective lenses. The document made no sense. I have worn glasses since the age of six, when I was unable to read the hymn num- bers in our Newmarket church. I had been hauled off to the optician's and made to wear the kind of NHS glasses that only became fashionable forty years later – a fate that I have held against the Church of England for almost half a century. Connie Babin would hardly need corrective lenses if her eyesight was perfect. So we issued a subpoena for the original prescription, and it reflected that her eyes were actually 20/40 *with* corrective lenses[39] – the doctor's record had been doctored.

The shenanigans did not end there. When the original trial had been in full flow, four lads who had been playing in the basketball game at the time of the murder showed up at the courthouse. They had read in the paper how the prosecution was casting doubt on Shareef's alibi and wanted to testify to his innocence. But one of the prosecutors intercepted them and instructed them to leave the courthouse and report to the DA's office for the duration of the trial.[40] Effectively, they had been kidnapped against their will. As a result of this, Shareef's lawyers were unable to locate them and they never testified.[41]

Shareef's conviction and death sentence were ultimately reversed, but on the basis of a technical legal issue, rather than as a result of this litany of misconduct. One of the chief prosecution witnesses, a friend of Shareef's called James Rowell, had recanted his statement that Shareef boasted about the murder. Jordan had nevertheless presented the original statement as 'evidence'. The full story was more alarming than the term 'legal technicality' might suggest. Rowell described how the prosecutor had coerced him into lying about his friend.

'My lawyer came to me and told me I was looking at 800 years unless I had something for them on Shareef committing the murder,' he said. Rowell, then just sixteen himself, had been charged with a number of other robberies.[42] 'Then I'd get fifteen years, otherwise life. I argued about taking fifteen years and being able to tell them nothing since I did not know anything.' But the lawyer insisted that he needed to give up Shareef to get the lower sentence.[43]

Rowell described two meetings that he had with the prosecutor. 'Jordan provided me with the questions I would be asked in court, and the answers, always telling me "the main thing is just to emphasise how Shareef was bragging to you all about doing the murder",' he reported.[44] Rowell told the jury that he had an agreement with the prosecution. If he helped out, he would get the lesser sentence – harsh enough for armed robbery, given that Rowell was a juvenile as well, but infinitely preferable to life in prison.[45] 'Jordan told me to lie about whether I had a deal with the State,' he said. 'But I knew that the reason my sentencing date kept getting moved back was to make sure that it would occur after the trial date, so they could hold that over me.'[46]

As he sat in the Orleans Parish jail, waiting to make his appearance in his friend's trial, Rowell's conscience caught up with him. When Jordan called him as a witness, Rowell admitted that his earlier statements had been false, and denied that he knew anything that might link Shareef to the murder of Michael Gerardi. Nevertheless, Jordan went through the statement Rowell had recanted, and argued to the jury that it was true. He knew he was not allowed to do this – once recanted, a statement is not 'evidence' – and the conviction was reversed for this,[47] while Jordan's other transgressions, far worse, received virtually no mention by the Supreme Court of Louisiana.

In America, when a conviction is reversed, the prisoner may be prosecuted again – and again and again, if necessary. We prepared for Shareef's retrial, but the District Attorney dismissed the charges on the Friday before the trial would have started.[48] They concluded that they could not win the case. Shareef and I discussed suing the prosecutors and the police for what happened to him. He was keen to do so, but said that he did not care whether he received compensation: he would settle for a simple apology, and proof from Harry Connick's office that they had introduced rules that would prevent anyone else from suffering the same fate. Perhaps we could force them to adopt open-file discovery, where the defence would see in advance of trial everything in the possession of the prosecution.

Far from issuing an apology, Jordan continued to insist publicly that Shareef was guilty.[49] So we sued everyone involved in placing Shareef on Death Row, laying out the full spectrum of Jordan's misconduct in the complaint: he had apparently kidnapped witnesses, falsified evidence and covered up the proof of Shareef's innocence.

Many observers would find it difficult to conclude that Jordan was anything other than corrupt. I felt rather differently.[50] I felt that Jordan suffered from the 'Tony Blair Syndrome'. Blair doubtless began his relationship with George W. Bush thinking that the President's general aims in stamping out terrorism were good, but worrying that Bush might go overboard in his reaction. So Blair resolved to play an important, moderating role, for which he needed to be Bush's friend.

Gradually, as the piece developed, Vice-President Dick Cheney and the American Neocons proposed ever more extreme responses from their Washington armchairs. Incrementally Blair found himself justifying actions that he would earlier have rejected out of hand. Eventually he found himself a fully-fledged member of the Neocon bash-Islam brigade. Crucially, though, if he took a lie-detector test on whether he had always been honest about Iraq, or whether he thought he had made mistakes in his response to the threat of terror, he would forever maintain his line and pass.

Similarly, Roger Jordan. He no doubt began with his law-enforcement bias, but his intentions were heartfelt within those parameters: he would have felt that the voice of the victim's family was being drowned out by the defendant's clamour for constitutional rights and the defence lawyer's manipulation of the jury. He doubtless believed that people who came to his attention, arrested by the police, were almost always guilty. His ally was the police officer; his enemy, the opposing advocate. More and more his bias would have drawn him to search for the underhand tricks that he expected the defendant's lawyers to employ to get their guilty clients off the hook, such as using a video that had an inaccurate time setting.

In Shareef's case, he would have talked to Connie Babin, the eye-witness, and then seen the video alibi. He knew Babin as a person and a victim, but the video only as a defence plot to weasel out of a crime. When he managed to undermine the latter, far from thinking that he was condemning an innocent person, Jordan would have congratulated himself on cracking a scam. When he promised several decades off James Rowell's sentence if James identified Shareef, Jordan would have viewed this as a necessary price for the truth; later, he would have deemed the recantation the lie, not the original statement. He probably did not even notice some of the exculpatory evidence in the file: Shareef was guilty, so how could this detritus genuinely absolve him? By the time we later piled up new evidence that undermined the prosecution case, Jordan was so firmly committed to his edition of the truth that he would have been unable to believe it: the wish would have become father of the thought.

So were I on Roger Jordan's jury, and he was charged with the *purposeful* attempt to convict an innocent person, I would be bound to acquit him. I don't think he did it intentionally. I suspect he genuinely believed that what he was doing was just and right, and that he still thinks – years later – that Shareef Cousin was the killer. In this sense he is like most prosecutors I have encountered over the years, and his mindset is far more dangerous than someone who is venal. The problem posed by corruption is recognised, and everyone agrees that it should be rooted out; the profound imbalance created by the hiring patterns and work environment of virtually every District Attorney's office in America is not even acknowledged. Nobody, then, is even on the lookout for a cure.

Meanwhile this had resulted in a young man on Death Row for a homicide that he did not commit. And Jordan would face no meaningful punishment for what he did: we would lose our lawsuit against him; he would never be prosecuted for what might have been crimes, and even the Bar association would impose nothing more than a slap on the wrist.

A sensible legal system would be structured to identify misconduct by a prosecutor that put an innocent person on Death Row. It would then provide a strong disincentive against this ever happening again. Sadly, not in the United States.

America is famous for its compensation culture, but Shareef never received a cent in recompense for the time he spent growing up on Death Row for a crime he did not commit. I have worked on the cases of half a dozen innocent people who were on Death Row in Louisiana, and the most that any of them received was ten bucks – I still have the cheque on my wall that was issued by the State of Louisiana to Dan Bright, dated June 14th, 2004.[51] I bought it off him for twenty dollars. In part, this is a reflection of a prejudice against 'criminals' – one that the British seem to share,[52] and one that is rarely dissolved by proof that the individual did not actually commit the crime. Even when the prisoner has been freed, there is a sneaking sense that he was probably guilty anyway and should feel fortunate that he has been released at all.[53]

Prejudice compounds itself. When society adopts the position that prisoners are somehow less than fully human, it becomes increasingly acceptable to put in place rules that reinforce that notion. After all, the prosecutors are the good guys, and they should be allowed free rein to protect us from criminals. There are many examples of this creeping devolution – the denial of the vote to prisoners, for example, removing any last vestige of power from the powerless[54] – but none perhaps as insidious as the rule, created by lawyers for lawyers, that prosecutors should have absolute immunity from being sued by prisoners, no matter how blatant their malfeasance. This rule – grandly called the 'doctrine of the prosecutor's sovereign immunity' – was exhaustively detailed in Shareef Cousin's application to the federal Court of Appeals. The court assumed that all the allegations against Roger Jordan were true, but dismissed Shareef's case on the grounds that Jordan enjoyed immunity for anything he may have done.[55]

The 'doctrine of prosecutorial sovereign immunity' is not codified in American federal law.[56] It is one of the rules made up by lawyers to protect members of the club. It is very difficult to see the justification for it. There is no proof that there would be more frivolous lawsuits by those proven to be innocent than there are by those who claim to have slipped on the wet aisle of a supermarket. And yet, because we despise 'criminals', we have allowed the creation of a system where it is impossible to sue a prosecutor who frames an innocent person for capital murder.

There is a second way in which a prosecutor might be brought to account, and encouraged to do the right thing: discipline by the Bar association. Shareef's outspoken sister, Tonya Cropper, was outraged at Roger Jordan's single-minded efforts to put her kid brother on Death Row and insisted on reporting him to the Bar.

The Louisiana Bar Disciplinary Board refused to sanction Jordan at all, but eventually his case percolated up to the Louisiana Supreme Court. The court found that Jordan had violated his ethical duties in suppressing the evidence favourable to Shareef, and emphasised that there are few ways of holding a prosecutor to account. 'Prosecutors are in a unique position from other members of the Bar as they are immune from civil liability,' the court noted.[57] Bar disciplinary sanctions were, then, all the more important to ensure the integrity of the process.

The court canvassed the various states, and determined that the harshest punishment they could find that had been meted out to a prosecutor for hiding evidence that could prove someone innocent was a suspension, with the possibility of reinstatement after three months; there were only half a dozen cases nationwide where there had been any punishment at all, and normally the worst a prosecutor could expect was a 'public reprimand' – a mild slap on the wrist.[58] The court then voted for what they believed to be the second-harshest punishment ever imposed: a three-month suspension from the practice of law. However, the suspension was itself suspended. In other words, Jordan would not be suspended at all.

The entire discussion showed a remarkably cavalier attitude to the seriousness of the offence: kidnapping witnesses and putting a child on Death Row. Indeed, a footnote in the history of the Jordan family serves to illustrate the value the profession puts on integrity when it comes to prosecuting 'criminals'. When I was browsing the Bar reports one evening, I came across mention of Roger W. Jordan Junior's father in the archives. Jordan *père* had been referred for a disciplinary violation some years before. He had apparently received $3,000 for the settlement of India Matlock's personal-injury case. After deducting his third – the contingency-fee arrangement that the British legal system is so keen to emulate – he should have passed the remaining $2,000 on to Ms Matlock, but he apparently failed to do so. While at one point the older Jordan had offered to repay the money in instalments, the Supreme Court ruled this was insufficient. He should be permanently disbarred.

'The conversion of a client's funds is one of the most serious violations of an attorney's obligations,' wrote the court. 'For the protection of the courts and the public, we have concluded that [Roger Jordan Senior] must be disbarred.'[59] So for pinching $2,000 from a client – which could readily have been reimbursed – Roger Jordan Senior lost the right to practise law for ever. Yet for committing acts that the Fifth Circuit Court of Appeals assumed were criminal, and which put a kid on Death Row for a crime he did not commit, Roger Jordan Junior received no more than the mildest rebuke. This is how the legal system values the principle that we would rather 999 guilty go free than one innocent should be convicted.

If we took seriously the goal of protecting the innocent from being framed by a prosecutor, we might even consider prosecuting those who kidnap witnesses or falsify evidence. That is not going to happen: prosecutors don't prosecute prosecutors for sending an innocent person to prison.[60] Prosecutors rarely even get held in contempt for a direct violation of a judge's order that favourable evidence should be turned over to the defence.[61]

Contrast this with the way in which defence lawyers are treated. If we want to ensure that defence lawyers are vigorous in their labours, we should at least have a level playing field. Yet the field on which justice plays out slopes steeply in one direction. Perhaps the greatest indicator of this is the fact that prosecutors can actually charge defence lawyers with crimes. Consider just the two lawyers who were now defending Kris Maharaj in his challenge to the death sentence: Ben Kuehne[62] and me. Ben recently had to defend himself against highly publicised criminal charges brought by prosecutors who assumed that criminal defendants were paying legal fees with the proceeds of their criminality – an allegation that presumed them guilty before they had been tried. The prosecutors charged Ben with offences that carried fifty years in prison. The federal court eventually tossed the case out, vindicating Ben, but not before it had caused him immense hardship.[63]

Similarly I have been put on trial for contempt – facing prison – for nothing more than advising my client that he could assert his right to remain silent under the US Constitution, when the prosecution tried to force him to take part in an illegal mental-health evaluation.[64] The prosecutor had the untrammelled authority to charge me with criminal contempt of court without any input from a judge or a grand jury, and I had to go through a full trial to prove that it was nonsense. The defence lawyer has no reciprocal power.

Both for Ben and for me (and our families), such experiences have been intimidating, and they run a brightly coloured highlighter across the imbalance between defence lawyers and prosecutors. This speaks eloquently of the justice system and its priorities: the interest in prosecution far outweighs the desire to ensure that we prosecute the correct person.

7

The Police

If the capital prosecution of the sixteen-year-old Shareef Cousin illustrated the inherent bias of the prosecution, any decisions made by the prosecutor came on top of work already done by the police. Shareef's case led me to coin a new rule for our office: if you want to expose police corruption, search out the lead detective's soon-to-be-ex-spouse. The principle worked well for Shareef. Regina Small explained how her husband, Detective Anthony Small, had falsified a Crime Stopper tip against Shareef,[1] so he could collect the $10,500 reward. This was apparently how he used to supplement his police income.

I had not considered it before, but the Crime Stopper process is very dangerous in the wrong hands. Crime Stoppers take anonymous tips from citizens about crime. When you call in with information, you need not leave your name; rather, you are given a code number. When the subject is arrested, you call back and give your number to collect your reward. In the UK you then give Crimestoppers the branch of the bank where you would like to pick up your loot, and the date. You go there, give your number and take the money – tax-free. In America the system varies, but effectively you name the particular alley where you would like to collect your cash in a brown paper bag. Again, you pay no taxes. Now there are even encryption systems to ensure that the informant remains secure in his anonymity.

Regina Small explained how her husband phoned in the tip on Shareef, then arrested him and had a friend – she knew the name, but would not tell me – collect the cash. Circumstantial proof in the police records supported her story. On March 24th, 1995, at 10.05 p.m., Detective Small wrote a report saying that he had received Crime Stoppers Tip #3519. Supposedly the tipster heard Shareef Cousin boasting that he shot and killed a white man coming out of the Port of Call restaurant. The caller added that Shareef lived in the basement of 3811 Marais, and described him as 'dark complexion, skinny, short'.

Even before talking to Regina I had been suspicious of this report. It did not match the Shareef Cousin that I knew. He was six feet tall and solidly built. However, I had noticed in the police file that the only document they had that gave a physical description of Shareef before the Gerardi murder involved an arrest for 'truancy' four years before, when he was only twelve – and the description of a twelve-year-old Shareef was consistent with the Crime Stoppers tip.

According to Regina, her husband had boasted about many other sidelines to his law-enforcement business. He was drunk on the power of his police pistol, and he would play for any side that paid him. Many times she witnessed him bringing his police reports home to doctor them, to help those who were willing to buy their way out of justice. He had fixed a drug offence for a resident of St Croix for a fee of several thousand dollars, altering his reports to facilitate the suspect's continued liberty. He sold confidential information that he obtained in the police department. He stole jewellery from crime scenes whenever he could get his hands on it. If I ever got him on the witness stand, under oath, Regina said I was to ask him where he got the Rolex watch that he always wore. It came from a homicide victim, she said, though the man who was later put on trial for murder had been convicted of robbery as well, for taking the watch. Small had a particular fondness, she said, for tropical fish, and when he had executed a search warrant on the home of a fellow enthusiast, he netted some of the rarer specimens and brought them home to his own tank.

Detective Small was also proud of his win-loss record. He would boast that he had never failed to convict someone charged with murder. He told Regina that he was going to make sure he did not start losing with the case against Shareef Cousin.[2]

Detective Small's practices were, I very much hope, an extreme case. There is pure corruption, where the goal is simply to line one's own pockets, and then there is a different form, where the officer's motive is not personal gain, but is based on his belief that the prisoner is patently guilty, but might be set free by a worthless judicial system. Both 'corrupt' the system, in the sense that they hinder justice. It is a sad fact that policemen often lie to get the result they want, thinking they are acting for the greater good. I worked in New Orleans for eleven years, and officers from the NOPD would boast that they were going down to court to 'testi-lie', rather than testify, in order to ensure a conviction. We caught police committing perjury in eight consecutive capital cases. Their lies were not just a passing recharacterisation of a disputed fact, but a full-on falsification of evidence that might send a person to his death.

I met the police authorities to try and persuade them to take action. I met with local politicians. I met with federal prosecutors in an effort to persuade them to bring a case against those who were proven perjurers. After all, actively lying in a capital case could theoretically send you to prison for life. But nobody was interested. I lived close by the St Thomas Projects, where sixteen of the 1,600 residents had been murdered in one year – one in 100, roughly the same death rate suffered by American soldiers in the Vietnam War.[3] The police were meant to be the last line of defence between the people of St Thomas and a tsunami of crime, and the authorities did not want to be heard saying that the Thin Blue Line[4] was actually the crest of the crime-wave.

I felt so thwarted by the failure of the legal system to take testi-lying seriously that I decided the only alternative was to take the issue to the court of public opinion. We set up a watchdog frivolously called Stop the P.I.G. ('Perjury In Government'). We would make a very public award to the officer whom we had caught committing perjury in court that month. At the same time, to ensure balance, we would give a Serpico[5] award to the officer who had been fair to a criminal defendant – but we kept this award secret, to avoid getting him into trouble. We made little headway. Fairness for a person accused of a capital crime was a long way down the public's list of priorities.

When I had begun my independent investigation into the case of Kris Maharaj, one of my first moves had been a Freedom of Information request for the prosecutors' files. I did the same for the Miami-Dade Police Department. To the evidence custodian, this was all routine.

He showed me to an airless and windowless room and brought in box after box of materials. He pointed out the copying machine, and told me to Xerox anything I liked – I only had to keep a running tally, and pay ten cents a page at the end. He also kindly pointed to the coffee machine. It was free, it was dark (vintage from early that morning), but it was very welcome. I had not expected so many boxes. I was going to be in that room for a while.

I marvelled at my good fortune. Here was file upon file of material, thick seams of evidence that might save Kris' life. It was even tabbed.

The policeman who had done the most damage to Kris' defence at trial was Detective Buhrmaster. In particular, Buhrmaster had testified to various things that Kris supposedly said, and did not say, during questioning. He did not claim that he had recorded these statements in any way – he produced no tape, no signed statement, no notes of the conversation. Yet this testimony was central to the prosecution case. For example, if Kris really said he was never in Room 1215 that day, then how could he explain the fingerprints of his that were found all over the room?

Kris insisted to me (as he had to his lawyer at the time) that he told Buhrmaster the whole story – how he had been invited to the room by Neville Butler to meet a man called Eddie Dames, who might agree to distribute Kris' paper in the Bahamas. How he arrived around eight in the morning, waited an hour, read the paper, had some coffee, and finally got impatient and left – three hours before the murders.

In the file I had accumulated back in my office I already had evidence indicating that Buhrmaster's trial testimony might be false on one score. Indeed, Eric Hendon knew this at the time of trial, but simply failed to point it out to the jury.[6] Hendon had asked Officer David Romero in a deposition whether he knew what Kris Maharaj had told his colleague, Buhrmaster: in particular, had the accused admitted being in Room 1215 on October 16th, 1986?

'He had been there,' Romero swore at the time, 'prior to the homicides, that's correct.'[7] Kris might still be guilty, but Romero's testimony would have proved he had told Buhrmaster that he had been in the room and would have provided an innocent explanation for all the fingerprints.

But there was a step that Hendon could have taken before trying to prove Buhrmaster a liar in front of the jury. If a statement by a defendant seems to be inculpatory, any defence lawyer should first consider whether it might be excluded from the trial. Everyone knows about the famous Miranda rule, which requires the police to read a suspect his rights and only permits them to interview him if he agrees; certainly there can be no questioning if he asks to speak with an attorney. Kris had told me that, when Buhrmaster interrogated him late on the night of the Moo Youngs' murder, it became evident that the detective thought he was guilty, so he demanded access to a lawyer.

I was shocked when one of the first pieces of paper I found in Buhrmaster's file was the following note: 'Buhrmaster and Amato go to jail at 12.18 a.m. with Maharaj. (D invokes his right to attorney.) FORGET THIS. * BE CAREFUL ABOUT THIS.'[8] Someone had written a script for Kris' testimony. 'D' meant the defendant; the detective knew that if he conceded that Kris had asserted his rights, then anything Kris allegedly said would be inadmissible at trial.[9]

By now I was very excited. I knew that this, standing alone, provided a strong legal claim to raise in Kris' appeal. But my review of the boxes at the police department had hardly begun. One box was labelled as a complete copy of the contents of the Moo Young briefcase. I vaguely recalled a note that I had read in the defence lawyer's file: Ron Petrillo, the investigator, had gone to Buhrmaster's office and asked whether he could see the briefcase. The detective told him that it had been returned to the Moo Young family. Buhrmaster misled them, because here it was before me.[10]

The briefcase had apparently contained hundreds of pages, including all kinds of corporate documents, and there were copies in the police files. Kris had previously described for me his litigation against Derrick Moo Young. Derrick had been running Kris' Florida property investments, when rents worth $14,000 went missing. Then entire properties changed hands, and Marita Maharaj's car turned out to be in the Moo Young name. The embezzlement added up to more than $400,000. Kris had confronted Derrick. The Moo Youngs – father and son – had behaved as if they would make good. Duane had written Kris cheques for $200,000 and $243,000, but both bounced. Kris had sued; it was a simple case, and he was confident of an easy victory. After all, had he not taken on the establishment in Britain in the famous banana case, winning a major court victory against Lord Cock-field? He hired Levi England as his attorney and went to court.

But even by the time I met him Kris did not fully understand how the Moo Youngs had ripped him off. The briefcase provided the answer. Kris had named his Florida holding company KDM International. The company was originally registered to Derrick's Florida address, and he was a signatory on all the KDM International accounts. Yet here in front of me were documents showing how Derrick and Duane had created a company with a very similar name, KDM Distributors, listed at the same address. They had begun to commingle the bank accounts, transferring money and buildings from one to the other. On March 3rd, 1986, they went one better. Duane filed papers removing Kris and Marita as officers of KDM International, substituting himself.[11] In this way the Moo Youngs concluded a stealthy takeover of the entire company.

The Moo Youngs' next move was equally subtle. Kris had insisted to me that his response to the defamatory articles in the *Caribbean Echo* was not – as the prosecution suggested – to ride around South Florida hatching bizarre plots to kill people. Rather, relishing a new game of business chess, Kris had established the *Caribbean Times*. Nothing about the Moo Youngs or the *Echo* ever appeared on the pages of the *Times*; Kris simply planned to drive the *Echo* out of business by publishing a better alternative for the Caribbean community in South Florida.

Here, in the briefcase file, I found the Moo Young countergambit. Apparently Kris had not completed the technical documents establishing his new paper, so on July 11th, 1986, Derrick and Duane registered a company with another similar name, the *Caribbean Times International*, in an effort to take over the paper as well.[12] On August 12th, 1986, just two months before they died, Derrick started writing to the Barnett Bank demanding all the financial records for Kris' paper. Derrick said he was president of the *Caribbean Times International*, and demanded to know what accounts had been opened in the company name, hinting darkly at financial impropriety.[13]

I was thrilled with what I was finding in the police file, and I was making copies of everything.[14] The air conditioning was running, it was hot outside and I had no interest in taking a break. I skipped lunch and concentrated on a new pot of coffee and a snack machine that dispensed small packets of peanuts. As I continued, the briefcase gradually unlocked more convoluted secrets.

The next discovery I made was a set of life-insurance policies. On January 26th, 1986, Derrick applied for $1 million in 'keyman' life insurance, naming the beneficiary as NEC International, a Panamanian corporation.[15] Why Panama? In 1986, that would have still been the fiefdom of the notorious General Manuel Noriega.[16] Although the prosecution had described Derrick at trial as disabled, and effectively retired, the older Moo Young claimed in his insurance application that he had been employed by NEC for a year.[17] I had no idea what NEC was all about, or why Derrick would take out a huge life-insurance policy on himself. But I had a general idea of what keyman insurance was – something about reimbursing a company for the loss of an important employee.[18]

As I leafed through the pages, I found more policies. On August 7th, 1986, Duane Moo Young also took out half a million dollars in insurance on himself. The same day, Paul Moo Young, Shaula Ann Nagel and Kerry Lee Nagel (all family) applied for a total of $1.3 million in insurance through a corporation called DMY International, obviously another company named after either Derrick or Duane Moo Young – presumably Duane, as he signed each application as president. On October 13th, 1986, Alan Stuart Carr and Andrew Wong, more members of the family, applied for a total of $800,000 of insurance with DMY.[19] I briefly totted it up. The family suddenly took out more than $3 million worth of life insurance, some of it just three days before Derrick and Duane died. Why? Did Derrick and Duane know that disaster was looming? Had someone threatened them? Had someone threatened Derrick that his children might be targets? This was more helpful than the earlier materials. It did not yet point at another suspect, but who, or what, did they fear?

And here were the deeds of another Moo Young company, Cargil International SA. The name Cargil was vaguely familiar to me. If memory served, this was a huge multinational corporation, maybe from Canada. When I looked it up later that evening, I learned my mistake: it was based in the Midwest. Cargill (it had an extra L) was a multibillion-dollar food and agriculture company.[20] The Moo Youngs lived in South Florida but, as with NEC, Cargil's main office was in Panama. There was also a branch of Cargil in the Bahamas.

The next item of interest that I noticed was a copy of Derrick's and

Duane's passports, along with various credit-card records. It was now clear where some of the money they had embezzled had gone. The Moo Youngs had taken at least thirteen international flights in the nine months leading up to their murder, staying in expensive hotels wherever they went.[21] They went to Europe (staying two weeks on two occasions), the Cayman Islands, Mexico, Panama (a total of six times), Puerto Rico (twice), Trinidad, as well as all over the United States.

I came across a letter dated June 6th, 1986, purporting to be from someone called Richard Solomon, sent to Derrick Moo Young at an address in Panama, discussing some gems.[22] Not just 'some' gems: stones worth more than $130 *million*.[23] I had no idea what to make of this. There were also notes in what I now recognised as Duane Moo Young's spidery handwriting suggesting that the gems were being held in the Bank of Tonga.[24] Given that the other Bank of Tonga documents in the briefcase were clearly fakes – I could see one original, and a copy where the names had been whited out and retyped – this seemed to be some kind of fraud. But precisely what kind, I had no idea.

There were various other drafts of letters in the file that were in Duane's handwriting. They were extraordinary. They purported to offer loans of vast amounts to various governments around the Caribbean. There was a proposal from the Moo Youngs to someone called Dr Enrique Van Brown, offering to provide $100 million to the government of either Paraguay or Venezuela. Another letter offered $250 million to Trinidad.[25]

How, I asked myself, were the Moo Youngs in a position to offer this kind of money? My emotions were mixed. None of these materials had been turned over to Kris Maharaj's defence. They clearly should have been, and this made me angry. But these pieces of paper ought to be enough to unplug the electric chair as far as Kris was concerned.

At the end of a day in the police department, I made an appointment to go elsewhere the next morning. The Moo Young insurance was all taken out through the William Penn Life Insurance Company and it was apparent that the family had sued after Derrick and Duane died, claiming a seven-figure sum. Brenton Ver Ploeg was the lawyer who had been representing the William Penn Company. I called him, and he obtained permission from his client to share any materials with me that would not betray legal privilege.

In a capital trial the defence rarely has the resources to investigate the case as thoroughly as it should. Civil lawyers who are arguing over money tend to be funded much better. Ver Ploeg described how he had hired John Healey, a gumshoe out of New York. He was appropriately coy about confidential issues, but implied that William Penn had spent hundreds of thousands of dollars defending the suit, although it was finally settled.

Ver Ploeg described how he had received a copy of the briefcase documents years before. Detective Buhrmaster gave Healey the materials that he had withheld from the defence in Kris' criminal trial. The investigator, Healey, then trawled around the Caribbean trying to decrypt some of the notes. Ver Ploeg suggested that they spread a little largesse around Panama. From what they learned, he expressed concern that Kris Maharaj did not get a fair trial. He set me in front of another pile of boxes. The office was smarter than the police department; the copy machine was faster; and the coffee rather better. The level of my excitement remained the same.

Healey had been very thorough. He had uncovered documents reflecting how the Moo Youngs were negotiating to buy a bank in Panama for *$600 million*. He located the letters that the Moo Youngs actually sent, rather than drafts, offering loans around the Caribbean. With $100 million here, and $250 million there, the letters escalated to an offer they made to Trinidad to loan the country $2 billion.

Later I came across documents suggesting that the Moo Youngs had access to *$5 billion* in Japanese Yen bonds.[26] That evening I ran a quick check: in 1986 there were thirty-two countries that had a gross domestic product of under $5 billion a year.[27] How could the Moo Youngs have had access to enough money to buy various nation-states?

At trial, the prosecution had portrayed Derrick Moo Young as a retired, disabled businessman, with an income of no more than $24,000 per year. The bank statements in the briefcase included the Moo Youngs' legitimate private account, doubtless the one the taxman might have been allowed to see. It hit a February low of $6.85 on Valentine's Day 1986, and went into deficit (minus $14.65) on April 7th. By and large, the account reflected very modest balances.[28] During the same period, they were offering several nation-states billions in loans.

What on earth was going on with Derrick and Duane?

I trembled both with excitement and with frustration. These documents would have been dynamite in the hands of the defence lawyer at trial, but would I be able to find a jury to listen now? Kris was on Death Row. We had to persuade a judge to grant him a new trial before we could do anything else.

I had been looking at Buhrmaster's own homicide file, and I periodically wondered what all this said about him. He was certainly organised, which meant that he could not have overlooked these documents in their entirety. Was he like the prosecutors, simply focused on convicting the man he believed to be the killer, Kris Maharaj? Did he therefore ignore or simply not notice anything that didn't fit with his theory? Or was there something else going on?

Of the alternatives, police bias is the most insidious and wide-spread threat to justice. Indeed, the law-enforcement system is structured to select not the people best suited to the job, but rather those who are most likely to make mistakes.[29] This is defined initially by who applies to be a police officer, and why; next, by who is selected for the job; and, finally, by what becomes of these people once they are in post. The police have been sued so often for discrimination in hiring, or misuse of their power, that American police officers have undergone plenty of psychological profiling. Using well-worn testing techniques, law-enforcement agencies seek to hire people with 'police-oriented' attitudes.[30] If you are inclined to question authority, you are probably not going to make it as a policeman.[31] If you tend to think that the wrong people get banged up all the time, perhaps you are not the person for the job.

The studies demonstrate that there is a set of law-enforcement value judgements – a police 'subculture' – that has remained relatively unchanged over many years.[32] Descriptive terms applied to 'the policeman's character profile' include 'conservative', 'suspicious' and 'cynical',[33] and sometimes 'authoritarian'.[34] Unfortunately, 'suspicious' does not imply self-doubt; rather, it indicates a willingness to believe the worst about the suspect. 'Cynical' tends to indicate a refusal to accept a plausible explanation, if it is made by the 'wrong' person.

Some social scientists are unsure whether these 'typical characteristics' merely typify those attracted to police work, or reflect the moulding influence of the police environment once they are employed.[35] From the perspective of the criminal defendant, it does not matter which is the chicken and which is the egg, for the result is the same: the officer who arrests them is predisposed to disbelieve claims of innocence and to forge towards proving guilt. There seems to be little recognition of the problem and still less effort to turn the tide. Indeed, it is remarkable the degree to which advertisements for jobs in the world of law enforcement omit *all* reference to the possibility of doing justice, and focus solely on apprehending someone as the criminal.[36] With such an approach, the execution of the innocent becomes inevitable.

8

The Expert

'Is it your conclusion that this man is a malingerer?' the judge demanded of the expert.

'I wouldn't be testifying if I didn't think so,' testified Dr Herbert Randolph Unsworth, 'unless I was on the other side. Then it would be a post-traumatic condition.'[1]

Expert evidence played a significant role in the case against Krishna Maharaj. There was no murder weapon, but that was not so unusual. Any killer with half a brain would dump the pistol after killing two people, and there were plenty of waterways around Miami where a gun could vanish for all time. The prosecution nevertheless put together a fairly compelling case against Kris with regard to the gun used in the crime. Detective Buhrmaster again provided key evidence: he said that he had questioned the defendant, and Kris had denied ever owning a handgun. As with all assertions attributed to Kris by the lead detective, there was no tape, no signed statement, not even any notes. The jury depended on the policeman's say-so.

The prosecution proved that Kris had, in fact, bought a Smith & Wesson pistol some months earlier. Indeed, he had bought it through a friend who was a police officer, Lieutenant Bernie Buzzo, and the prosecutors laboured intentionally over proving this, as each witness underlined the idea that Kris must have lied to Buhrmaster. Detective Bellrose of the Miramar Police Department described how he wanted to sell his gun, and Buzzo told him that he had a buyer. Bellrose did not even know who this was until much later, when he 'found out' that it was Krishna Maharaj.[2]

Next, the prosecution proved that Kris carried the weapon with him. Officer Gregory Jansen, of the Plantation Police Department, was called as a witness to describe how other officers stopped Krishna Maharaj for speeding on the Florida Turnpike on July 2nd, 1986, three and a half months before the homicides. Jansen responded to lend assistance at 2.40 in the morning. He searched Kris' rental car, and his report reflected that there was a Smith & Wesson nine-millimetre handgun in the boot. The serial number was A235464.[3] More than a year later, having briefly seen him in the dark, Jansen said he could identify Kris as the driver of the car.

Finally, the prosecutors summoned Thomas Quirk, the expert firearms examiner from the Miami-Dade Crime Laboratory, to discuss ballistics.[4] Again they purposely belaboured the point. They had various bullets taken from the bodies of the two victims, Derrick and Duane Moo Young, as well as the shell casings that had been ejected around the room. Quirk's task was to determine whether it was possible to say which gun had fired them.

'I don't think it's necessary for someone to tell how a weapon works,' said Judge Solomon, trying to move the case along. 'Believe me, when those jurors go in there, men with experience in weapons will tell the ladies how a weapon works, if people don't know. But if you insist on telling how a weapon works, without objection from defence, we will listen to this gentleman.'

In fact Thomas Quirk did far more than explain how a weapon works. He essentially told the jurors that the bullets found at the scene came from the type of gun that Kris Maharaj had owned – a Smith & Wesson. Quirk opined that it was immediately clear to him that the bullets had been fired from one of six brands of weapon, all nine-millimetre semi-automatics – guns made by Browning, Leyte, Llama, Sig-Sauer, Smith & Wesson or Star. He had then test-fired all six types of guns, recovering the slugs, and decided that the Smith & Wesson was the most likely, since the striations on the bullets (the marks made as the bullet went down the rifled barrel of the weapon) were the closest match.

After discussing the slugs, he moved on to the bullet casings.

'The only fired standard that I have in the lab,' Quirk testified, 'that matches the same type of morphology on the casings from the scene is a Model 39 Smith & Wesson.' In other words, he was saying that the casings found at the scene were probably also from a Smith & Wesson. All in all, he concluded that these bullets were probably fired through just such a gun as Maharaj had owned.

The prosecutor marked a photograph of a semi-automatic Smith & Wesson pistol for Quirk to show the jury. At last, Eric Hendon objected. What was the possible relevance of this? It could not be the actual gun.

'Overruled,' snapped Judge Solomon. 'This is demonstrative. Go ahead.' He nodded the case on.

Here, the prosecutors were playing with a psychological phenomenon known as 'Wigmore's Horse': if a horse is brought into the courtroom where the man on trial is accused of horse theft, the jurors will automatically – albeit irrationally – leap to the conclusion that it is *the* horse he stole, and he must therefore be guilty. No doubt, when they looked at Quirk's photograph, some of the jurors subliminally thought they had seen the murder weapon.

On cross-examination Hendon did point out that perhaps 270,000 Smith & Wesson handguns were produced from 1954 to 1986, any of which could have been the murder weapon. But by now the damage had been done, and Hendon's focus on the number of such weapons would have left the impression that everyone agreed that a Smith & Wesson had been used in the crime.

Quirk had focused the jury's sights directly on Kris Maharaj.

To understand the extraordinary influence of the expert in a courtroom, we don't need to go much beyond the intimidation that many people feel among scientific whizz-kids in school. But there are deep-rooted cultural reasons for our deference to science: in an earlier era of experimentation, scientists came generally from the moneyed classes. They studied the world, they asked questions, they discoursed in the Royal Society or in the coffee houses, and they proposed the rules that governed the confusing world around us. They were viewed as the unbiased intellectual cream of society. In 1673, an unknown Dutchman called Antonie van Leeuwenhoek advanced a novel theory of biology. Since nobody else had studied it, the Royal Society simply asked him for character references from the ministers and lawyers of Delft.[5] It was a matter of honour: if he was from the right social class, his conclusions should be accepted on trust. It is only more recently that some scientists have been married to Mammon, work-ing for corporations, so that their credibility has come into question. Yet because few lawyers – and fewer jurors – feel inclined to challenge witnesses in their field of expertise, their testimony still carries over-whelming weight.

The scientific method,[6] developed over many hundreds of years, is designed to test whether a particular hypothesis truly reflects the operations of nature, whether the observer has happened upon a theory that can honestly be replicated, or whether it is just an allur-ing but random happenstance. The true scientist comes up with a hypothesis, and then tests it: for example, does a particular medica-tion actually help cure the illness? The scientist does randomised, controlled, double-blind studies to see whether the results of admin-istering a new pill are significantly better than the benefits of the currently available medication, of a placebo or of no treatment at all. The scientist then publishes both the methods and the data, so that others can attempt to reproduce the result, level criticism and help to establish the truth.

In order for the scientific method to operate, there must be others in the field who have an incentive to cast a critical eye over this work, otherwise it cannot truly be deemed reliable. If these other experts come from within the company, they may be keen to ensure that a very expensive development of a particular medicine will not go to waste. That is one form of bias. Those from a rival company may have a different partiality, hoping to demonstrate that the new pill is an expensive fraud. Ideally, then, the peer review comes from an independent body, whose only motive is to establish the efficacy of a medication before another drug like thalidomide is unleashed on the market.[7] But while such a scientific watchdog may be impartial, who is going to fund it?

The central problem with 'forensic science'[8] is that there is no scientist with an incentive to question the proposed hypothesis. Take forensic hair analysis, for example. Every day a 'Trace Evidence Expert' looks down his binary microscope. This is a microscope with two lenses, so that he can see two hairs at the same time, side by side. He compares a hair found at the crime scene with one belonging to the suspect. He runs his eye along the two hairs until he comes to the point where the two look most similar, and then he starts identifying an intimidating array of characteristics – the hair's colour, to be sure, but also its buckling, cortex, medulla, and so forth.[9] He may opine on the racial class of the hair, often – remarkably – still describing it in arcane terms such as Caucasian, Negroid or Mongoloid.[10] He then reaches an opinion as to whether the two are microscopically similar, sometimes loosely referred to as a 'match'.

The forensic hair analyst then appears in court and takes the oath. The prosecutor has him list his qualifications, and the hundreds of cases where his view has been deemed important, before turning to the judge to ask that he should be respected as especially learnèd.

'In light of his years of training and practice,' the robed eminence on the bench will intone, 'I recognise this witness as an expert. He may state his opinions to the jury.'

There are many flaws in this process – some of them obvious on a cursory evaluation. What, for example, do they mean by 'Negroid' hair? I worked with a Mississippi lawyer years ago, who used officially to change race as he crossed the border with Louisiana. His blood was, he told me, one-sixteenth African American. In Louisiana he was deemed to be white, as a mixed-race person was only classified as 'Negroid' if he had at least one-eighth African American blood (one great-grandparent). But when he drove back into Mississippi he reverted to 'Negroid', defined there as one-sixteenth black (one great-great-grandparent). However fatuous and offensive such racial grouping might be, for a forensic-science category of 'Negroid' to mean anything, there has to be a definition – in order to distinguish between a spectrum of commingled genes. Yet I have never persuaded a hair-analysis expert to tell the jury what they mean when they use the term. Somehow they have got away with using such terms for decades, without meaningful challenge.

But there is a far deeper problem: there is nobody who spends his days looking down a binary microscope wondering whether he is wasting his time. In other words, there is nobody who questions whether what they see down the microscope actually tells them anything consequential about who dropped the hair. Everyone trained as a forensic hair analyst believes that his work is valid, yet there has been no independent study that meaningfully validates it.[11]

For me, this all came into sharp focus in the case of Randy Bevill, who was on Death Row in Mississippi. He was granted a new trial,[12] again to face the death penalty, and I was representing him with Jackson Brown – not the singer, but a loudly opinionated lawyer.[13]

Randy was charged with the rape and murder of Amy Clayton, in Tupelo, Mississippi, on July 31st, 1986. On retrial, as at the first trial, a central focus of the case was the hair testimony of a technician from the Mississippi Crime Laboratory. The crime scene was searched for physical evidence that might identify the perpetrator. The victim's clothing was combed for hairs. Nearby, on the ground, there was a bloody white T-shirt. That was combed as well. Later, known samples of scalp, pubic and chest hairs were taken from Randy when he was arrested.

The Mississippi Crime Lab technician, Joe Andrews, then compared the hundreds of hairs from the scene with those taken from Randy, and found ten 'matches' between Randy's chest hairs and hairs found on the white T-shirt and on the victim's clothes. He also found two pubic-hair 'matches' to Randy, one in the victim's pubic combing and one on her clothes. Since Randy denied committing the crime or having anything to do with Amy Clayton, the hair evidence took on huge significance: if it was to be believed, it proved that Randy was a liar and that he had been with the victim.

There were two key questions: first, was there any scientific evidence showing that a 'match' between hairs meant anything at all? And second, how likely was a false match? For instance, it is one thing to say that the perpetrator has blue eyes: if a crime occurs in Ghana, blue-eyed perpetrators might be very rare, but in Europe they are not.

Forensic hair analysis has been used in criminal trials since the 1850s. According to the Mississippi Supreme Court in Randy's original appeal, hair analysis is a 'very useful tool in criminology'.[14] It has been used as the basis for innumerable death sentences, right up to recent times. Indeed, there are at least fifteen cases in the past ten years[15] where hair analysis made a significant contribution to a capital conviction, later upheld through the entire state and federal system; there are many other death sentences that have not yet completed this legal journey; and hundreds, if not thousands, more people are serving criminal sentences based in part on this 'very useful' forensic tool.

Astoundingly, in the 140 years during which forensic hair analysis had been used prior to Randy Bevill's second trial, only two studies had been completed in an effort to determine what a 'match' might mean. Both had been done by the same person, Barry Gaudette, a trace-evidence expert from Canada.[16] Gaudette made his living at the time as a forensic hair expert, and was therefore hardly impartial:

if he were to conclude that his expertise meant nothing, not only would he put himself out of a job, but he would also be saddled with a Himalayan sense of guilt for all the Canadians he had sent to prison over the years.

According to Gaudette's study, the probability of a false match with respect to pubic hair was one in 800.[17] In other words, according to him, there was a 99.875 per cent chance that a single pubic hair found at Amy Clayton's murder scene matched the sample removed from Randy Bevill. If you are 99 per cent sure someone is guilty, is that enough to find someone guilty? As there was no innocent explanation for Randy's hair being at the scene, then the prosecution might argue that this evidence alone was proof beyond a reasonable doubt.

The Mississippi analyst, Joe Andrews, took the matches he had found, and had the bright idea of multiplying them: surely, if the odds of one false match are one in 800, then the odds of two hairs matching by chance would be 800 x 800, or one in 640,000, at which point we could be 99.9999 per cent sure Randy was guilty. And so forth. Andrews decided that with eight chest hairs and two pubic hairs matching, there was only one chance in several trillion trillion that Randy Bevill might be innocent.[18]

Mark Twain once commented on the dangers of statistical extrapolation. He had been told that the changes in the course of the Mississippi River had resulted in its shortening by 242 miles in 176 years, a change of just over a mile a year. 'Therefore,' suggested Twain, 'any calm person, who is not blind or idiotic, can see that during the Old Oolitic Period, just a million years ago next November, the Lower Mississippi River was upward of one million three hundred thousand miles long, and stuck out over the Gulf of Mexico like a fishing rod. And by the same token any person can see that seven hundred years from now, the Lower Mississippi will be only a mile and three quarters long, and Cairo and New Orleans will have joined their streets together, and be plodding comfortably along under a single mayor and a mutual board of aldermen. There is something fascinating about science. One gets such wholesale returns out of such a trifling investment of fact.'[19]

Indeed, Twain was right. Andrews' analysis merely illustrated that he had forgotten what little arithmetic he learned in grade school. If all of my hairs are similar, and if one somehow matches someone else's hair, then the chances are good that all of them will.

But there is a much deeper problem. Barry Gaudette's study was itself thoroughly unscientific. When I telephoned him to ask to see his raw data, he wanted to know my motives. I candidly explained that I doubted Joe Andrews' testimony, and was trying to ascertain whether his analysis was correct. Because I was a defence lawyer questioning his 'science', Gaudette refused to share his materials.[20] So much for scientific impartiality: he was only willing to share data with those who were committed to upholding his technique.

I was reduced to using the figures he had published, which were incomplete, but essentially sufficient for my purposes. Suffice it to say that Gaudette had made various assumptions that might be suited to a clean laboratory, but not to a grubby crime scene; he had also used an erroneous statistical method. By plugging the real-life number of hairs collected in the Amy Clayton murder into Gaudette's equations, the odds dropped dramatically: we would expect to see between one and two *false* matches, and Andrews only claimed to see two meaningful ones[21] – the evidence would then mean nothing. It would be bad enough if lawyers and jurors were blinded by true science, but in the case of hair analysis, they are misled by something masquerading as science – a technique that has never passed its most basic test. But who is going to challenge this? The courts are unlikely to, in part due to the fact that many lawyers chose their profession because they hated the scientific subjects that might have taken them into medicine.

Presenting any challenge to this kind of evidence before a jury highlights the next problem of forensic science. The judge in Randy Bevill's case was an amiable man, the Honourable Frank Russell. He had a distaste for Johnny Young, the local District Attorney. Young's dedication to securing a conviction was never quite matched by his ability to present a case. Judge Russell had not fully recovered from the time he directed a verdict against Young in a criminal trial, where there was insufficient evidence to allow the decision to go to a jury. Young had thrown a fit in the courtroom and then stalked out towards the back of the courthouse, where – Judge Russell soon learned – he had urinated all over the carpet of the judge's chambers. Such is the world of Mississippi trials.

Judge Russell was far from biased in our favour, but he was at least willing to listen. Nonetheless, his attention appeared to wander fairly soon after the first mention of statistics. He did bar Joe Andrews from sallying forth with his more outlandish numbers at the retrial: the state's expert could call his findings a 'match', but could not say what this meant. Yet this made the prejudice to Randy Bevill even greater, since the only way we could show that Andrews' findings were meaningless was to get into a lengthy battle over mathematics. If we tried this, we would lose the jurors' attention faster than we had Judge Russell's.

In the end I was reduced to playing a card trick on Joe Andrews. Fortunately he fell for it, and that partially made the point.[22] But a witness will only fall for such a ploy once, and it does not solve the problem of phoney science in the courtroom.[23]

When a potentially bogus science has been accepted into the law, it is difficult to challenge it. In the decade after Randy's trial, I toured the country giving talks about how unreliable the evidence gleaned from hair analysis was. But I could find no experts to testify to my view. Of course: the only people who qualify as experts in the field are those who believe in it. There is no such person as an Anti-Forensic Hair Expert, someone who trains in hair analysis and then spends her entire life testifying that it is a sham. Indeed, one time a colleague in Atlanta was so desperate for an expert to challenge hair analysis in a capital trial that he called me, simply because I had written an article on it. It was absurd that I should be considered an expert, and it only happened because there was nobody else.

The battle over hair evidence is not over, but it should be. Ron Williamson was a Minor League baseball batter for the Oakland Athletics. A shoulder injury and an unhealthy appetite for alcohol cut short his career. In 1988 he found himself facing a capital charge for the rape and murder of Debra Sue Carter. At his trial a forensic expert, Melvin Hett, testified that thirteen hairs found at the scene were consistent with either Williamson or his co-defendant, Dennis Fritz. Hett testified that he found two pubic hairs on the victim's bed, where Williamson had supposedly raped the victim.

'They were consistent microscopically and could have the same source as Ron Williamson's known pubic hair,' Hett concluded.

The prosecutor asked what he meant by this.

'When a hair matches, if you will, it is consistent microscopically to a known source,' Hett explained. 'The hairs either did originate from that source, or there could be or might be another individual in the world somewhere that might have the same microscopic characteristics.'

This, along with the testimony of an informant, Glen Gore, provided most of the evidence against Williamson, who was sent to Death Row. Fritz received life. His wife had passed away some years earlier, and he had been raising their daughter alone when he was arrested.

'I'm innocent! I'm innocent! I'm innocent!' Williamson screamed repetitively from his Death Row cell. He lost his appeals through the state courts and came within five days of dying in the chamber. By then he was well along the path to losing his sanity as well.

In 1994 federal judge Frank Seay stayed his execution. Judge Seay was from the old school, but he was shocked at the way Williamson's trial had gone. He penned a long, 176-page opinion tearing the prosecution case apart. In particular, he shredded the use of forensic hair analysis. He ordered a new trial,[24] writing an unusual epilogue to his opinion. Philosophically conservative, he had struggled with his duty to order a new trial: 'While considering my decision in this case I told a friend, a layman, I believed the facts and law dictated that I must grant a new trial to a defendant who had been convicted and sentenced to death. My friend asked, "Is he a murderer?" I replied simply, "We won't know until he receives a fair trial." God help us if ever in this great country we turn our heads while people who have not had fair trials are executed. That almost happened in this case.'

Williamson's trial had not been fair, but that did not mean he was deemed to be innocent. His exoneration did not come until much later. In 1999 DNA evidence proved that the 'inculpatory' pubic hair did not come from Williamson at all, but from the victim herself. In other words, the strongest 'scientific' evidence – offered to show both that he lied when he denied being at the crime scene, and that he raped the victim – turned out to be evidence that at some point Debra Carter had been on her own bed.

Another round of DNA helped prove that Glen Gore, called by the prosecution to testify against Williamson, had himself committed the murder. The police had taken samples from him at the time of the crime, since he had been the last person seen with the victim. Because they thought Williamson was guilty, they never bothered to test them.[25] In short, the 'forensic science' was bunk, and in Ron Williamson's case it was – belatedly – debunked by DNA.

After such a catastrophe, how can anyone still use this 'forensic science' today? One illustration of why this is comes in the shape of a bibliography of articles about forensic hair analysis compiled five years after the Williamson case. Max Houck, an FBI 'physical scientist', emphasises in it that forensic hair analysis has been used for sixty years, and references many articles supporting its use.[26] Houck ignores the articles and legal decisions that have found the procedure wanting, and explicitly omits DNA studies that have disproved hair testimony, such as those in Ron Williamson's case. Instead he quotes from an article published five years before Williamson was exonerated: 'Hair is extremely important as physical evidence. It must be collected in every case in which it occurs, and subjected to thorough study … [and] it is dangerous to depend on any but expert study of hair found in evidence.'[27]

'It is hoped,' Houck concludes, 'that this listing will provide some assistance to forensic hair examiners who are seeking information and support for courtroom forensic challenges.' Translated into plain English, Houck means that experts must stick together to defend themselves against interlopers who are challenging their livelihood.

Does this mean that Houck is a conscious charlatan? Not at all. It simply reflects the pervasive human bias that allows junk science to continue long past its sell-by date. Houck has devoted his professional life to this 'science', and both his job and his reputation depend on it being valid. How likely is it that he would agree that the reports he issued in 800 cases for the FBI, and hundreds more in Texas[28] – the hub of capital punishment – relied on bogus science,[29] and had helped consign many to prison or the death chamber? The same osmotic pressure forces virtually all exponents of this science towards defending it.[30]

If only hair analysis were the solitary example of this phenomenon. Unfortunately it is as much the rule as the exception in 'forensic science'. Recently a number of forensic sciences previously considered to be established have come under fire, including fibre analysis, ballistics, bullet content analysis, neutron-activation analysis, bite marks, handwriting and shoe-print identification. All suffer from the same profile: they are techniques masquerading as science that essentially serve only one purpose, which is to assist in the prosecution of those accused of crime.[31]

Even fingerprinting has not been immune from criticism. Brandon

Mayfield is a lawyer in Oregon who was arrested for his alleged involvement in the Madrid train bombing in 2004. The terrorist attack killed 191 people and injured as many as 2,000. A fingerprint was found at the scene that the FBI matched to Mayfield. No doubt the decision to arrest him was partly prompted by his recent conversion to Islam.[32] The Spanish authorities, sceptical that someone 5,403 miles away could have left a fingerprint, ultimately convinced the FBI that their method was flawed and the print was not Mayfield's. The US government paid Mayfield $2 million to settle his claims against them.

Some apologists point to DNA as the silver bullet that will solve all the problems of our flawed forensic science. This optimism is again misplaced, for a number of reasons. One is the limited relevance of DNA to criminal cases. At best, only perhaps 2 per cent of forensic science involves DNA testing, and in only fifteen of the first 124 Death Row exonerations did DNA play any role.[33] I was struck by my own experience in New Orleans, where we resolved a total of 171 capital cases in three years – and DNA was not relevant in a single case. The reason for this is obvious: DNA may be left at many rape scenes, but if you commit an armed robbery, the chances are that you will leave none, or the police will fail to collect it.

Indeed, while DNA testing may itself be an entirely valid area of science, *forensic* 'DNA fingerprinting' is something else altogether. The very use of the term 'fingerprinting' indicates an unscientific bias. When forensic DNA was novel, its promoters were seeking to benefit from a public perception that the fingerprint technique was infallible. But it is one thing when a careful and well-trained scientist performs the work in a pristine laboratory; quite another when an overworked and underpaid technician labours under pressure on a jumble of soiled samples found at the crime scene.[34]

The testimony of Thomas Quirk, the firearms expert in Kris Maharaj's trial, stretched out over seventy-nine pages of transcript and had the imprimatur of 'science', but what did it really prove? In Britain, the mere fact that Kris owned a handgun would be enough to raise a presumption of guilt. Indeed, if the police had found one in his car on London's North Circular, rather than on the Florida Turnpike, he would have been arrested on the spot. But swathes of Americans view the 'right to bear arms' as the most vital of their constitutional protections, necessary to hold back a repressive government, or drive off the criminal forces who may burst into their homes at any moment. As someone who has periodically had a gun pointed at me on the streets of New Orleans, my own view is that advocates of the Second Amendment[35] are in the lunatic fringe, but it is a large fringe, and I am surely in the minority.

For years, few truly believed that the Constitution protected the citizen's God-given privilege to tuck a concealed semi-automatic weapon into his belt each time he went out. Rather, liberals insisted, it was a hold-over from the late eighteenth century when the US had no standing army and felt under threat from the perfidious British. Maintaining a well-armed part-time national militia (or national guard) was considered necessary to the defence of the new nation, and the best way to arm them was for each member to keep his own rifle to hand. But those days are long past. Now, while arming the people does not protect America from invasion, it does expose Americans daily to the dangers caused by millions of guns. Firearms are the cause of more than 10,000 homicides a year,[36] close to 20,000 suicides,[37] and more than 75,000 injuries.[38] Surely the government had the right to regulate this carnage?

Unfortunately, in a bitterly divided opinion, five votes to four, the conservative wing of the Supreme Court informed us in 2008 that the government has no such power. Because the lack of a weapon would otherwise leave American citizens 'vulnerable to criminals', the five conservative justices determined that all Americans have the right to arm themselves.[39]

Florida has been at the forefront of the pro-gun movement. Starting in the mid-1980s, Florida incrementally became a 'shall-issue, concealed-carry, stand-your-ground, take-your-gun-to-work' state, with the passage of a series of gun-friendly laws.[40] This meant that the state had no discretion to refuse a gun licence; citizens were allowed to carry concealed weapons – indeed, this was encouraged, and carrying guns openly was generally forbidden. In Florida, if someone wanted to pull a weapon on you, you had no duty to retreat or avoid a confrontation: 'Make my day!', as Clint Eastwood used to put it. It meant that it was illegal for an employer to discriminate in any way against someone who wanted to come to work fully armed. Yet even this was not the most extreme end of the spectrum. When I lived in Atlanta, the residents of a small town nearby – Kennesaw – were so offended by an ordinance passed banning handguns in a

Chicago suburb that they passed a law *requiring* that everyone should have one.[41]

All this is a roundabout way of saying that owning a gun in America is not viewed as suspicious. There are an estimated 200 million guns in private hands.[42] Of these, perhaps 65 million are handguns and 26 million are semi-automatics.[43] It seems highly likely that the Moo Youngs were killed by one of these 65 million American handguns.[44] The challenge for Thomas Quirk should have been whether his 'science' could meaningfully narrow the pool of possible murder weapons. He thought he could. Indeed, his testimony left the jurors with the clear impression that only one of these guns – the one belonging to Krishna Maharaj – was likely to have committed the crime.

Was his evidence reliable?

As with hair analysis, forensic efforts to identify the bullet used to commit a crime began in the nineteenth century. Apocryphal or not, the first expert to testify in court is said to have been Oliver Wendell Holmes, later a justice on the US Supreme Court. In 1902 he is supposed to have fired a bullet into some cotton wool and then used a magnifying glass to compare the markings on that bullet with those on the bullet retrieved from the victim at autopsy.[45] If this story is true, then not very much changed between then and Kris Maharaj's trial nearly a century later. Ballistics testimony went unchallenged for decades. Indeed, some purveyors of the trade had taken to calling it 'ballistics fingerprinting',[46] again hoping to piggyback on the perceived reliability of fingerprinting.

It was not until recently that lawyers began to question whether there was any scientific basis for the testimony that had been used to put so many people in prison. Sure enough, the 'science' had never been verified: no independent, unbiased studies had been done to prove whether it was possible to distinguish the bullets fired from one gun from millions of others. In 2008 Jed Rakoff, a respected federal judge in New York, finally held a series of full hearings on whether ballistics qualified as scientific, provable expert testimony.[47] Judge Rakoff was clearly nonplussed by the fact that ballistics had been accepted in the courts for more than a century.[48] He speculated that the process might once have been more reliable, when firearms were effectively hand-made, and therefore more distinct one from the next. This notion, if it was ever true, had long since evaporated with the mass production of identical weapons.[49] Ballistics experts purported to match bullets under a microscope, but when their own practice was put under close scrutiny, Judge Rakoff could find no evidence that they were capable of making the distinctions they claimed.

'Whatever else ballistics could be called,' Judge Rakoff concluded, 'it could not fairly be called "science".' According to Judge Rakoff's view of the testimony, Thomas Quirk would not have been allowed to limit the possible murder weapon to 225,000 of a particular type of Smith & Wesson. He would have been forced at least to concede that several million Brownings, and similarly large numbers of Sig Sauer pistols, were candidates.[50]

Judge Rakoff's decision came too late for Kris Maharaj and others on Death Row. Indeed, Quirk had grossly overstated his conclusions in a number of capital cases. For example, in helping to place Juan Carlos Chavez on Death Row, he assured the jury that the bullet could come from no other gun in the world but the one the defendant was supposed to have been carrying.[51] Giving evidence against Michael Griffin, Quirk appeared as an all-purpose expert, both on firearms and shoe impressions. He stated his conclusions in absolute terms, and again Griffin went to Death Row.[52]

But of the small number of capital trials where Quirk's name appeared as a witness, the most worrying – as far as Kris Maharaj was concerned – was that of Dieter Riechmann. Riechmann, a German national, was charged with a capital murder that took place in Miami on October 27th, 1987, six days after Kris Maharaj had been found guilty in a nearby courtroom. Once again, Quirk's testimony was important to Riechmann's subsequent conviction and sentence of death. At Riechmann's trial, Quirk testified that only certain weapons could have fired the fatal bullet, including an Astra revolver, a Taurus revolver and an FIE Derringer. Riechmann had two such guns in his hotel room at the time of his arrest. The relevance of Quirk's testimony was particularly dubious since he tested both Riechmann's guns and concluded that neither was the murder weapon. The best that might be said was that Riechmann had two such guns, so perhaps he had previously had a third. However, the confusing power of expert testimony is illustrated by the decision upholding Riechmann's capital conviction: the Supreme Court of Florida found the evidence significant to the outcome.[53]

Almost ten years later the new lawyers representing Riechmann had done their ballistics homework. At an evidentiary hearing, Quirk conceded that there were numerous other guns that could have fired the fatal bullet – guns that he failed to mention in his trial testimony. The database he had used to make his ironclad assertions at trial included only the guns that had passed through the Miami-Dade Crime Lab – essentially covering just Miami – as opposed to the FBI database,[54] which included tens of thousands of weapons.

In other words, Quirk's ballistics testimony, offered against Riechmann as it had been against Kris Maharaj, was unscientific in the extreme. One was bound to conclude in Maharaj's case that there was no reliable evidence the murders were committed with a Smith & Wesson, let alone one that Kris Maharaj may have owned.

Yet there is an even more profound point to be made about the 'science' presented to secure a death sentence against Kris Maharaj: even truly scientific conclusions are only as good as the information that is fed into the formula. If garbage goes in, then garbage comes out. For Quirk's testimony against Kris Maharaj to have any meaning, it had to be true that Kris owned the relevant type of gun at the time of the homicides.

There were already doubts about Detective Buhrmaster's 'recall' of Kris Maharaj's statements on the night of his arrest – including whether Kris had told the policeman that he had been in Room 1215 that day. Buhrmaster also told the jury that Kris denied ever owning a handgun. Kris claimed not only that he told Buhrmaster about the Smith & Wesson he had bought, but also that it had disappeared during a police patrol stop more than three months prior to the crime.

As I waded through the documents in the police files, I found a note where Buhrmaster had seemingly scrawled what Kris had actually told him: 'Approx. six months – $150 for protection. F.H.P. took gun Orlando, Fla. $1,000.00–$700.00 & gun.'[55] The first line was readily understood, and it fitted with what Kris had told me. Around March or April 1986, six or seven months before the murders, he had bought the gun through Police Lieutenant Bernie Buzzo – a friend – for $150, as he was concerned about his safety as he delivered copies of his newspaper to distributors late at night. This, alone, proved Buhrmaster's testimony false – Kris not only admitted to owning a gun, but said when he got it.

The second line of the note was also easily interpreted: Kris had apparently said that, some time later when he was driving back from Orlando on the Florida Turnpike, he was pulled over by the Florida Highway Patrol (the 'F.H.P.'). He described how they took a large proportion of the cash ($700) that he had in the boot of the car, as well as his gun. Again, this was precisely what Kris told me, and it was direct proof that Kris told Buhrmaster the complete story.

The cynical Detective Buhrmaster might have thought Kris made it up, though that would not excuse his misleading the jury. But if that was his motive, he was wrong. We had tracked down a Greek man called Manuelos Stavros. Mr Stavros told me that in July 1986 Kris had generously offered to loan him $1,000 to travel home to Crete for a family emergency. However, when he went to see Kris to pick up the money, Kris was 'emotionally upset'. He told Mr Stavros that he had been stopped by the police, and some of the money and 'a gun' had been taken from his car. Stavros remembered the incident clearly. Though he was several hundred dollars the poorer, Kris had still retrieved more cash to lend to Stavros. Here was independent proof that Kris was telling the truth. It was hardly likely that he had falsified the story in July so that he could commit a double-murder three months later.[56]

While Buhrmaster appeared to be completely impeached at this point, none of this reflected well on the prosecution, either. They were clearly aware of the exchange. I found another note, this time in the prosecution file. Paul Ridge had written to Buhrmaster to 'speak with FHP liaison about money and gun'.[57] In other words, Ridge wanted the detective to talk with the Florida Highway Patrol to see whether Kris Maharaj's story checked out. For Buhrmaster to testify that Kris denied ever having a pistol was therefore patently false.

Garbage in, garbage out. Thomas Quirk went to great lengths to convince the jury that the gun that Kris Maharaj owned was almost certainly the one that fired the fatal bullets. The 'science' was unreliable in the first place; but if Kris had anyway lost the gun three months before the crime, it proved nothing.

9

The Defence
Lawyer

When Kris Maharaj was thrust into the maelstrom of a capital prosecution in October 1986, he began by calling an attorney with whom he was acquainted – Robert Trachman. Trachman knew nothing about death-penalty cases, but he did perform two crucial services: first, he hired an investigator to look into Kris' alibi and take statements from the witnesses; and second, he told Kris that he needed to find a real capital-defence lawyer.

Kris himself could have testified that he was forty miles away from the DuPont Plaza Hotel at noon – the time that everyone agreed the murders took place. He had at least six alibi witnesses who backed up his story. First, there was Tino Geddes, put under oath by Ron Petrillo, the lead investigator.[1] Geddes said that around eleven o'clock on October 16th he was at the Kenyaan Press, on West Sunrise Boulevard, which is where they produced the *Caribbean Times*. As he left the building, he encountered Kris, driving his wife Marita's blue car. Kris asked where he was going. Geddes replied that he had planned a quick drink with his friend Clifton Segree, and Kris invited himself along. They went to the Disco Lounge, where Tino asked for a rum, but the barman there said they were not serving strong drink at that time of day.

'Well,' Kris interjected, 'one beer won't hurt.' So they each had a beer, downing it quite quickly. Geddes remembered that Kris was wearing what he referred to at the time as a 'bush jacket', which he said was white.

'Kris paid for the beer,' Geddes laughed. 'Kris always pays the bill, uh, whenever we go out.' He added a detail – Kris used a ten-dollar note.

Kris then left in his car, while Geddes and Segree went to the office to work on the paper.

'Have you given this statement of your own free will and voluntarily?' Petrillo demanded.

'Voluntarily and of my own free will and it is the truth,' Geddes replied.

Geddes' version of events was backed up by Arthur McKenzie, a diminutive, shrivelled black man, an immigrant from the Caribbean, who gave a statement just a week after the murders. He owned a garage next to the Disco Lounge in Fort Lauderdale and, as a favour to the owner, would open the Lounge up in the mornings. He said he knew Tino Geddes, and saw him some time before noon on October 16th, accompanied by one or two other people – he could not be sure how many. One was an Indian who was a little taller than himself, wearing some kind of 'bush jacket'.[2]

George Bell was a sixty-year-old accountant from Jamaica. He also gave a statement soon after the murders took place, when he could clearly remember what had happened on the day.[3] Bell was working on some documents when Kris arrived in his office at ten minutes before noon – in other words, ten minutes before the murders took place forty miles to the south in the DuPont Plaza. Douglas Scott, who worked with Bell, was also there.

'Let's go,' Kris announced, in typical manner. He scooped George up and they went to the 420 Club, to rendezvous with a friend of Kris, someone who went by the name 'Gang'. From there, they drove in Kris' car to the Margate Shopping Center on Southwest 7th Street, where Kris wanted to look at a store that he was thinking of renting. They left there around half-past twelve and went to Tarks restaurant for lunch, arriving around 1 p.m.

At Tarks there was someone George did not know, a slim man with a beard, who greeted them. George had chicken wings and corn-on-the-cob, and Kris ordered oysters. As ever, Kris paid in cash. After lunch they drove through the Margate area again, as Kris wanted to see what kind of neighbourhood it was. Around 2.45 p.m. they dropped 'Gang' off at the 420 Club and Kris left George at the office. It would have been around 3.20 p.m. by then.

'I'll see you later at about seven o'clock,' Kris said as he left.[4]

Douglas Scott also gave a statement.[5] His regular employment was for a real-estate company, but he had recently done some work for Kris Maharaj's new paper, the *Caribbean Times*. On October 16th he had been in George Bell's office in the Romark Building in Fort Lauderdale – a fact he remembered clearly, as it was payday. Shortly before noon Kris walked in, wearing a cream safari-style jacket. Mr Scott received his pay packet, and Kris left with George Bell soon afterwards.

As with all the other alibi witnesses, the jury never heard from Douglas Scott, but years later we called him as a witness when we were seeking a new trial for Kris, challenging Eric Hendon's performance.[6] He repeated his story, adding only that George Bell was his brother-in-law.

'And do you recall roughly what time that was?' I asked him.

'It was – it was before noon,' he replied.

'When you say before noon, was it way before noon, close to noon?' I tried to narrow him down. 'Roughly when?'

'It was close to noon,' he said.

Scott firmly denied ever talking to Tino Geddes about the alibi. 'I have never spoken to him about any of the issues.'

Gangabissoon 'Gang' Ramkissoon had known Kris for thirty years. Kris picked him up in the parking lot of the 420 Club. It was October 16th, shortly before noon. Gang remembered the date and time – he had given the statement soon after the murders, on November 5th, and the particular day was clear to him because that morning he had purchased a radio. He described going to see some property, before heading for lunch at Tarks around one o'clock.

Kris had shaved his moustache off. Gang remembered someone at Tarks asking, 'Kris, how come no more 'stash?'[7]

His memory was consistent with George Bell's – they left and went by the property again, before Kris dropped him off back at the 420 Club. Kris looked totally normal to him – certainly not like someone who had just killed two people.[8]

*

Ronald Kisch was then twenty-seven years old, and had been manager at Tarks restaurant for more than two years. He was the 'slim man with the beard' whom George Bell had not recognised. But Kisch knew Kris well, as Tarks was one of Kris' favourite restaurants. Kris came in for lunch on October 16th, and was there from some time around noon until two, with two friends. Kisch was sure of the date as he normally worked evenings, but had to come in early that morning, at eleven o'clock. He remarked on the fact that Kris did not have his usual moustache that day.[9]

These six statements were taken by three separate investigators, at the behest of Robert Trachman, the civil lawyer who had first taken on Kris' case.[10] Each investigator was a notary public, licensed to place the witness under a formal oath, and each witness was simply asked to give a statement into a tape recorder about what he knew. It could hardly be suggested that the three investigators were confabulating a consistent story. Indeed, I later found another witness who corroborated what they said.[11]

According to John Kastrenakes, when later interviewed by Channel 4, the prosecutors talked to each of the alibi witnesses.

'They, in fact, confirmed Tino Geddes' original story,' he said. Kris was elsewhere at the time of the crime. 'The prosecution was presented with evidence of fingerprints, a motive, identification by disinterested people at the scene which pointed one hundred per cent to guilt and, on the other hand, this seeming air-tight alibi that Krishna Maharaj had on the day in question.'[12]

What was the prosecution to do about it? It turned out they didn't have to do anything.

Fortunately for Kastrenakes – and much to his surprise – Eric Hendon chose not to call any of the witnesses at trial.

'I advised Mr Maharaj that in my opinion he really did not need to call these alibi witnesses,' Hendon said later, when we called him to court as a witness to explain his actions (or inaction).[13] If there had been no evidence against Kris, perhaps this would have been true. But nobody could sensibly suggest that the prosecution's presentation had been weak. Years later we had undermined it, but at the time of the trial there was no proof in Hendon's hands that the Moo Youngs might be corrupt, and the jury heard no evidence that Buhrmaster might be testi-lying. Neville Butler had testified to looking on while

Kris killed both Derrick and Duane, and there was powerful evidence of motive. The prosecution case was substantial, so why was it that Hendon gave Maharaj this advice?

'At the time the only witness listed by the state was Neville Butler and the police-related witnesses. My review of the information from those witnesses suggested that the state's case was a very weak case,' continued Hendon, in a self-justifying tone. 'Mr Butler's testimony was beyond belief and if that was all the state had, my advice to Mr Maharaj was to proceed without supplying the state any additional information.'[14]

Yet this could hardly be a valid explanation, either. Neville Butler's testimony became difficult for me to believe when I later dissected it, but at the time of the trial Hendon barely touched him on cross-examination. What had Hendon done to prove Butler a liar? Hendon had advanced the ridiculous notion that Butler was conspiring with the tabloid publisher Eslee Carberry to commit a double-homicide and pin it on Krishna Maharaj in order to improve the circulation figures of the *Caribbean Echo*. If he felt Butler's testimony was so weak, then he did very little to make his point to the jurors.

'I advised him that I was not completely satisfied with the affidavits that had been prepared by his investigator and that I did not believe he would gain by filing this alibi list,' Hendon said, retreating somewhat. 'Mr Maharaj advised me that he wanted the list filed, those were his witnesses. So I filed the list. Shortly after I filed it I believe the state attorney adopted the list and indicated they would call them as state witnesses.'[15]

So Hendon was saying that he believed the prosecution was going to call all of the alibi witnesses to prove that their testimony was false. With respect to just one of the six, this was true. Tino Geddes had suddenly recanted his testimony, saying that he had fabricated the alibi for Kris Maharaj shortly after the arrest. He testified for the prosecution at trial and, while his evidence was not proof of guilt, the notion that Kris had asked him to falsify the alibi would have weighed heavily against the accused.[16] Indeed, this would have made it even more important for Hendon to present the other five alibi witnesses. Any lawyer would have deemed it crucial – if it were possible – to impeach Geddes with proof that Kris' story was not concocted. Had Hendon only talked to the five other witnesses, he would have learned that they were firmly sticking to their guns, contradicting

Geddes' assertion that he had confected the alibi.

As Hendon fell back from one position to the next, he ultimately insisted that he had not wanted to pursue an alibi because he considered an alibi to be dangerous. He felt that his position was illustrated by Kris' case – look what had happened: a witness had recanted. There are, in truth, traps for the unwary lawyer in presenting such a defence. When the person on trial attempts to show that he could not have committed the crime because he was elsewhere at the time, there is a danger that the jury will allow the burden of proof to shift to the accused: if he says he was somewhere else, and if he cannot show that to be true, then he must be guilty.

It is important to recognise the problem, but that should not mean that the defence lawyer capitulates. The jury had to be reminded over and over again that the prosecution bore the burden of disproving Kris' alibi.[17] If Kris said he was in Fort Lauderdale at noon on the day of the murders, the prosecution had to show beyond a reasonable doubt that he was in the DuPont Plaza. Obviously, if there was a serious question as to whether Kris was even at the crime scene, then there must be doubt that he was guilty.

Hendon also repeated his concerns that the witnesses might not hold up to cross-examination. Putting any witness on the stand is not easy – it is far easier, even for the marginally competent lawyer, to attack the case presented by the other side. But this cannot be a reason to forgo putting on a defence; the defence must be properly prepared, albeit perhaps not in the manner that the prosecution had prepped Neville Butler. In contrast, Hendon originally said that he did not talk to any of the alibi witnesses, but relied solely on Ron Petrillo, the investigator.[18] Later, when his competence at the trial was challenged, he insisted that he only ever spoke to 'a couple' of the alibi witnesses.

'I can't tell you specifically what names these witnesses had,' he said, 'but the ones I spoke to really wanted nothing to do with any further involvement with this case.'[19] Whether we believe his first statement, or the self-serving version he told later, there was no suggestion that Hendon talked to *all* the alibi witnesses, or sought out other people who might have been missed in the initial investigation. When I talked to them later, none of the witnesses voiced any qualms about testifying.

'Well, what I can tell you, Counsel, is when I reviewed the affidavits, the affidavits did not meet the standard that I would have required,' Hendon insisted, when we pressed in court our challenge to his decision. 'The affidavits were affidavits that I thought would cause Mr Maharaj more harm than good. It appeared to me as if these were alibi witnesses who had been sought out, trying to account for every half-hour of the entire time surrounding the incident and it seemed all too convenient, and I just felt that going forward with these alibis would not be in Mr Maharaj's best interest.'[20]

In other words, Hendon said that the alibi was too good – not a complaint that many lawyers would be heard to make. The witnesses had, he thought, been sought out. But seeking out witnesses is the essence of investigation; rarely do they come forward on their own. Hendon said he was not satisfied with the 'affidavits' of the witnesses; in this he was again demonstrably mistaken. They had not given affidavits, but had rather recorded complete sworn oral statements, without prompting.[21]

So who was this Eric Hendon, and what was going on with him?

Hendon was recommended to Kris Maharaj. He had been with the Public Defender Office before going into private practice; he later found it hard to make ends meet and returned to the PD Office, perhaps for a more reliable pay cheque. I called some lawyers I knew at the PD before meeting him, and they confirmed my own impression: he was not the hardest-working lawyer, but pleasant and mostly well intentioned.[22]

Kris told me that Hendon had boasted to him of a perfect record: seven capital cases tried, seven won. Many years later Kris would learn that this was not quite the case. At the time – 1986 – Hendon was only eight years out of law school, and he had never actually tried a capital case to a jury at all. But Kris was partly the cause of his own downfall. Hendon's fee was very reasonable: $20,000.[23] That was one reason Kris went with him rather than someone else. Kris was a businessman. He recoiled at the notion of spending enormous sums on proving something he viewed as self-evident: that he should be found innocent. Some will blame him for this, for what could be more important than his liberty? But while Kris could be generous, he was not a spendthrift; he had not become an effective businessman by throwing money away – except, perhaps, on horses. In this regard, though, perhaps the innocent man was his own worst enemy.

The set fee caused many of Kris's ensuing problems. There should always be at least two lawyers on any capital case: one person cannot handle such a task alone.[24] So Hendon should have hired someone to help him, but that would have cut his fee in half from the start. Because the fee was fixed, every hour Hendon worked cut back on his profit – if he could have settled the case with the prosecutor in just sixty minutes' negotiation, his rate would have been $20,000 an hour; two hours, $10,000; three hours, £6,666;[25] and so on. If he worked 1,000 hours, he would receive no more than twenty dollars an hour. This is a structural disincentive that encourages a lawyer to do less work. Indeed, while he might deny it, this consideration inevitably played a role in some of the advice that Hendon gave Kris. When it came to deposing the witnesses, Hendon wanted only fifteen minutes per person; the prosecutors had to urge him to take longer.[26]

Anyone familiar with complex capital litigation would know that Hendon's fee was far too low. Here we encounter another element of the judicial system that makes little sense. Presumably most people would agree that no legal case is more significant than a death-penalty trial, with human life at stake; litigation between corporations over contractual disputes pales in comparison. We might expect someone on trial for his life to receive the very best defence available, paid at the highest rates. If, again, we want to avoid the conviction of the innocent at all costs, we will ensure that the defendant is provided with all the resources and tools necessary to him. We will pay the capital-defence lawyer more than anyone else, to ensure that those on trial for their lives receive the very best representation possible.

The real world is an inverse reflection of this. New York corporate lawyers have starting salaries of more than $150,000.[27] Partners make far more, often in the $2 million-a-year range. In Britain, there are at least 800 lawyers earning this kind of money.[28] The median rate for New York lawyers of all stripes is $252 per hour,[29] but this masks some who demand $1,000[30] (or $16.67 for each minute they work). The cup of coffee you have with your lawyer may cost $5 to buy, but by the time (the lawyer's time) that you have finished drinking it, it will cost $100, even if you scald your tongue trying to slurp it in just six minutes.

What justifies all this largesse? While corporate lawyers may think they work hard,[31] they probably put in fewer hours than a capital trial lawyer. At $1,000 an hour, and with two lawyers working on the case, the legal fee alone in a capital case would be $2 million.[32] Would this be too high a price to pay for the defence of human life?[33]

It is certainly far more than society is willing to pay. Frederico Martinez-Macias was represented at his capital trial in El Paso, Texas, by a court-appointed attorney paid only $11.84 per hour,[34] roughly one-hundredth as much. A federal court later reviewing the death sentence noted caustically that you get what you pay for: as with Kris' case, the lawyer failed to present an available alibi witness, and failed to interview and present witnesses who could have testified in rebuttal of the prosecutor's case.[35] Martinez-Macias was inevitably sentenced to die. On appeal he had volunteer lawyers who did everything that his trial lawyer should have done. He was granted a new trial, whereupon the grand jury refused an indictment, and he was released[36] – but not until he had lost nine years to Death Row.

The court seemed to think that $11.84 was an extraordinarily low hourly wage for a trial where a man's life was at stake. It is far from the lowest I have seen. When I began trying capital cases, several states paid a maximum of $1,000 for the entire process – this included the attorney's costs, expenses, as well as investigation and experts. I have kept my time for many years, and I average more than 1,000 hours for a complicated capital case, so the hourly rate would fall below one dollar per hour. Indeed, we once sued the State of Mississippi because the fee for four capital trial lawyers varied from $1.28 to a high of $2.22 per hour.[37] We demanded that they be paid at least the federal minimum wage – which is now around $6.55.[38] We won, and the rate eventually rose to $25, but that is still well below what it would cost to keep a law office open.[39] In other words, for every hour a lawyer works on a death-penalty trial in Mississippi, he loses money.[40]

There is another division among criminal defendants – between the well heeled and the downtrodden. O.J. Simpson is reputed to have paid around $10 million for his acquittal for two murders.[41] At the time when all America was transfixed by defence attorney Johnny Cochran's clever rhymes ('If the glove don't fit, you must acquit'), I was feeling rather lonely in a parish somewhere in the middle of Louisiana. Eight people were facing the death penalty, and the total budget for the defence of everyone in the parish for the year – all trials, both capital or not – was $16,000, or around what O.J. was paying a single expert in a day.

Surprisingly, despite this, lawyers can still make a reasonable living off court-appointed cases, but only if they ignore the needs of their clients and focus solely on trawling for money. Linda Carty, a British woman on Death Row in Texas, was represented by the infamous Jerry Guerinot. Counting Linda's case, Guerinot managed to lose twenty capital trials[42] – resulting in more people on Death Row because of his personal ineptitude than there are in thirty-one of the US states.[43] Thankfully, he had retired from capital 'defence' by 2008 – but he still managed to pull in $100,000 a year on felony cases. He achieved this by taking on as many as 2,000 felony cases in two years.[44] To set this number in perspective, most people only know about 300 people in the entire world; Guerinot was meant to be representing seven times that number, each of whom was relying on him to establish the degree of their culpability and achieve a fair verdict and sentence. But since he would have to resolve several cases each day, the prisoners would be lucky if he spent a few moments with each of them.

Guerinot is not unique. Other lawyers encounter similar caseloads without the same venal motives. In Calcasieu Parish, Louisiana, we did a survey of the parish jail to assess the quality of defence that the prisoners were getting. We had the full cooperation of the sheriff, who was tired of fielding the prisoners' complaints.[45] Each year the Public Defender Office was assigned roughly 2,400 new felony cases by the court. The lawyers averaged 587 open cases; one had 3,395 misdemeanour clients, many of whom could face several months in jail. Because the system was so overloaded, a prisoner would not be charged for six months, and would not generally appear in court for the first time until he had spent nearly a year in jail. We checked the visitation logs at the jail: each month, fewer than 1 per cent of the prisoners received a lawyer visit.[46] There were only two brief investigative reports in hundreds of client files. Only twice in three years (out of perhaps 20,000 cases in total) did the Public Defender Office use an independent expert to challenge the state's case.

While 6,950 criminal cases were filed by the prosecution in one year, there were only ten jury trials. This meant that 99.86 per cent of those in prison did not receive a jury trial – and therefore ended up pleading guilty (often simply to get out of jail) or, after months, having the charges dismissed for want of evidence against them.[47] Reprieve's young British volunteers found forty-two prisoners in the jail who had no case pending in the courthouse – in other words, they should never have been locked up. At least thirteen people were languishing there although their sentences had long since expired. For example, Eddie James should have served six months, but he had been in jail for two years. Jeremiah Rodriguez had been sentenced to sixty days but was still in prison fifteen months later. Mark Celestine received only thirty days, but he had not been released eighteen months later.

Thirty people had not gone to trial, though they had already been held in jail for longer than the maximum possible sentence. Of these, one man had been incarcerated for three months on a charge of trespassing, although even if he were guilty, the crime was not subject to jail time, but merely to a fine. Another man had been in jail for six months despite having the charges against him dismissed three months earlier – the District Attorney had decided there was no evidence, but had failed to tell the jail. In all, then, eighty-five of the prisoners clearly should not have been in jail at all under any interpretation of the facts.

Calcasieu Parish was a shambles, but it was not unique. Indeed, compared to Orleans Parish, it was rather well organised.[48] When Hurricane Katrina hit New Orleans, it took months to work out who had been in the jail, and much longer to resolve who should have been there. The story told by these figures is a depressing one: if capital defence is hopelessly underfunded, then the plight of those facing felony criminal cases (carrying the potential for years in prison, or even life without parole) is even worse.

Systemically it is clear that the US does not take seriously its obligation to avoid the conviction, or execution, of the innocent. At $110 per case, each Calcasieu Parish prisoner would receive only twelve minutes of a New York corporate lawyer's time. Nationwide, the accused could not expect much more. Meanwhile a business client spends more than this when he shares a café latte with his lawyer. Such is the value we place upon life and liberty.[49]

The Fifth Circuit Court of Appeals said that you get the kind of defence you pay for. How does the underfunding of criminal defence translate into an effective, or ineffective, effort by the lawyer? While there will always be zealots who choose a calling for reasons other than money (and I count myself among their number), it is the nature of the capitalist system that price affects quality. Those with effective counsel tend not to get sentenced to death.[50] However, the structural problems with the system make it inevitable that the people who receive the death penalty tend to have a selection of the worst lawyers available.[51] More than 100 condemned prisoners have been exonerated from Death Row in the USA in recent years,[52] and the State of Illinois enjoys the dubious distinction of having exonerated more condemned prisoners (thirteen) than it has executed (twelve).[53]

The stories of incompetent lawyering make depressing reading.[54] In George Dungee's case, the lawyers begged to be relieved from the appointment, as they feared the bad publicity they would receive in their local community for representing someone accused of a terrible crime.[55]

'This is the worst thing that's ever happened to me professionally,' complained one man assigned to George's defence.

'I only stayed on the case because to refuse would be a contempt of court,' said another apologetically. During trial they referred to George as a 'nigger'.[56]

Various lawyers have shown up intoxicated to represent their clients.[57] In Talladega County, Alabama, we did a study looking into the time each lawyer spent with the client before trial. This ranged from fifteen minutes to a couple of hours. One local attorney turned up to court drunk. At least the judge recognised it, and jailed him for contempt; sadly, the spell in the cells was the only time he seems to have spent with his client preparing for trial.

In more than one case the lawyer slept through part of the trial.[58] In Texas, Joe Frank Cannon was the court-appointed lawyer assigned to defend Calvin Burdine. He said that he became bored and was finding it hard to remain awake.[59] The state judge gave short shrift to Calvin's complaint: 'The Constitution does not say that the lawyer has to be awake,' he opined.[60] Indeed, even the first panel of the federal court reviewing the case found no error, since Calvin had failed to prove that the lawyer slept through parts of the trial that really mattered.[61] I was at the argument in the appellate court where these issues were discussed. It was surreal: at one point a judge asked whether there was a constitutional distinction between an attorney sleeping during a death-penalty trial versus one who only dozed. Prior to the hearing Cannon had died, and I had the bright idea of checking out his tombstone. I thought perhaps we could get a good photograph that would illustrate how his motto was the same in death as it had been in life – unfortunately, the epitaph did not read 'Rest in Peace', as I had hoped.[62]

Of course, Calvin might have been better off had his lawyer slept through the entire trial, rather than clambering to his feet to speak. With a defence lawyer like Cannon, Calvin hardly needed a prosecutor: Cannon referred to his client as a 'queer' and a 'fairy', and made no objection when the district attorney told jurors that 'sending a homosexual to the penitentiary certainly isn't a very bad punishment'.[63]

I can never make up my mind which example of defence-advocate ineptitude is my favourite. One contender would be the Mississippi trial of Alfred Dale 'Woodrow' Leatherwood. He was a mentally disabled young black man, accused of raping a young girl (a capital offence at the time). He had been represented at trial by a third-year student from Ole Miss law school, doing her clinical work experience,[64] and I ended up doing the appeal.

'Excuse me, Your Honour, can I have a moment to compose myself?' she said at the start of the trial. 'I've never been in a courtroom before.'

While the justices were aghast during the oral argument, in the opinion reversing the conviction the Mississippi Supreme Court did not even mention that a student had been involved in the trial, as it would have added further fuel to the criticisms of Mississippi justice. Again, then, there was no public acknowledgement of the problem and therefore little effort was made to avert a recurrence.[65]

It is not only the court-appointed lawyer who comes under a series of financial and psychological pressures to underperform. Sometimes retained lawyers are even worse. A person facing a death sentence will hear that legal-aid lawyers are hopeless and will search around for a lawyer to hire. But if a real capital defence would cost hundreds of thousands of dollars and the typical prisoner is impoverished, who is he (or his desperate mother) going to find to hire? Only the courthouse bottom-feeder will be willing to take a case on for the kind of fee that the family can afford. When I was in New Orleans, before 2004, the public defenders were terrible, but they were not as bad as the retained lawyers, who paced the halls of the Orleans Parish court building, cornering the weeping families of prisoners charged with serious crimes. For $500 they would *really* mess up the case.

Every courthouse has this breed. Some wear sharp suits, with slicked-down hair, giving off a greased air of financial success to lure their prey. Others cannot afford the costume, and spin a line to account for their threadbare suits – they are the true defenders, they say, dedicated to preserving the rights of their clients, intent on keeping their fees as low as humanly possible.

The defendant also plays a little-recognised role in this judicial train wreck. While this may be the lawyer's hundredth trial, it is very often the prisoner's first. He may suspect that the lawyer is no Perry Mason, but he is unlikely to know what to do about it. No surprise, then, that he rarely stands up to complain that his lawyer – his only ally in the courtroom – is not living up to expectations.

Even those who try to help themselves have a steep mountain to climb. Soon after he was arrested Calvin Duncan – still a teenager, black, barely literate, but showing more initiative than most – filed a request with the trial judge: 'Motion for a Law Book'. Accused of a crime he had not committed, he realised that he had a problem with the law and needed to figure out what to do about it. He could see that his court-appointed lawyer was going to be of little help. But Calvin was convicted. While he taught himself a lot about the law in the ensuing decades, he had to wait twenty-three years in prison before he was exonerated. He could not investigate his own case from behind bars, and it was only when the Innocence Project of New Orleans took on his case that the facts were finally revealed that allowed him to go home.[66]

Was Eric Hendon just another example of a lawyer who was terminally inept?[67]

As it turns out, perhaps not.

When I went to see Ron Petrillo, the investigator who worked for the defence on Kris' case, I asked him why Hendon had not instructed him to spend more time on the case. There was, after all, so much he could have dug up to shape a proper defence. Petrillo claimed that Hendon had received a menacing phone call.

'A few weeks before the trial, Hendon called me early one morning,' Petrillo recalled. 'He told me someone had called him at home and threatened him.'[68] The caller apparently said that if it looked like Hendon was doing too much to get Kris Maharaj off, something might happen to Hendon's son. Petrillo said that from then on his job was mainly to keep an eye on the boy to make sure nothing happened to him.

Obviously, when we interviewed him, Ben Kuehne and I confronted Eric Hendon with this. He denied there ever was a threat. But he would, wouldn't he? If it really happened, admitting it would place his son in jeopardy, as well as raise questions concerning his own actions at trial. On the other hand, I wondered what motive Ron Petrillo might have for making up such a story. I could not think of one.

10

The Other Suspects

The popular stereotype of the Death Row prisoner is that he constantly seeks to avoid his punishment by filing frivolous appeals: 'Never put off until tomorrow that which can be put off indefinitely.' Yet the reality for many condemned prisoners is that they want to move their cases forward as quickly as possible. When he had first been convicted, Kris had still been able to pay for his own attorney and had pressed his new lawyer, Ken Cohen, to move forward with his quest for a fresh trial as fast as possible. Kris had yet to learn that nothing can expedite the capital appeals process unless the state scents the opportunity for an imminent execution.

Meanwhile Kris had been getting a taste of what it really meant to be on Death Row. His wife Marita travelled more than 700 miles to see him every other weekend. As a companion, she had located Katherine Tafero, who lived near her and was the mother of another Death Row prisoner, Jesse. On May 4th, 1990, Jesse was executed. It went spectacularly badly. Jesse's death, with flames flickering around the skull cap that delivered the electricity to his brain, was a gruesome reminder of what Florida had in store for Kris. It shook Marita even more than Kris, and she no longer had Katherine with whom to share the ride to prison and the cost of petrol.

That year, 1990, saw three other men die in the electric chair in

Florida, followed by two more in 1991. Six of Kris' neighbours had been killed before the Florida Supreme Court finally handed down an opinion on his direct appeal, four years after the trial had ended. The justices unanimously affirmed Kris' conviction without any question that he might not have done it. They stated, as uncontroverted fact, that 'these murders occurred as a result of an ongoing dispute between Derrick Moo Young and Krishna Maharaj'.

The new lawyer, Ken Cohen, had argued that the gossip in Carberry's newspaper, the *Caribbean Echo*, should not have been introduced as evidence against Kris. The appeals court ruled that even though Hendon had asked prior to trial that the newspaper stories be excluded from the case, the trial lawyer had failed to object a second time when they were actually offered, so the issue was barred from review.[1] Various other concerns that Cohen raised were likewise 'procedurally barred' because Hendon had failed to object. With respect to every other challenge to his conviction that Kris presented, the court airily dismissed them in one sentence: 'We find that the remaining claims are without merit and need no further discussion.'

'Furthermore,' the court unanimously concluded, 'the evidence is sufficient to sustain the convictions of each of the offenses for which Maharaj was found guilty.'

With respect to the death sentence, the review was even more cursory. A legal mistake had been made in allowing the jurors[2] to find the crime to be 'especially heinous, atrocious or cruel'. Under the proper standard the case did not qualify, but the error was harmless, the court said. Two of the seven justices did not agree with their colleagues' analysis here, and a third, Justice McDonald, thought the sentence should be reversed, but none of them bothered to explain why. 'Accordingly, for the reasons expressed,' they summed up, 'we affirm the convictions and sentences, including the sentence of death for the murder of Duane Moo Young.'

Kris had then unsuccessfully sought review from the United States Supreme Court in Washington, before his case came back to Florida to begin the next round of proceedings: state habeas corpus.[3] This is the point where new lawyers generally investigate the case afresh, and present evidence showing that the original trial was not fair. It was here that Ben Kuehne and I had assumed responsibility for Kris' appeals.[4]

Those unfamiliar with the legal process are often flummoxed by the notion that there is ever a time when the state no longer has the obligation to prove guilt. Yet once the original trial concludes, so does the prosecution's burden of proof. It then shifts very clearly to the prisoner to come up with a compelling reason why he should not be executed. In Kris' case, it was never going to be an easy task. Unlike the screen appearances of legendary and entirely fictitious lawyers like Perry Mason, no real killer – stricken by remorse – was going to burst through the double-doors at the back of the courtroom to make his confession.

Yet, early on in our investigation, we had come across the Moo Young briefcase, withheld from Hendon by the prosecution at the time of trial, and this gave us plenty of hints as to where we might look for those who actually killed Derrick and Duane Moo Young, and why. Another clue came from the original files of defence lawyer Eric Hendon, where I found a copy of a letter written by Kris' friend, US Congressman Mervyn Dymally, to a certain Adam Hosein. Without explanation, Dymally demanded to know whether the Cargil International of which Hosein was a director related in any way to the Cargil International in the Bahamas? And was the address on a letter that Dymally had received from Derrick Moo Young correct: Frederick House, PO Box 4839, Frederick Street, Nassau, Bahamas?

There was nothing in Hendon's file that elaborated on Dymally's letter. Hendon had apparently cast it to one side as Kris' case headed for trial. When I went to his office later to talk about it, Hendon insisted that he knew nothing about this Cargil International. Kris could not have explained the importance of the company, as he knew even less. However, documents concerning Cargil were littered throughout the Moo Youngs' briefcase. It seemed to be the main front that they had set up for whatever it was they were involved in. Whatever this Dymally letter was, it merited a full follow-up.

Former Congressman Dymally had been one of Kris' character witnesses at the penalty phase of his trial. I called him to see what he could tell me. He might have been an important person, but he picked up the phone at once and sounded the courteous Caribbean gentleman. He was in his eighties, and the events I was asking him to recall took place long ago, but he remained convinced that Kris was innocent. He told me how he had received a letter from the Moo Youngs with the Bahamian address and Adam Hosein's name on the letterhead.

Something made him think that the corporation had to be dodgy. He couldn't recall the contents of the letter – probably something about a favour they wanted from him. He promised to look out the letter for me, but called back the next day to say that records from that year had been destroyed. He could tell me nothing more.

It was frustrating. Nevertheless I planned a trip to the Bahamas, as I had various leads to chase there. It was a cheap twenty-minute flight from Fort Lauderdale, and I arrived in Nassau early one morning. First, I knocked on the door of Eddie Dames, the man in whose name Room 1215 had been reserved. He was immediately and vehemently hostile. Before I was thrown off his porch, I warned him that the investigation was going to go on regardless, until we learned the truth about Kris' case. Later that day I received a call from Prince Ellis, who had testified against Kris at trial, describing his trip to Miami with Dames, allegedly to buy music and restaurant equipment. Ellis wanted to meet. When he came to the hotel, he told me that he felt racked with guilt and wanted to provide me with a statement concerning the case. He subsequently went on-camera; he felt that Kris had been framed, and he described how Dames was involved in the drug trade in the Bahamas.

Meanwhile I went to Frederick House, at the address Dymally had mentioned in his letter, and discovered that it was the law office of Bowe & MacKay – and the first listed member of the partnership was F. Nigel Bowe. Now, immediately, I knew we were getting somewhere. That was a name with interesting associations.

By the late 1970s the Bahamas had become a major conduit of drugs into the United States, and money out of it. Of the 700 islands, Bimini was the closest to the US mainland, just fifty-three miles due east of Miami. It was ideally suited to transit the cocaine and marijuana that flooded in from Colombia.[5] As a result the Bahamas attracted all sorts of ne'er-do-wells (albeit those involved in the drug trade were doing pretty well). It helped that the Prime Minister from 1967 to 1992, Sir Lynden Oscar Pindling, was a crook himself, perennially on the take from almost anyone willing to pay. He was knighted in 1983, the Queen apparently choosing to overlook a recent NBC television report entitled *The Bahamas: A Nation for Sale*, which made a strong case that Pindling was facilitating the massive drug shipments of Carlos Lehder, a major figure in the Medellin Cartel.

If Pindling was the Prime Minister of Bahamian narco-crooks, then the lawyer F. Nigel Bowe was their chief advocate. And the biggest name on Bowe's dance card was Carlos Lehder. Lehder 'was to cocaine transportation as Henry Ford was to automobiles', said US Attorney Robert Merckle, who would later prosecute him.[6] His innovation was to build a heavily protected 1,000-metre runway on Norman's Cay in the Bahamas, an island that he bought to create a waystation for the mass transit of cocaine. By 1982, 300 kilograms (660 pounds) of the drug, worth perhaps $10 million, would arrive on the island with every flight.[7] It would then be divided into smaller shipments that were essentially fired at the US coastline in small planes and high-speed boats. The US Coastguard was overwhelmed, and was lucky to intercept one shipment in fifty.

Lehder's personal wealth mounted into the billions.[8] He used some of his money to keep the locals onside. On the ninth anniversary of Bahamian independence, July 10th, 1982, a large crowd gathered to celebrate in Clifford Park in Nassau. Lehder dropped leaflets into the crowd from a light aircraft, with the message, 'DEA GO HOME'. He did not like the attention he was receiving from the US Drug Enforcement Agency (DEA). To help bring the Bahamians around to his point of view, he attached $100 bills to his promotional material.[9]

Despite Lehder's efforts, by then the Bahamian Government was beginning to buckle under intense American pressure. Lehder needed local agents to negotiate with the authorities to keep his Bahamian estate secure. He hired F. Nigel Bowe to help him, paying Bowe to 'persuade' the Bahamian authorities to stop causing him trouble at Norman's Cay. Lehder also needed a front company to give a semblance of legitimacy to his accumulating wealth. That company, International Dutch Resources Ltd, was set up by Bowe.[10]

Notwithstanding his retainer, Bowe proved unable to keep the Americans off Lehder's back.

'I know Nigel is ripping me off,' Lehder complained to another Bahamian fixer, Everette Bannister. 'And, when I get proof, I'm going to have him removed from the population count.'[11] Bowe got into further trouble with Lehder when the drug king sent a $250,000 necklace to Lady Pindling as part of his ongoing efforts to keep the Prime Minister sweet. When she rejected the present, Lehder found that he could not retrieve it. Bowe denied that he was responsible for its loss.[12]

Eventually Lehder lost the battle and was evicted from Norman's Cay. But this did not slow Bowe down. He served other members of the Colombian cartels by introducing them to smugglers and continuing to facilitate transit through the Bahamas. In one instance that would later come to haunt him in federal court, Bowe accompanied smuggler Jack Devoe to Cartagena, Colombia, hooking Devoe up with José 'Pepi' Cabrera Sarmiento, considered a 'pioneer' in the cocaine trade for his imaginative ways of evading law enforcement. Devoe flew Cabrera Sarmiento's cocaine into the Bahamas, and subsequently on to the United States, earning about $10 million over just nine months. He kicked back 10 per cent to Bowe, who was also being paid by Cabrera Sarmiento.[13]

By now the US authorities were heavily focused on Bowe. In 1985 the US began to seek his extradition,[14] but they were blocked by Pindling. Five days after the Moo Youngs were killed, on October 23rd, 1986, a new indictment was published in Miami accusing Bowe and Cabrera Sarmiento of importing 7,304 pounds of cocaine into the US,[15] with a street value of $100 million. Soon afterwards the same Miami grand jury released indictments against Pablo Escobar and Carlos Lehder.[16]

Bowe remained a free man in the Bahamas, thanks to Pindling's patronage. However, the Prime Minister's luck ended with the 1992 election when, based largely on the recurrent stories of narco-corruption, his party lost for the first time in a quarter-century. He had had a good run, and took his defeat well.

'The people of this great little democracy have spoken in a most dignified and eloquent manner,' he said in his concession speech, 'and the voice of the people is the voice of God.' His retirement plan was, of course, well funded.

Simultaneously, Bowe's freedom ran out. He was finally extradited, but the ongoing influence of his money was such that the Bahamian Government struck an agreement eliminating some of the more serious charges against him. He went to trial without his retained lawyer, David Markus, who had just been arrested himself on narcotics charges.[17] Bowe was convicted and sentenced to fifteen years in prison.

*

With the knowledge that the Moo Young company, Cargil International, had a branch office at Bowe's address in the Bahamas, I later tried to trace Bowe through the US prison system, but they said he was no longer being held. He apparently received remission on his sentence and had just been sent back to the Bahamas. Joe Hingston, a Reprieve stalwart, was then an investigator with our office in New Orleans and went back to the Bahamas with a BBC reporter, Tim Samuels, to try to talk to Bowe.

When they knocked on the lawyer's door he was expansive in his welcome, although he soon retreated into suspicion. Tim covertly filmed the conversation.

'I wanted to ask you about Derrick Moo Young …' Joe began.

'Who?' Bowe leapt in. 'Don't know the man.' He was emphatic, and rapid with his denial.

'What about the company, Cargil International?' Joe persisted. 'Can you tell me anything about them?'

'Cargil?' Bowe replied. He said he knew nothing about it.

Joe mentioned the letter sent by Derrick Moo Young from Bowe's own address to Congressman Dymally, representing it as the Cargil office in the Bahamas. He described how Adam Hosein was a director of the company.

'That is impossible. That's simply not true!' Bowe said.

While Joe had failed to extract any information about Cargil, Bowe spoke openly about how close he was with Hosein, though when Joe pressed him on their business associations, Bowe said it was a strictly social friendship.

Time went by, and we made no further headway on the Bahamian issue. We had not even been able to corroborate Mervyn Dymally's letter, or his memory. But then a friend who had developed a deep interest in Kris' case was dabbling one evening with an online research tool that could identify anything and everything about corporations around the world. And there it was: Cargil International Corporation SA (Bahamas). Sure enough, just as Dymally recalled, the records showed that its registered office was to be found at Bowe & MacKay Attorneys, Frederick House, PO Box 4839, Frederick Street, Nassau, Bahamas.[18]

So Nigel Bowe had not been forthright. Had he been lying about his relationship to Adam Hosein?

*

Adam Amer Hosein was a Trinidadian acquaintance of Kris from England who, like many others, had been attracted to Kris' wealth and success. Kris thought him a mildly irritating but harmless poser.[19] Hosein bore a close resemblance to Kris, and in Kris' horseracing heyday used to pass himself off as the millionaire, to get into the better stands at the track. Like Kris, Hosein had made a home in Florida and had set up a business running a garage.

In Hendon's file, I had found a significant piece of information: a sworn statement from George Abchal, who had worked at Hosein's garage at the time of the Moo Young murders. Ron Petrillo, the defence investigator, had spoken to Abchal two months after the crimes and taken a sworn statement from him which was full of allegations about the Moo Youngs being mixed up in drugs. But when I now spoke to Petrillo on the phone, he said he had run into Abchal again, and even though the investigator was no longer on the case, he felt he owed it to Kris to do what he could. Abchal had filled in a few crucial details – apparently speaking more freely now that he was no longer working for Hosein.

'Abchal said Hosein kept a gun and a silencer in the drawer of his desk, and on the morning of the murders, he said, Hosein took the gun and left,' Petrillo told me. Abchal claimed that the gun was a Smith & Wesson nine-millimetre, the type of weapon that Thomas Quirk thought was used to kill the Moo Youngs. I still doubted the ballistics expert's opinion, and was unwilling to rely on it for anything, but Petrillo thought a silencer could explain how seven or eight shots could have been fired in the DuPont Plaza Hotel without alerting security.

'Ask yourself,' demanded Petrillo, 'why is it that nobody heard anything?'[20]

This linked in with another piece of evidence connecting Hosein to the crime scene. In the police files I had come across voluminous telephone records. A message had been left for Room 1215 on the day of the murders: the call came from Hosein's number.[21] Yet the police never investigated Hosein in the murders of the Moo Youngs. He wasn't even questioned.[22] He returned to Trinidad shortly afterwards.

I decided to go to Trinidad to talk to Hosein, but first I wanted to catch up with Petrillo's witness, George Abchal. He added some facts to his earlier statement: a few days before the Moo Youngs were killed, he said, Hosein had tried to buy six kilos (13¼ pounds) of cocaine from them on credit. They kicked him out because he allegedly owed them too much money.[23] On the day of the murders Hosein had returned to the garage, obviously nervous, and told Abchal not to mention to anyone that he had gone out, or where he had been.[24]

I went to Trinidad to see what I could learn. Hosein had apparently been in legal trouble since returning there, and we wanted to find some physical evidence – perhaps his fingerprints – that I could link to the Miami crime scene. I was taken aback when I learned that Hosein's defence lawyer on the charge had been Ramesh Maharaj, Kris' younger brother. I had hoped that Ramesh would be an important ally. He was a famous lawyer in Trinidad, and owed a debt to his brother. Kris had paid for him to come to London to complete his legal studies. Ramesh then returned home to make a name for himself as a human-rights advocate when he represented the members of Jamaat Al Muslimeen, a Muslim group charged in the wake of an attempted coup in July 1990.[25] Ramesh rose to become Attorney General of Trinidad and Tobago in the 1990s – their chief prosecutor. I had heard rumours, but it was only when I arrived in Trinidad that I discovered how fully he had abandoned his earlier commitment to human rights. While his older brother Kris languished on Death Row in Florida, Ramesh had been fighting 'tooth and nail' to implement the death penalty back home, once authorising nine hangings over a four-day period.

'For Trinidad on Friday, hanging day was rife with irony,' commented the *Los Angeles Times*. 'It was a major victory for Attorney General Ramesh Maharaj, a onetime lawyer for Death Row inmates and a human rights crusader, who partially withdrew from international rights bodies while pushing hard for the hangings. His own brother is on Death Row in Florida. After years of frustrating judicial delays, Friday's hangings, Maharaj said, "will build confidence in law and justice". '[26]

When I arrived at the small hotel in Port of Spain, I switched on the television and found, to my pleasure, that there was little but cricket to watch. Secretly I wanted to stay in the room and watch for a while, but I dutifully telephoned Ramesh, to seek his help. I left him several messages, but he did not reply. Eventually I spoke to his wife. By now I was thoroughly annoyed, so I told her I'd be dialling the local newspaper in half an hour if I didn't get a return call.

Ramesh called back at once. We did meet up briefly. He was a handsome and charismatic man, with gold chains flashing around his neck and his wrists. But he was obviously concerned about the impact that publicity might have concerning a brother on Death Row; less obviously concerned with his brother's plight. He palmed me off on an aged retainer in his law firm, who lectured me on the superiority of British law and the importance of barristers' wigs, and was of little help with my mission. Adam Hosein would not meet me. Ramesh did nothing to help make it happen.

Later, Joe Hingston went on another trip to invite Hosein to tell us what he knew. In the few snatched and hostile moments that Joe spent with Hosein, the man denied having anything to do with the Moo Youngs. He had no dealings with them, he said, business or otherwise. He knew nothing about them. But the evidence suggested otherwise. According to Congressman Dymally, Hosein had been a director of Cargil. He was close friends with Nigel Bowe. And the documents in their briefcase showed that the Moo Youngs incorporated a company in Panama called Amer Enterprises. It took me a while to crack the code, until I remembered that Amer was Hosein's middle name.

But why were most of these businesses registered in Panama?

As the tropical islands of the Bahamas became increasingly hot for the drug trade, the Bahamian connection did not close down. There were plenty of people like Nigel Bowe who had no other way to make up for their lost earnings. By now they were experts in the field, and they simply branched out, using other countries to run their narco-business. Panama was a favourite change of venue,[27] largely because Manuel Noriega was then in power and it had a convenient border with Colombia, not too far north-west of Medellin.

For a while the US considered Noriega an ally in the 'War on Drugs'. He used to show visitors the letter of appreciation that he received from American legislators, praising his efforts. Gradually, though, the Americans came to appreciate something rather different about him. 'Noriega turned a blind eye to ... corruption and dealing,' reported the US Congress, 'as he was emerging as a key player on behalf of the Medellin cartel.'[28] It was not so much a blind eye as an open hand. By the 1980s 'staggering sums of currency, amounting to at least several billion dollars, were being laundered each year' in Panama,[29] and Noriega was insisting on his percentage.[30]

Panama was an obvious point of interest in our investigation, in part because of the copies of the Moo Youngs' passports, which, along with their credit-card records, I had found in the police files. Derrick and Duane indulged in an extraordinary amount of travel for a family with a declared income of just $24,000 per year. Derrick first flew to Panama City on June 13th, 1985. He returned there seven times in 1986,[31] eating in exotic restaurants and staying at expensive hotels. The Moo Youngs' entire annual income, as declared to the taxman, would have been consumed by their travel to Panama alone.

The documents in the Moo Young briefcase revealed the existence of three Moo Young companies in Panama: Cargil, Amer Enterprises and NEC International. The Moo Youngs were, according to the documents, negotiating to purchase a Panamanian bank for $600 million.[32] 'By the early 1980s,' according to a US congressional report, 'there were well over one hundred banks in Panama and more than fifty of these were owned by Colombians.'[33]

11

The Jury

Here we were, amassing lots of new material in the hope of getting Kris a retrial, but thus far we had as many questions as answers. Although I had become personally convinced that Kris was innocent, one jury had already decided not only that he was guilty, but that he should die for the crime. Even if a court allowed us a second trial, we needed overwhelming evidence to ensure that a jury would reach the right conclusion. When it comes to jurors' decisions in capital cases, there are a number of problems that swing the compass towards convicting the innocent.

There are three general areas of concern: how jurors are selected, how jurors consider the case, and how the system covers up the bizarre mistakes that jurors make. In other words, the whole procedure is flawed.

This is not to say that the alternative – abolishing the jury, and replacing it with judges – is somehow better. Indeed, many of the same criticisms apply to judges. However, for now, let us focus on the concerted effort that is made to pretend that the naked jury is a fully clothed emperor.

An obvious place to begin is the rule that jurors can only serve if they swear, under oath, that they are in favour of the death penalty. In the American *voir dire* process,[1] prospective jurors are called into court where, in the presence of the defendant and the lawyers, they are questioned on all kinds of issues. If you are summoned for a capital trial, early in the process the judge and lawyers will ask you for your views on capital punishment. If the evidence proves him guilty, will you promise to follow the law and potentially sentence him to death? This will not be a public opinion poll, or a pub conversation; rather, you will be under oath, seated in the same room as the person whom you might have to sentence to death. You will probably be looking at him as you make your pledge: if he is found guilty, and if the prosecution proves the appropriate case for death, you *will* vote to end his life. If you reply that you are opposed to this, and will not vote to have a person killed, then you will be sent home and will have no more to do with the trial.

Only those who make this commitment in the defendant's presence can serve on the final panel of twelve.[2] Thus a large number of people are not eligible even to be considered for the jury – paradoxically, the more liberal the venue where the jurors are selected, the more of them will be excluded.

In Kris' case, Ms McKay lived in North Dade, between Miami and Fort Lauderdale. She did not favour the death penalty, she said, but it would not affect her ability to decide whether the defendant was guilty or not. She had, she pointed out, previously sat on a jury in a drug-trafficking case, where the defendant was acquitted. The prosecution struck her from the jury for her opposition to capital punishment. Three other potential jurors – Mrs Antrim, Mr Miles and Ms Roberts – went the same way. Mr Miles did no more than query whether he would feel able to impose a death sentence. This weighty issue was being dropped on him all of a sudden, and it was hardly surprising that he was tentative when asked whether he could vote for Kris Maharaj's death.[3] Indeed, a better system might have qualms about seating a juror who did not pause when faced with the idea of executing someone.

In most states a death sentence can only be imposed if the jurors are unanimous. Florida has retreated from the unanimity rule when it comes to capital sentencing. The state now uses the regime that governs most civil litigation: it is sufficient for a simple majority of jurors to vote for a death sentence. With respect to Derrick Moo Young, the jury vote was six-to-six and, because there was no majority for death, Kris narrowly avoided execution for that murder. But for the murder of Duane Moo Young one juror switched and, on a vote of seven-to-five, Kris was sent to Death Row. The hangman's rope was a rather thin thread.

Four people had been removed from the jury because they opposed capital punishment. Because Kris was sentenced to death by a single vote – the narrowest possible margin – any one of these four could have provided the swing-vote that might have saved his life; or they might have viewed the prosecution evidence differently and seen a 'reasonable doubt' in the strange case that was presented against him.

Anyone would agree that it is unfair if jurors are chosen with a bias that remains hidden. When properly conducted, American jury selection can be a fascinating and enlightening process, much my favourite part of any trial. Ideally, the *voir dire* process is a conversation with a prospective juror in a small and unthreatening room, with just the judge, the lawyers and the defendant present, rather than a vast courtroom with the public listening in. The discussion is partly to warn the jurors of what is coming, to educate them and allow them to work out for themselves whether they are right for this kind of case.

The theory behind the broad American right to question jurors is a good one; the practice in most states, and virtually all federal courts, falls far short. In federal court, the judge normally does most of the questioning. Judges are simply not very effective at it, and the questions they pose are ponderous. In a capital case a judge might ask the standard question: 'Do you have conscientious scruples concerning the death penalty?' Most jurors won't even be able to decipher the question, and do not respond in a meaningful way.[4]

Many prosecutors and defence lawyers proceed along equally pointless lines. After a lengthy explication of some arcane aspect of the law, the advocate will ask the juror whether he can follow the law. 'The difference between first-degree murder and second-degree murder involves the element of specific intent to commit the proscribed act,' the lawyer opines, in the patronising tone that he inherited from his law-school professor. 'This is the *mens rea* of the crime. To have specific intent means that the accused must actively advert to the proscribed consequences. This is not the same as motive, but it does mean that he must have the subjective desire or knowledge that the prohibited act will occur. Could you follow this law as stated to you by His Honour, the judge?'

How many prospective jurors, bleary-eyed by the end of the question, are going to say anything meaningful in response to that?

The Supreme Court itself proposed the following question when approaching the issue of race: 'The defendant is a member of the Negro race. The victim was a white Caucasian. Will these facts prejudice you against the defendant or affect your ability to render a fair and impartial verdict based solely on the evidence?'[5]

How often is someone going to say, 'Hell, yes, I'm a racist!' It does occur: in all the cases I have tried, it happened once, when the judge asked the question and a man with a crewcut held forth on his views about the superiority of his own race, in a surprisingly apologetic and forthright way. But such honesty is rare; if you want to expose people's racial prejudices, you must be rather more subtle. You never ask direct questions, since jurors know what the politically correct response is. Rather, you explore topics that will expose these opinions.

If you want to know jurors' views on race, it is more fruitful to ask them what they think of the O.J. Simpson prosecution. White racist jurors tend only to have discussed the issue with other white racist people,[6] and see nothing wrong with delivering a lengthy diatribe about how guilty O.J. was, and why. Once you have them going on the case, you can bring them gently around to a discussion of the lead detective on the case, Mark Fuhrman. After Simpson was acquitted, Fuhrman pleaded no contest to one count of perjury, which concerned his false testimony about whether he used the word 'nigger'. He had insisted that the word had not passed his lips in ten years. Yet he had been taped saying 'nigger' forty-one times, just months before the trial, by a writer who was preparing a screenplay about the police. One does not need to believe that Simpson was innocent to think that Fuhrman's racism was important to the case.[7] Would the fact that Fuhrman committed perjury about his own racism make you doubt other things he said? The racist juror, unwilling to loosen his hold on O.J. Simpson's guilt, is likely to deny it.

Thus to *voir dire* proceeds, sometimes for a couple of hours with each person. If you ask jurors to name their favourite verse from the Bible, or whatever scripture appeals to them, this will tell you far more than a person's religious denomination.[8] If you enquire what book the juror has most enjoyed recently, you will uncover those who can't or don't read and are likely to be intimidated by the prosecution's pseudo-science. And so it goes on. By the end of the process you have a real sense of who each juror is, and what language each will best understand. Without this, the lawyer is blind, relying on the kind of skin-deep judgement that gets us all into trouble, no matter what the circumstances.

Then there are jurors whose biases are specific to the case, who must also be removed for 'cause' (that is, for good reason). This is primarily thought to be because they know about the case and have formed an opinion,[9] but there are any number of other reasons to justify a 'cause' strike. For example, jurors must be excluded if they announce that they will believe anything a police officer says;[10] or if they have such close ties to the police as to make it unreasonable to think they will not lean in the direction of law enforcement;[11] if they will not respect the law concerning the defendant's right to remain silent;[12] if the jurors have been victims of similar crimes, and that would affect their judgement;[13] and for many other such reasons. It is difficult to argue with these decisions: if jurors cannot be fair, then how can they be permitted to sit on the jury?

I have never tried a case where we did not identify a substantial number of jurors with such biases.[14] But if the process is done superficially, or if the jurors are only asked legalistic questions that are incomprehensible, there is no telling who may end up deciding the prisoner's fate.[15]

The next flaw in the American jury system involves a devotion to the pretence that nothing is awry.

The US right to free speech means that nobody can be banned from speaking about the experience of serving on a jury. Indeed, jurors write books[16] or even – more recently – tweet about what happens.[17] A corollary of this is that there is generally no prohibition against lawyers talking to jurors when the trial is over – although, sadly for Kris, Florida is one of a small minority of US states that forbids a lawyer from initiating such an interview. Over the years I have made sure that we interviewed the jurors in virtually all the cases in which I have been involved. It is a fascinating and humbling experience, and for the life of me I can see no reason why jurors should be forbidden from talking, unless the government wants to hide the peculiar or illegal things that jurors periodically do. After a capital trial I always check out what the jurors thought, regardless of the outcome.

There is plenty to learn even when the trial comes out as well as could reasonably be expected.[18] I worked on the retrial of Outlaw biker Clarence 'Smitty' Smith. Smitty had been sentenced to death once, and we got him a new trial at which we presented a strong case for his innocence. The jurors had us all twisting in terror when they deliberated for three hours before they finally acquitted him. It transpired, when I later talked to them, that one of their number had been holding out for conviction. Watching the courtroom carefully over the two weeks of trial, the juror had developed a theory: every time I stood on the sides of my shoes when I was talking, I was not telling the truth – he thought he had developed a kind of footwear polygraph. He correlated this idea with his observations during my closing argument and decided that whenever I said Smitty was innocent, I did not believe it.

His theory was very wrong, as I was convinced of Smitty's innocence of the murder – the state's two informants, John Joseph 'J.J.' Hall and Carl 'Sick Quick' Holley, had manipulated the FBI, and cut a deal for themselves not only to avoid the death penalty, but to get into the cushy Federal Witness Protection Program. They were, I firmly believed, the ones who wired a bomb to the brake lights of a federal witness' pickup truck – a belief the jury came to share. Yet the holdout juror's bizarre thinking is far more common than jury advocates might hope, and it certainly meant that I have never stood nervously on the sides of my shoes since then.

The juror in Smitty's case would no doubt have sent him back to Death Row, had the rest of the jury not talked him around. Indeed, the most important conversations with jurors concern those who actually vote to condemn someone to death. Sam Johnson was a black man from New York who had been convicted and sentenced to death for killing a white police officer in rural Mississippi. The local sheriff was Lloyd B. 'Goon' Jones, who acquired his moniker when crushing civil-rights demonstrations. He was the man who ordered the Mississippi State Highway Patrol to open fire on the black students at Jackson State University in 1970.[19] He also achieved some infamy when a number of demonstrators dared to enter Mississippi from such communist-infested states as California. He arrested them, took them to the local jail and dry-shaved their heads with razors, before pouring moonshine over their scalps. With the leader of this rabble Goon went to the additional trouble of sticking a fork up his nose.

Things were not looking good for Sam Johnson when I started work on his appeal. I was young and very inexperienced. Early in the

case I ventured to Pike County to talk to the jurors who had condemned him and see what I could learn. I was too young and foolish
to have any trepidation about my task. I did not realise the pattern of
Ku Klux Klan behaviour in the state at the time. I later learned that
the KKK generally kept a low profile in the Mississippi Delta counties, where there was a large majority of African Americans, since
whites simply had to reach an accommodation there; neither did the
Klan bother with the north-eastern counties, where whites were in a
clear predominance. The Klan focused, instead, on counties where
there was – or should have been – a rough parity in political power,
where either whites or blacks were in a slight majority. Pike County is
51.5 per cent white, 47.4 per cent black.[20] It was, I should have known,
prime Klan Kountry.

One of the first jurors I talked to invited me in warmly for a glass
of iced tea. She loved – l-u-u-u-rved – my accent, she said. At some
point her husband mentioned how much they liked the English:
'Y'all helped us out during the war.' He meant the American Civil
War – the 'War between the States', as it is still occasionally called
down south. The two of them began regaling me with her experience
as a juror at Sam's trial, a moment's excitement for the sleepy town of
McComb. She told me that one old black lady on the jury had been
no problem ('She knew her place'), but there had been a black man
who had caused trouble, and who had not wanted to vote for the
death penalty.

'It weren't no problem really,' she said in a cheerful sing-song. 'We-
all jus' told him we'd send the Klan round if he didn't make good.'

I thought she was joking. She was not. As the conversation pro-
gressed, her husband said that he was a Klan member and mentioned
that they had a meeting the following evening – would I like to go
along? Again I thought he was pulling my leg. He was not. I politely
declined. Ever since I have regretted my cowardice, but I was terrified
they would discover that I was some commie-pinko-liberal and I'd
end up with my own noose.

I spent several more days in Pike County, avoiding lonely roads
late at night. There was only one black male juror, so he had to be the
one who had been coerced into sentencing Sam to death. I went to
see him one evening. His dark face paled when I explained why I was
visiting; he denied ever being picked for the jury, let alone sending
Sam to Death Row. I left his house perplexed and frustrated. I sought

the support of the local chairman of the NAACP,[21] the civil-rights organisation, and explained to him that this could be life-and-death for Sam. He went to visit the juror himself and argued that it was the man's duty to reveal what had happened in the case. The juror ultimately admitted that he had been on Sam's jury, but he adamantly refused to accept that he had ever voted to send someone to the gas chamber, or that he had been threatened with a visitation from the Klan. Given that he and his family lived in McComb, I could understand why.

Sam Johnson eventually got a new sentencing trial on technical legal grounds entirely unrelated to the coerced juror.[22] Prior to the resentencing trial, we held a hearing on our claim that those associated with the prosecution were racist, and the process should therefore be invalidated. 'Goon' Jones came to testify in coveralls, an enormous man who chewed tobacco throughout the hearing, spitting the juice out as he pondered each reply. I asked him whether he still called black people 'niggers'.

'Nope,' he said, looking down at me with disdain. 'Someone told me that was rude.'

So what would he call black men today? I demanded.

He pondered a moment, masticating. 'Coloured boys,' he finally said, with emphasis.

And when, I asked querulously, would he stop doing that?

'When someone tells me it's rude.'

I took a deep breath, and suggested that perhaps it was rude.

'Well, boy,' he said, with another spit into his plastic cup, 'I guess I just don' appreciate your opinion.'

As he walked past me, leaving the witness stand, he suggested in turn that I should not come by his county after dark.

The judge refused to bar a retrial because of this racism, and Sam only narrowly avoided a second death sentence when four African American jurors declined to go along with the majority viewpoint.[23]

If they are permitted to speak, jurors can also show great courage when they come to question whether they made a mistake. Murray Barnes was at Creola's Bar in New Orleans, on Super Bowl Sunday, and he won the $1,000 pool on the game. As he left with his winnings, Barnes was robbed and killed. Dan Bright was charged with the crime and Kathleen Hawk Norman, a successful white businesswoman, later found herself selected as foreperson of his jury. The evidence seemed strong, and she felt she had little option but to sentence Dan to death.

Some years later the charity where I worked had taken over the appeal, and we approached her to discuss her role in the case and share new evidence with her. Most dramatic was an FBI report, generated long before the trial, that we had obtained during Dan's appeal through Freedom of Information litigation. It read as follows: 'The source further stated that Dan Bright, aka Pooney, is in jail for the murder committed by ▆▆▆▆▆▆▆▆▆.' The name of the perpetrator had been redacted from the document: the FBI argued that this was necessary to 'safeguard the privacy' of the real killer.

We ultimately identified the man whose name was blacked out in the FBI report as Tracey Davis, and accumulated other evidence to prove that he was the murderer. We learned that the state's eyewitness, Freddie Thompson, had been drinking heavily on the day in question, and was on parole for a prior felony when he was encouraged by the police to identify Dan, weeks after the murder. We located alibi witnesses who placed Dan elsewhere at the time of the crime.

When we showed all this to Kathleen Hawk Norman, who had presided over the decision to impose death, she felt betrayed by the government. She had been called upon to perform the hardest task of her life: to consider taking another human life. The prosecutor who asked this of her had hidden evidence from her and the other jurors that would certainly have changed her mind. She was furious. She began a campaign called 'Jurors for Justice', and came to court every day that any kind of appeal hearing was scheduled in Dan's case. She became such a vocal critic of the judge that he set hearings earlier and earlier in the morning, finally delivering his opinion denying Dan a new trial before eight o'clock, in an effort to avoid the wrath of 'The Angry Diva', as Kathleen had been dubbed by the local media.

Kathleen then filed a legal brief in support of Dan's appeal, describing what all this evidence would have meant to her and the other jurors.[24] Despite this, the Louisiana Court of Appeals found that the new evidence provided 'no reasonable probability that the outcome of the case would have been different'.[25] In other words, they felt they were better placed to decide what the jury would have done with all this new evidence than Kathleen was. She became even more determined.

Fortunately, the story had a happy ending; the Louisiana Supreme Court ordered a new trial,[26] the prosecution dismissed the charges, and Dan was a free man. Kathleen felt responsible for almost taking his life and consigning him to prison for nine years for a crime he did not commit. She dedicated herself to helping him establish a new life – helping him with employment and standing at his shoulder, no matter what challenge he might face.[27]

On the many occasions when I have talked to jurors I have learned some interesting things, and some horrifying ones. Generally the jurors were not members of the KKK and were struggling to do their best at a difficult task. Very often, though, their misunderstanding of the law left them ill equipped even to approximate to what the system expects of them. Judges read over lengthy, impenetrable instructions[28] and think that the jurors are thereby ready to apply complex legal doctrines. Nothing could be further from the truth. My own experience is reflected in various studies of real jurors in the US:[29] perhaps as few as one-third of those who have actually sat through a criminal trial understand that the prosecution bears the burden of proof,[30] let alone what it might mean to carry such a burden beyond a reasonable doubt.

I talked to all twelve of the jurors who had sentenced Jack Davis[31] to death. One of the legal issues we were raising was whether the jurors would have understood the arcane instructions that defined how they were to consider aggravating and mitigating circumstances – the factors presented at the penalty phase of a capital trial to determine whether the correct punishment should be life or death. There are all kinds of complexities that keep appellate courts entertained: what counts as a mitigating circumstance? Can there be any limit on mitigating circumstances? What is the burden of proof on mitigating circumstances? And so on.

In the real world the issues are more mundane. Not one of the twelve jurors knew what the word 'mitigating' meant, and one suggested it was a synonym for 'aggravating'. It was difficult to believe, then, that they had properly considered the evidence before sentencing Jack to death. Yet this was not the most troublesome fact that emerged from the interviews. I engaged one of the jurors – the foreperson, as it happened, a woman with a PhD in English – on evidence that suggested rather strongly that Jack was innocent of the crime. The prosecution had used some outmoded serological testimony to implicate him at trial; our recent use of DNA demonstrated that this blood-test result had been false. At the same time, the government's informant had recanted, admitting that he had made up the story to avoid prison himself. None of this bothered her.

Why not? I politely enquired.

In addition to her PhD, she said, she had the benefit of ESP (Extrasensory Perception), and this allowed her to know beyond per-adventure that Jack was guilty not only of this murder, but of four others. She therefore had no qualms about sentencing him to death.

There is no escaping the inevitable truth that any human enterprise will be beset by bizarre interventions, such as a juror with ESP. But presumably most people would agree that appellate judges should take note when jurors inflict a sentence of death based on ESP, or on the racism in Sam Johnson's case. It would be difficult to justify ignoring this kind of thing. Yet this is ignored on a daily basis in courts across the United States.

If the US generally allows jurors to speak their minds, that does not translate into action when the truth seeps out. The Florida law is the archetype that holds sway across the United States: first, because Florida's rule is incomprehensible; and second, because it allows virtually nothing to affect the finality of the conviction.

'Upon an inquiry into the validity of a verdict or indictment', says the Florida law, 'a juror is not competent to testify as to any matter which essentially inheres in the verdict or indictment'.[32] If you don't understand what this means, you are in good company. It is the type of nonsense that lawyers speak when they are trying to set them-selves apart from the population at large. What Florida means is that the juror is allowed to state the facts as they observably happened, but they cannot comment on what the consequences might have been. For example, they can describe how a particular book in the jury deliberation room should not have been there, but they cannot discuss whether the contents had any impact on them. In this way, judges authorise themselves to hear what happened, but then require themselves to guess whether this had any impact on the verdict.[33]

Then there is an additional wrinkle that hauls the process even further away from common sense: if the item was properly in the jury room in the first place, no challenge may be raised at all.[34] Rather, the influence has to come from outside – such as a dictionary that should not have been there, which jurors might have used to look up the meaning of legal terms.[35] In other words, it is wrong for jurors to seek definition of terms they don't comprehend.[36] But if the jurors decide to check whether the white substance that the police say they got from the suspect is actually cocaine – if they crack open the evidence bag and snort a few lines – that fact can't be used to challenge the conviction: the drugs were properly introduced at trial and were therefore legally in the jury room. The fact the jurors were stoned when they decided to vote guilty – ignoring the prisoner's defence that the drugs were planted on him – would count for nothing.

This may seem far-fetched. Unfortunately, it is not. There is, the Supreme Court has noted, a 'strong policy against any post-verdict inquiry into a juror's state of mind'.[37] But this is not a rational argument; it is just a statement. Why is there such a policy? Could it be because the alternative would expose the bizarre truths all around us? Consider the case cited by the Supreme Court for this 'strong policy': a man called John Dioguardi had been convicted for violating the securities laws, for trying to manipulate the price of some stocks. After the trial he received a letter from one of the jurors,[38] in which she explained that she had 'eyes and ears that … see things before [they] happen', but that unfortunately her eyes were 'only partly open' because 'a curse was put upon them some years ago'. Armed with this letter, Dioguardi's lawyers consulted seven psychiatrists, all of whom thought this juror was probably suffering from a chronic mental disorder, and may well have been psychotic while she was on the jury. Each doctor suggested that she receive a mental-health evaluation.

The judge refused even to look into the issue, satisfied that he had, from his bench on high, noticed nothing strange about her during the trial.[39] Unless it was patently obvious to people in the courtroom that a juror was in the midst of a psychotic breakdown, the judge held, no steps should be taken to remedy the issue, even if it later came out that she was insane.[40]

If this is odd itself, the lead Supreme Court precedent on juror testimony is even stranger. In 1987 the court was presented with a demand for a new trial by Tony Tanner, who had been convicted of receiving a $30,000 kickback on a road-building contract in Florida.[41] One of the jurors who had voted Tanner guilty, Daniel Hardy, had subsequently given a sworn statement expressing misgivings about his experience.

'I felt like ...' he began, 'the jury was one big party.' Seven of the jurors, including Hardy himself, drank alcohol through the trial; they would split several pitchers of beer during the recesses. The foreperson, an alcoholic, downed more than a bottle of wine at lunch. Juror Hardy admitted that he and three others smoked marijuana quite regularly during the proceedings, although he did not join the two jurors who regularly used cocaine. One juror brought various drugs and paraphernalia into the jury room, and sold a quarter-pound of marijuana to another juror during the trial. Hardy said that some of the jurors were falling asleep during the witness testimony – a fact that the lawyers had noticed.[42] One of the jurors, John, described himself as 'flying' during much of the case.

'I felt that the people on the jury didn't have no business being on the jury,' Hardy summed up, pricked by his conscience. 'I felt ... that Mr Tanner should have a better opportunity to get somebody that would review the facts right.'[43]

Hardy had admitted to committing a series of crimes himself during the trial, and accused others of serious felonies for which they could have received far more time in prison than Tony Tanner himself. Tanner faced a maximum of twenty-five years.[44] The juror who brought the cocaine, marijuana and drug paraphernalia into the courthouse, either selling it or giving it away, might have been looking at sixty-three years in prison.[45] Even those who simply used the drugs could be facing two to six years.[46]

Surely, then, this would be sufficient to require a new trial?

Certainly not. The Supreme Court agreed with the lower courts that there was no point even holding a hearing. The rule against 'impeaching a juror's verdict' forbade overturning the conviction, even if everything that Juror Hardy said was true.[47] All of this talk about intoxication referred to the jurors' mental state, and that could not be explored after the verdict. The Supreme Court went on to suggest, however, that the trial judge might have made a mistake in a complicated and arcane interpretation of the law. Tanner ultimately walked free on this point,[48] and never went to prison at all. Why, one might well ask, were the courts afraid of disturbing the 'finality of the jurors' verdict' based on their drug distribution and intoxication, and yet were happy to do so on a hyper-technical interpretation of the law?

As with many such doctrines, the rule against hearing jurors' testimony originated long ago. Lord Mansfield's opinion, expressed in 1785, that jurors' deliberations should be sacrosanct, sealed off from review, was imported without debate into the United States.[49] Those who would defend this rule worry that questioning jurors will 'operate to intimidate, beset and harass them' and thereby destroy 'frankness of discussion'.[50] This makes little sense because American jurors are generally free to talk with anyone they choose. The reason that judges do not want to hear their testimony in court is that looking closely at the conduct of jurors would result in too many reversals, or too *much* justice.

In many areas where the government exercises power over the individual we would be horrified if it were done in secret, insulated from any review. To be sure, politicians often wish that their actions could be immune from public review – when it comes to their expenses, to mention just one notorious example.[51] Yet when people are carrying out the functions of government, it is vital that they be subject to close scrutiny. There are few occasions when the government's power is greater than the criminal trial where jurors, acting on behalf of the state, have the authority to deprive the prisoner of liberty, or even life. Why should this be done in unreviewable secrecy?

What we are witnessing here is yet another effort by the criminal justice system to achieve 'finality' – a euphemism for ensuring that there is a conviction, without worrying whether it is an appropriate one. Allowing jurors to speak out, and lifting the veil on the kind of bizarre issues that I have witnessed, would result in the reversal of a number of convictions. But the idea of justice is not to conclude a trial, no matter what its flaws, and then defend the result at all costs. The consequence of taking a realistic approach to the conduct of jurors would be a *fair trial*, which, it bears repeating, is the actual purpose of the process.

For the doomsayers who argue that transparency here would spell the end of the jury trial after 800 years, let us set it in perspective. Focusing on capital cases alone, from 1973 (when capital punishment was effectively reinstituted in America) until 1995, 40 per cent of cases were thrown out on their first state appeal for 'serious error'. Of those that made it through to federal court (599 cases), a further two out of five were vacated for 'serious error'. In other words, serious mistakes required reversal in roughly two-thirds of all cases. The process took an average of nine or ten years to complete in each case.[52]

The courts are finding mistakes in two-thirds of capital cases. It is unlikely that a thorough investigation of the jurors would result in two-thirds of all cases being vacated for misconduct, yet we are willing to accept such a reversal rate on other grounds. Indeed, critics would say that the 'mistakes' that are being identified are technicalities. Why would an appellate court be willing to reverse a conviction on something technical (the wording of an instruction, for example), but not on something of profound significance (jurors distributing and experimenting with drugs during a trial)?

Since 1995 there have been no comprehensive figures on reversals in capital cases, but my experience has been that the rate has declined substantially. This has been occasioned, though, not by any reassessment and correction of the faults in the system.[53] Rather, the political solution has been to pass legislation to make sure that fewer cases can be reversed. As ever, the government has attempted to address a patent problem by wishing it away – by insisting that the naked emperor is fully clothed – rather than by addressing the root causes.

British lawyers tend to look askance at the American judicial process, confident that such a nightmare could never happen at the Old Bailey. This confidence is misplaced. If the rules governing jurors seem strange in the United States, in Britain they are significantly worse. The number of cases resulting in acquittal or reversal in the UK is similar to that in the United States.[54] We are willing to tolerate a system where (for one reason or another) we may have got it wrong a significant proportion of the time. However, we are most certainly not willing to look closely at the jurors who are making these mistakes. In the UK lawyers are no longer permitted to question the jurors prior to trial (in the *voir dire* process), making it intuitively more likely that biased or inappropriate people will make it onto the jury. Once jurors have served in England, the lawyers (and everyone else) are barred from talking to them, and the jurors themselves are legally forbidden from revealing what happened in the jury room.[55] Then, if some bizarre happening does leak out by chance, the British courts follow a rule very similar to that of their American counterparts – barring consideration of the jurors' misconduct. In other words, in the United States the legal system learns about its faults and refuses to redress the problem; but at least the flaws are known. In the

UK, in contrast, we jam our judicial head firmly into the sand from the very beginning and never look up. Such is the secrecy surrounding the British jury that it is probably as easy to obtain information about the latest decision by MI5 as it is to challenge something that happened during jury deliberations.[56]

The next institutional problem is perhaps more insidious, and concerns how the jurors consider the evidence that leads to a guilty verdict. This applies in all cases, not just those where the death penalty is at stake. The proponents of the jury system[57] proudly point to the fact that twelve people must unanimously find that the person on trial is guilty 'beyond a reasonable doubt', before they are permitted to convict him. At the penalty phase in Florida the individual juror must be sure 'beyond a reasonable doubt' that death is the appropriate punishment, before voting for it – although the jury does not have to be unanimous. Ultimately the judge imposes the sentence in Florida, but in imposing death on Krishna Maharaj, Judge Solomon had to be sure 'beyond a reasonable doubt' that he should go along with the jurors' recommendation.

This all sounds very meticulous, but what does it really mean? We know that it falls far short of eliminating any possible mistake – otherwise the standard would be 'beyond all doubt'. More than 120 prisoners have been exonerated from Death Row since the reintroduction of capital punishment in 1973 – and these are only the people whose innocence has been established with sufficient certainty to convince conservative appeal courts bound by strict rules of procedure.[58] Yet in each of these 120 cases all twelve jurors were convinced beyond a reasonable doubt that the individual was guilty and deserved to die; in each case they were emphatically wrong.

In an American trial (as in a British one) the lawyer is not allowed to ask jurors what they mean by 'beyond a reasonable doubt'. Why not? Could it be because we are deeply uncomfortable about what jurors (or even judges) might say? I have conducted a fairly unscientific survey over the years, asking audiences at conferences where I was speaking to try to place some kind of definition on the term – to quantify it as best they can with statistical probabilities: what degree of certainty would they demand before voting guilty? In a civil case it is 'by a preponderance of the evidence' – or just 50.1 per cent against the other side's 49.9 per cent. So what does it mean to be convinced 'beyond a reasonable doubt'?

Lawyers and judges tend to respond: that it is a concept that cannot be quantified; but this is the refuge of scoundrels. We cannot loudly proclaim that the burden of proof is central to the system, yet then assert that we cannot begin to define it.[59] When people wish to avoid public debate, it tends to mean that they are not very secure in their position. Indeed, the refusal to confront what the definition of 'reasonable doubt' should be tells us that the answer to the question is so potentially embarrassing that it is Pandora's box, best left sealed.

Jurors in Florida are specifically told by the judge that they should not eliminate all doubt. 'Whenever the words "reasonable doubt" are used,' they are told, 'you must consider the following: A reasonable doubt is not a mere possible doubt, a speculative, imaginary or forced doubt. Such a doubt must not influence you to return a verdict of not guilty if you have an abiding conviction of guilt.'[60] But at what level is the elimination of doubt sufficient to justify incarceration, leaving aside the question of execution? Would the jurors have to be 75 per cent sure that Kris Maharaj really did it? 90 per cent sure? 99 per cent sure? In my unscientific study I drew up a form for members of the audience to fill in whenever I was giving a presentation on the subject. I passed my forms out at a Louisiana judges' conference to see what they would say, and I was taken aback at the results. No judge wrote more than 95 per cent, so everyone was *aiming* to get it wrong at least one time in twenty. Roughly 7 million people are behind bars, on probation or on parole in the US – so all have been convicted in a criminal proceeding.[61] If we were to *aim* to make a mistake once in every twenty cases, the US judicial system would be *aiming* to have a total of 360,000 innocent people in prison – and if you aim low, you probably miss your target. The average among the judges I canvassed was far worse (just 83 per cent), and one liberal federal judge indicated that 75 per cent certainty would be acceptable, thus aiming to convict around 1.75 million innocent people.

Only a tiny percentage of people plead guilty to an offence that carries the death penalty;[62] the large majority go to trial. Thus, of the 3,200 people on Death Row, aiming to be 95 per cent sure we get it right means that we hope to execute just 160 innocent people; shooting for 83 per cent, the goal would be 544 innocents. It is difficult to believe that jurors take a much more careful view of their responsibilities than judges.[63] By insisting that nobody should discuss the most central point in the decision-making process – what degree of doubt should lead to an acquittal – we are making it absolutely certain that mistakes will be commonplace.

Thus the law is structured to make sure that we don't know what went on in the jury room when Kris Maharaj was sentenced to death; we have no idea whether the jurors understood their role properly; we can't tell them how they were misled, or what new evidence has arisen; and even if we could, and they wanted to do something about it, the courts would refuse to listen to them.

12

The Laundry

Our attempt to find out what really happened in Room 1215 of the DuPont Plaza Hotel was taking us into dangerous territory. When I started to look into a possible relationship between the Moo Youngs and the drug cartels, I was told that we needed to get a sophisticated program to encrypt our emails, because the cartels had a far greater capacity for snooping than the CIA. If they were to get the sense that our investigation might harm their interests, there would be few corners of the Earth where we would be able to hide.

The profits in the drug business are enormous. In the 1980s, at the time of the Moo Young homicides, three of the five richest men in the world were members of the Colombian cartels: only the Sultan of Brunei and King Fahd of Saudi Arabia were richer.[1] In 1986 General Motors had sales of $102.8 billion[2] and ranked in the top-ten traded companies in the world, with more than 200,000 employees; yet the Cali Cartel alone had greater annual profits.[3] This was hardly surprising given the demand for cocaine in the US. According to a report prepared for the US Congress, 'the American market for drugs produce[d] annual revenues of well over $100 billion at retail prices' – twice what US consumers spent on oil each year.[4]

In the 1980s, the Medellin Cartel was larger than the Cali,[5] and was deemed, in relative terms, rather less subtle. The man in charge at Cali, Gilberto Rodriguez-Orejuela, was nicknamed the Chess Player and tended to bribe everyone in government to achieve his goals.[6] Not so the Medellin Cartel, which preferred to kill officials rather than buy them. 'The Medellin people are much more violent. They are operating in the Stone Age, killing whoever gets in their way,' said one Colombian expert at the time. 'The Cali people are much more elegant. They buy people, they buy into the system, they do not offend. They buy police, politicians, whole towns.'[7]

To be sure, the Medellin Cartel was not above buying up the police, and when the Medellin constabulary once arrested Pablo Escobar, it was generally accepted that the officers had done so by mistake.[8] But violence was their recognised calling card, and the policemen who had committed this error ended up dead. The drug lords raised private armies, and as many as 70,000 well-equipped thugs roamed Colombia, enforcing the will of their employers.[9] Since these people were given weapons in order to use them, it was no wonder that the national murder rate was inordinately high.

The Medellin Cartel was known, and feared, around the world. Escobar set the tone. 'More than anybody in the Medellin cartel, Escobar was known as an enforcer,' wrote Guy Gugliotta, in *Kings of Cocaine*. 'He never forgot an insult. He held grudges. He took revenge.'[10] Anyone who ripped him off could expect to pay the price. And his colleagues in the cartel learned to apply the same rule.

The cartels recognised that one danger point in the export-import process was moving the drugs *into* the US to a 'legitimate' client – someone who was not working for, or compromised by, US law enforcement. The Cali solution (starting in the early 1980s) was to use Mexico as the conduit for their product, selling to Mexican narco-traffickers, who were then left to assume the risk of distribution into the US.

Yet getting drugs in was the easy part.

The point of maximum exposure for the cartels came when they moved their profits back out of the United States.[11] It is an axiom among American law enforcement that they 'follow the money'. Long ago, Al Capone went down on tax-evasion charges rather than one of many potential murder charges.[12] Likewise, the Drug Enforcement Agency (DEA) – scenting capitalism at work – knew that tracing the money leaving the United States was easier than tracking the drugs coming in. Extracting their loot from America would be the cartels' main challenge.

Ensconced in Colombia, the drug lords agonised over how to bring the money home to continue to fund elephants for their ranches, and to pay off the police and politicians.[13] To quantify their dilemma, the half-trillion dollar bills they needed to launder each year would weigh more than the entire population of Washington DC – more than 500,000 well-fed people.[14]

In the early days Colombians were notoriously ethno-centric, refusing to trust anyone but a fellow Colombian to handle their drugs and money. However, the task simply became too large for their compatriots to handle, so they had to look elsewhere for help. The Medellin Cartel recruited ever more widely for the launderers of their profits. 'Because of the staggering sums generated daily by street sales in the United States,' wrote a journalist in the 1980s, 'the normally nationalistic Colombian traffickers are willing to step outside the Hispanic community to find professionals who can launder their money quickly and efficiently. They want service from US residents with expertise in accounting and a high comfort level around big bucks – "respectable type people from the suburbs", as one DEA agent puts it.'[15]

Indeed, the cartels put out a profile of the kind of 'employee' they needed, called the 'Traffickers' Bible'. It reads like a job description for Derrick and Duane Moo Young. The laundryman must have his own house – the 'operating centre "par excellence"'. He must try to 'imitate an American in all … habits, like mow the lawn, wash the car, etc. He must not have any extravagant social events, *but may have an occasional barbecue, inviting trusted relatives*' (the emphasis on permissible barbecues came directly from the cartel HQ in Colombia). The 'minimum standards' for the employee's house must include a 'residential location, lots of green space, garage for two cars, garage hopefully not within the neighbours' sight, swimming pool (arguable).' The laundryman must always have 'a trusted lawyer' and a 'vehicle ready for escaping'.[16]

Kris Maharaj's defence team now had all kinds of interesting material from the Moo Young briefcase, supplemented by several thousand pages of documents from Brenton Ver Ploeg, the lawyer for the William Penn Life Insurance Company, gathered in their defence of the Moo Young claim. Laura Snook, a forensic accountant with Ernst & Young in London, agreed to do a close analysis of all the material without charging us a fee, so that we could try to prove what the Moo Youngs were up to.

'The Moo Youngs were involved in potential arrangements to launder illegal money,' she told us, after analysing the documents we sent her. That the money was headed to various Caribbean destinations was one factor in her reasoning. 'I understand that back in 1986 there were far fewer regulations concerning the laundering of illegal (particularly drug) money than exist today. Additionally, the Caribbean and Panama were among the regions of the world that delayed enacting tough banking legislation to prevent the laundering of these illegal monies.

'Furthermore, it appears that the Moo Youngs were trying to include secret arrangements in the details that would allow them to receive part of the interest payments directly,' Snook explained. 'There are specific admonitions not to tell certain parties to the negotiations about these arrangements. For example, while some loans initially provided for a commission of five percent, and an interest rate of six percent, the documents reflect Derrick Moo Young's attempt to raise the commission to six percent, and the interest rate to seven percent, with the additional commission and interest payable to Mr Moo Young's business interests. This would, of course, represent a very substantial amount of money. A one percent commission on $1 billion would be $10 million. The vehicle that the Moo Youngs planned to use for these arrangements was, apparently, St Jude Investment Co. Ltd.'

In other words, the documents seemed to say that once they had got onto this cash cow, the Moo Youngs had decided to do some milking on the side, skimming 1 per cent of the cream off the top. St Jude is the patron saint of desperate causes. The only people who had this kind of money to launder through the Moo Youngs were the cartels; if they found out that the Moo Youngs were ripping them off for $10 million, the Moo Youngs would find themselves acolytes of St Jude very quickly. The cartels would kill people for looking askance at them; if the Moo Youngs were suspected of trying to steal millions, that would be a sure way of dying.

We still had a great deal to learn. Money-laundering was not high on the list of my areas of expertise. I had represented around 300 people on Death Row, but every one of them had been poor – including Kris, by the time I met him. Indeed, I'd only ever been paid an attorney's fee by one client in my life, and that was my friend Ruth Friedman when I got her acquitted for a traffic ticket in Atlanta. She bought me two six-packs of Newcastle Brown ale. My one fee-paying case came to an unhappy conclusion. I took the beer to Mississippi when I was visiting Death Row en route to somewhere else. When the guards found the bottles in the boot of the car, they told me I had to take the alcohol off the penitentiary grounds. I obeyed this, hiding it in a ditch, but when I came back at the end of the day it had vanished. I suspect the guards had watched me as I stashed it.

Studying the cartels' business, I quickly discovered that there are many ways to wash money. One technique is to buy a business, preferably in the service industry, and create a false record of the amount of your custom. A clothes laundry is itself a classic: unlike the manufacture and sale of televisions, for example, where there will be a trail of components that you need in order to manufacture them, and a traceable number of TV sets that you sell, the only barometer that will indicate how many items you have actually cleaned is your soap consumption. You are not required to keep the contact details of those who bring their clothes in, so you can make up receipts and nobody will be any the wiser. The problem, of course, is that washing clothes does not involve enough money. If you owned every launderette across the globe you would not cover the billions of dollars at stake for the cartels.

Another variation on the theme is to deal in goods that are extremely valuable. Here, the problem is the identity of the items. If you buy the *Mona Lisa*, it is unique, and there will again be a paper trail between your purchase and the source of your money. If, on the other hand, you buy a gold bar, it may be uniquely identifiable – it may have a stamp on it – but that can be removed without destroying its value if you melt it down. In this sense, all gold is fungible. But gold is heavy, and does not easily pass the metal detectors. If a launderer were to be caught carrying a couple of ingots, he would have some explaining to do.

There is a way around the problem, and an imaginative launderer figured it out long before I did: you buy a small number of legitimate ingots in America, ensuring that when you buy them they have no serial numbers or any form of unique identification. You put them in a safety-deposit box in a highly respectable bank with all the proper paperwork. Nobody knows whether the ingots are there at any given time, as you can take them out without giving notice to anyone. Therefore you immediately remove them to hold them elsewhere. Meanwhile, you convert your illegal money into gold of any kind, which you melt down into ingots that match the legitimate ones for which you have the paperwork. Each time you travel out of the country to your chosen destination, you carry another couple of ingots, along with the same paperwork. If you are stopped you have the documentation to prove their provenance, and you can even take the authorities to the bank and show them the empty deposit box. Until you are stopped you can repeat this process any number of times; even then, nobody can prove whether you have brought the ingots back into the country in the interim.[17]

The more valuable the commodity, the easier it may be to move large amounts of money out of the country quickly. For example, Raul Vivas had the perfect profile for the Colombians, because he traded in jewellery in Los Angeles, he was respectable on the surface, and he was greedy. A jeweller can create original pieces that are much more valuable than the constituent parts, and jewellery is another example of a fungible valuable – the jeweller can create many copies of the same item for transport. In two years Vivas laundered $1.2 billion for the Medellin Cartel, before the Feds caught up with him.[18]

In the Moo Young briefcase, in addition to letters offering billions in loans around the Caribbean, I had found evidence that the pair were negotiating over millions of dollars' worth of jewels. What was going on?

William Caswell 'W.C.' Bryant died on January 13th, 2008, at the age of eighty-nine.[19] Some would rue travelling through life with the moniker W.C., but he rose above such puerile humour. He was the picture of a southern Baptist minister, so it was only young lads, bored in his congregation, who must have sniggered behind his back. He was born in Hood County, Texas, on November 12th, 1918, the day after the end of the Great War. His marriage was early and lasting. He and Evelyn would remain married for three days shy of seventy years, though the wedding only came about because W.C.'s father drove over to Amarillo to issue the proposal on his behalf. W.C. was a diffident young man.

Although W.C. always felt called, it was not until 1943 that he enrolled in the Southwestern Baptist Theological Seminary. When he and Evelyn moved to Amarillo in 1947, W.C. did not know what God had in mind for their future. When he prayed, he asked God for only three things: a lot upon which to build a church, an interim meeting place and somewhere to live with Evelyn. He began his new church with just thirteen charter members, yet within three years he was seeing almost a thousand parishioners a week in Sunday School.

They had planned to live in Amarillo all their lives, but God had other ideas. After a stint establishing Baptist churches in Colorado, they moved to California in 1959. During his twenty-one-year stint as pastor of the First Baptist Church of Norwalk, one of his roles was as Western Director of the Baptist Church Loan Corporation, an entirely legitimate organisation that helped foster the establishment of Baptist churches around the world.[20] He was also a director of the less obviously licit Los Angeles Church Loan Corporation.[21] It was to the LACLC that Derrick Moo Young came to do business in 1986. When the Moo Young family later tried to collect on the life-insurance policies that Derrick had taken out, the William Penn Life Insurance Company sent its lawyer, Brenton Ver Ploeg, to LA to try and figure how the Church Loan Corporation was involved in the Moo Youngs' business. Ver Ploeg gave me a copy of the deposition he took from W.C. Bryant.

'What was this Los Angeles Church Loan Corporation?' Ver Ploeg had demanded.

'To furnish loans to churches, primarily buildings and ground land, and to help to promote and institute senior citizens, and whatever – world hunger needs, and that sort of thing,'[22] W.C. said, rather vaguely. The nebulous ambit of these goals did not seem to have deterred donors. W.C. talked – again without any great precision – about staggering sums of money that supposedly flowed into the coffers of the company.

For example, Derrick Moo Young and he had discussed what could be done with some gemstones that the LA Church Loan Corporation owned. They were worth, W.C. estimated, somewhere around $500 million.[23] Later, W.C. brought up the subject of the Japanese yen bonds that he said were held in trust for the church.

'And what was the total amount of the Japanese yen bonds?' demanded Ver Ploeg.

'About twenty billion dollars,' W.C. replied calmly, as if this were the normal endowment of a church, as opposed to a nation.[24] The two other men in the room, and even the stenographer, must have gulped. Reading this later in my motel room, it brought to mind the Reverend Creflo Dollar, the televangelist whose billboards shouted at me for tithes as I drove around New Orleans. Reverend Dollar advertised the inadequacy of the $69 million that his church already had in the bank, but he now seemed to be an amateur compared to the LA Church Loan Corporation.

Hard as Ver Ploeg pressed him, it was difficult to divine exactly what W.C. Bryant and the Church Loan Corporation did. Whatever it was, Derrick Moo Young clearly wanted in on the action. For their first meeting, W.C. would have us believe that Derrick just walked in, uninvited, to W.C.'s office in Norwalk, a suburb of Los Angeles, and asked a lot of questions about the gems.[25]

'He told me that he was connected with the banking institutions in South America and the Virgin Islands, the Bahamas, Panama, Mexico, Costa Rica,' W.C. recalled. 'He gave me the idea that he was in a commodities business, and he had a way of using the bonds back through the commodities business that he had and through the banking institutions.'[26]

'He represented his main place of business to be Mexico?' demanded Ver Ploeg.

'That's what I understood, yes.'[27] This was curious. We still had not located any Moo Young company in Mexico. As I read the deposition, I jotted down a note to myself to check into what we might have missed.[28]

Derrick's initial interest was the gemstones. The jewels were an enigma. While W.C. told Ver Ploeg they were worth $500 million, there was a letter dated May 1st, 1986, in which W.C. said the gems were valued at $94 million.[29] I found another valuation close to $150 million.[30] Did this mean that there were different valuations? Different gems? Or was it all some kind of scam?

W.C. identified three men who wanted to give such great gifts to the church: a Steve Bailey, a Mr Janovich and a Mr Kazangian.[31] Bryant wrote to Derrick that the church's gem collection included the 'Liberty Bell and the Star of Queensland, which are of undeterminable value'.[32] The only reference to a 'Star of Queensland' that I was able to find was the famous Black Star. This seemed to be the gem he meant. The original uncut crystal had been 1,156 carats, but it had been purchased in 1947 by a jeweller, Harry Kazanjian, whose name was spelled slightly differently, but was close to matching the benefactor listed by W.C. When it was cut and polished, the jewel was a six-ray star of 733 carats.[33]

If the church really had this gem, it alone was worth about $50 million.[34] Yet I had two immediate questions: first, the Black Star was permanently on loan to a museum, and was hardly going to be freely offered as collateral to the unregistered LA Church Loan Corporation, let alone by a dubious character from Fort Lauderdale like Derrick Moo Young. Second, while W.C. wrote about this stone in one document, elsewhere he had listed the gems in 'his collection',[35] and none matched the description and weight of the Black Star. However, his catalogue did include several uncut sapphires, which, if they really existed, were far larger than the 'legendary' Australian jewel. One was meant to be 11,250 carats, which would make it ten times as big. I do not pretend to be an expert in jewels, but this seemed to be as large as some of the most famous sapphires ever found.[36]

It was difficult to know what to make of W.C.'s claims concerning his jewels.

When it came to the yen bonds, the most obvious question was who might have provided $20 billion to the LA Church Loan Corporation. W.C. was under oath, but he could not, or would not, say. This seemed highly suspicious. W.C. did describe how the Church Corporation wanted to convert the bonds into dollars, but when they approached potential buyers, most felt the bonds were fraudulent, and anyway it was next to impossible for someone who was neither Japanese nor in Japan to negotiate them.[37] The bonds were apparently from the Dai-Ichi Kangyo Bank Ltd. While the bank was itself legitimate, my research threw up a scandal connected to the company in the 1980s, apparently involving shady connections with organised crime.[38] Again, what this meant was an enigma: were the bonds real, but dirty? Or were they fake?

None of these questions seemed to deter Derrick Moo Young. In September 1986 he wrote to W.C. from Panama. He said he wanted to use $5 billion of the Japanese yen instruments as collateral for transactions in Barbados, Trinidad, Costa Rica, Panama, Venezuela and Paraguay. They would, he said, each be loans of twenty years and one day, with interest paid biannually.[39] He was talking huge sums: he was asking for 6 per cent interest on $5 billion, which would be $300 million a year.

And Derrick talked to W.C. about other high-flying finance. 'There was a bank in South America that Moo Young said he had owned or he controlled or something to this effect,' said W.C., who went on to explain that he knew some people who wanted to buy a bank or two, so he thought they might be able to do some business there as well.[40]

What did Derrick plan to do with a few hundred million dollars' worth of gems, and $5 billion in yen? There was one possible, arguably legitimate hypothesis: in return for helping W.C. realise the value of some dodgy donations, Derrick wanted a commission on their sale. Ver Ploeg had a letter offering Derrick a commission of $600,000 if the gems were sold.[41] Then there was a second document that purported to guarantee the Moo Young company, Cargil International, 'a commission of 4% of the transactions made with gemstones, bonds and checks of the Los Angeles Church Loan Corporation. Said comission is already agreed in contract held in Costa Rica.'[42]

Again this 'guarantee' might provoke misgivings simply because it was so amateurish: the word 'commission' was repeatedly misspelled in a document that purported to be about such enormous sums. But the Moo Youngs' lawyer, sitting in on Ver Ploeg's deposition, wanted this to be true, as he had to prove that the Moo Youngs had been into legitimate business in order to collect on the life-insurance policies. He pressed the witness to help his case.

'Obviously, if anybody converted them to cash, they would have received some kind of commission or bonus for it; you wouldn't expect people to do that for nothing?' he asked W.C., knowingly.

But he did not get the answer he wanted.

'Most folk aren't that generous, but we weren't paying any commission—' began W.C.

'You mean to tell me, if somebody converted these to cash—' the lawyer interjected.

'We would not pay any commissions. We never paid any commissions,' W.C. insisted. Those who dealt with the church were not expected to seek out a profit (all of that was meant to go to the church). They were meant to be supporting the church's work, whatever that might actually be. 'What Mr Moo Young was – he told me he was purchasing the instruments through Cargil ...'[43]

That ruled out one hypothesis. According to W.C., Derrick had told him that he wanted to *buy* the gems and the yen bonds. This fell squarely into my original theory. To purchase the gems, Derrick would have to come up with somewhere around a $100 million; who knows how many billions he would need to buy the bonds? There was a question hanging over the room: where was Derrick going to get money like that?

It all came back round to money-laundering. There was only one client (or co-conspirator) in 1986 who could have supplied that kind of money: one of the cartels. Derrick might not have to actually buy either the gems or the bonds for his purpose. He could have used them as a kind of collateral in the 'substitute' laundering scam. If there were a huge amount of money in America that Derrick's 'client' wanted to export, one way of doing this would be to borrow documents relating to extremely expensive and portable items, like gemstones. If Derrick was going to carry gems through customs, he would need the right kind of documentation in case he was stopped. He could not carry documentation for the items that he actually bought, because then he would have to explain where the money originated to make the purchase. But if he had documents that purported to show that the gems belonged to the LA Church Loan Corporation, and that he was merely taking them to a prospective buyer outside the country, then he would be covered … notwithstanding the fact that the gems he was ferrying were not the ones reflected in the documents. So long as he was not questioned too closely, he could make the same trip many times.

One matter was clear: nothing Derrick was doing was above board. W.C. stressed that the Church Loan Corporation had never given Derrick authority over the gems or the yen bonds. Nonetheless, the vice-president of Cargil, one S. Scott, wrote to the Ministry of Finance of the Government of Barbados: 'Our corporation is currently holding the equivalent of one point five billion of US dollars in Japanese Yen instruments.' They were triple-A-rated bonds, Scott assured the minister, and Cargil had many years of experience in international banking.[44]

I did not need to spend much time investigating the validity of this letter. I had long since figured out that 'S. Scott' was an alias used by Derrick Moo Young. In her deposition in the life-insurance case, Derrick's daughter Shaula had identified Shernette Scott as the name of the woman who had been the kids' babysitter in Jamaica years before. Presumably this faithful family retainer was not the vice-president of Cargil who had years of international banking experience.

*

Ver Ploeg pulled other documents out of his briefcase during W.C.'s deposition. There were two letters of credit issued by the 'International Bank of the South Pacific', each for $100 million. In one, the name of the beneficiary had been whited out.[45] The second had the names filled in, in favour of Banco Continental / Amer Enterprises SA and Cargil International Corporation.[46] Yet both were dated September 17th, 1986, and both bore the same identifying code ODA-170986-SL5-10: in other words, they were the same document, but the Moo Youngs had used white-out on the real name and simply typed in their own company in an unsophisticated forgery.[47]

'This document says it's an "irrevocable and transferable letter of one hundred million dollars of credit",' Ver Ploeg noted, dubiously.

'It's only worth the paper it's written on, probably,' replied W.C. Bryant, amending the aphorism.[48]

'Do you recall telling me several months ago that Mr Brimberry had investigated the Moo Youngs and told you not to have anything further to do with them?' asked Ver Ploeg, as their interview drew to a close. Robert Brimberry was W.C.'s lawyer in California.

'I know he did investigate, and that something was said between us that he was not ...' WC hesitated, looking for an acceptable word, '... that Derrick Moo Young was bad medicine ... There was something, you know, bad about the situation.'[49]

As the dates on the correspondence between the Moo Youngs and W.C. got closer to the day when father and son would die in the DuPont Plaza Hotel, the Moo Young side of the exchange seemed increasingly desperate. For example, on September 22nd, 1986 – just over three weeks before he would die – Derrick wrote to W.C. Bryant about 'problems' that had arisen with the International Bank of the South Pacific. 'To have received this news so soon after the Dai-Ichi Kangyo Bank incident, with respect to the bonds, is,' he observed, 'to say the least most disheartening, discouraging and disappointing.'

W.C. testified that he could not remember what these banking 'problems' might have been, but it only took a moment on the Internet to figure it out. The International Bank of the South Pacific was the brainchild of another man of the cloth, this time a Mormon called Glen Bell. Rev. Bell had promised high rates of interest to fellow Mormons, and invested the money in local ventures in the US, before apparently emptying the coffers and absconding.[50]

Derrick ended his letter with the rather peremptory demand that

W.C. provide him with a signed form of 'irrevocable commitment' to release the gems to him. 'We trust that you will provide us with this immediately,' he wrote.[51] Again, he seemed almost despairing, hoping, but barely expecting, that he would get what he sought. I wondered to myself: perhaps Derrick or Duane had made some promises? Perhaps they were facing some angry and disappointed 'investors' of their own?

W.C. Bryant told Ver Ploeg that he had informed Derrick that the 'church' would not give him authority over the gems.[52]

'What happened in your relationship with Mr Moo Young after you told him that you were not going to sign the form letter, which he said he needed to deal with the bank?' Ver Ploeg demanded.

'I don't remember the date of that, but I do …' He hesitated, as if there was something he wanted to add, but thought better of it. 'I don't recall … The weeks before he left he was aware of the fact that we were not going to sign it, the document, that he had sent us to sign.'[53]

W.C. seemed to be trying to leave the impression that he had nothing to do with the Moo Youngs after that September 22nd letter – which came just over three weeks before the murder. But Ver Ploeg pulled out another document dated the end of September, when W.C. had written to Derrick again. In the interim there must have been a phone call. Then, twenty-four hours later, there was another letter from W.C. to Derrick, offering the yen securities for twenty years at 6 per cent interest a year or, if he preferred, allowing him to buy them outright for 20 per cent of their value – a cool $1 billion. When confronted with this, W.C. initially said he did not think this was a letter that he would have written, but he had to admit that it looked like his signature.[54]

Derrick appeared to be trying to fill an enormous financial hole in his affairs two weeks before his death. W.C. must have been a possible lifeline. The credit-card receipts in the Moo Young briefcase described how Derrick and Duane left Miami for LA at eight in the morning on October 6th on Eastern Flight 533.[55] When they arrived, they checked into the Hyatt Anaheim,[56] not far from W.C.'s office, staying for four days, and twice dining out at the Chin Ting restaurant.[57] They returned to Florida on October 10th.

What deals they struck on that visit, W.C. Bryant never said. Ver Ploeg did not ask him,[58] and W.C. took the knowledge to his grave.

*

There had to be some connection between W.C.'s carats and the cartels. From the very beginning I had been certain that the name Jaime Vallejo Mejia somehow held a key to the case. He was the Colombian occupying the suite across the corridor from the double-murder in Room 1215.

A reporter from Miami latched onto this hole in the original police investigation and confronted Detective John Buhrmaster about it in an interview.

'I questioned him,' the indignant policeman retorted. Buhrmaster explained how he chatted with Mejia from the doorway to his hotel suite. He peered inside the room, without entering, and 'everything seemed fine'. Mejia was ruled out as a suspect, according to Buhrmaster, because he 'seemed legit'.[59] The officer never looked into Mejia's claim that he had been on a different floor of the hotel at the time of the crime; he did not take Mejia's fingerprints to compare to the various unmatched prints found in Room 1215; he did not look into precisely how 'legit' Mejia was; and unless it had been purged from the file, at no time did he run a criminal background check on Mejia.

Prior to trial, the defence similarly made only the most desultory effort to follow up on Mejia. Kris Maharaj was no idiot. He knew that if he did not commit the crime, then someone else must have. He wondered whether the Moo Youngs were involved in drugs. The fact that a Colombian was so close to the crime scene was an obvious lead. But his defence counsel, Eric Hendon, later gave his excuses, saying that he could not find anything to confirm Kris' suspicions.

Mejia had an import-export business that he ran out of the DuPont Plaza, but Derrick and Duane hardly had time to get to the morgue before Mejia checked out of the hotel for good. Was it not worth looking a little closer at him? After all, Sylvia Romans, the state evidence technician, had found blood on the wall and door outside his room.

Jaime Vallejo listed his address as Pereira. When I looked it up, I found that Pereira was twinned with Miami.[60] Miami city council must have been having a private joke, high on Colombian cocaine, when they voted on this. The city may not be as well known as some other places in Colombia, but it is halfway between Medellin and Cali. Carlos Lehder, a co-founder of the Medellin Cartel, was born close by. Pereira has a strong presence of both the major cartels, as well as its own much smaller and more discrete Pereira Cartel.[61] In the Seventies and Eighties, Pereira was one of the most important centres of the world for processing Quaaludes (methaqualone). The powder was imported from Germany or Holland and then manufactured into 'jumbo' pills.

At the time of the murders Detective Buhrmaster took a very brief statement from Mejia, in which the Colombian named his company, All Leather Import & Export Inc.[62] Perhaps, borrowing from James Bond, drug dealers like to use an import-export company as their front,[63] since this is obviously their business: the import is drugs; the export, money.[64] Mejia gave Buhrmaster another business card, reflecting that he was Agente General for the American Protectors Life Insurance Company. The address was listed in Pereira, Colombia. A life-insurance business is almost as good as a clothes laundry as window-dressing for the exportation of drug money, since an insurance policy is no more than a piece of paper – there is nothing physical that must be bought and sold, nothing that needs to be manufactured.

What role did Mejia play in this 'import-export' business? Did Mejia's sense of irony prompt his choice of the second business card – was he a life-insurance agent, or did he deal more frequently in death?

It was some time before we were able to make any headway tracking Mejia down. At the time of Kris' trial in 1986 a records check on Mejia would have been impossible for the defence, easy for the prosecution: they could simply run him through the law-enforcement computer.[65]

Today, with the availability of the Internet, more information seeps out. Mejia had tried to establish another business in Miami. He aspired to be a liquor salesman. In 1986 he had applied to set up a business selling alcoholic beverages. If he was in the drugs business, this was a rather bold plan, as any such licence would require a full investigation of his moral and financial background, performed by the Florida Division of Alcoholic Beverages and Tobacco. Perhaps he thought they were incompetent; I leaned towards the view that enough people in law enforcement had long since been bought and paid for.

On October 15th, 1986 – the day before the Moo Youngs were murdered – Mejia's personal banker wrote a letter in support of his application. 'Mr Vallejo has always handled all his accounts in a most satisfactory manner,' wrote Alexis Gomez. His account had varied from $120,848 – the lowest balance – up to $524,529, a little over half a million dollars.[66] Mejia did seem to be a very good customer. One day in June he had deposited $100,000 into his current account, where he earned very little interest.[67] I compared this to the 1986 profit-and-loss statement for All Leather Import & Export that Mejia attached to the application. The total business income for the year was $42,961.26; the expenses were $82,967.02, for a net loss of $40,005.76. The telephone bill alone – $8,497.63 – was almost as much as the money made from the sales of leather goods.[68] What was going on here?[69] Where were the hundreds of thousands of dollars coming from that flowed through his account?

Eventually the Florida Department of Business Regulation sent an investigator to analyse Mejia's latest venture. 'The premises is located in a small shopping mall in the center of the downtown Miami shopping district,' noted Earl Simmons, 'a strange place for the receiving and distributing of alcoholic beverages.' However, this was a minor criticism when compared to other information that came Simmons' way – he learned from the Drug Enforcement Agency (DEA) that Mejia was 'believed to have hand carried more than $40 million to Switzerland for deposit to Swiss bank accounts on behalf of Colombian drug smugglers'.[70] In March 1987, seven months before Kris Maharaj's trial for the murder of the Moo Youngs, indictments and arrest warrants were issued in Oklahoma City against Mejia and one Francisco Javier Ocando Paz. The DEA had been watching a man called Lizardo Marquez Perez, considered a key player in the drug trade.[71] Perez had been involved with Pablo Escobar in the management of hotel properties in Venezuela.[72] Perez had a contact for ongoing shipments of Medellin Cartel cocaine: Francisco Ocando Paz, also a Venezuelan.'[73] Ocando Paz was a retired military officer. On February 26th, 1984, the Venezuelan police authorities found 136 kilograms (300 pounds) of high purity cocaine inside a Super King 200 plane owned by Ocando Paz.[74] This would have been worth roughly $5 million. He was later arrested in Denver, Colorado and sent to Oklahoma for trial.

The charges alleged that Ocando Paz, Mejia and another man had arranged the transfer of $40 million in cash from the United States to a numbered bank account in Switzerland. They had achieved this in four separate flights, using a private plane, between October 1984 and August 1985.[75] Unless the leather trade was remarkably vibrant during those ten months, there was only one plausible source for this money.

Mejia had been arrested in Miami, just as Kris Maharaj was going on trial. His bond was set at $600,000, an alarming amount for a leather dealer teetering on the verge of bankruptcy, yet he had no problems bailing himself out. He faced up to five years in prison and a fine of up to $250,000, but he never served a day. On May 4th, 1989, Bonnie del Corral, from Coconut Grove, Florida, flew out to Oklahoma and entered her appearance for Mejia.[76] She was a highly regarded – and expensive – defence lawyer from Miami, who had previously done defence work for accused drug dealers.[77]

A deal was struck somewhere in a back room. The allegations against Mejia were suddenly scaled back in dramatic fashion. An assistant prosecutor now suggested that Mejia had 'willfully' failed to file a report on the transportation of 'more than five thousand dollars' from the US to Switzerland.[78] With the amount of money cut by a factor of 8,000, his punishment was also reduced. He was sentenced to two years' probation and a $1,000 fine – with a requirement of 200 hours of community service each year. All the plea proceedings were placed under seal.[79] Ocando Paz was never even prosecuted, but was simply deported back to Venezuela in the same month.

It seemed likely, in the end, that Mejia used one of the tried-and-true Colombian responses to a criminal indictment: he bought his way out of jail. Between them, the three defendants forfeited more than $8 million to the government,[80] ten times what they could have been fined had all three gone to trial and been convicted. State law-enforcement agencies were happy to get their cut.[81]

Mejia was safely back in his home country, but we needed to find out more about him. We learned that Mejia, now in his seventies, was living in his home town of Pereira. The house was not in his own name – according to the computerised records, nothing appeared to be. It was listed as the address of his sister. He was one of a dozen siblings with a well-known family name; his brother Hernán was Minister of Agriculture and Treasury in Misael Pastrana Borrero's government of Colombia in the early Seventies, and in Belisario Betancur's government from 1982 to 1986. Mejia was still said to be a 'businessman', but nobody knew what type of business. When we called officials at both the town hall and the local government of Risaralda, we were told that Mejia was a 'real ghost'.

Colombian business records also revealed no evidence that Mejia's leather company or life-insurance concern ever existed. However, there was one company where Mejia's name did appear. He was in a partnership with a man by the name of Ramiro Gonzalez Betancourt in a 'chemical' company, Proquim Industrial Ltda. Proquim had offices, described as a closed-down warehouse or factory, in a dangerous part of Cali. The stated aims of the company were to produce and distribute cleaning products and chemicals under the name Bellot. However, the Colombian Registry of Companies contained no evidence that the firm ever distributed a product under that name. The company was wound up in 2002.

It does not take a degree in chemistry to figure out what was probably going on. The mass production of cocaine requires an enormous amount of chemicals – ether being the main one. In the early days of the cartels this was readily obtained: it was a case of the capitalist selling the noose for his own hanging – or, more precisely, the drugs for his child's addiction. Many of the chemicals were imported from the US.[82]

Eventually the US started to 'crack' down. The cartels simply turned to Europe, Germany being the main source. In searching for a legitimate cover for importing large quantities of chemicals, the Cali Cartel adopted a typical solution – they established Rebaja, the largest drug company in Colombia, providing the perfect front.[83] Mejia seems to have been part of the same game, using his Proquim company to help import the necessary ingredients. Was this the way in which his superiors in the trade rewarded him for his loyal service? Perhaps.

There was more to come. On May 13th, 2008, when Rodrigo Tovar Pupo was extradited to the US, various other things leaked into the public domain. Tovar was the real name of Jorge 40, the notorious leader of a paramilitary bloc (called the AUC). Tovar controlled drug trafficking on the eastern half of Colombia. His computer was seized in 2006 and the hard drive contained details of 558 murders that Tovar had ordered in one area alone – hits that took place even as he had been negotiating an amnesty for himself and the AUC. But the bigger scandal involved the names of the living, rather than the dead. Tovar was in the blackmail business, and his computer contained a compilation of individuals – from high-ranking politicians to dealers – with connections with the drug cartels and the paramilitary.

J. Mejia V. was a name on the list.

How could a man with so many suspicious links to a Colombian cartel be in the room across the hall from the scene of a double capital murder and yet attract no attention from the police? How did Buhrmaster come to the conclusion that Mejia 'seemed legit' simply by standing at the door, peering into his hotel room? Were the police being inept? Or was there a darker explanation?

If the goal of the cartels was to get their cocaine into South Florida, then the goalposts were spaced hundreds of miles apart; hundreds of balls were in play at any given moment, and the goalkeeper was a policeman wearing a blindfold, who periodically turned around and kicked a few balls into his own net. Gradually the players have been willing to start telling the story, as some did in the extraordinary documentary *Cocaine Cowboys*. Drugs would come in with 'mules' on cruise ships or commercial aircraft. Drugs would arrive, dart-like, in high-speed powerboats that slid into the Everglades. Drugs would fly in on light aircraft that ducked under radar.

'Hell, they even fly coke in from a ship in one of those remote-controlled toy planes and land it on a bayshore condo,' said Patrolman Doug Morris of the Miami-Dade County marine patrol.[84] If the DEA stopped the occasional shipment, such losses presented a very small tax on the business.

Drugs brought violence and corruption. By 1986 there was plenty of both in the Miami-Dade Police Department – the same bureau that would investigate the murder of the Moo Youngs in the DuPont Plaza. As the immigrant population grew rapidly – in the 1980 Mariel Boat Lift, 125,000 Cuban exiles came to South Miami in one flotilla – the MDPD underwent a massive hiring spree. While it could not rival Colombia, Miami was the murder capital of the United States, with a higher homicide rate than New York or Washington DC. Yet training experienced police officers takes many years; by late 1985 a chief of police who was reputed to be barely competent himself led to what one commentator described as a Miami police force of 'too many ill-trained, undisciplined, anarchic and corrupt officers ...'[85]

A branch of the MDPD called Centac (the Central Tactical Unit) was put in charge of stemming the flow of drugs. It was made up mainly of homicide detectives, drawn from the same office as Detective John Buhrmaster. Centac burned brightly for a few months,[86] but there were pervasive allegations of corruption against its lead officer, Raul Diaz, who was accused of taking kickbacks from the people he was meant to be arresting. Another MDPD officer, Aldo Suero, got stung when he went into the market for a bazooka so that he could blow the doors off the US customs building in Miami and steal the seized cocaine.[87]

An even more celebrated instance of corruption was dubbed the Miami River Cops case, involving six homicide detectives who were arrested and charged with murder and drug dealing. Police detectives had been ripping off the drug dealers. By 1985 one of the MDPD officers, Rudy Arias, had banked a little over a million dollars – $1,080,000, according to his meticulous records later found during a search. When the federal agents began closing in, the six Miami River Cops confected plots to eliminate six witnesses against them, either by hiring assassins or doing the work themselves.[88]

Had Arias not been arrested on untimely corruption charges, he was to have been nominated as Miami 'Officer of the Year'.[89]

This was just one example. The corruption in the police force was pervasive. 'We are literally on the ragged edge of anarchy,' a federal judge told a private audience by May 1986. The lawlessness had taken on a different quality, beyond cocaine wars between rival drug dealers. Miami, the judge said, 'was now experiencing the double jeopardy of rampant, violent crime *by* the police, and on an extraordinary scale.'[90]

Up to this point, I had my doubts about the work that had been done by John Buhrmaster, the lead homicide detective on the case. His file was full of material that would have been helpful to the defence – yet Kris' trial lawyer had seen none of it. And what had Buhrmaster himself made of it all? Surely he would have pondered some of the same questions that struck me when I looked through the contents of the Moo Youngs' briefcase.

Buhrmaster supplied critical testimony against Kris, making the fingerprints and the ballistics evidence appear to be incriminating – and now his version of events had been cast in grave doubt, while Kris' version had been corroborated, suggesting his innocence. How could any competent police officer investigate a crime like this, with a list of players who seemed inevitably to have links to drug crime, without digging deeper? How could he fail, for example, to run a quick computer check on Jaime Vallejo Mejia, the man from Pereira in the room across the hall?

All of this could be explained by police bias of the kind that I had often seen in New Orleans, when officers came to court to testi-lie, intent on ensuring the conviction of a defendant they deemed to be guilty. Was that the sum of it? Or had rampant crime *by* the police somehow spilled over into Kris' case?

Unfortunately, I doubted that we had the resources to do a full investigation of the police for corruption. Indeed, unless someone were to come forward with some inside information, the best we could hope for was that one day the Florida authorities would wake up and insist on such an investigation. There was clearly something very fishy about the way Kris' case had been investigated, from start to finish.

13

The Judge

Gradually we were unravelling the prosecution's case against Kris Maharaj. Neville Butler, the star witness for the prosecution, had not passed a polygraph: he had failed, and the prosecutors had misled the court about this. Such an act, alone, might be considered enough for a new trial. We could also show how Butler's version of events metamorphosed over the course of a year. Every time he came up with an assertion that differed from another witness or the physical evidence, the prosecutors would adapt his story until it was consistent, and then argue to the jury that the independent proof corroborated Butler's sworn testimony. If he testified again today, he would leave the stand in tatters.[1]

The forensic 'proof' against Kris had also been neutered by evidence withheld from the jury. Detective Buhrmaster had testified that Kris denied being in Room 1215, making all Kris' fingerprints that were found there seem inculpatory. But the sworn statement of Officer Romero corroborated Kris' account that he had told Buhrmaster from the start that he had gone to the DuPont Plaza for a meeting with the elusive Eddie Dames and left when Dames was a no-show. If Kris had an innocent reason for visiting the room, the fingerprints proved nothing – except that Buhrmaster may have conveniently mis-remembered what Kris said.

Buhrmaster's testimony that Kris denied ever owning a handgun had likewise fallen apart. Buhrmaster's notes showed that Kris told him about the gun he had owned. It seemed most likely that the gun had been stolen during the traffic stop by the Florida Highway Patrol in July 1986, three months before the murders. Regardless of this, the ballistics evidence was valueless as Thomas Quirk, the state's witness, far overstated any valid conclusion.

Next, there was the suppression by the prosecution of boxes of information about the case. I had never in my career seen anything like it. The contents of the Moo Young briefcase alone transformed the entire story. These documents painted Derrick not as an innocent semi-retired businessman on $24,000 a year, but as a money-launderer for the drug cartels, trying to shift *billions* of dollars around the Caribbean. Perhaps more important, they provided a motive for a cartel plot to kill Derrick and Duane: the documents indicated that they were trying to skim 1 per cent off the top of these deals.

And what of Adam Amer Hosein? Records showed that he telephoned Room 1215; George Abchal said he apparently went there that morning with a gun that could have been the murder weapon; Hosein was linked to the dubious Moo Young businesses in Panama and the Bahamas; he was friends with convicted cartel lawyer F. Nigel Bowe, whose office served as the business address for the Moo Youngs' main company, Cargill International (Bahamas); and there were indications that he might have confessed to being involved in the murders. One of the prosecution witnesses, Prince Ellis, had now gone on-camera to admit that Eddie Dames, the man used to lure both Kris and the Moo Youngs to Room 1215, was another member of the Bahamian drug conspiracy. Ellis asserted that Kris had been framed.

The tentacles that had enfolded Derrick and Duane Moo Young seemed to begin with the man in the room across the hall from their murder. We now knew that, at the time of Kris' trial, Jaime Vallejo Mejia was being investigated for carrying $40 million in drug money to Switzerland. What was the probability that the Colombian from Pereira had nothing to do with it?

Surely the evidence pointed strongly to a complicated drug hit – and surely this was more than enough material to warrant a new trial?

And what of Eric Hendon? One witness suggested that he might have been intimidated by threats against his family. He denied this, but he did an abysmal job, failing to hire the help he needed, conducting no meaningful investigation, failing to present the alibi, and failing vigorously to cross-examine witnesses or offer a coherent alternative to the prosecution case.

Eric Hendon also made another, fatal, error, which gave us plenty of ammunition to demand a retrial. This was in the advice he gave Kris about how to deal with Judge Howard Gross.

Long before his trial began, a flustered Kris Maharaj had asked Hendon to come for a legal visit. He was confused and concerned.

'What happened, one evening my client, Krishna, called me to the jail,' Hendon later explained. 'He was quite … I don't want to say upset, but quite agitated about a conversation he indicated he had had. He had a card bearing the name of a member of the local bar. He indicated that he had been approached by a lawyer in the Dade County jail and the lawyer asked him to retain her and quoted a price of $50,000 and indicated to him if she were retained, she had a relationship with Judge Gross and he would definitely be allowed to be released on bond. He advised me that this lawyer told him that she knew he was innocent and that she knew he had passed a polygraph and that she knew Judge Gross and Judge Gross knew her and if she were retained, he would definitely be released on bond.'[2]

Kris showed him the card he had been given. Hendon didn't remember whether an office designation was given with the name. It seemed to him, Kris said, that she was demanding a bribe, and he had angrily sent her on her way.[3]

'I advised my client,' Hendon went on, ' "Kris, this doesn't make any sense. This person is a prosecutor. This person couldn't have approached you. But definitely, don't – this is first-degree murder. You are not going to be released on bond on a charge of first-degree murder." And with respect to … I just sort of dismissed it. I told him I found it hard to believe.'[4]

Hendon recognised the name on the card as that of a lawyer who worked in the Office of the State Attorney, alongside Paul Ridge and John Kastrenakes. But a few enquiries revealed that she was leaving to set up her own practice. He did not know what to make of it, but he did pass the information to the prosecutors and asked them to look into it. I later found reference to this in the prosecutors' file,[5] but neither they nor Hendon took any further action.[6]

Then, on the morning of October 8th, 1987, with the third day of the trial about to begin, Judge Howard Gross did not appear on the bench. Chief Judge Herbert Klein summoned the lawyers into his chambers. Gross had, Klein told the lawyers in private, been arrested that morning, and would be taking no further role in the case. It was shocking news. Nobody could remember a time when a judge had been carted off in chains in the middle of a capital murder trial. Judge Klein told Kris Maharaj and the lawyers to consider how they wanted to respond to this news and he would speak with them soon. The jury was not given any details about what had happened, but was told to go home for the day and await further instructions.

Judge Howard Gross went by the nicknames 'Mousey' or 'Howie the Mouse', derived from his childhood when playmates teased him about looking like a small rodent. It had become his motif. He had a swimming pool constructed in the shape of a mouse. When he was married, his wedding cake was decorated with two mice holding hands. A group of attorneys once burst into his courtroom wearing Mickey Mouse attire. Far from holding them in contempt, Gross loved it, and the incident was written up in the *Miami Herald*.[7]

Well, the Florida Department of Law Enforcement (FDLE) had set out some cheese for the mouse, and early on the third morning of the Maharaj trial the trap was sprung. Gross, who had once been hailed as both brilliant and compassionate, was the target of an elaborate sting operation. An agent, posing as a drug suspect called Orlando Zirio, was being held in the same jail to which Kris Maharaj returned each night from the courtroom. 'Zirio' was meant to have been caught with twelve kilograms (twenty-six pounds) of cocaine, with a street value of close to $1,000, and his bond was set at $750,000.

Another agent took the part of a cartel representative[8] called Ernesto Cassal, and approached attorney Harvey Swickle, a longtime friend of Gross who was thought to be one of his bagmen.[9] Cassal explained that Zirio was his employee and that he needed Zirio to get out of jail. Once out, Cassal made it clear to Swickle that Zirio would vanish and never be seen again. While the cartel needed to take care of its own, the $750,000 bond – on top of the loss of the drugs – was too steep a price to pay. Cassal asked if he could get a judge to lower the bond to around $150,000.

This might be possible, Swickle said. 'If my guy is on duty.'

Some negotiations ensued, and Cassal suggested that his people could meet a $200,000 bond. Swickle indicated that his fee would be 10 per cent up front: $20,000. Cassal brought him $10,000 in cash. Swickle was leery of accepting only 50 per cent.

'This creates a problem because, ahm, my situation is that I can't, I say, I can't have somebody do something,' he explained, 'unless they know that, ah, I'm fully represented.'[10]

Cassal assured him that the rest of the money would be coming his way soon.

Using wiretaps, the FDLE then eavesdropped as an unwitting Swickle called Gross at home. Swickle made twelve calls in the space of just twelve minutes, perhaps some kind of code. Then Gross called him back, and the call lasted for two minutes and forty-three seconds.

'Yeah, okay,' Swickle began. 'I've … ah, I've got the signed contract.'

'So they did … this man now has a lawyer?' asked Judge Gross.

'Yes sir.'

'Okay, if you are his lawyer and you tell me those are the facts, I'll reduce the bond accordingly,' the judge assured him.

'Ah, what time you going to be in?' Swickle asked, wanting to meet the judge in the courthouse the next day.

'I'll be in, ah, probably … eight fifteen,' replied the judge.

'Urn,' was Swickle's enigmatic reply.

'I'll be there all day. I've got that murder trial,' Gross explained.

'That's right.' Swickle remembered that the high-profile Maharaj case had just started.

'I am, I'm going to be tied up.'

'How about if I meet you in the morning at the house?' Swickle asked.

'Where? Here?' Gross sounded surprised.

'Yeah.'

'Well, I don't care, it doesn't matter,' Gross conceded.

'About eight?'

'Yeah.' This would be just before Gross left to go to the courthouse.

'Okay.'[11]

The next morning Swickle drove to the judge's Normandy Isle home and handed him $6,300 in marked bills. The first $5,000 was apparently the bribe for fixing the bond for 'Zirio'; the additional $1,300 a separate illegal payment to Gross for passing a criminal case

Swickle's way.[12] Gross stashed the cash in his garage before climbing into his Camaro to drive to the Miami-Dade courthouse to continue Kris Maharaj's trial. As he was about to leave his driveway, the FDLE agents arrested him.[13] Gross would have no further involvement in the Maharaj case, and henceforth his problem would be to find a judge who would allow him bail, so that he could prepare for his own prosecution.

When Kris had initially raised the issue of bribery, Hendon had not taken him seriously. Perhaps he was not sure what to believe – the lawyer who had allegedly asked for $50,000 was leaving the prosecutor's office and going into private practice, so she might have been trying to steal his client, making inflated promises of what she could achieve for him. But the larger reason was obvious: no lawyer who planned on making a living in Miami was going to be the one to bring up questions of judicial corruption. Yet Gross' arrest added extraordinary weight to Kris' allegations, and surely now was the time to revisit what had happened.

Years later, when Ben Kuehne and I asked him about all this, Hendon said he had not put the jigsaw puzzle together at the time of Kris' trial. He had been confused, he said, at the hostile reception that he had received in Gross' courtroom. Now he gave it some thought, it all began to fit together.

'Well, it appeared to me following that,' he said, meaning the solicitation of a bribe from Kris, 'we – we not get any favourable treatment.' He paused. 'If I can explain "favourable". I don't mean favourable being something we are not entitled to, but simple nuances such as scheduling, consideration of scheduling difficulties; from that point on my relationship with Judge Gross in this case, nothing that would have been convenient to the defence was ever done.'[14] At the trial itself there were all sorts of incidents where Judge Gross seemed biased, including the way he misrepresented the outburst in court by one of the Moo Young family members.

When Gross was arrested and taken away in chains, Hendon had many options. First, this was strong evidence that Kris' original complaint had been valid: if Gross was arrested now for taking his 50 per cent cut on a $20,000 bribe in a drug case, that was powerful proof that half of the $50,000 demanded from Kris would have ended up in his pocket at well. Hendon's first duty was to demand that there be a full investigation into the allegation of bribery in Kris' case.

Second, Hendon could obviously put a stop to the trial. Surely no proceedings should simply continue when the judge is arrested. The argument carried still more force in Florida, one of only three states where the judge would be the ultimate sentencer in a capital case. Two days of evidence had already been completed, including half of the testimony of Neville Butler, the key prosecution witness. If another judge took over now, he would be asked to impose a life or death sentence without hearing a vital part of the case.

So what did Hendon do? He advised Kris to waive his right to start the trial afresh. He did not raise the idea of an investigation into whether a bribe had actually been solicited. He did not even mention how Gross' rulings had seemed so biased over the preceding months.

'My client asked me what my advice would be,' Hendon began. 'I advised him that I believed it would be in his best interest to continue and not ask for the mistrial. I was quite pleased with the jury that we had. I was quite pleased with the nature of some of the testimony that had come forward … I advised my client I thought it was in his best interest to proceed and not ask for a new trial at this time, or mistrial.'[15]

Who was Kris to reject his lawyer's advice? He knew he was innocent, and expected to be acquitted. But I thought there was a different, and quite human, truth here. Hendon was on a set fee. If the case had to start again, he would have to spend days picking another jury and going over the evidence again. It would all eat into what he had been paid.

So a week went by, a new judge was installed, and the trial continued.

If Judge Gross' name appeared to be rather appropriate, the name of his replacement was not: Judge Harold Solomon.[16] I found some interesting facts about him when I took advantage of Florida's 'Sunshine Law', looking through the prosecution's files. I had a list of Hendon's file and our own to cross-check against the state's and would copy any document that seemed incongruous.

I also had my notes concerning various exchanges that had taken place at trial that I did not fully understand. One had occurred on December 1st, 1987, immediately before Judge Solomon had imposed a death sentence on Kris.

'I understand that there is a supplemental order that you have drafted here,' remarked Judge Solomon.

'There were two packages submitted to the court,' said prosecutor Paul Ridge.[17] I did not know what either 'package' was, or what order the prosecutor referred to. Hendon was no help.

As I rummaged through the prosecution file, in the mid-afternoon I became confused at the number of copies of the sentencing order in the prosecutor's file. There was a signed copy, dated December 1st, 1987, but there were other unsigned copies, which I noticed were slightly different from each other.[18] This was unusual, as I had never seen a sentencing order before the judge signed it. My first impression was that perhaps things were done differently in Florida, and the judge had given copies to both parties beforehand so that they could correct mistakes or make objections.

But then I noticed that at the bottom corner of one unsigned version there was an annotation: '*JSK.smc:11/18/87*'. It did not take too much sleuthing to figure out what JSK meant – I had no idea what John Kastrenakes' middle name was, but it was a good bet that it began with an S. So this document showed that one of the prosecutors had been typing a sentencing order on November 18th, 1987, some days *before* Kris' judicial sentencing hearing. This meant that Kastrenakes had given the judge a draft order sentencing Kris to death *before* the judicial sentencing hearing took place. Again, Hendon knew nothing about this. It had been done without any involvement from Kris' lawyer.

Later I made some calls to Florida lawyers who might be able to help me figure this out. It turned out that Judge Solomon was a singularly lazy adjudicator. Jimmy Lohmann was a lawyer working on the case of Dieter Riechmann, the German citizen who, as we have seen, had been sentenced to death a year after Kris for killing his girlfriend. The crime had taken place in Miami; the judge had been Solomon. Lohmann had called Riechmann's prosecutor to the witness stand at a hearing challenging the death sentence. The state attorney testified that he had run into the judge in the hall of the courthouse one day. They had talked for the briefest of moments, before each continuing on his way. Solomon wanted a sentencing order written up.

'I don't recall the judge asking me to include any, you know, include anything specific in the – in the order,' the prosecutor said.

'Well, did he tell you the contents of the order?' demanded Riechmann's lawyer.

'No, I don't ... well, I don't recall him telling me the contents of the order,' the prosecutor said, in acute discomfort. 'I mean, all I remember from that exchange was "Prepare an order." '[19] In other words, Solomon did not bother to do any judging. He simply told the prosecutor – *ex parte*, without bothering to tell the defence lawyer – to write up an order sentencing Riechmann to death. It was not immediately clear when this was done in Riechmann's case, but with Kris the dates were clear: the judge wanted such an order before he heard the evidence.

This was extraordinary; the order was no mere formality. The judge is the ultimate authority when it comes to sentencing in Florida, and the law specifically requires him to write his own judgement, balancing the evidence and personally determining whether death is the proper punishment.[20] The Riechmann order was very similar to the one they had written in Kris' case: it went on for ten pages, and included conclusions that should be made by a judge, but had been written by the prosecutor.[21]

Kris had been convicted and sentenced to death, with one judge in shackles and the other chumming up with the prosecutors in secret. With Kris' appeals, the Florida judiciary still had a third chance to get it right. The judge who had come to the plate had been Leonard Glick. Glick had been the one who would decide whether Kris would be allowed a hearing on any new evidence that he produced challenging the fairness of his trial. In capital cases, evidentiary hearings are common at this stage of the Florida process. But there had been no such hearing with Judge Glick in charge. He had affirmed the death penalty imposed on Kris in a summary order.

In the prosecution file I found another unsigned order – again drafted by the prosecutors, awaiting the signature of Judge Glick. It went step-by-step through the prosecution's argument for upholding the death sentence on this appeal, without hearing any new evidence. Again, the lawyer representing Kris knew nothing about it. All Glick had done to the prosecutors' draft was change the date from October to November, and sign it.

Who was this Leonard Glick? Was there an epidemic in the Miami courthouse, where all the judges left the judging to the prosecutors?

I immediately made a request for Glick's personnel file,[22] to see what had been motivating him. Before denying the petition, Glick had pointed out to Kris' lawyer that he was an acquaintance of the two government prosecutors, Ridge and Kastrenakes, because he had worked in the same office before he became a judge. What he had failed to mention was that, at the time of Kris' trial, he had been their supervising prosecutor: he had taken part in the process of approving the death penalty, and had probably had discussions with them about the case.

No doubt few judges are as overtly venal as 'Howie the Mouse' Gross; we might hope that few are as obviously biased as Harold Solomon and Leonard Glick. But we must ask whether the system is structured to discourage corruption or bias in the judiciary. It does not help the troubled profile of the American justice system that most judges are selected at the ballot box. Forty-two of the fifty states elect them.[23] Of the thirty-seven states with the death penalty,[24] thirty-one elect their judges.[25] Nobody has ever run a judicial campaign on 'being fair to criminals', and securing votes is an increasingly expensive exercise.

Some of the stories that emanate from American judicial elections would seem very foreign to the decorous, wigged world of the British Royal Courts of Justice.[26] One of the sadder recent examples involved the race for Chief Justice of the Alabama Supreme Court. The challenger accused the incumbent of shaking down attorneys who were appearing before the court for contributions to his expensive re-election campaign; the incumbent ran advertisements where the father of a murder victim accused the challenger of being an accomplice to murder, because he had not been harsh enough in a capital case.[27]

There must be a suspicion that US judges who must raise large amounts of money to prevail in contentious elections are more subject to corruption than those who are appointed with tenure. This might result from bribery, which is not as uncommon as one would hope;[28] but electing judges also injects corruption in a more subtle form, where the candidate avoids making a particular decision that will haunt him the next time he goes to the polls.[29]

In the early 1980s the California Supreme Court, led by Chief Justice Rose Bird, had a reputation for being liberal, and for not brooking any unfairness in capital cases. Bird had been Chief Justice for ten years, and in the sixty-one capital cases that came before her, she voted to reverse each and every one.[30] In 1986 the Republican Governor of California was George Deukmejian. He announced that he would seek to unseat Chief Justice Bird at the election that year, and he publicly warned two other justices, Cruz Reynoso and Joseph Grodin, that he would oppose them as well unless they voted to uphold more death sentences. This pressure failed to persuade the justices to change their votes, so he carried out his threat to go after them. They all lost their seats after a bitter fight dominated by the death penalty, with Bird outspent by two-to-one during the campaign; Deukmejian appointed their conservative replacements.[31]

The other justices on the California Supreme Court got the message, and they wanted to keep their jobs. Over the five years that followed this power play the court affirmed almost 97 per cent of death sentences;[32] previously the reversal rate had been 95 per cent. Indeed, the court rapidly became radically pro-capital punishment, to the point that by the 1990s the Mississippi Supreme Court was viewed as significantly more liberal. The phrase 'to be Rose Birded' entered the lexicon, and Mississippi Supreme Court Justice Jimmy Robertson would soon face a Birding of his own. Jimmy was a very decent person, certainly more liberal than most. He, too, became a victim of the law-and-order forces and was voted out of office. His opponents were cunning as well as well funded: in addition to outspending him by wide margins, they ran a candidate against him called Jimmy Roberts – a singularly unqualified individual whose name came first on the ballot, and was sufficiently confusing that some people would end up voting for him by mistake.[33]

The politicisation of the death penalty is not the monopoly of elected judges. By 1994 crime had eclipsed all other political issues in the US, such that an official of the National Governors' Association suggested that the 'top three issues in gubernatorial campaigns this year are crime, crime, and crime'.[34] In theory, the judiciary is meant to protect the citizens, especially minorities, from being drowned by populist tides. Yet even where the judges are appointed rather than elected, anyone who voices qualms about the death penalty will face opposition. The nomination of federal judges is, in theory, straightforward: 'the President shall nominate, and by and with the Advice and Consent of the Senate, shall appoint … Judges …'[35] In practice, it is more complicated. For district and appellate judges, by an unwritten convention referred to as 'Senatorial Courtesy', the senators from the relevant state will forward the name of a proposed judge to the President. This is the first layer of the political onion: to get the nod from some of the most powerful politicians in the state, the candidate must fit a certain mould. This person will generally be nominated by the President, taking into account a heavy bias in favour of candidates from the President's party.[36] Arriving at the US Senate, the candidate then faces what may be gruelling confirmation hearings designed to ensure that he does not harbour any views that would offend the politicians in power that year. One red-button issue is almost certain to be the death penalty;[37] others will include abortion and same-sex marriage. It is very difficult – but not impossible – for outspoken opponents of the death penalty to be appointed as federal district judges, but if they want to advance to the Court of Appeals or the Supreme Court, they had better start laying a track record of upholding the death penalty in the cases before them.[38]

The British will nod knowingly: 'The election of judges is an absurdity. Of course, we would not do that.' But to what extent do British judges reflect Britain's diverse population?[39] Members of the working class might wonder whether the judiciary is simply biased against them or just does not understand their predicament.[40] It would be hard to deny that the legal system in general favours the rich and powerful. 'Laws are like spider webs,' said the Scythian philosopher Anacharsis, speaking of Athens in the sixth century BC. 'They will catch the weak and the poor, but would be torn to pieces by the rich and powerful.'[41]

There used to be plenty of stories about old white male British and American judges guffawing at their own sexist jokes, or opining that women in short skirts should expect to be the objects of unwanted sexual advances.[42] The question is how far this has changed. In the US the number of women on the bench has risen to around one in five, which is a vast improvement on the past, even if women are a majority of the population.[43] Yet the voting pattern of this 20 per cent does not ultimately 'represent' women; it reflects the partialities of those who are focused on appointing women who are thought to be 'equal' to men. In other words, affirmative action ('positive discrimination') is often applied to women and minorities in order to push forward those whose views come closest to mirroring those of the majority group (white men); this does not solve the problem posed by a lack of diversity on the bench.[44]

Consider a hypothetical drive for equality in the military: it is sometimes said that if women were in charge of the army, there would be few wars. However, that would not be true if the women chosen to run the army were selected largely because they held views as close to their militaristic male predecessors as possible: some might suggest that Margaret Thatcher projected more 'testosterone bias' than her allegedly 'wet' predecessor, Edward Heath.

There are plenty of examples of this 'white male in drag' tokenism in the legal world. US Supreme Court Justice Clarence Thomas was the beneficiary of affirmative action programmes himself; given the segregated world into which he was born, there is little chance that without positive discrimination he, as a black man brought up in the south, would have been offered many of the educational opportunities that he enjoyed. Ultimately, President Reagan and the Republicans had to find a person to fill the massive shoes of the only African American who had previously served on the Supreme Court, Thurgood Marshall. Thomas was an individual of unproven intellect and limited qualifications, and he would never have made it to the court without positive discrimination. He was chosen not because he 'represented' the general interests and beliefs of black Americans – as Justice Marshall clearly had – but because he was a black man who came closest to fitting the mould of conservative white America. He was, if not an Uncle Tom – the term used by some – then at least a Cousin Thomas. The choice was, from Reagan's perspective, an inspired one: Thomas turned his back on any issue that could advance minorities with a dedication that could not have been outdone by a former Klansman.[45]

Britain and other common-law countries[46] lag behind even the US in redressing the discriminatory sins of the past.[47] It would be surprising, then, if the bias were less obvious in the British system. The highest court in the UK[48] has in the last 500 years only ever had one member who was not a white male.[49] Indeed, when a position comes vacant on the UK Supreme Court, the next justice is selected by a panel comprised of the president and deputy of the court itself, plus one member each from the three Judicial Appointments Commissions.[50] The various commissions themselves are barely more representative of the nation than is the court,[51] and they make their selections from a pool of like-minded, similar people. It would be surprising, then, if the British courts saw a rapid evolution in the outlook of judges, even if genuine efforts are being made to improve the racial and gender profile of the bench.

So Judge Howard 'Mousey' Gross was on the take. Some ask: what does it matter? How does this make the conviction of Kris Maharaj 'unsafe'? Kris did not pay the bribe that was apparently solicited; the prosecution argued that Kris had offered no evidence that Gross was biased against him. Though Eric Hendon thought the judge had taken it out on Kris, the appeals courts viewed this as insufficient proof of partiality and affirmed Kris' conviction.[52]

Perhaps, as he sits alone in his cell twenty-five years later, Kris allows himself a moment of regret. After all, he paid about $20,000 to Eric Hendon and got only a very lukewarm defence for his money; had he gone along with the proposal to pay off Judge Gross, it would have cost a bit more, but he might have been back home in England twenty-five years ago.

14

The Road to Nowhere

When Ben Kuehne and I first got involved in the case in 1994, Judge Glick had just denied Kris's request for a new trial, without any kind of a hearing. By now Kris had been in prison for seven years. We had to appeal Glick's order to the Florida Supreme Court simply to ask for a hearing on all the new material we had developed. Fearful that Kris' case might be ignored by the court, we got a group of several dozen MPs to file a brief on his behalf, to highlight the British interest in the case. There were some unknown names back then – Stephen Byers, Harriet Harman and Kim Howells, for example – as well as the occasional ranking member of the Labour Party, such as Jack Straw. Ken Livingstone signed up. There was also a smattering of Tories, including Peter Bottomley, who would soon make Kris' well-being a focal point of his parliamentary life. Geoffrey Robertson QC, showed up to argue as a friend of the court, representing the eighty-six British MPs who were asking that Kris be given a new trial. I begged him to wear his wig and gown, as the more he looked like Rumpole of the Bailey, the more the justices were likely to be impressed. He declined. Geoffrey expected justice to matter more than appearances.

Our request of the court was a modest one: just let Kris have his day in court. But the government argued that Kris had not objected in a timely manner to the fact that Judge Glick had a supervisory role over Paul Ridge and John Kastrenakes at the time of trial, or that the prosecutors had authored his order. When the Supreme Court of Florida issued its opinion, it was half-defeat, half-victory. They went out of their way to note that a number of Kris' claims ought not to be considered, because his lawyer should have raised them at trial, so he was 'procedurally barred'.[1] By now, Kris was becoming depressingly familiar with the notion of a 'procedural bar' – a rule which states that if a lawyer fails to object to something in the original trial, that objection cannot be raised at a later stage. The idea is that the judge should be given every opportunity to ensure a fair trial in the first place, so the defendant should be forced to raise every issue on the spot, at trial. The defendant should not be allowed to keep claims in his back pocket, so that, if the trial comes out the wrong way, he can sandbag the system by bringing them up later on.

Superficially the rule may seem to make sense; in practice, is an entirely counterproductive doctrine when it comes to ensuring that the trial reaches the right result. It is not the prisoner who is raising or 'waiving' claims that might be important to his case, but the lawyer. Effective lawyers will not sit back and sandbag anyone; rather, they will raise every issue, forcing the judge to rule on each one, any of which might later secure the client a new trial. They will then present a powerful case for the defence, maximising the client's chances of being acquitted. The inadequate lawyer, on the other hand, will raise no issues before or during the trial and will muddle through the case, ensuring that his client is convicted.

The way the procedural bar doctrine 'works' in reality is therefore as follows: if you have a good lawyer at trial, your chances of a fair jury verdict are much greater. Even if you are convicted and sentenced to death, you are more likely to win on appeal, because your lawyer will have objected to anything that may have gone wrong. If, on the other hand, you have an inept lawyer, your chances of a fair result at trial are slim, and you have little or no chance of winning a new trial on appeal: your lawyer 'waived' the claims by failing to raise them during the original trial, so you are 'procedurally barred'.[2]

Capital punishment therefore becomes a penalty that is reserved for the defendant with the worst lawyer, rather than for the person who committed the worst crime.[3]

While the Florida Supreme Court suggested that many of the

claims in Kris Maharaj's petition should be dismissed because Eric Hendon had failed to raise them, the court did rule that a hearing should be allowed on some of the issues in his petition. Eventually, on September 19th, 1996 (one month shy of Kris' tenth anniversary in prison), the court remanded the case to a new judge, Jerald Bagley. Kris was glad to hear that they set a deadline of ninety days for Judge Bagley to rule; by Christmas he hoped he would be free.

I was mildly panicked – we had a great deal to do in three short months. We filed an enormous petition, running to more than 300 pages, detailing the mistakes that had been made by defence lawyers, prosecutors and judges, as well as the new evidence of Kris' innocence. Much had already been done, but the case was far from complete. It had been exciting work, but it was bankrupting the charity for which I worked.

Christmas 1996 came and went. Two more men died in Florida's electric chair. Kris had still received no hearing. The problem was one of money. We had very limited funds and Kris' investigation had already cost us far more than we had to spend. Along with investigators and volunteers, I had already spent weeks in Florida, combing through the files of the prosecutors, the Miami-Dade police, and the federal court records of cartel lawyer F. Nigel Bowe, as well as interviewing all the witnesses who remained in the state.

But the hearing was going to cost far more. In addition to paying the transport to Florida of those whom we had already interviewed, so that they could appear to testify, there were hugely important witnesses in several other countries who still needed to be investigated: people in Britain who could attest to Kris' past; the highly suspicious Jaime Vallejo Mejia from Colombia; those associated with Cargil International in Panama; Eslee Carberry of the *Caribbean Echo*, who had since been deported to the Turks and Caicos Islands; Tino Geddes in Jamaica, the man who insisted that Kris' alibi had been concocted; and several others across the USA. We did not have sufficient funds to do what was needed.

Neither did Kris, nor had he for a long time. His main concern was his wife Marita, whose situation was becoming increasingly perilous. She had lost their house, and had gradually sold her possessions in the home she now rented.

The State of Florida should have paid us, as Kris' lawyers – after all, if the government wants to execute someone, they cannot expect random citizens to subsidise the defence. On top of this, the cost of preparing and presenting the hearing would more than double our expenses to date. So we turned to Judge Bagley and asked him how we were meant to represent Kris effectively without any funding.

I had high hopes of Jerald Bagley. He was a young African American who had recently been appointed by Governor Lawton Chiles – the liberal Democrat 'Walkin' Lawton', named for the miles he strode in his election campaign. He was therefore unsullied by the corruption that had provoked Operation Court Broom, the full-scale investigation of the local judges that followed on from Judge Gross' arrest. Kris, on the other hand, did not trust the new judge, partly because Bagley had previously been in the Miami-Dade prosecutors' office that put him on Death Row.

I felt I had a rather broader experience of judges than Kris – and Kris' view was certainly coloured by the sequence of events he had faced to date. To me, Bagley seemed a likeable person, and from what little I could tell, and what others reported, it seemed improbable that he was much of a fan of the death penalty. Whether he had the courage to do what was right was open to question, but then who among the elected judges of Miami-Dade County could be relied upon for that?

Sometimes the client is much wiser than the lawyer.

Paying to defend those on Death Row was very close to the bottom of the priority ladder for the Florida legislators, who thought the money better spent on cranking up 'Old Sparky' and disposing of the problem on a more permanent basis. By now, the Capital Collateral Representative (CCR) had been created to provide help to Death Row prisoners, but they told us they were out of funds and could provide Kris with neither a lawyer nor expenses. There were more than 300 people condemned to death in the state, and the office had enough money to represent perhaps a dozen of them effectively. Provision had been made in a separate budget for cases where CCR could not take the case. The total available for 1997 was $236,084 (perhaps enough to pay for one case) and when, early in the year, we asked for funds, other lawyers had already submitted bills for $360,584.

It was, ultimately, Judge Bagley's job to make sure that Kris got a fair hearing. Time and time again we asked for funds and Judge Bagley turned us down, saying that he could not find any. In the end, a year had gone by since the Florida Supreme Court's ruling. Kris was now fifty-eight years old.

Meanwhile Pedro Medina had just become the twenty-second person electrocuted by the state since Kris lost his liberty. Medina had been one of the Cuban refugees who had fled Castro in the 1980 Mariel Boat Lift, but his welcome to America had not been all that he had hoped. By 1982 he was on Death Row, and in 1997 he went to his death insisting that he did not commit the crime.

'I am still innocent!' Medina exclaimed in his broken English just before he was strapped into the chair. When the electric current came, as with Jesse Tafero, fire burst from his head and there was an acrid smell of burning. He continued to take laboured breaths as his body cooled, before the doctors could check his heartbeat. Then they juiced him again.

'People who commit murder better not do it in Florida,' remarked Attorney General Robert Butterworth in the wake of Medina's death. 'Because we may have a problem with our electric chair.'[4]

Judge Bagley suggested that if we were to wait another year until 1998 there might be funds in the budget to pay for Kris' hearing. Of course the court and the prosecution had the resources they needed. Only Kris' lawyers were not being paid; only Kris could not pay the expenses of his witnesses. We reminded the judge that it had already been twelve months, and the Florida Supreme Court had ordered the hearing take place in ninety days; Kris could not be forced to abandon his right to a timely appeal simply because Florida was not willing to pay for it. We suggested to the British Government that they might like to help Kris fund his case. Nothing came. In the end we felt we had no choice. We had to go forward, rather than wait for funding that would never materialise.

As I sat in a rather sordid motel across the road from the Dade County courthouse, the television sombrely reported that Diana, Princess of Wales, was feared dead in an accident in Paris. It was Monday, August 31st, 1997, and Kris had been in prison for almost eleven years. Diana's funeral took place on September 6th, and I was one of the 2.5 billion to watch it on television, while preparing for Kris' case. The hearing was set to begin two days later. Britain seemed far away. It was much further for Kris Maharaj, but perhaps the next week would bring a change of fortune. Notwithstanding our lack of resources, we still had more evidence to prove an unfair trial than I had ever seen before in a capital case.

I hoped that Judge Bagley would act to mitigate the lack of money. He might press the state to concede to issues that were not in real contention. He might agree to waive formalities such as bringing a witness across the Atlantic Ocean merely to ratify the authenticity of a particular document. But when the time came, he did the opposite. Prince Ellis had recanted his trial testimony, expressing the view that Kris was innocent, and had given a taped statement that Eddie Dames was a drug dealer. As part of our cost-cutting system, Ellis' statement had been filmed for free by a Channel 4 cameraman, with an agreement that in return it could be shown on television. This was hardly an ideal way to go about an investigation, but we had few options.

Judge Bagley would not give us the funds to go and take a sworn deposition from Ellis in the Bahamas. We suggested simply admitting the videotape. He said the cameraman who shot it had to testify to its authenticity. We suggested a telephone call to the man in Britain. He said that was not good enough. We told him that we needed funds to fly him over. He said there was no money. So he excluded the tape, and refused to consider a statement from a man who had testified against Kris at trial, yet who now said that Kris had been framed.

The state lawyers were intent solely on winning, without regard to what might be fair – no doubt because they believed that Kris was guilty, or certainly could not bring themselves to consider his innocence. Sally Weintraub was the lead prosecutor for the hearing, since the original trial lawyers (Ridge and Kastrenakes) were to be witnesses. Local lawyers told me that she had come out of retirement because she missed the excitement of being mean to people in criminal trials. I thought they were probably being unkind, but it became clear they were merely being descriptive.

We had to prove that Kris had passed a polygraph, and that Neville Butler had in large part failed his. Weintraub initially insisted on contesting this. She could simply have agreed that the experts' reports said what they said, nothing more. Instead we had to pay for polygraphers George Slattery and Dudley Dickson to come to court. The moment she knew that they were on their way – and we had already shelled out a $1,000 for travel – she backed off and agreed to admit their reports as evidence.[5]

And so it went on. For a week. It was unpleasant at the start; it got uglier.

We had had no funds to do a crime-scene reconstruction that would have shown how Neville Butler's version of events was inconsistent with the physical facts. Ron Petrillo, Hendon's investigator, believed Kris was innocent. He had agreed to testify to his review of the scene, giving his own opinion based on years of experience, without charging us anything. Judge Bagley excluded his testimony altogether. Laura Snook was the forensic accountant who had voluntarily evaluated the documents in the Moo Youngs' briefcase and would have testified that they were laundering drug money all around the bowl of the Caribbean. Judge Bagley refused to hear her testimony unless we paid to fly her over from London. And he would not allow George Bell, one of the alibi witnesses, to testify at all, even though he was present in court.

The hearing was frustrating and deeply flawed. Nevertheless I agreed with my co-counsel Ben Kuehne that there was plenty of evidence to enable Judge Bagley to throw out Kris' convictions. Kris had watched the week's testimony and was even more optimistic. He now knew that he really would be home by Christmas 1997. I did not disabuse him, but was not sanguine that Bagley would do the right thing. By 1997 I had been doing death-penalty work for thirteen years, and an elected state trial judge had *never* granted a new trial to one of my clients challenging a death sentence – in dozens of cases, no matter what the evidence.

Judge Bagley issued his opinion several weeks later – in time for Christmas, but Kris was not going to be spending it at home. My first reaction was that it was very badly typed. I realised my criticism was petty when it came to the content. There was one bright spot: he had thrown out the death sentence, since the order sentencing Kris to death had been written by the prosecutor rather than the judge. But that was of little solace to Kris or, by now, to me. To an innocent person it makes little difference if he dies in prison at the time the State of Florida decrees, or if he has to spend many more years there before dying of natural causes.

As for the overwhelming evidence that cast the case into doubt, Bagley glossed over the facts, or dismissed them out of hand. Of the hundreds of pages of incriminating documents in the Moo Young briefcase, he wrote that Kris was the one at fault: he was 'procedurally barred' from complaining. His lawyer, Eric Hendon, had known about the briefcase prior to the trial and had not chased it up. This was absurd. Neither Kris nor his lawyer had any reason to suspect that the briefcase was a goldmine of information, because they knew only of its existence, not what was in it. Ron Petrillo, the investigator, had actually asked to see it, but Detective Buhrmaster had replied that it had been returned to the family. From this, Petrillo concluded that it was not relevant. Buhrmaster never told anyone he had retrieved it; I had happened upon its contents years later.

The conviction was safe, Judge Bagley concluded. Kris should have a new trial, limited solely to punishment – whether he should be executed, or held in prison until after his hundredth birthday.

I was crushed by the decision. Somehow, Kris brushed himself off, announced that we would win next time and demanded that we move forward. So it was off on appeal again – another exercise in futility that would take three more years. Kris continued to sit on Death Row, even though he was no longer under a death sentence. Ten more men died in Florida's execution chamber as we waited for the court to rule.

In the brief to the Florida Supreme Court I led off with the issue of Judge Gross' arrest. I thought this would set the tone. Surely the judges would be ashamed of a judge who had been hauled off in shackles on the third day of the trial and, even if they could not bring themselves to impugn the judiciary by writing something scathing about 'Howie the Mouse' himself, it would provoke them to find another reason to reverse the case.

I was wrong. The appeal decision made my blood boil.[6] Judge Bagley's decision was summarily affirmed. 'These murders,' the unanimous court repeated, with the certainty of the zealot, 'occurred as a result of an ongoing dispute between Derrick Moo Young and Krishna Maharaj.'[7] There was no pause for consideration. No moment of doubt.

We had claimed that the hearing before Judge Bagley had been inadequate because we had no funds to investigate or call the vast majority of our witnesses. The Florida Supreme Court made no mention of the fact that they had ordered the hearing to take place within three months. Kris had waited a year, constantly asking for money to pay for the expenses. The court blamed Ben Kuehne and me, suggesting that we were somehow trying to sandbag Judge Bagley. The issue was barred, the court said. 'Postconviction counsel, for strategic or other reasons, chose to proceed without the funds being available. Had Maharaj's attorneys chosen to [put off] his hearing until October and funds had not been forthcoming, he would have a better argument before this Court on this issue.'[8]

This was hard to take. What possible strategic reason could we have had, except that Kris wanted Judge Bagley finally to hold a hearing after waiting four times the period originally allowed by the Supreme Court? As everyone knew, there were no more funds in October than there had been in September – the entire budget for 1997 had long since been exhausted.

If that was disingenuous, then the court's treatment of Judge Gross' arrest was its equal. Here, we were told, Kris had failed to prove that Gross had actually solicited a bribe from him. 'Maharaj has not demonstrated that Judge Gross was in fact involved in a bribery solicitation in this case,' the justices wrote. 'We cannot base our conclusions on such a serious matter on the fact that the judge was involved in bribery in some other matter.'[9]

What more could we have done? Kris had complained about the bribery attempt to his lawyer, before Gross' cankerous character became public. Hendon passed the complaint to the prosecutors, who saw no reason to act. Hendon testified that Gross' rulings became hostile after Kris spurned the solicitation. Gross actually referred to Kris' case in the monitored telephone conversation with his bagman, made on the morning of his arrest. Short of Gross volunteering his criminality, what more could we have proven? Meanwhile the court failed to mention that we had asked for the state to make disclosures: the Florida Department of Law Enforcement had been investigating Gross, and presumably had plenty of evidence that might support our case, but refused to turn it over.

The justices repeated their mantra – the issue was procedurally barred, because Kris 'waived' it by agreeing to go forward with the trial, before a new judge.[10] Yet Kris had relied on Hendon's advice, and Hendon had admitted that he never even put two and two together at the time. Only later did he link Gross' arrest with Kris' earlier report of the attempted bribe. Regardless, surely there was also a societal interest in refusing to allow a trial to go forward when the judge had just been taken away in chains?[11]

And what of a simple claim that Kris was innocent? Surely the courts would hear that? The answer to this was not just *No*, but *Never*.

At this point the State of Florida had to resentence Kris, which would involve a complete trial before a new jury. Both sides had a choice to make: before any resentencing proceeding, Kris wanted to continue with the challenge to his conviction, taking his case to the federal court. I agreed with him: I remained convinced that a court where the judges were not elected would toss out the guilty verdict, so it was pointless having another trial on the sentence if that was founded on the quicksand of a flawed conviction.

At the same time the prosecution could simply elect to forgo a new penalty trial – the result being that Kris would be given another life sentence, and would be ineligible for parole until after his hundredth birthday. Ben and I told the prosecutor – Sally Weintraub again – that to go back to another jury on sentence was a waste of everyone's time. The original death sentence had been imposed by the slimmest of margins, a seven-to-five jury vote. Now a great deal of new evidence had come to light and this, combined with a much better-prepared defence, would make it very unlikely that Kris would be sent back to Death Row.

But Weintraub was insistent: the state wanted to sentence Kris to death again, and they wanted to do it now.[12] So in 2002 we moved on to the next farcical procedure in front of Judge Bagley.

In the real world, any doubt surrounding the defendant's guilt is perhaps the most important factor that impels a jury to vote against the death penalty. One might expect this to be particularly true in Florida, where there have been many highly publicised exonerations of those formerly on Death Row – indeed, the state leads the league table when it comes to miscarriages of justice.[13] A study of Florida juries reveals that lingering doubt is the factor that recurs most often when jurors explain their life recommendation:[14] 69 per cent of the jurors interviewed after capital trials said they still had some doubt about the guilt of the accused, and this was their main reason for recommending life.

Like any sane person, then, Florida jurors worry about condemning a person to die who may be innocent.

Judge Bagley, on the other hand, told Ben Kuehne and me that it was illegal for us to suggest to the jury in any way that Kris might not be guilty. This is Florida law: if you have been found guilty, then you are guilty. Evidence challenging this is just not admissible.[15] Indeed, evidence that someone else committed the crime would, we were told, be 'misleading' and might 'confuse the jury'.[16]

The idea that a juror should not be permitted to consider the prisoner's innocence when deciding whether he should die invites every hackneyed expression of incredulity, from 'Kafkaesque' to '*Alice in Wonderland*'. In a resentencing trial such as Kris', the argument for allowing evidence of innocence is even stronger. Kris had been convicted in 1987 – his original jury heard the evidence as to guilt, and the five jurors who voted for life were clearly able to take into consideration any reservations they might have had. Now he was to face a second jury more than fourteen years later, when a vast amount of new evidence had come to light, casting far more doubt on his culpability. To proceed as if nothing had changed was a fraud on the jury.

But Judge Bagley was emphatic: Florida law was Florida law. That did not mean we had to accept it without a challenge. So we set about forcing Judge Bagley to face the logic of his ruling in every way we could imagine. We filed a *Notice Of Intent To Prove Mr Maharaj Innocent Of These Charges, Or To Allow The Jury To Hear The Evidence That It Considers The Most Significant In This Capital Case Where Life Is At Stake*. In addition to arguing that the Florida rule was plain silly, we pointed out that one of the listed mitigating factors under Florida law was that the accused had no significant prior history of criminal activity.[17] Here, because Kris was innocent, we should be allowed to show that he had no criminal history at all. Judge Bagley ruled that this was improper.

Another listed mitigating factor was that the victim was partially to blame for his own death.[18] We asked for permission to prove that the Moo Youngs were actually killed in a Colombian hit, because they were skimming 1 per cent off the cartel's money. Judge Bagley excluded the evidence.

We offered to prove another mitigating factor – that Kris would not be a future danger[19] – because he had never been a danger in the past. We wanted to prove the mitigating circumstance of Kris' good character,[20] by showing that he had never committed a crime at all. We lined up an expert who was prepared to testify that Kris suffered from a serious mental problem: clearly a mitigating circumstance under Florida and federal law.[21] Kris was, the expert said, suffering from Post-Traumatic Stress Disorder (PTSD). The cause? Suffering for many years on Death Row for a crime he did not commit. Judge Bagley, increasingly irritated, shook his head vigorously at all this.

We filed a modestly styled *Notice that Mr Maharaj intends to testify to his Innocence*. Bagley said that he could not.

Eventually Bagley got impatient, and told Ben Kuehne and me that if the word 'innocent' came out of our lips once during the trial, we would be held in contempt. Neville Butler testified for the state. I was not allowed to cross-examine him about how his story was a lie, let alone go into the fact that he had failed a polygraph on some of the very details he was again telling a jury.

We were reduced to presenting a case for mercy that focused solely on Kris as a person, which was compelling in itself. Four Death Row guards voluntarily testified for him, risking the opprobrium of their employers, who did not think they should take the side of a condemned prisoner. They all believed in the death penalty, and none had ever been moved to testify for a Death Row prisoner before.

'If'n all the prisoners were like Kris Maharaj,' testified one gruffly, 'we wouldn't need all of us guards.'

'The only danger I see in setting him free,' said another, 'is the culture shock ... he's been locked away so long.'

All of them, after being around Kris and studying his character for years, thought he was probably innocent, but even though this was a large part of their reason for testifying, they were not allowed to say so.

Various of Kris' friends testified by satellite from London. I had warned each person that we were banned from suggesting that Kris did not commit the crime. Peter Bottomley MP was outraged by this and nearly got me thrown in jail.

'Why are you testifying for Mr Maharaj?' I asked him, expecting a testament to Kris' good character.

'Because his case is a miscarriage of justice!' Peter responded vigorously.

Judge Bagley started in his chair, and sent the jury from the room, before giving Peter a lecture about what he could not say. He assured me that I would be facing jail myself if any other witness made a similar comment.

The zeal with which prosecutor Sally Weintraub argued for Kris' execution should not have surprised me, but as far as I was concerned, it was one of the most bizarre capital trials I have ever defended. Little of the normal pressure was there. It didn't seem to matter what the jurors decided to do, because Kris might be strategically better off with another death sentence. He was already sixty-three years old and in bad health. The courts have a strange sense that a Death Row prisoner who later receives a life sentence has already used up his stock of good fortune – glossing over the notion that he might be innocent. When DNA cast doubts about the guilt of Earl Washington, a mentally disabled prisoner on Death Row in Virginia, the governor commuted his sentence to life without parole.[22]

But it was impossible for Marita to take such a view, after all her nightmares about her husband's execution over many years, waking in the night with visions of flames licking around his head.

The courts look more closely at a case that involves the death penalty, and back in Britain it would be easier to get people interested in Kris' plight if he were awaiting execution, rather than 'merely' serving another three or four decades in prison. Unless we could get his conviction reversed, one thing was already certain: Kris would die in the Florida state prison system, either at the hands of the executioner, or when his battered body could take no more of the abuse that prison life was handing out.

A death sentence, we agreed, would be no big deal.[23]

When the closing arguments were over, as the jury listened to Judge Bagley intone the interminable and incomprehensible instructions of law, I watched them, with an arm over Kris' shoulder. I did not feel there was much chance they would come back against us. It all seemed rather anticlimactic. It was difficult to believe that anyone could take seriously the idea of sentencing Kris to death when he didn't do the crime, even though the jury had not heard any of our evidence about his innocence.

The tension began to rise later, though. I had thought optimistically that it would be a simple matter for them to go back to the jury room, check with one another and come back with a verdict of life. Not so. After a while they said they wanted to quit for the night and start deliberations again in the morning. They had to go to a motel, and Ben Kuehne joked that perhaps they wanted one free dinner on the county's expense for all they had been forced to endure.

It was going to be a difficult evening for Marita, home alone waiting to hear if her husband would go back to Death Row. It was going to be a lonely evening for Kris in his cell, waiting to hear if another group of jurors would decide he was not fit to breathe the same air as them. I went out to the county jail to see him. The guards had got to like him too, and they treated me well on my visits. Kris and I talked about the challenge to his conviction, with him putting on a brave face about the twelve jurors, now probably back in their motel rooms looking at their Gideon Bibles, contemplating what they should do in the morning.

After an unsettled night, everyone reassembled in the courtroom to do some more waiting. There was a clock on the wood-panelled wall. It slowed time down. I had my laptop and tried to do some work on another urgent case, in between telling Marita periodically that everything was going to be fine.

But nothing ever prepares you for that knock on the door, when the jury slips a note out to the judge announcing that they have a verdict.

They filed into the courtroom. The foreperson handed a piece of paper to the bailiff. He studiously did not look at it, walking ponderously up to the bench to hand it to Judge Bagley. The judge glanced at it, his face giving nothing away, before he handed it to the court clerk.

'Please publish the jury's recommendation as to punishment,' he said.

They were eleven-to-one for life. The tension suddenly gone, I was unreasonably angry at the one juror who had voted to kill Kris.

15

The Appeal Court

The State of Florida could do no more to Kris Maharaj. From their perspective, Kris had a totally valid life sentence and would die behind bars unless, by some miracle, he lived into his eleventh decade. We now went to the federal court. Here at least they would not be elected, but appointed for life.

We filed in the federal district court on July 26th, 2002, as soon as possible after the jury at Kris' resentencing trial came back with life.[1] By now, Kris had served almost sixteen years in prison. The state then took ten months to file a brief that could have been written overnight, essentially regurgitating everything they had said in the state court: ten long months during which Kris sat in a prison cell, with Marita coming to see him for three hours every fortnight. We responded to the prosecution within days with 103 more pages – twice the length of their pleading – to show how very wrong they were.

Federal District Judge Paul C. Huck had the power to right everything that had gone wrong. He assigned the case to a magistrate, William C. Turnoff, for a preliminary review. A year and a half after we first filed, on February 23rd, 2004, Turnoff issued an order denying all of Kris' claims. He refused us funds for investigation. He wouldn't let us test the unmatched fingerprints that had been found in Room 1215, any of which might point to the real killer. He wouldn't let us summon any of the witnesses whom we had not been allowed to call in state court.

It was depressing, but there was still hope. Judge Huck could reject the magistrate's report. Indeed, we had a telephone conference with the judge on June 23rd, and it seemed that someone – probably his clerk – was going through the record quite carefully. I still hoped for a proper hearing at which we could present Kris' evidence. Six months after the preliminary review, on August 30th, 2004, Judge Huck issued his order. The first question he addressed was whether he should allow funds for us to conduct the investigation in several countries that we had previously been unable to visit. The state court's refusal to provide Kris with any funds to present his defence was 'unfortunate', Judge Huck thought, but he was not going to exercise his discretion in Kris' favour.[2] Indeed, he wrote that he might have been inclined to allow funds if Kris still had a death sentence, but with the case no longer being capital, he felt he had no right to intervene.[3]

As I had feared, Kris would have been better off on Death Row.

Judge Huck recognised that he could still order an evidentiary hearing, allowing us to present the witnesses who had been excluded from the state court hearing. He accepted that Ben Kuehne and I, working voluntarily as Kris' lawyers for a decade, had 'diligently' tried to secure the witnesses we needed, without any funding. But, just when I thought he was coming to the sensible conclusion, he stood logic on its head. Based on the case of *Murray v. Giarratano*, he concluded that there is no 'right to adequate funding in state post-conviction proceedings'.[4] Because the lack of funding meant that Kris could not show whether the witnesses would actually say what we promised, Kris could not have a hearing.[5] That was some catch, that Catch-22.

Lawyers like to set themselves apart from the rest of the world, sometimes perhaps to justify their fees. They do this in various ways. The most fraudulent is to hang a certificate on the wall to reassure clients that they are members of the bar of the United States Supreme Court. This impressive credential implies membership in a most exclusive club. I have such a document stashed away somewhere, and it cost me $130. I did not even have to go to Washington to get it. A second stratagem is to hurl around phrases in Latin or some other incomprehensible dead language that others won't understand – hence a series of phrases that could perfectly well be said in English – from *respondeat superior, voir dire* and *non compos mentis,* all the way to *de minimis non curat lex* (which I had begun to think should, in the context of Kris' case, be amended to *de maximus non curat lex* – 'don't bother the law with any serious thing').

However, the final frontier in our legal apartheid is the use of case names as shorthand for broad principles. They mean nothing at all to the rest of the world, and yet they allow lawyers to speak in a code worthy of Da Vinci. Thus, we have *Murray v. Giarratano.*[6] Permit me to translate. The case arose when Joseph Giarratano, on Death Row in Virginia, submitted a radical proposition to the courts there, that he should be allowed legal aid to help him with his capital appeals.[7] But the Supreme Court ruled against him: a prisoner on Death Row – whether adult or juvenile,[8] scholar or mentally disabled, sane or insane – had no constitutional right to the assistance of a state-funded lawyer to help him with a couple of decades' appeals in the most complicated field of law imaginable.[9]

The Supreme Court felt it was justified in this fantastical rule because no prisoner would actually be left to die without a lawyer stepping in and offering to work for free, as Ben and I had agreed to act for Kris.[10] This was the Big Society run riot: the government was in the business of killing people, but felt it could depend on some do-gooder lawyer volunteering time to provide a basic defence to the condemned prisoner. As ever, those designing such a happy social order apparently did not live in the real world.

As I read Judge Huck's decision concerning Kris' appeal, I fell into a deeper depression. I knew which way he was going to go on our evidence that Kris was not guilty of the murders of Derrick and Duane Moo Young.

'Although [Mr Maharaj] vigorously resists clear legal precedent,' the judge wrote, 'claims of actual innocence based on newly discovered evidence have never been held to state a ground for federal habeas corpus relief …'[11] In other words, Judge Huck agreed that Kris' proof of innocence was simply not an issue under the federal constitution. The reason for this apparently unassailable rule, he went on to explain, is that 'federal habeas courts sit to ensure that individuals are not imprisoned in violation of the Constitution – not to correct errors of fact'.[12] Kris' innocence was an error of fact, not a technical legal matter, and thus beyond the purview of the federal court.

Judge Bagley had threatened to throw Ben and me in jail if we mentioned the word 'innocent' to the jury who resentenced Kris. That was bad enough. But to comprehend how Judge Huck could rule that proof of a prisoner's innocence was not a reason to set him free, we need to understand the shameful hidden meaning behind another case name: *Herrera v. Collins*.[13] Lionel Herrera had been convicted of the murder of two policemen in the Rio Grande Valley, in Texas, but four witnesses came forward with proof that his brother Raul had actually committed the crime. His lawyers argued that, because he was probably innocent, he should not be executed. This left the majority of the Supreme Court unmoved.

'This proposition has an elemental appeal,' opined Chief Justice William Rehnquist piously. 'After all, the central purpose of any system of criminal justice is to convict the guilty and free the innocent. But the evidence upon which petitioner's claim of innocence rests was not produced at his trial, but rather eight years later. In any system of criminal justice, "innocence" or "guilt" must be determined in some sort of a judicial proceeding.'[14]

Rehnquist acknowledged that Herrera was prohibited from bringing his claim of innocence in the Texas courts by an arcane rule that required the prisoner to present evidence of innocence within thirty days of conviction, or be forever barred.[15] This may seem extraordinary, but similar rules apply in forty-one of the fifty states.[16] You might be a teenager when you are convicted, but you still have to spend the rest of your life in prison (or even be executed), no matter what proof of innocence you finally assemble.

Why, Rehnquist queried, should the federal courts take a step that the state courts refuse? 'Claims of actual innocence based on newly discovered evidence have never been held to state a ground for federal habeas relief,' wrote Chief Justice Rehnquist.[17] You might get your case reversed on any number of technical legal grounds then, but not on the question of whether you actually committed the crime.

Herrera's lawyers retreated a step: how about agreeing that the Constitution bars the execution of an innocent person? At a minimum, they suggested, the prisoner should not be killed. At least then he might find someone to listen to his proof of innocence at a later date.

'Petitioner urges not that he necessarily receive a new trial, but that his death sentence simply be vacated if a federal habeas court deems that a satisfactory showing of "actual innocence" has been made,' Rehnquist went on. 'But such a result is scarcely logical ... It would be a rather strange jurisprudence ... which held that under our Constitution he could not be executed, but that he could spend the rest of his life in prison.'[18]

A minority of three justices, out of nine, disagreed. They felt that a conviction should be overturned if the prisoner could show that he was 'probably' innocent. But their argument carried no weight with the Chief Justice and the other members of the court. 'The dissent fails to articulate the relief that would be available if petitioner were to meet its "probable innocence" standard,' wrote Rehnquist. 'Would it be commutation of petitioner's death sentence, [a] new trial, or unconditional release from imprisonment?'[19] Surely to ask the question is to answer it: if someone is 'probably' innocent, then no sensible person could find him guilty beyond a reasonable doubt, and he would have to be released.

Common sense is, unfortunately, not terribly common in some of the opinions of the United States Supreme Court. There has never been a case, either before *Herrera* or since, when the court has accepted that the 'mere' fact that a prisoner is innocent should be a constitutional basis for ordering his release.

Over the years I have been charged with contempt of court on more than one occasion. While I have always been acquitted, it is sometimes difficult not to have disdain for judges who come up with this kind of nonsense, whether they are the Supreme Court justices who lay down the precedent or the lower-court judges who fail to resist it. Yet for all the folly of denying Joe Giarratano the right to counsel, or the refusal to pay attention to Lionel Herrera's evidence of innocence, at least these are human issues that can inspire anger, action and, ultimately, perhaps reform. *Giarratano* is still the law, but gradually the states are providing more resources for those appealing a sentence of death. While the Supreme Court still applies the rule of *Herrera*, it has been disparaged by commentators, and one day good sense will surely prevail.

These issues are sufficiently comprehensible to provoke a public debate. But there are far more insidious rules in the law that are so convoluted that they lead to no headlines. Indeed, there are very few among the 1,227 people executed in the US since Kris Maharaj went to prison[20] who did not fall victim to procedural rules that were better suited to the medieval law courts of Henry IV than to the twenty-first century.

The American legal system uses various pretexts to prevent judges from considering the 'merits' of any claim – in other words, the judge is not even allowed to decide whether an error requires a new trial, but rather must rule that the prisoner failed to present it properly, so any mistakes should be ignored altogether. One is the perceived need for the 'finality' of judgements. Endless appeals, we are told, prevent the government from obtaining its pound of flesh and diminish the citizen's regard for the legal system. Yet presumably the state should only be allowed to impose punishment if the punishment is just.

A second excuse is highly political, and is dressed up in a dubious characterisation of the relationship between the federal government and the states. We are told that the federal courts must respect a state court judgement. But why defer to a judgement if it is wrong?

In denying Kris Maharaj a new trial, Judge Huck applied a number of procedural twists and turns from this armoury. One was the doctrine of 'procedural bar'. The British Government had intervened in the case, belatedly – because Florida failed to notify them that a British citizen had been arrested. Had the British known from the start, the local consulate would have ensured that Kris had competent assistance; he might never have been convicted. But Judge Huck ruled that Kris was 'procedurally barred' from arguing the point because his trial lawyer did not raise it.[21]

Unless you are a member of the legal profession, and enjoy debating the number of angels who may dance on the head of a pin, it is difficult to comprehend how Kris could have 'waived' his right to be told that the consul could help him: the very purpose of the consular notification rule is to tell a foreign prisoner of this right. Obviously Kris did not know about it; if he did, there would be no need to tell him. Once informed, a primary task of the consul would be to ensure that Kris had an adequate lawyer; one proof that Eric Hendon was not up to trying a capital case is that he did not tell Kris he had the right to consular assistance, and therefore 'waived' it. This is an example of the cat chasing its tail round and round and round. It does not contribute to the reliability of the verdict; it merely cuts the prisoner off from justice.

Procedural bar was just one of the 'doctrines' that led Judge Huck to ignore the merit in Kris' case. Throughout the Eighties, the death penalty became increasingly politicised; indeed, crime itself became a political football on both sides of the Atlantic. There were many valid criticisms of the system, from the sluggish way in which justice was served up, to the mistakes that steadily came to light. However, there is no meaningful 'criminal constituency' – no vocal group of the electorate demanding respect for the rights of convicts. In contrast, the volume of those representing the victims of crime has been increasingly loud, so efforts to redress the systemic flaws are one-sided.

Professor Jim Liebman's study of all 4,578 capital cases between 1973 and 1995 found that serious error, undermining the reliability of the case and resulting in a new trial, occurred in two thirds of cases.[22] He identified two major structural flaws in the process: the systemic mistakes that infected trials,[23] and the length of time (an average of ten years) that it took to identify those mistakes. If politicians were to accept Liebman's analysis, then they would look for a cure both for the sloth of the system and for the grotesque error rate (with a fifty: fifty coin toss, the process would be more likely to reach a reliable verdict). As the Liebman study documents, 'judicial review takes so long precisely *because* American capital sentences are so persistently and systematically fraught with error that seriously undermines their reliability'.[24] But rather than addressing both ills, the politicians tried to cure only one: they sought to speed up the process with the 1996 Anti-Terrorist and Effective Death Penalty Act. The only effect of this legislation was to reach the *wrong* conclusion faster, because it made no effort to address the root causes of the errors.

Nowhere does the Effective Death Penalty Act seek to redress how a trial court might make a mistake. The Act does not make innocence a federal issue, or mandate that particular procedures should be used to assess the reliability of eyewitnesses or informants. Instead, the Act imposes harsh deadlines, where the prisoner has to bring his case before the federal courts within a one-year deadline or forever lose his right to habeas review.[25] And the federal courts of appeal and the US Supreme Court have since been falling over each other to enforce the rules with rigour – to the point that Death Row prisoners are deemed to have 'waived' their entire right to seek a remedy in the federal court simply because their lawyer was a day late filing their appeal.[26]

Judge Huck applied the Effective Death Penalty Act against Kris Maharaj: the question before him was no longer, he wrote, whether the state courts were wrong in interpreting the law. Rather, it was whether they were *unreasonably* wrong.[27] What does this mean? They could be wrong, but not awfully, awfully wrong? They could make a mistake, but the result would be good enough for government work – adequate to send someone to prison for ever, or to the chamber?

The Florida Supreme Court had opined that Eric Hendon knew that the prosecution's star 'eyewitness', Neville Butler, had failed a polygraph at the time of trial; Judge Huck accepted that we had presented plenty of evidence to show this was wrong, and that Hendon only came to learn that Butler failed the test years later, when I told him. However, Huck thought that the state court was not 'unreasonable' in its wrongness.[28] Quite what this means is difficult to divine: the state was either right, or it was wrong. If it was wrong, then Kris did not get a fair trial.

Likewise, everyone agreed that Butler had originally told a false story, but Butler insisted to the jury half a dozen times that he came forward of his own accord to change his testimony. This obviously made him look good. Judge Huck believed, to the contrary, that Butler had changed his testimony because he had been threatened with the negative results of his polygraph.[29] Logically this meant that Butler had perjured himself at least six times. But while Huck thought the Florida courts were wrong to hold otherwise, he thought them not 'unreasonably wrong'.

It went on and on. The state court had blamed the defence for not uncovering the briefcase, notwithstanding the fact that the defence did not know what was inside it, and that Detective Buhrmaster had explicitly told the defence investigator that he no longer had it. Again, the state decision might be wrong, but it was not 'unreasonable'.[30] Any notion that Adam Hosein or Jaime Vallejo Mejia was involved in the case was no more than 'speculative',[31] and while the state courts probably should have allowed us the money to prove Kris' case, this was not sufficiently wrong to result in a new, fair hearing.

It is a serious charge to accuse the nine US Supreme Court justices of maintaining a legal system that achieves a goal that is quite different from its stated purpose: to ensure the safety of society by imprisoning only those who should be imprisoned. But the way in which the system induced the error in Kris Maharaj's case must be understood, if we are to remedy it and reform the process.

First, we must look at who becomes a Supreme Court justice. The candidates are drawn from a very shallow, privileged pool, where nobody experiences the storms that beset the everyday life of many citizens. What is more, none of the current crop of justices in the US Supreme Court has spent time defending criminal cases, so they have never experienced the impact of the laws they interpret from the other side of the bench. There is a clear set of criteria that must be met for the applicant who wants to be a justice, so that anyone with even marginally 'radical' views need not apply. The Senate confirmation hearings provide a stringent vetting procedure, where those nominated for the job promise under oath that they will respect the prevailing interpretation of the law, and will only diligently refer to the will of the elected legislature in applying statutes passed by Congress. This process is designed to place justices in a straitjacket, where they essentially reflect the populist 'tough on crime' views of politicians. While this is powerfully enforced in the US, the philosophy is stronger still in Britain, where the notion of parliamentary supremacy is so imbued in judges that few contemplate the possibility that they might strike down laws as contravening fundamental rights.[32]

Even the justices chosen by recent Democratic presidents closely fit the mould, differing only in minor degree, just as Democrats themselves vary only slightly from Republicans. Distance is a matter of perspective. President Barack Obama doubtless believes himself far to the left of George W. Bush and, from where he sits, he doubtless is. From the vantage point of a European, though, he is very closely aligned, as are all Democrats. Twenty years ago, purely for my own entertainment, I did a rather unscientific review of the voting patterns of Margaret Thatcher as contrasted to Teddy Kennedy, on the principle that she was vocally on the right wing of the Conservative Party in Britain, and he was then deemed to be the most liberal member of the Senate. Kennedy's votes were consistently less moderate than Thatcher's.[33] This reflected a fact that is generally missed by British people: for the most part, American politics begins at the right wing of the Tory Party, and moves to the right. Indeed, with limited exceptions,[34] American political discourse is all to the right of *all* European debate.[35]

Most nominees to the US Supreme Court adhere closely to the established line. Like the police, most have also entered into a 'training programme' that reinforces this line. This means that they generally come from privileged backgrounds and go to top law schools (there are 200 accredited law schools in the US, yet the nine current justices attended just three between them – Harvard, Yale and Stanford); they clerk for other judges who teach them how it *has* to be done; they work for the government and then are appointed to lower courts where their many judgements provide plenty of material for public scrutiny – fearing the consequences of this, they don't take risks.[36] In a phrase: if they are not predisposed to walk in the footsteps of their predecessors, the shoehorn of their experience soon squeezes them in.

Once there, the doctrine *stare decisis* keeps them there – it means literally that judges should 'leave standing that which has been decided'.[37] This chains a judge to a past decision for the simple fact that the decision was made, rather than because it was correct. Thus, for example, there is currently no justice who has publicly stated that the death penalty might be unconstitutional, because thirty-six years ago a narrow majority thought it legal.[38]

Shackled in this way, the best that the so-called liberal wing of the Supreme Court can offer as its 'radical' work has been finally to suggest, in 2003, that gay people should not be imprisoned for consensual sexual acts in the privacy of their bedrooms.[39] This is the furthest that the liberals creep from the past. *Stare decisis* recently found its ultimate expression in the opinion of Justice John Paul Stevens, who decided at the end of his long tenure that the death penalty was – under all circumstances – a cruel and unusual punishment and therefore a violation of the US Constitution. Yet, notwithstanding his conclusion that capital punishment involved the 'pointless and needless extinction of life', he still determined that the particular method of execution in the case before him (lethal injection) met the requirements of earlier Supreme Court decisions.[40]

So that was that. Perhaps we should not have been surprised when we lost Kris' case in federal court. Judge Huck followed the lead of the Supreme Court and dismissed most of Kris' petition without even discussing its merits. My hands compulsively crumpled the legal opinion.[41] On October 2nd, 2006, Kris' appeal to the American judiciary effectively came to an end. He had spent two weeks short of twenty years in prison for a crime he almost certainly did not commit.

In the case of Lionel Herrera, Chief Justice Rehnquist had justified the refusal to admit new evidence of innocence in part because there was the option of a pardon, if the courts got it wrong. This would be the valve that would correct any mistakes made by the courts.[42] In the case of Herrera, the prosecution moved quickly to prove Rehnquist naïve. The Texas Pardons Board did not recommend clemency for Herrera, which meant that the governor therefore could not grant it, even had he been inclined to.[43] Texas executed Herrera on May 12th, 1993, just four months after the Supreme Court ruling. He refused the ritual of a final meal, but did take the opportunity to make a final statement shortly before his execution.

'I am innocent, innocent, innocent,' he said. 'Make no mistake about this; I owe society nothing. Continue the struggle for human rights, helping those who are innocent, especially Mr Graham. I am an innocent man, and something very wrong is taking place tonight. May God bless you all. I am ready.'[44]

In mentioning 'Mr Graham', Lionel Herrera was referring to Gary Graham, another young man on Texas' Death Row with a strong claim of innocence. Graham had been just eighteen at the time of the crime alleged against him, and had doubled his age on Death Row. But they got him all the same, and he was put to death on June 22nd, 2000. 'This is nothing more than pure and simple murder,' he said. 'This is what is happening tonight in America. Nothing more than state-sanctioned murder, state-sanctioned lynching, right here in America, and right here tonight.'[45]

For Kris, once we had lost in every court in the land, the only place to turn was the Governor of Florida in a quest for executive clemency. It was not a game where I would want to bet much money, yet there was no other table at which we could gamble. Years before, we might have had a chance. Between 1924 and 1966 nearly a quarter of those on Florida's Death Row received some form of mercy from the governor – either having their death sentences overturned or their convictions thrown out.[46] By the time Kris needed compassion, there had been three decades of intense politicisation: Florida had issued no positive clemency decision to a Death Row prisoner in twenty-seven years.[47] While statistics do not tell the whole story, there is no number so emphatic as zero.

The Republican former State Attorney General, Charlie Crist, was now Florida's governor. He was the very man who had been prosecuting the appeals against Kris for four years, opposing Kris' request for a new trial. Even so, as the date approached in June 2008, we had cause for some optimism. Our pro bono allies in London, the law firm Freshfields Bruckhaus Deringer, had been working the political side as effectively as anyone possibly could. Freshfields partner Paul Lomas and his colleague Clarissa O'Callaghan were flying to Tallahassee to put Kris' case to the Clemency Board.

I got a call from Kris' wife Marita. She sounded very excited.

The British Consul had been to see Kris the day before and had told him to get ready to leave prison before the end of the week. The plane, she said, should be flying out of Miami. The consul had assured Kris that he had a valid passport ready to go. I was sceptical, but I got caught up in Marita's enthusiasm; she seemed very certain. She had begun to make arrangements to put her few remaining possessions in storage, so that she could catch the flight back to Britain at Kris' side.

It was wonderful news. It had to mean that the string-pulling by the British Government had finally paid off. I passed Marita's message along to the other members of the legal team and it buoyed Paul and Clarissa as they headed to the US to make their pitch. When Tim Samuels, with the BBC, called me to ask whether it was true, I called Marita back and begged her to be more circumspect. If it came out in the media that a decision had been made to grant clemency before the hearing was complete, no matter how much influence the British Government had, the deal would be squashed. It was paradoxical to think that, twenty-one years after the prosecutors wrote the judge's order sentencing Kris to death before the hearing began, perhaps someone had written the final order ending Kris' nightmare before the clemency hearing had even started. Such symmetry would be perverse, yet appropriate.

The time difference meant that much of the day in England had passed before we knew the result of the hearing. I was busy, caught up on another case, and had almost managed to stop worrying when the email came through.

'Denied,' wrote Paul.

We later caught up on the phone. Derrick Moo Young's family had turned out in force, and tearfully told the Board how important it was to them that Kris Maharaj should serve the rest of his life in prison. Governor Crist had not even bothered to consult the other members of the Board, but summarily cast his vote against commutation. Crist was, after all, still holding out hope that he might be Senator John McCain's vice-presidential running mate in the November 2008 elections.

Marita's account of what the consul had told Kris came into belated focus. The official must merely have told him that they were prepared – should the miracle occur. Kris had heard what he had so desperately wanted to hear and relayed it, excitedly, to his wife.

16

The Victims

No matter who killed Derrick and Duane Moo Young, there can be no doubt of the impact of the murder on the rest of the family. While the term 'victims of crime' is often used to refer only to people left dead or injured, violent crime may leave an indelible mark on whole families, which is why I will refer to the Moo Young family as victims of the murders committed in Room 1215 of the DuPont Plaza Hotel.

The grief and anger expressed by the victims at the clemency hearing are understandable, especially when you consider what the criminal justice system has put them through. No one should have to lose anyone they love in such sudden and terrifying circumstances, and the family has clearly been attended by pain and despair for each of the twenty-five years that Kris Maharaj has been in prison.

But what has the criminal justice system offered the Moo Young family to support them in their ordeal? First, they were offered a promise of closure via Kris' execution, premised on their cooperation with a system that speaks the language of 'an eye for an eye'. Second, they were told to stand by for closure for years, while the case began its way through the courts. Third, the death sentence was overturned, and the Moo Young family would have to come and ask for the death penalty anew. Fourth, they were told that they would have to make do with Kris dying in prison at some indeterminate date in the future. This was followed by more years of appeals. Finally, they were told that Kris would get out of prison and be returned to the arms of his family – in a way that Derrick and Duane could never return – unless they trekked to Tallahassee to relive their grief all over again in front of the Clemency Board.

If this is what 'victims' rights' get you, all the more reason to pray that your loved ones are never the victims of a violent crime.

But if you are such a victim, is there an alternative? Parents encourage their children to resist the urge to hit back. Religious traditions foster similar values. Most Christians would bless the merciful. The ninety-nine names of Allah include the Exceedingly Merciful, the Exceedingly Compassionate, the Subtly Kind and the Much Forgiving. Nowhere will we find 'Hatred' or 'Vengefulness' in the list of virtues – or prescribed by any god since Thor.

Why, then, has inspiring a victim towards revenge become the primary focus of politicians on both sides of the Atlantic? This relatively recent trend has inverted the legal process, which had been evolving to substitute society as a more consistent arbiter of justice.

A Texas leaflet called 'A Walk Through the System' that I came across in a recent case describes the rights that victims are typically told to expect in our 'modern' era. They have the right to know where the convict is being held. There is a hotline that is operational twenty-four hours a day for them to check on whether he is seeking parole. They can seek assistance in preparing a 'Victim Impact Statement' detailing why a particular punishment should be imposed, or a 'protest letter' if the prisoner is being considered for release. Indeed, they can pre-empt the prisoner's request for freedom: 'As often as you wish,' the leaflet assures the reader, 'you can send protest letters to our office to be included in the inmate's file.'[1] Virtually all of these rights assume that the victims seek revenge, and that their only interest is in keeping the prisoner locked up for as long as possible. Indeed, in a capital case the members of a murder victim's family are given the explicit right to watch the execution.[2]

This interpretation of 'victim's rights' has involved a U-turn. In the 1970s a movement arose for 'restorative justice', which sought to educate the perpetrator to appreciate the impact of the offence and simultaneously begin to repair the damage that he had inflicted by allowing the victim to meet him, and thereby better understand why it happened.[3] But restorative justice was a threat to those who would rather inspire hatred. Politicians – including many elected prosecutors – shoved psychologists and therapists to one side, terrified that an emphasis on healing would deprive them of the opportunity to parlay the politics of fear to their advantage. Those who push for the death penalty, or other harsh punishment, doubtless believe they are helping the victims of crime, but at the same time they are using victims, forcing them into confrontation both with the defendant and with the judicial system, and profoundly damaging their chances of ever recovering from the trauma of bereavement or a terrifying attack.

The Moo Youngs, shattered by the savage murder of both Derrick and Duane, seem to be prime examples of people who have been revictimised by what has become known as 'victimology', where they are promised the false catharsis of revenge. Look at the case from the point of view of the surviving members of the Moo Young family.[4] The family's pain, lasting for a quarter-century and passed down through the generations, is patent in their submissions to the Clemency Board.

'This man murdered my father and brother,' wrote one family member. 'MURDERED. This man used up his one life when he had his sentence reduced from death to life imprisonment. I had hoped prior to that that he would be put to death. For people who have not lived through family members being murdered, they will not be able to comprehend the feelings I have, so be it. This man should have been put to death, as was the original sentence. I want this man murdered for what he has done to my family and I. Clemency should never be granted. What has changed over twenty years? Nothing. This man has never shown any remorse, and I certainly have never been able to find any for him. If he is destined to live out the rest of his life in prison, it will be too long. This man needs to suffer as much as possible until the day he takes his last breath, which will never come soon enough.'[5]

'Every time the phone rings,' wrote another family member, 'or an envelope arrives at my office with the address of the State of Florida Victims' Advocate or State Attorney's Office a cold sweat runs down my entire body as I think, "What else is he claiming?" I implore you to please find it in your hearts to make this hearing today the last of my family's seemingly endless tragedy. Enough is enough. Mr Maharaj has drained our family enough over the … years. He has exhausted enough of our State's resources on pointless, ridiculous appeals.'[6]

Here's what a third wrote: 'Repentance and the admission of guilt and unchangeable exile is the beginning of hope. The least

Mr Maharaj could do is pay with his own life for the lives he has taken.'[7]

The deaths of Derrick and Duane, and their aftermath, have devastated the Moo Young family. One of them described this. 'The psychological effect already pervades and affects our lives. It reveals itself in the way we handle problems in our everyday living and relationships. We have been demoralized, lacking confidence, devoid of trust, and often experience periods of depression, mood swings, and impulsive behaviour as well as angry outbursts of indelible anger, trying as we may to remove the hurt from our hearts. He betrayed our kindness and acceptance of him into our family. This is the man the children once called "Uncle". '[8]

For twenty-five long years a spectre has haunted the Moo Young family of a maniacal Krishna Maharaj, released and hell-bent on his own revenge. The saddest of the statements to the Clemency Board came from one of Derrick Moo Young's grandchildren. 'Although I never met my grandfather,' wrote the child, born at least a decade after the crime, 'his death has not only affected my mother or anyone else who knew him, it has affected me and all my cousins – even the little ones, they will never know their own grandfather. I dread the thought of Mr Maharaj's release, if he may come after me. I often have dreams about my grandfather being murdered, I see the killer's face and feel as if I were to scream, but I know it is just a dream.'[9]

The justice system encouraged the Moo Young family down a particular path; it is not the only one available. I have met scores of family members of murder victims, and some of them have been allowed the space to respond in a way that is very different – one that seems more likely to lead to some degree of peace, even when it is clear that the person in prison is actually guilty of the crime.

Paula Kurland's daughter, Mitzi, was murdered in 1986.[10] In September 1998 Ms Kurland was able to meet Jonathan Nobles, the man who took her daughter's life. She favoured the death penalty, she said, and did not oppose his execution. But she wanted to tell him that she forgave him – largely, she said, because this was the only way to get back her relationship with her other children. Nobles was also able to apologise to her for what he had done.

'It taught me to breathe again,' she said. Nobles died two weeks later. She attended the execution and, before he died, Nobles told her how grateful he was to her. He was singing 'Silent Night' as the executioner started to go about his business.[11]

However, it is the rare exception where offender-victim mediation is permitted in a capital case. The system is structured to make it very difficult for victims to attempt any kind of reconciliation. For example, in Texas (where Nobles died) the process is implemented by the Texas Department of Criminal Justice (TDCJ),[12] the prison system. The TDCJ does not allow violent offenders to begin mediation until after their legal challenges to their conviction and sentence are complete. We are told that it takes four to six months of training in the Victim-Offender Mediation (VOMD) programme before the victim and the offender can expect a first meeting.[13] Yet a condemned prisoner almost always continues with his appeals until the eleventh hour. As a result, it is not normally possible for someone on Death Row to engage in mediation.

This forces victims who want mediation to elbow their way into the process without official aid, as best they can. A small number of those who already know they want reconciliation may know to seek out the small charity called Murder Victims' Families for Reconciliation (MVFR),[14] but most must make it up as they go along.

Take the remarkable case of Rais Bhuiyan.[15] Rais came to the United States from Bangladesh on February 22nd, 1999. He was twenty-five, formerly a pilot with the Bangladesh Air Force. He arrived in New York, saw the Statue of Liberty and was thrilled by the prospect that stretched before him. His plans were flexible, but he hoped to pursue further education and bring his fiancée to the US. They had both applied for a green card. In the meantime Rais had to earn some money to make the dream possible. A friend told him to try life in Texas. Another Bangladeshi contact offered him a job at a filling station, the Buckner Food Mart in Dallas. In July 2001 the filling station was robbed. Rais was not unduly intimidated by this – he was not hurt – but he began to see that the American tableaux had dark shadows. Two months later came 9/11, and with it a surge in Islamophobic attacks. Now Rais was nervous, but he could not make do without the job.

On September 21st, 2001, Mark Ströman walked into the store, shortly after noon, and put a shotgun in Rais' face. Ströman's rap sheet listed an astounding array of minor crimes stretching back to his childhood. Now, though, he was stepping up a league. He had decided that the Bush administration were wimps, unwilling to exact revenge on the 'towelheads' who had attacked America, so he took the task upon himself. Rais Bhuiyan had brown skin (so he must be from the Middle East) and spoke a funny language (Arabic, Strōman assumed).

Rais thought it was another robbery, but it soon became clear that money was not the intruder's motive. 'He didn't even look towards the money, rather he asked me a question.' Strōman appeared to be drunk or high on drugs, and he was mumbling. Rais could not understand what he said. 'I asked him, since I didn't understand the question, I asked him, "What was that?" And then he shot me.'

Rais felt a pain 'like a million bee stings'. He heard the echo of the gun blast, and blood poured out of the side of his head. He thought he was going to die, and images of his parents flew before him. 'I saw images of my parents, my siblings and my fiancée and then a grave-yard and I thought, "Am I dying today?"' he recalled later. 'I screamed, "Mom!" I looked and he was still staring at me and I thought he might shoot me again if I don't fall and he doesn't think I'm dead. The floor was getting wet with my blood. Then he left the store. I could not believe he shot me. I thought I was dreaming, going through a hallucination. I didn't do anything wrong. I was not a threat to him. I couldn't believe someone would just shoot you like that.'[16]

When Strōman left the store, Rais was still conscious, and struggled to his feet. He went to the barber shop nearby. 'They ran away. They saw me full of blood running like a slaughtered chicken and they thought the guy was behind me. I saw my face in the barber-shop mirror and I couldn't believe it was me.' The journalist who was interviewing Rais noted that he began to cry as he talked about this. 'A few minutes before, I had been a young guy in a T-shirt and shorts and tennis shoes.' The tears came faster. Rais briefly apologised for his emotion. 'I was lucky because there was an ambulance in the area.'[17]

Rais survived, with the scars of shotgun pellets down the side of his face. Over a three-week period two others were not so fortunate. Indeed, Mark Strōman had already committed one murder before he came for Rais. On September 15th, 2001, four days after the terrorist attack in New York, Strōman had walked into the Mom's Store where Waqar Hasan had recently invested his savings. The forty-six-year-old Pakistani immigrant was cooking hamburgers. Strōman simply shot the man and left. There was money lying around, but none was taken.

Detective Daniel Wojcik was perplexed. Robbery did not appear to be a motive of the crime. The original police report on the Hasan murder was stark: 'No motive, no robbery, no suspects, no witnesses.'

Rais came next. Then, on October 4th, 2001, Ströman walked into the Shell Station on John West Road and Big Torn Boulevard in Mesquite, to murder once more. This time, Vasudev Patel pulled a gun in response, but the magazine was not locked, so the weapon could not fire. Patel was the one left dying on the floor. Ströman had strewn a trail of misery behind him. There were two widows, and several children who had no father.

Rais had survived, but he was learning what it meant to be without medical insurance. He needed multiple operations to try to save some of the sight in his right eye, as well as lengthy medical treatment for his other injuries. This being America, he was constantly sent bills for his treatment. His doctor did apply to the Texas Crime Victim Compensation Program, but the request languished without approval for two years. Rais, still a recent immigrant, was trapped between his fear of the debt collectors who appeared on his doorstep, and missing out on the medical care he needed. Some of the time he treated himself as best he could with samples that he begged from doctors, mainly painkillers and eyedrops.

Meanwhile, two days after Rais almost died, his father suffered a stroke. Rais could not return to Bangladesh since he was undergoing treatment himself. Later he did not have the money. He slipped into a deep depression. His fiancée severed their engagement, feeling estranged by the distance and his impenetrable melancholy. In early 2002 the friend who had let him share an apartment asked Rais to move out – suggesting that he needed to be in a nursing home. He was reduced to sleeping on couches, staying as long as each friend could bear, until he felt bound to move on.

Mark Ströman, the man who had destroyed Rais' life, was certainly a racist. When he arrived at the jail he penned a form of poetry: 'Here sits the Arab Slayer. For what he did, we should make him mayor,' he wrote. 'Patriotic, yes indeed, a true American, a special breed.'[18]

The man prosecuting Ströman met Rais. He did not explain any of a victim's rights, but stated that the death penalty was essentially a fait accompli, and Ströman would become the twentieth photograph on the trophy wall of the District Attorney's Office. Rais had little comprehension of the American legal process. He thought the determination to execute Ströman had already been made and that he had no role in the decision. He didn't realise that he was being asked to play a part in producing that result.

'This man needs to die, pure and simple,' said Assistant District Attorney Bob Dark, in his argument to the jury. Rais was called as a witness at the penalty phase of the trial. He was told only to answer the questions he was asked. Ströman's defence lawyer had not even had the courtesy to contact Rais. At the end of the trial the judge entered an order forbidding any contact between Rais and the man who had tried to kill him.[19] The Texas Department of Criminal Justice had the same rule, and barred Ströman from all contact with Rais Bhuiyan.

While Mark Ströman went to Death Row, Rais gradually pulled his life back together. In June 2003 he got a job at the Olive Garden restaurant. In 2005 he became aware of a charity, the Pathways Clinic, and started receiving therapy for his trauma. Meanwhile he trained in computers, so that he would be able to move on from working as a waiter. He was able to pay for a trip with his mother to go on the Hajj, to Mecca.

By 2011 Rais was thirty-seven. He still had the physical scars – he was effectively blind in one eye, and the right side of his face was pockmarked. 'I'm still carrying more than thirty-five pellets on the right side of my face. If I touch my face, my skull, I can feel it's all bumpy.' It was increasingly clear to him that he should take affirmative steps to understand what had happened to him, and why. However, he did not know how to engage with the legal system. The trial seemed far in the past.

It all suddenly began to come into focus in March 2011, when Rais read that a date had been set for Mark Ströman's execution: he was to die on July 20th of that year. Rais was horrified. He asked around to see what, if anything, might be done to prevent this. For the first time he learned that his status as a victim gave him rights. How, though, was he to assert them? Rais went to the media. On May 16th, 2011, he did an interview with the *Dallas Morning News* in which he stated publicly for the first time that he wanted to work on reconciliation with Mark Ströman. 'There are three reasons I feel this way,' he said. 'The first is what I learned from my parents. They raised me with the religious principle that he is best who can forgive easily. The second is because of what I believe as a Muslim, that human lives are precious and that no one has the right to take another's life. And, finally, I seek solace for the wives and children of Vasudev Patel and Waqar Hasan, who are also victims in this tragedy. Executing Ströman is not what they want, either. They have already suffered so much; it will cause only more suffering if he is executed.'

When she read the article, Ströman's new lawyer took action. Lydia Brandt[20] had wondered whether it was permissible to contact Rais, given the prison rules, but now she was satisfied that such an approach would be welcome. She delivered a letter from her client expressing his deep remorse for his crimes. Rais soon learned more about the man who had shot him. While perhaps typical of many prisoners on Death Row, Ströman's history was nevertheless shocking – and revealing – to Rais. From the moment he was born, Mark Ströman's mother, Sandra Baker, consistently rued the fact that she ever had a son, saying that she had only been fifty dollars short of an abortion. She used to say this in front of Mark. She said it to anyone who would listen.

'She wished she had had a dog,' reported her sister. 'That it would have been better if she'd had dogs instead of children.'

Sandra married Doyle Baker, who became Mark's stepfather. They were heavy drinkers. Mark rode his bike thirty miles at the age of eight to escape briefly to his grandparents' house. Perhaps Sandra and Doyle were well matched; he certainly complemented her cruelty. If ever Mark came home from school complaining that he was being bullied, Doyle sent him back to fight the other children. The alternative was a whipping at home. Mark was required to be in his room at all times when the parents were downstairs, including Christmas Day. And so it continued.

There is no such thing as a dog born bad, thought Rais, but there are certainly bad dog owners. It seemed to him that his terrible experience was gradually becoming more comprehensible. He heard stories of how much Mark had changed in ten years as well: a bevy of penpals across Europe vouched for his efforts to improve himself. Mark had been a white supremacist, a racist, but now he rejected this creed.

'It's not been easy to unlearn everything my stepfather taught me,' Mark wrote. 'And I'm not there yet. I may not have time ever to get there. But I'm trying.'

Rais publicly dedicated himself to working on Mark Ströman's rehabilitation. That was the wrong word, he thought; perhaps he should call it 'habilitation', since Mark never received a decent upbringing in the first place. He wanted to meet Mark in person.

He still felt it was important for his own recovery that they should talk, so that he could hear directly from Mark why that shotgun had shattered his new life in America. Ströman told the prison authorities that he was willing to undergo mediation with Rais.

'I requested a meeting with Mr Ströman,' said Rais. He was told by the prison authorities that various officials had to approve his application, and the Attorney General (the person trying to ensure Ströman's execution) would anyway have the power to veto any mediation. 'I'm eagerly awaiting to see him in person and exchange ideas. I would talk about love and compassion. We all make mistakes. He's another human being, like me. Hate the sin, not the sinner. It's very important that I meet him to tell him I feel for him and I strongly believe he should get a second chance. He could educate a lot of people. Thinking about what is going to happen makes me very emotional. I can't sleep. Once I go to bed I feel there is another person that I know who is in his bed thinking about what is going to happen to him – that he is going to be … killed. It makes me very emotional and very sad and makes me want to do more.'[21]

Nobody from the Department of Corrections got back to either Mark or Rais concerning their request – ever. Rais Bhuiyan, the victim, who was supposed to have rights, became the only person in the world who was barred from meeting Mark Ströman. As the execution date loomed, some of Mark's penpals had travelled over from Europe to help him through the last days of his life. They were allowed into the prison. Rais was not.

Next, Rais decided he would address the Clemency Board, so that he could explain why he wanted them to show mercy – or at least delay the execution long enough for him to seek mediation with Mark. The Board rules specifically made provision for a victim to speak.[22] Rais never received a call, a note or even an email in response to his request. Twenty-four hours before the scheduled execution, the Board summarily denied clemency.

Rais wrote to Governor Rick Perry, who could – independently of the Board – stay the execution for long enough for Rais to meet Mark. He never received a reply.

Rais found himself confused and upset. He had expected to be treated with some dignity, or at least basic politeness. After a decade of Islamophobia, here was an opportunity for reconciliation and understanding. Rais had been the victim of a 'hate' crime. In the wake of

9/11, such offences against Muslims in the United States had leapt from twenty-eight in 2000 to 481 in 2001 – a sixteenfold increase.[23] Here was a victim trying to repay hatred with mercy, just as his parents and his Qur'an had taught him. After a decade of articles about the savagery of Shari'a law, here was a Muslim victim who wished to illustrate the compassion in Islamic law, rather than the vengeful caricature that appeared in American newspapers.

Rais was quoting Qur'anic verses to anyone who would listen. 'If anyone kills … it would be as if he killed all people. And if anyone saves a life, it would be as if he saved the life of all people.'[24] He explained how charity and forgiveness were essential to his own salvation: 'if a person forgives and makes reconciliation, his reward is due from Allah'.[25] Under Islamic law, Rais would have had the power of forgiveness. Because he said that he did not want the death penalty – and was supported in this by the widows of Mr Hasan and Mr Patel – then there could be no execution. In whose name, Rais demanded, was the State of Texas planning to kill Mark Ströman?

But nobody in Texas was listening.

Finally, Rais found he had drained the considerable reservoir of his patience. He set out to sue the State of Texas. He did not have the money to pay, but Khurrum Walid, a Muslim lawyer from Florida, agreed to represent him without charge. Rais' lawsuit simply sought to enforce the Texas Constitution, which imposed a duty upon government officials to treat a victim with respect.[26]

'All we are seeking is an injunction to stop Mr Ströman's execution so that we may grant an American victim of violence the same rights under the law as are granted to many other Texan victims,' Khurrum told the media assembled outside the courthouse. 'This is not about Mr Ströman. It's about victim rights. Do we believe they exist or not? Because if we cannot enforce them they don't exist for any of us.'

The spotlight swung back on Governor Rick Perry, even then dipping his toes in the electoral waters, wondering whether to issue a challenge to President Obama in the 2012 election. Rais found Perry's conduct particularly galling. Perry had recently declared Victims' Rights Week in April 2011. 'I encourage all Texans,' the governor proclaimed, 'to join in this effort by learning more about victims' rights and supporting victims of crime whenever possible. We can help our fellow Texans on the road to recovery with compassion and respect.'[27]

Rais felt this was pure hypocrisy, and Perry was named as the first defendant in the complaint. The case would be *Bhuiyan v. Perry*. It was filed in state court, since it primarily involved victims' rights under state law. Texas state court was surely where Governor Perry would want to resolve the issues: he held himself out to be a vehement advocate of states' rights, a critic (in the Tea Party vein) of the intrusion by federal courts into Texan affairs. Indeed, he had recently complained that the federal courts were 'oppressive'.[28]

Even after all these years I was surprised at Perry's response, through his lawyers. He removed the case to federal court, where he could argue that the State of Texas had immunity from being sued.[29] In case this stratagem did not work, his lawyers were to argue that the Texas Victims' Bill of Rights was merely 'symbolic' and unenforceable.[30] Perry may have been a hypocrite, but the governor won, and Rais' case was dismissed.

Meanwhile Mark Ströman was in his prison cell, waiting to die.

'I sit here with a Cup of Coffee and some Good ole Classic Rock playing on My radio, how Ironic, the song "Free Bird" by Lynyrd Skynyrd …' he wrote, his grammar all his own. 'Yes, Mr Rais Bhuiyan, what an inspiring soul … for him to come forward after what ive done speaks Volume's … and has really Touched My heart and the heart of Many others World Wide … Not only do I have all My friends and supporters trying to Save my Life, but now i have The Islamic Community Joining in … Spearheaded by one Very Remarkable man Named Rais Bhuiyan, Who is a Survivor of My Hate. His deep Islamic Beliefs Have gave him the strength to Forgive the Un-forgiveable … that is truly Inspiring to me, and should be an Example for us all. The Hate, has to stop …

'Texas Loud & Texas proud … TRUE AMERICAN …' Mark Ströman signed off. 'Living to Die – Dying to Live.'[31] There was a brief stay, which extended his life by three hours before he was executed.

Rais felt that he had failed, but he had not. He had upheld the principles that his parents instilled into him. But the criminal justice system of the State of Texas had failed Rais Bhuiyan, just as the Florida system has been failing the family of Derrick and Duane Moo Young for twenty-five years.

17

Getting Closer

On January 26th, 2009, Kris turned seventy. Since his trial in 1987, every court available to him had rubber-stamped his original verdict, refusing even to consider his claim of innocence. By now he had served twenty-three years in prison for a crime he did not commit. I wouldn't say he celebrated his birthday, as there was nothing to be joyous about, but at least he had made it that far: life expectancy in prison is far lower than in the free world. Kris was now considered a geriatric prisoner, and as such he was transferred to another institution in Miami. This made travel easier for his wife Marita who, steadfast as ever, continued to visit Kris as often as she could. Now she could see him for three or four hours on Saturdays. The rest of the week she devoted primarily to waiting for the next visit, and taking brief calls at night when he was given access to the phone.

To me, on the other hand, life had been kind. My wife and I had moved back to England in 2004, and I was full-time with Reprieve, the legal services charity I'd helped to establish in London in 1999. Life had been full of challenges – capital cases around the world and the battle against Guantánamo Bay – but Kris' case continued to nag away at me. Every once in a while, Marita would call me at home to find out whether there was any progress. Her calls spurred me on. It may have been the law that had let Kris down, but I couldn't escape the feeling that it was my responsibility. I would pass through Florida every few months on the way to Guantánamo Bay, where

I was representing several detainees. If I could, I would stop in on Marita in Fort Lauderdale and, when the prison visitation schedule allowed, on Kris too.

Equally sporadically, back at the Reprieve office in London, we would plan investigative forays to try to find something new that might finally convince the courts to show Kris some justice. I hoped a witness might come face-to-face with his conscience as he thought of Kris as an old man, wasting away in his cell. Generally, I was disappointed. We tried to locate more material on the drug prosecution of Jaime Vallejo Mejia in Oklahoma, but documents relating to his guilty plea and sentence had been placed under seal. Jim Drummond, a friendly local lawyer, agreed to press for access but progress was slow. Every few years one of our investigators would reach out to Neville Butler, who was now pushing eighty but still refusing to talk.

In time, one focus of the work started to bear fruit. It involved the curious testimony of Tino Geddes.

Eric Hendon had done a hopeless job representing Kris, most especially with respect to his alibi. If it was true that Kris was miles away at the time of the crime – even if there had been some question in a juror's mind that this might have been the case – Kris should have been acquitted. Key to the case against him was the turncoat witness, Tino Geddes, who testified under oath that he had concocted the original alibi at Kris' request, and that it was false. When, long after the trial, I told the other five witnesses that Geddes claimed to have hoodwinked each of them into their original stories, they said that he was lying: he never talked to them. They would not be swayed: all of them insisted that, at the time of the Moo Young shootings, Kris was several miles north meeting with people who worked with him, then having lunch with friends, and scoping out new premises for his newspaper.

I found these witnesses credible; apparently, when they were originally interviewed, so did the prosecution. If the alibi was honest, then Geddes was lying. But why? Geddes had always been central to our investigation as we tried to work out what prompted him to invert his original story.

Geddes stood an inch over six feet tall, and had a dark complexion. He had a reputation as a smooth talker, a ladies' man. I got the sense he had a bit of a crush on Marita, though she was certainly never going to see him as anything other than the man who betrayed her husband. At the time of the Moo Youngs' murder, Kris had recently given him a job working for the *Caribbean Times*, and treated him well.

Several people who were present in the courtroom at the time of the trial told me that Geddes was the most persuasive of all the prosecution witnesses. He was glib, his story was shocking, and it painted Kris in a terrible light. According to Geddes, Kris had enlisted him in a series of attempts to kill Derrick Moo Young. Geddes told the jury that he was present for a 'dry run' of the actual murder in the DuPont Plaza a couple of weeks before the crime itself. He said that he had duped all the witnesses who had said Kris was elsewhere at the time of the murders: he said they were describing what happened the day before, the Wednesday, not the day of the murders. His testimony managed to turn Kris' solid alibi into an incriminating albatross.

'Why, Tino?' Marita had cried, as Geddes had walked back through the courtroom after leaving the witness stand. 'Why?'

Geddes did not respond. Over the years, he had never given a good answer.

I had pored over his testimony a number of times and by now I had no doubt that he was being deceptive about a number of things. But it was important to work out precisely how he was lying and, more important, *why*. If I could understand his motivation that would go a long way towards proving that his whole volte-face was a sham.

The record at trial – what the jury heard – was not much use since not only had Eric Hendon ignored the alibi evidence, but he had conducted an anaemic cross-examination of Geddes. When I first took up Kris' case I gathered up a number of statements Geddes had made – something Hendon appeared not to have done. On the day after the crime, Geddes had given an interview to the *Miami Herald* in which he said that Kris was totally innocent, and that he could not imagine why his boss had been arrested. About a week later, he told defence investigator Ron Petrillo in a sworn statement that he was with Kris on the morning of the crime, several miles north of Miami.

Yet eight months later his entire story changed: now, appearing for a deposition, he said that the alibi had been confected, and Kris had connived with him in several bizarre attempts on the lives of Derrick Moo Young and Eslee Carberry.

As with so many witnesses in this strange case, my initial reaction had been to stand back and assess the overall plausibility of their story: did Geddes' testimony pass the test of basic common sense? He said that Kris had hired him away from the *Echo*, to work on the *Caribbean Times*. Soon after Geddes took the job, Kris began to hatch plots against Carberry and Derrick Moo Young. First Geddes had described a midnight plot to shoot Eslee Carberry as he took the *Echo* proofs to the printer.

'Mr Maharaj told me that he was going…' Geddes had paused, perhaps for effect. 'He was going … to blow away Mr Carberry.' He said he saw Kris buy two crossbows, which were to be used against Carberry. Kris also had two hunting knives, Chinese throwing stars and camouflage gear.

As I read this, I could imagine the way one might cross-examine such a witness – with a rising inflection of incredulity. *How was middle-class Mr Maharaj, in his jacket and tie, going to carry out this homicide? Was he going to use the bow like William Tell? The hunting knife like Jim Bowie? Or the Chinese throwing stars – would that be Bruce Lee?*

Geddes testified that he and Kris had gone up together to West Palm Beach, where the *Echo*'s printer was located. The plan was to do Carberry damage on the 'lonely stretch of road which runs from Wellington down to Fort Lauderdale'. At trial, Hendon did not press Geddes on where exactly the crime was slated to take place, but a journalist had later asked this question in an interview for a British paper.

'You must understand where this is,' Geddes told him. 'You would drive for miles and see no sign of life or light.' It took me only a moment on Google Maps to prove that this was bogus. The Town Crier printer was, and still is, in the same building as the Publix supermarket in Wellington, Florida. The road was solid with houses between there and Fort Lauderdale. It was not a venue for a secretive assassination. According to Geddes, the plot petered out when they got bored and hungry and went looking for a deli. If this had been true, they would not have had to go far: there was a deli right there, in the Publix.

Next came the effort to kill Derrick by running him off the road. Geddes testified that Kris rented a Ryder truck for the task, and planned to kill Derrick at the intersection of Griffin Road and the Expressway, as Derrick drove home. 'It is not a very well-used highway that very many vehicles travel up and down,' Geddes said. This was, again, demonstrable nonsense. It was a busy intersection. How was Kris to know which route – I looked on a map and there were several –Derrick would use coming home? (Indeed, according to Geddes they never saw Derrick pass.) What was Kris going to do – take the large bright-yellow Ryder truck, careen across the road, smash Derrick's car into the ditch and then do the man in with his crossbow?

Perhaps because they noticed more potential flaws than did Kris' lawyer, the prosecutors decided to 'corroborate' Geddes' claim that he had rented a truck for this assault. The only record that they could find of a truck rental in his name was for July 25th, 1986, a date that was many weeks earlier than Geddes had suggested. Kris said this was just one of several times he needed a truck to handle the distribution of his new paper, the *Caribbean Times*. Unfortunately, Hendon let all of this go by.

Then there was the 'dry run', perhaps the most vital episode from the perspective of the prosecution. Geddes described a plot that was remarkably similar, in every detail, to Neville Butler's version of the actual murders on October 16th. It was obvious how he might have made it up: he was friends with Neville Butler and they had spoken about the crime. The question was whether it was true. The 'dry run' supposedly took place in room 408 of the DuPont Plaza Hotel (not room 1215 where the murders actually took place). Once Derrick Moo Young arrived, the plan was for Kris to burst in from the adjoining room. In the early years of my own investigation – on Wednesday, February 5th, 1997 at 11.00 a.m., to be precise – I did what Eric Hendon should have done before trial: I went to the DuPont Plaza, met with Ken Kalish, the hotel manager, and asked him to take me to room 408. The room itself was occupied, but those on either side were not. It did not take long to determine that there was no door connecting either room with 408. There never had been. A maintenance man in the hall confirmed this.

The prosecutor, Kastrenakes, had promised evidence of a fourth assault in his opening statement, but he and his witness apparently forgot to include it in the sworn testimony before the jury. It involved the incident that I thought of as the 'Marriage Day Massacre'. In his deposition, Geddes had said that Kris had planned to kill Derrick Moo Young at Duane's wedding – Geddes knew this because he had helped Kris plan the hit. But Duane had never married. At best, Geddes was mistaken and it was the wedding of Derrick's other son, Paul. Regardless, the story was omitted from the trial for good reason: the spectacle of the portly, middle-aged defendant swooping into the wedding party to commit mayhem seemed more James Bond fantasy than Kris Maharaj reality.

There were plenty more problems with Geddes' testimony, but he had faced little challenge from the defence. I found a letter in Hendon's file. Not long after the trial, Kris had written, asking him why he had seemed to be in a 'frozen stupor' throughout Geddes' testimony. The lawyer had not replied, and Kris had fired him soon afterwards.

Why did Geddes flip to become a witness for the prosecution? He told the jury that what made the difference to him was learning the 'real' timing of the murders.

'Did you know, in fact, that the murders were committed between eleven thirty and twelve?' Kastrenakes asked. No, Geddes replied. Knowing the time of the murders made him realise how important his alibi evidence was, and he felt a duty to set the record straight and tell the court that the alibis were fabricated. I dismissed this explanation. It was just silly. If Geddes had been asked to create an alibi for his boss, then he would have had to know when the crime had taken place. After all, an alibi is by definition a story that accounts for the suspect's presence elsewhere at the time of the crime.

An alternative reason for working with the prosecution had been apparent at the trial: the prosecutors had threatened to charge him with perjury for the concocted alibis. Geddes reported that Kastrenakes had promised him complete immunity if he would testify against Kris; if he did not cooperate, however, Kastrenakes said he would make life difficult for him. During the pre-trial deposition, Kastrenakes essentially confirmed this. He stopped Geddes from speaking.

'I would interrupt that,' the prosecutor told Eric Hendon, who was in the process of questioning Geddes about his new story, 'with saying that we did advise Mr Geddes that he could not be prosecuted for perjury because he has, in fact, recanted and I advised him of Florida law with respect to that.'

Imagine the power of those words: the state prosecutor told Geddes that if he upheld Kris' alibi, he would be perjuring himself. In a capital case, lying under oath can get you locked up for fifteen to thirty years.[1] Kastrenakes was insisting that he – the prosecutor – could divine truth from falsehood and it was, he had decided, perjury to say Kris was elsewhere at the time of the crime. Imagine, also, if Eric Hendon had plucked up the courage to tell Detective Buhrmaster that he had better change his story or he would face prosecution for perjury: Hendon would have been charged with intimidating a witness, for which he could have received life in prison.[2]

The prosecutor also told Geddes he could go to prison for what he had said happened. 'Because I had been with Kris on a number of occasions,' Geddes later told a British reporter, 'even if no criminal activity took place, there was criminal intent which I think … um … could be looked at as, you know, conspiracy or aiding and abetting.' So if he was telling the truth, he was involved in conspiracy to commit murder. But that was okay, as Kastrenakes gave him immunity for this as well.

If the prosecution used the threat of a stick, they also held out a carrot. Not long before Kris' trial, Geddes had been arrested in Jamaica on a weapons charge. He downplayed its seriousness – there was no gun, he told the jury, he'd just forgotten to take some ammunition out of his suitcase when he flew back from Miami. Nevertheless, this was potentially a serious offence: gun crime was rampant and, under Jamaican law, Geddes could – once again – have faced time in prison.[3]

At Kris' trial, Geddes placed the blame for this arrest on his former employer. 'I purchased that gun because I had become involved in these escapades which I have already described with Mr Maharaj,' he told the jury, 'and I was, in fact, fearful for my own safety, and this is why a I purchased this firearm.'

Geddes got off lightly in Jamaica – with a $1,000 fine – in part because not one but both Florida prosecutors – Paul Ridge and John Kastrenakes – flew there to support him.

'They simply produced a public document before the Court in

Jamaica,' Geddes testified, downplaying their role.

This made no sense. What was the point of travelling all the way to Jamaica simply to bring a document? Indeed, Eric Hendon had some of the tools to challenge Geddes even before the trial: Ridge had written to him disclosing that he and Kastrenakes had gone to Jamaica to testify at Geddes' trial, rather than just carry a piece of paper.

When Geddes said he had bought the gun 'a couple of weeks' before the murders, in response to Kris' homicidal escapades, again this had to be untrue. The plots he described all occurred – by his account – in the two or three weeks leading up to the Moo Youngs' deaths. In other words, they took place either in late September or October, 1986. But a receipt produced by the prosecution at trial proved that Geddes bought the gun on July 19th – two months before the earlier attempts on Derrick's life. For once, Hendon noticed the discrepancy, and brought it up.

'A couple of weeks, like eight,' Geddes had explained. 'And when I say a couple, I do not necessarily mean two. This is how we speak. This is standard Jamaican.'

All this we knew in 1997, when Ben Kuehne and I filed Kris' state petition for a writ of habeas corpus. Was it sufficient to explain Geddes' about-face? After all, who among us would not do as a prosecutor asks to avoid fifteen years in prison for perjury?

Regardless, I was sure this was not the full story. How could a man who was once close to Kris have concocted such a deliberately damning testimony? Marita told me she'd heard that Geddes had received $50,000 for his amended testimony. She could not recall the name of the man who had told her this, but we continued with our efforts to build on her memory.

Meanwhile, once Kris was safely on death row, Geddes spoke to various journalists who wanted to interview him about the case. What he said was hardly an admission that his testimony was false, but it did colour the way in which he and the prosecutors negotiated his change of heart. 'For a time when they came over to interview me, I took them over the north course and I took them around Jamaica,' Geddes told a British journalist. 'I think they had a wonderful time.' *The Caribbean Echo* carried a picture of the two prosecutors and Geddes drinking at a bar. They also accompanied their star witness to a lap-dancing establishment.[4]

Then a remark Geddes had made on tape caught my attention.

'Is, is…' a British reporter had stuttered during an interview. 'Is part of the reason for the traumaticness of it because of the threats that came from other Trinidadians?'

'Well, I mean the threat is always there,' Geddes replied. 'Um … and that certainly helps.'

What threat was he talking about? And where did these threats come from – Trinidad? Or elsewhere?

'If I am lying to this jury,' Geddes had concluded his trial testimony in 1987, with high drama, 'I would pray to God He would punish me in the worst way possible. Everything I have said to this jury has been the truth.'

By 2010, the unfortunate man was suffering from cancer. The smart suits that had once fitted his heavy frame now hung on him like sacks. He was sixty-two, but he looked twenty years older. While I would not wish cancer on anyone, I hoped his illness would make him ready to come clean before he died. We had also learned of a scandal that had broken in the local media: he had been fired from his job as a journalist in Kingston because of associations with an infamous gangster, a member of the Jamaican Shower Posse.

When someone first mentioned the Shower Posse, I thought I had misheard him: it seemed a rather damp sobriquet. But then I was told that it came from the Posse's penchant for showering people with bullets. Notoriously violent, they controlled much of Jamaica's drug trade and were closely linked to narco-associates in Colombia.

At this point, an investigator whom I shall call Ken agreed to help us with the Jamaican end of things. That is not his real name, but it is safer not to say who he is – I won't include anything at all about him, as that might betray his identity. He gradually pulled together a slew of interesting information. He learned that while Geddes primarily covered sports media, he was also known for gritty 'in the streets' reporting. Younger journalists would be surprised at Geddes' bank of contacts in some of the roughest parts of Kingston, particularly in the Tivoli Gardens area – home to the Shower Posse.

Geddes, it turned out, was very well connected in the Jamaican underworld. He had grown up with the most disreputable of all the Shower Posse members, Carl 'Byah' Mitchell, and we learned the details of how Geddes – touted as the 'respectable journalist' at Kris' trial – came to be sacked from his job. He let slip in a loose moment of boasting that he hid Mitchell out for a year in his home during the 1970s state of emergency. The violence had been so bad then that the government had cracked down heavily on the gangs. While Jamaicans were used to a bit of wild talk, Geddes' admission that he had conspired with one of the island's most dangerous criminals proved to be too much, and he was fired.

With his health in rapid decline, Geddes finally agreed to an interview with an investigator for Kris rather than for a newspaper, and he met Ken at a Kingston bar. Ken called me to run through what he should ask. I was excited; at last, I thought, perhaps he would come clean. But Geddes had survivor's hope – the optimistic sense that cancer could not take him, no matter what the doctors were saying. He was surprisingly forthcoming about his connections to the underworld. He even talked about acting as an intermediary, arranging a hit for Jim Brown, the chief 'enforcer' for the Shower Posse. But he clammed up when challenged on some of his improbable testimony at Kris' trial.

Geddes maintained his party lifestyle almost to the day he died in 2011. Then doors began to open. Churchill Neita was a local attorney who had represented Geddes at the trial on weapons charges. Neita had never spoken about his client before, but when Ken went to see him at his office and started asking questions, Neita felt that Geddes' legal privilege had died along with him. The facts of the case were very different from the story relayed to the jury in Miami a quarter-century earlier. It was not just a matter of a bullet or two in his suitcase; Geddes had been arrested at the Norman Manley International Airport in Kingston with two or three guns, ammunition and a silencer. Neita said he was facing a long stretch in jail.

The lawyer understood that Geddes had had a contact in customs who was going to let him get through with the hardware, but the man got cold feet. Neita said the guns were intended for the drug gang. Geddes was mixed up in something much bigger than the gun charges, but his client pleaded guilty and instead of being given a custodial sentence, which could have run to life in prison, he was simply fined – largely due to the intervention of the American prosecutors.

While Geddes was alive, it had been impossible to get information about him from any member of the Shower Posse, past or present, but after his death Ken located a veteran gang member who went by the name Cowboy.[5] Cowboy had been close to Geddes, and was shocked to learn that Geddes had been a witness for the state. He said that if he'd known, he would have 'paged' Geddes – in Jamaican terms, this might cover anything from a strong word to serious physical injury. Cowboy could not understand how a man who was considered a 'hard rock' could switch and become a 'stool pigeon'. He said there was no way his old friend would have done it unless someone had had something on him. Thinking back over their long association, he wondered aloud whether Geddes had been caught importing drugs into America, and guns back to Jamaica.

Ken got even more out of his next interview. He tracked down Peanut, a Posse 'legend', a man who by his own admission had been involved in 'a lot of things' over the years. Peanut, Geddes and various Posse dons would regularly go clubbing at two bars in Kingston – Epiphany and Exodus. In the 1990s Peanut had been wanted 'dead or alive' by the police, and that normally meant dead. Extrajudicial killings were just a lot quicker than trials. But Geddes had arranged a meeting with the Senior Superintendent of Police; Peanut was held for forty-eight hours and then released. Peanut described how Geddes had achieved the same thing for Byah Mitchell in the 1970s, after hiding his gangster friend at home for a year.

Peanut agreed that the guns Geddes brought into the country were likely for the Posse, but he declined to go into further detail. He said he had always assumed that Geddes had 'bought out of the case' – local slang for paying off the relevant officials. He was shocked that his old friend had been testifying against Kris. He never thought that a man like Geddes would go to 'Babylon' (the prosecution). He was even firmer than Cowboy: if the Posse crowd knew he had been working for the other side, he would have ended up dead. Peanut thought the Feds must have had a hold over him.

Ken then went back to Miami. If you want to know what is happening in South Florida, a good place to start is with John Hodgson, a radio presenter at WAVS, a South Florida radio station, who goes under the name 'John T'. Hodgson knew Geddes from the early days, when Geddes was a journalist and he was a Jamaican police officer. They would go drinking together in Tivoli Gardens. He met many of the Shower Posse's dons through Geddes – who introduced him to Carl 'Byah' Mitchell, Claudius Massop and Posse hit man Lester Lloyd Coke, aka 'Jim Brown'.

Hodgson told Ken he had also met Kris Maharaj on a number of occasions. They would run into one another regularly at the Carib 420 Club. When he heard of the murders, he was shocked; the story did not fit with the Kris he knew. He related to Ken how Geddes later told him he'd testified against Kris because he was afraid he'd end up in the dock himself: the prosecutors had let him know that he had to testify or face being charged with conspiracy to murder. Despite being a 'hardcore' man, Hodgson said, Geddes had a mortal fear of jail. Hodgson also thought the prosecutors must have known about Geddes' involvement with Carl Mitchell's gang, running drugs into the US and guns back to Jamaica.

I wondered at all this. It suggested that the authorities knew that Geddes was part of a smuggling ring. That would have upped the ante for Geddes considerably. The inclusion of a silencer in the weapons Geddes had with him was particularly significant, since that would certainly imply criminality.

As Ken relayed information to us back in London, I felt we were edging towards a fuller picture of Geddes and his motivation, but we weren't all the way there yet. I hoped against hope that his conscience had got to him before he died, and he'd made a confession to someone, probably someone close to him. Under the rules of hearsay, a so-called dying declaration, a statement made by someone who knew he was dying, would be admissible – on the rather arcane theory that he would be too afraid of his impending encounter with St Peter at the Pearly Gates to dissemble. If he had made a deathbed confession that he had lied against Kris, that could really help us.

Not long after, Ken managed to track down Tino Geddes' brother David at the Jamaica Water Board, where he worked. The siblings had been close, and David knew intimate details of his brother's life. Ken asked whether there were any pressures weighing down on Tino that might have persuaded him to change his statement about the murders.

'Yes,' David replied, simply. Initially, he would not elaborate. Ken pressed him, reminding him that this could do Tino no harm now, but that an innocent man was in prison in Florida. David thought about it, and went a little further at a second meeting. He confirmed that his brother had testified against Kris because he had been told by the prosecutors that if he did not, he would be on trial himself. After that, he clammed up again.

'What was Tino mixed up in?' Ken asked.

'My brother was always mixed up in things,' he said, enigmatically.

'Well, there's mixed up and then there's mixed up.'

'My brother knew a lot of people, especially in the Garrison areas,' he said, referring to the Shower Posse's stronghold.

'What criminal activity was he mixed up in?'

'I don't see what the relevance is of that,' David replied, testily.

'If the prosecutors had known it, they could have used it to make him come testify.'

'I don't know what they knew and didn't know,' David said. 'I was told certain things by my brother in confidence, and I'm not going to reveal them even after he's dead.'

Ken tried to take the interview on, and David conceded that Kris' case had affected his brother badly. When Tino came back to Jamaica he went into a depression and was taking medication for it.

'He was having nightmares.'

But that was as far as he would go.

It seemed from what we were learning that Tino Geddes lived a compartmentalised life that offered variable images to the different people in it. His family saw a man who was deeply traumatised. He told them about his alcohol abuse, his abuse of prescription drugs and the nightmares that plagued him. He told them he felt he was being watched. With others – especially those in the Shower Posse – he insisted he was strong and loyal, giving no hint that he had become a stooge for the prosecution. As a journalist, Geddes was used to juggling stories. That was his talent.

Uncovering these links with the Jamaican Shower Posse, and the facts surrounding the weapons charge, were both massive breakthroughs. Geddes clearly had a great deal to fear on various fronts: from the American prosecutors, their Jamaican counterparts, and from the people in the drug trade. The Posse had close connections with the Colombian cartels. They did a lot of business together, and while there was never much trust among drug lords, they knew they had common enemies: the DEA, prosecutors, and snitches. Was Geddes perhaps an 'authorised snitch', giving out a story he had been encouraged to tell by the lords of the drug domain? Had Geddes

received a visit from a drug dealer or a middleman who was keen that
Kris should be the fall guy for the Moo Youngs' murders?

We had made some headway, but Geddes was now dead, and Kris
would soon follow him if he remained in the harsh conditions of his
South Florida prison.

18

Getting Even Closer

Tino Geddes had carried many secrets with him to his grave. Nevertheless, his death had loosened several tongues. If people began to talk so soon after his funeral, there was a chance that we would learn more in due course. Tino had lived life to the full, at least when he was able to mask his depression, and was liked by many in the community. While witnesses often do, indeed, speak ill of the dead, this is less likely to happen while the funeral eulogies are still in the air. I hoped that, in time, perhaps, those close to Tino would come to see that helping the living is more important than worrying about the dead.

There were opportunities, too, in changes at the Miami Dade Police Department.

John Buhrmaster, the lead detective in Kris' case, had taken another law-enforcement job after his retirement in 2012. David 'Pete' Romero, another officer who had been closely involved, retired at the same time, but had then committed suicide. Sad though this was, it might make others more willing to speak. It seemed like a good time to look again at the MDPD.

When I first took on Kris' case, I knew little about Miami. As the years went by, though, the sheer weight of material that seemed to have escaped the attention of the Miami Dade Police Department meant they were either incompetent, biased even beyond the testi-lying cops I had encountered in New Orleans, or something worse.

By now I knew that almost every player in the case against Kris was somehow involved in drug dealing. I knew a bit about the MDPD, and what they had been up to in the 1980s, and that made me wonder whether the police had to be involved in the narco-corruption too. With the limited resources available to the charity where I worked, Reprieve, I began to put together a more detailed picture of the MDPD back then.

At the time of Kris Maharaj's arrest on October 16th, 1986, the FBI labelled Miami the 'murder capital of the USA'. Dade County's murder rate was 23.7 homicides per 100,000 people, surpassing all other major metropolitan areas, three times the national average.[1] Rioting and violence in the area had made law enforcement a dangerous profession and, as the population increased, the number of officers dropped alarmingly. Politicians knew something had to be done. In one year in the early 1980s, 714 new police officers joined the force in a hiring frenzy, more than doubling the department. The rush resulted in applicants slipping past relaxed screening standards: they might have had poor work and driving records, credit problems, even criminal records and drug abuse histories – they still got work. Training was inadequate and promotion expedited.

Meanwhile, more than two-thirds of the cocaine coming into the United States was entering through the Miami area, bringing billions of dollars into the city, involving thousands of residents, and reaching every stratum of society. Because those in the police force doing the hiring wanted officers who could connect with the burgeoning foreign-born populations, including the Spanish-speaking influx who arrived on the Mariel Boat Lift, 'a lot of cops had either drug dealer friends or drug dealer relatives or drug dealer informants.'[2] It was a family affair.

Officers on a low salary might find themselves making a traffic stop and being offered a month's or possibly a year's salary simply not to look in the trunk.[3] There was little chance that beat officers would resist this temptation without strong leadership, and this was a commodity that Miami law enforcement lacked. The police chief was said to be inept, and several officers were indicted on drug-related offences including, almost amusingly, Raul Martinez, who was head of the Police Anti-Corruption Unit. Another was George Staphylaris, who ran the Treasure Island Elementary School 'Just Say No' anti-drugs campaign.[4]

Between January 1985 and November 1987, seventy-two officers were suspended, fired or asked to resign due to acts of misconduct. By 1988, this number had risen to 100,[5] a significant proportion of the entire force. And these were only the people who were caught.

Police corruption was such that many Miami cops were essentially part-time: they enforced the law some of the time, but also ran their own criminal enterprises. 'We're not just talking about taking bribes or giving protection to criminals,' opined Miami Police Captain Judith Bennett in a newspaper op-ed published just ten days before Derrick and Duane Moo Young died in the DuPont Plaza. 'We're talking about setting up a criminal enterprise ... the police themselves pulled the robberies. They themselves stole the drugs. They were thugs, operating under a whole different set of rules.'[6]

In some instances the local prosecutors were little better. They worked daily with the very police who they should have been investigating, and sometimes they joined in with the corruption.[7] Judges, too, got in on the act. Operation Court Broom resulted in several judges being charged and either convicted, removed from office or disbarred. One such person had been Judge Howard Gross, who had been sitting for the first three days of the Maharaj trial when he was arrested for accepting a bribe from an agent with the Florida Department of Law Enforcement (FDLE) who had been posing as a drug trafficker.

It did not stop at state level. The corruption spilled over into the federal agencies,[8] and even the federal judiciary. In 1981, US District Judge Alcee Hastings had been charged with seeking a $150,000 bribe from a convicted drug dealer. Although he was acquitted at a jury trial in 1983 – the key witness refused to cooperate against him – in 1988 he was impeached for bribery and perjury by a vote of 413 to 3. He became only the sixth federal judge in US history to be removed from office by the Senate.[9]

At the time I started to take a fresh look at corruption in the MDPD, some extraordinary stories were floating into public view, like scum on the top of the Miami pond. In one bizarre example, a journalist alleged that a CIA agent called Ricky Prado (who later worked for Blackwater) had been a cartel hit man in Miami in the early eighties.[10]

Ricky Prado should not be confused with Manuel Pardo, executed for murder on December 11th, 2012. Manuel Pardo had been a law-enforcement officer before he was sentenced to death for killing nine people in a ninety-six-day spree in 1986 – again the year of the Moo Young murders. Pardo faithfully recorded each crime in his diary, taking instant photographs of his victims and collecting newspaper clippings about the murders in the aftermath. A search of his apartment revealed a collection of Nazi memorabilia; he had also tattooed a swastika on the leg of his dog.

Pardo had been hired by the Sweetwater Police Department, in a Miami suburb, in 1979. This came two months after being forced to resign from the Florida Highway Patrol, where he falsified 100 traffic notices. In 1985 he was fired, in turn, by Sweetwater because he had gone to the Bahamas to testify for a former colleague who was being held on narcotics charges. Pardo identified himself to Bahamian officials as an 'international undercover officer' investigating drug trafficking between South America, the Bahamas and Jamaica. Apparently, being fired just led Pardo to change his narco-trafficking role: the following year he murdered his nine victims, while in the employment of Ramon Alvero, a local drug kingpin.[11]

Yet, despite all the information I was gathering, the task of unearthing everything that was going on in the Miami police force at the time of the Moo Young murders was daunting. I'd tried to do something like that in New Orleans, years before, and got nowhere. Some lessons had been predictable: when cornered, crooked police officers fight back, and fight ugly. But my most important education came from the authorities who might have kept the police honest: nobody wanted to accept that the Emperor was wearing no clothes. The political stakes were high and, if we all agreed that the police were part of the crime problem rather than its solution, politicians had no alternative to offer.[12]

The challenges in Miami were vastly greater: I was not living and working in Florida, as I had been in New Orleans. And no matter what I had learned about the police in Louisiana, they were amateurs stealing a few thousand dollars, nobodies on the scale of Miami narco-corruption.

Gradually, though, I was able to develop some sources in Florida. I cannot say who they are. I cannot, for now, even hint at their true identities, for reasons that will become obvious. Suffice it to say that various intermediaries proved willing to intercede with other intermediaries and lead me to some potential witnesses who I thought might be able to help. It was a slow and dangerous business.[13]

For example, I learned that Jaime Vallejo Mejia, the mysterious Colombian in room 1214, had long been known to the Feds. By the time of Kris' trial in 1987, Mejia had been the focus of a federal investigation. One former officer had been undercover with the cartels for much of the eighties. Another man, who had been deep inside some of the Miami mayhem as a police informant, began to tell stories about corruption but then clammed up again, worried about his own security.

With respect to a third man, a former policeman, it took a year for my intermediaries to get him to agree even to talk to me. I'll call him Fred, for want of a better pseudonym. It took a second year to gain Fred's trust. I would stop by on my periodic trips to Florida, often en route to Guantánamo Bay. I had to provide assurances that I would protect his identity, as I had no other means at my disposal to guarantee his safety. At Kris' trial, prosecutors had been able to ensure immunity to various people in exchange for their testimony against Kris. This included both Neville Butler and Tino Geddes, perhaps the two most important witnesses, each of whom escaped possible life sentences. The government could have put them in a witness protection programme if there had been a serious threat against them. But Fred knew that I, a mere defence lawyer, had nothing to offer but a salve to his aching conscience.

Fortunately, there are a lot of Catholics in South Florida, whether their affiliation is based on their South American drug dealing, or their Cuban, Irish or Italian ancestors. Though most have probably omitted attending a confessional for decades now, old habits ultimately die hard. Guilt is a great motivator.

The emerging story of corruption in the Miami Dade Police Department and the associated law-enforcement agencies in South Florida was astounding. Some officers' duties were wide-ranging. Members of the MDPD would ensure that a shipment of narcotics was allowed safe passage into Florida via boat or aircraft, sometimes acting as escorts for drug shipments coming via Caribbean islands such as the Bahamas.

Oscar Cuni was a name that came up a great deal. My sources described how he organised some of the 1980s murders in Miami for all the Colombians, whether for the Medellin, the Cali or the North Valley Cartel. The cartels competed to a certain extent, but they had a common interest in eliminating informants and those who might try to rip the primary players off. Cuni went down in the 1990s for his involvement in a drug conspiracy.[14] He later died in prison – on November 29th, 2009 – once again beginning to loosen a few lips when it came to the criminal conspiracies of the 1980s.

I learned that Cuni had relied primarily on two people when it came to actually pulling the trigger – 'Chino' and 'Tatta' were their *noms de guerres*. Not all of Cuni's team had been retired, forcibly or otherwise. My sources warned that one of his men was still working in the area – making the investigation rather more hazardous.

Cuni had a main man inside the MDPD Homicide Division. Apparently Cuni would run the names of those he proposed to have killed by this man, to make sure they would not cause the MDPD particular problems. In other words, his contact knew that a murder would happen beforehand. When the homicide took place, someone else was framed as the killer, evidence went missing or the homicide investigations conveniently bore no fruit.

This was horrific enough, but I learned that there was a second layer to the agreement between corrupt police officers and the cartels: an officer would generally be present at the murder scene, on duty, to make sure that the hit man didn't get into trouble. This was taking the police motto – 'To Serve and Protect' – to a different level.

While MDPD officers generally played only a support role for the cartels' crimes, sometimes they were recruited to take part in home-invasion robberies and street robberies of other drug dealers or – most sinister of all – actually carry out some of these killings themselves. Indeed, based on the various sources who were willing to talk, I gradually built up information on a number of homicides that seemed to have been perpetrated with direct police complicity but were listed as 'unsolved' or had been covered up by officers in the Miami Dade Homicide Department. I came to think of the office as the Miami Department of Homicide. In the end, I knew of about twenty or more murders where the police may have been involved.

For example, in November 1982, there was a multiple murder in the area of 97th Avenue and Coral Way. The victims were in a white cargo van. They were conducting surveillance, planning a home invasion. The killer worked for Oscar Cuni as a regular shooter, and he was tipped off that he was himself the target of the narcotics robbery. He took out the victims with his favourite weapon, a machine gun. The investigation into these murders was 'discontinued'.

Skipping forward to 1988, various officers were apparently involved in the murder of Roberto Suarez in the El Barrilito restaurant. While it was reported that Erasmo Torrez killed Suarez, actually MDPD officers are said to have killed both Torrez and the wheelchair-bound Suarez. The officers supposedly took nine kilograms of cocaine from the restaurant.[15]

In 1997, five people were killed in a notorious case at NW 6th Avenue and 63rd Street. An officer was designated to be near the scene when that took place. He apparently went into the apartment where five people had been lined up, gagged, and shot; he knew that the mayhem had been caused by 'Chino', the name of one of Cuni's two main hit men. The person who got the death penalty for this crime seems to have had nothing to do with it.

In 2002, members of a Jamaican drug gang were robbed in their vehicle on their way to collect a shipment. One individual was killed. This was covered up by the MDPD. The incident was written up by the MDPD as an automobile accident that took place on the Florida Turnpike. The vehicle was towed to a storage lot on Sunrise Boulevard. Police officers were tipped off by a Jamaican male and recovered $50,000 from the passenger side panel of the vehicle.

And so the list goes on. In each case, we tried to corroborate the information that came from various sources. It was far too big a task for our small office, but we found nothing to undermine what we were learning. All of this seemed to be increasingly relevant to the case at hand.

Then there was the double homicide of Derrick and Duane Moo Young in the DuPont Plaza Hotel in Miami on October 16th, 1986. This was, I was told, a cartel hit. My sources said the police framed Kris. Indeed, one source claimed to have had a conversation with 'Pete' Romero, who was partnering John Buhrmaster on the case.

'Gotta stick this guy,' Romero told him, referring to Kris Maharaj. That was MDPD code for framing someone.

Romero was close to Oscar Cuni. Romero was, I was told, definitely one of the cartel men inside the MDPD.

*

I have not often worked closely with law enforcement over the course of my career. That does not stem from an implacable refusal on my part; often it would suit justice well to do so. Indeed, the charity where I worked in New Orleans had a tremendous working relationship with the prosecution for one – sadly unique – three-year interregnum, where we would share our investigative findings with the prosecutors before they made their assessment of the case. They briefly showed great flexibility, and we are able to agree – extraordinarily – that the police had arrested the wrong person in 126 out of 171 potential capital cases. The decision to dismiss the charges was almost invariably made before indictment by a grand jury, which meant that the prosecutors were not responsible for the earlier mistakes; but this record was quite an indictment of the New Orleans Police Department. They had been arresting the wrong person three times out of four; substituting a coin toss for a trial would result in a far better chance of convicting the right person. The other slant on the story, of course, was that three-quarters of the real killers were still out there.

More recently, I've been working closely with the Metropolitan Police on their torture inquiry, looking into British complicity with the misguided rendition policies of the Bush administration. Most of the victims were Muslim men with beards who were understandably suspicious of authority. The Met officers have accepted that those who are being represented by us do-gooder lawyers are much more likely to trust us than they are an officer with a badge. The former prisoners also feel more comfortable telling the whole truth if they have someone in their corner. As such, police who are keen to get to the truth of the matter know it serves their purposes to include us in the discussion.

Of course, this analysis only applies if the police want to get to the bottom of what is going on.

I needed the help of US law-enforcement agencies if I was to take Kris' case forward. The information detailing how the Miami police had been conspiring with the cartels to commit murder was explosive, and it could also provoke the perpetrators to commit a few more homicides – of the witnesses against them. Obviously, Reprieve could not put someone in a witness protection programme. That option was only open to the authorities.

I made a few calls and, in late March 2012, I managed to set up a meeting with a senior lawyer with the Department of Justice. I went to his main office near the Mall in Washington, and waited in a library for twenty minutes: the leather chairs were surrounded by leather books, and some grim-looking jurists peered at me from the walls. The lawyer eventually showed up, apologised for being late, and listened to the synopsis of what I had learned.

He walked me across the street to meet with the head of the FBI Civil Rights division. This man, likewise, listened patiently to what I told him. I promised to send him a report outlining some of the material. In turn, he promised to get back to me. We discussed how this could not go to the Miami field office: they had, after all, been involved in some of the crimes. He said he would consider whom best to assign.

I emailed a preliminary memo shortly after leaving the capital.

After some months, I sent the FBI agent a follow-up email, asking what progress he had made.

I heard nothing.

I have heard nothing to this day.[16]

19

Waiting

It's August 2011, and I'm in Florida. Though we have been in frequent communication, it has now been two years since I last visited Kris and I am keen to update him about progress in our ongoing investigation into the various links that we have uncovered to drug smuggling in the Bahamas, Colombia and, more recently, Jamaica and Miami itself. I'm also anxious about him. I've been told that he's been seriously ill and is in hospital. He's seventy-two, and I'm worried that if and when our investigation bears fruit, it will be too late.

I arrive in Fort Lauderdale late in the evening. Marita pours me a drink and we sit, talking. She describes how she was burgled some weeks back. It was early afternoon, and she had stepped out of the house briefly. Someone must have been observing it. So was Marita's eighty-year-old neighbour, who saw two well-dressed young men at the door and assumed they were her guests. They had, indeed, come for a visit, but they entered by breaking through the dining-room window, then opened up the front door and started loading their car.

When she returned, Marita was heartbroken. On her fourteenth birthday, in 1953, her father gave her a gold bracelet that had belonged to her grandmother. For more than fifty years Marita had worn it almost every day. As she went out, she noticed that she had forgotten it and nearly went back. Now it is gone, along with a five-year-old computer that contained all the files she held for Kris. The machine was ancient in computing terms, worth little to the thieves, but the Internet was her only means of contact with the outside world.

Perhaps, Marita reflects, she was lucky. Her neighbour's appearance seemed to have scared the men off before they took the last of her possessions.

Losing her jewellery was one matter, but more recently Marita has been worried more than ever about losing her husband. Whenever she can, she has spent three hours with Kris every Saturday, fifty-two weeks a year, for a quarter-century. That is more than 1,300 weekends, hardly ever missing one. Once Kris' sentence was commuted to life, he was allowed to call her each evening for a maximum of fifteen minutes. He never used up the whole time. He did not want to be cut off, to be told by a guard that he had to stop. And there were other prisoners to think of, since there were only two phones for forty-six men. Still, the phone calls have been their lifeline.

Then ... nothing. The phone calls suddenly stopped. Marita rang the prison. Initially they told her only that Kris was sick.

'Where is he?' she demanded.

'We cannot say,' they replied. Security.

This brave woman, who has stuck by her man for a quarter-century, was not allowed to know whether he was dying or just had a cold.

After the burglary, kindly supporters bought her a new computer. She immediately emailed us in England with her concerns about Kris' health, but other crises had been consuming me. In one Texas case we had two months from start to finish to try to stave off the defendant's execution, and I had little time for anything else. The last two weeks I had averaged thirteen hours a day, seven days a week. When they finally killed him, I was fit for nothing. I had to quit the world for a while.

For ten weeks Marita had no idea how Kris was. After daily telephone conversations – silence. Finally a prison staffer let slip where Kris was: the Kendall hospital, with a vicious bacteria eating the flesh off his leg. But even then the authorities would tell Marita nothing about her husband's condition. According to someone's uncivilised rules, she was not allowed to visit him.

She was not even meant to know that he was in hospital. I think of a capital case we've got going in Yemen: Sharif Mobley, an American, was shot while he was being arrested by the security service in Sana'a. He vanished. His wife had no idea where he was. Eventually we learned that he had been in a hospital run by a German company. Only pressure applied back in Berlin got us a few meagre details:

there was a secret ward where Sharif was labelled 'Prisoner X'. We had derided President Saleh and his totalitarian regime and yet here, in metropolitan Miami, the State of Florida had 'disappeared' Kris for ten whole weeks.

When I called the prison I was told that I was the only one who could get in to see Kris, as his lawyer, and then only if it was an emergency. Sitting on the sofa opposite Marita, I now feel a surge of guilt that I didn't come sooner. Marita has shed so many tears that she looks drained. I am shocked at my own insensitivity.

I am up the next morning at six, bleary with jetlag. Marita sits across the breakfast table from me, clinging to her fond memories of life in Britain, with toast and Robertson's Original English thick-cut marmalade. I leave her house in a rental car, promising to report to her as soon as I get out from my visit. I am going to be there far too early, but I do not want to be late. Kris has waited a long time for a visit.

I park at the Kendall Regional Medical Facility. It takes me a while to settle on a space, as there are signs that threaten to tow away unauthorised vehicles, but give no indication which places are authorised for visitors. At the front desk it seems like any other hospital, but when I announce the purpose of my visit, the receptionist summons three burly corrections officers, who lead me through several security doors into the prison section of the hospital. One guard takes me to a bed, but Kris is not there. He must have been moved. We circle around a dozen cubicles, each with a hospital bed, each open at the front so that the panopticon guard in the centre can observe them all. The patients are all old men, lying prone. One has a bandage wrapped around his head. Most look close to death.

The guard points at another bed. For a moment I question whether it can be Kris. The man is clearly asleep, snoring quietly, his mouth open wide to the ceiling. He has a beard, something I have never seen on Kris. But then I realise it is indeed him. The guard asks what to do. I reply that I am sure Kris won't mind me waking him. I gently press his shoulder. He opens his eyes. He is confused. He tells me later that nobody had informed him I was coming. He has been waiting for ten weeks without any contact with the outside world.

I think of the vigorous man I first met in 1994. I sometimes wonder at the grey hair those years have put on me, but they are nothing compared to Kris' decline. His hair is very thin now, though the grey beard has come in full. One of his lower teeth is missing – if he were free, he'd have the dental work done; as it is, he just has a gap. He is breathing with a little difficulty, so we move the oxygen tube to hiss into him gently. It doesn't fit properly, so we can only get one jet into his nose. At the foot of the bed there is a fancy electronic readout that purports to tell his weight and monitor various vital signs. It is obviously not working, weighing him in at 200 pounds: he was 180 pounds when he came into hospital, and one of the nurses agrees when Kris says that he can't be more than 160 pounds after weeks of barely eating.

Kris is uncomfortable and wriggles. He needs to move his foot, but when I lift up the sheet, I see that he is shackled to the bed. His left ankle, so emaciated, is wrapped in bandages to limit the chafing. It makes me angry to see this. Here is a man who is barely alive, who cannot walk, surrounded by half a dozen guards, behind several locked doors, chained down … What is the point? As tends to happen at such moments, Wilfred Owen's poem 'Futility' intrudes on my mind: 'Was it for this the clay grew tall?' The toenails on Kris' right foot are crumbling, fragmented, orange, like the sandstone that collapses to the foot of the cliff near my home. On the inner shin there is a foot-long gouge where the bacteria have been scraped away. It is currently taped up, with a tube dripping antibiotics directly into it.

'My God! I am glad to see you!' Kris exclaims. He leans back in momentary pain, closing his eyes again briefly. A tear runs, trembling, down the side of his eyelid.

It's been ten weeks, I think to myself.

'I asked to see you, my lawyer,' he says. 'They said no lawyer, I couldn't even write. I asked to see the British Consul. They said no consul. I asked to see Marita. No visit from my wife. Paper. No. Television just to watch the news. No. Letters. No. Writing letters. No. Books. No. The only thing except the Bible I can have is some Christian thing, something written in 1994.'

1994? I wonder, abstractly, at his mention of the date. Did he mean George Orwell's *1984*?

The neon strip-lighting above the bed is his only companion. I am concerned at the flickering, and ask whether it is affecting him. Kris says it's all right – that's the least of his concerns.

'For weeks I cried,' he admits, uncharacteristically. Kris does not willingly share emotion. 'I felt like they put me here as the final act to kill me. Back in the prison, I was in South Unit. There were forty-six people in the dorm, and they put me in Bunk 2106. The last two people who'd had that bed had an infection. The man next to me, only three feet away, had an infection too. It came on all of a sudden, one morning – June 1st, I think. I asked to see medical.'

The prison doctor came and looked at him. She recognised the problem at once: a flesh-eating bacteria, with the alarming name 'necrotising fasciitis', and said he'd need surgery right away. They took him to the Kendall hospital. They treated the move like a presidential trip to Afghanistan, as if someone might attack the prison van at any moment. Kris was unconscious for most of the first few days on the ward and is not sure whether the operation was on June 1st or 2nd. Since then they have been opening the wound up every two days to clean it out.

At one point the surgeon said they might have to amputate. 'I nearly gave up. When the doctor said she might have to take my leg off, I nearly gave up,' Kris says, grimacing in pain once more. 'I prayed that they would save my leg. It was like an elephant's. But I want to be able to walk normally when I get back to England.

'I'd never been in hospital before I was in prison. Not as a patient, though I'd visited a few people there. But here, it's two hours of begging for a cup of water before a nurse will bring it. One of them said she'd slap me if I complained. Slap me!'

By and large the nurses seem to like Kris more than the other prisoners on the ward. It makes me wonder how the other prisoners get on. Kris does not complain much, and is unfailingly polite to everyone, in a very English way.

To me, he begins a lecture about the NHS. 'People in Britain don't know how fortunate they are. God blessed them by making them British.'

A nurse interrupts. Kris has pointed her out as one of the difficult ones, but she is civil enough with me there. She injects him with his four-hourly painkiller and it eases Kris' discomfort. She also checks his blood sugar, which is just within normal limits.

Sometimes, Kris says, the nurses have shown some kindness. 'Yesterday the nurse made me sit up on the side of the bed,' he explains. This was the first experiment in physical therapy. 'It made me feel like a human being for the first time in weeks.'

Did they take the shackle off his leg for this? I ask him. 'No, no!' he exclaims, surprised that I would think anything so foolish. Letting him sit on the side of the bed in chains once in ten weeks hardly defines kindness, I think, but I keep my opinion to myself.

Kris is due for a skin graft on the leg today, at three o'clock. I agree to be gone by then, to speed his chances of recovery. He has not been able to eat or even drink water, in preparation for the operation, which worries me. I know I wouldn't be able to talk for the next four hours without a sip of water. Kris is not bothered. He's just happy to have the chance to talk at all. One of the female guards provides him with two cold flannels to mop his face.

I try to do most of the talking for an hour or so. I fill him in with messages from Marita, catch him up on world events, update him on our investigation into his case. But our conversation doesn't get far before he starts insisting, as he does on every visit, that he did not do it. He does not have to win me over, but he knows he still has to convince the world, and there is frustration in his voice.

'I didn't kill the Moo Youngs,' he begins, as he always does. 'I didn't pay someone to kill them, I didn't do a bloody thing. What I'm saying is not ninety per cent true; it's one hundred per cent.'

Kris has had a quarter-century to try and puzzle out what was meant to happen in Room 1215 of the DuPont Plaza on October 16th, 1986. He's shared this theory before, and I suspect he is right. 'I was meant to be dead that day. I would have been another body in the room. They would have killed me too, to make it look like I killed the Moo Youngs and then committed suicide when I realised what I had done. They'd have left the gun in my hand.

'Neville Butler tried to make me stay,' he reminds me. 'But I wouldn't. I had another appointment. I don't like to be late for appointments, so I insisted. I had to go.'

After a while I worry that I'm not going to be able to think of enough things to say to fill the four hours. I'm not very good at just talking, but I want to stay the full time available to me, and Kris has no intention of letting me go early. The kinder of the guards takes me out to the toilet – you have to go through the prison doors – and that gives me a moment to remember how to keep Kris chattering happily for hours. I can't have been thinking straight – it's the jetlag. All I have to do is get him to tell a few stories about how he out-manoeuvred a business rival.

When I go back into the ward the guard asks if I would like some coffee. I hate to drink it while my client is barred from a sip of water, but Kris insists, and I am grateful. Tiredness is catching up with me. I start on a large cup as Kris takes us back to when he was fifteen, in Trinidad in 1954. It was his first employment outside his family shop, and it was a car dealership. All the other salesmen were in their thirties and forties. When Kris applied for a job the owner initially sneered, but eventually took him on a three-month trial – no salary, just a promise of a 5 per cent commission.

'The other salesmen were given their own car, a basic two hundred dollars a month, and a two per cent commission on top,' Kris recalled. But he went to a family friend, a banker who acquired cars for a large corporation. Kris gave him a good price, expecting several sales, and cut him in for 2 per cent for each car sold. 'In the first month, I took in fourteen hundred dollars. The other salesmen were angry. I was making a lot more than them and I only just started.' In the second month, Kris promised the receptionist her own 2 per cent on any other calls that came into the dealership. He sold even more, and made $2,000 – a fortune for 1955.

'I've never had one week of unemployment in my life,' Kris says. He's not being critical of others. It's a pride that was drilled into him by his father. 'When I first got to England, I went down to the Labour Exchange for five weeks looking for work. They said I could get ten pounds a week on the dole, but I refused. I didn't want something for nothing.'

Kris tells me the story – for the tenth time – of his stallion, King Levenstall, and how he beat the Queen's horse, Parnell, at Royal Ascot. I like to see him removed from his current situation, but my attention wanders a little from stories of the past to the grim present. Kris' universe is daubed in grimy orange-yellow paint. There are no pictures hanging on any wall. There is a small closet behind me, which I take to be a toilet that I am not allowed to use, and that Kris cannot get to. I adjust the pillow behind his head and he shifts in pain again. I notice that there is no sound from any of the other beds. No movement, either. It is as if they have all been drugged into oblivion – perhaps the kinder alternative.

Kris drifts back to his case.

'I didn't believe they were serious about having me killed until after the trial,' he says. 'When I got up in the morning after I was sentenced, I felt it was my last day on this planet. I felt I had lost my mind. I thought I may as well be dead.'

I comment on how I would like to talk to the jurors, but under Florida's restrictive law I cannot, unless they come forward. 'The jurors had their minds poisoned by the prosecutors,' Kris says. He does not blame the twelve people who condemned him. He sees it as almost inevitable, given what he has learned about the process. 'In a way I think the death penalty is more humane than what I have suffered. Many days I have woken up saying to God: take me home. It's only because of Marita that I am still here.

'My advice to jurors in future is that they need to demand the facts,' he says. 'Don't accept it if you're not told. And you've got to be sure beyond a shadow of a doubt.'

It's been a long time – almost twenty years – since we first met. Once we get going Kris and I are comfortable, like an old couple. We can talk about difficult things.

'What have I missed? My wife. My freedom. But what is freedom? To me, it would have been the chance to open up a few more businesses. To try to help people have some jobs they need, and they like.'

I ask him whether he would have done other things – maybe get involved in sport. He reminisces briefly about his passion for cricket. 'But I probably wouldn't have played cricket again if I'd been freed. It would have been going backwards, and I don't go backwards. Besides, I always want to be the best at what I do, and I wouldn't have been the best at cricket.'

He has missed travelling.

'I'd like to have taken Marita travelling. I always wanted to go to Red Square in Moscow, because I read about it as a child. I was going there once, but the *News of the World* ran a story just before I went. Some British businessman had been arrested for spying. That was enough for me.'

Then he moves into the future tense. Kris can never stay long in what might have been. He prefers to paint a picture of what is to come – if only a court will listen to his case.

'I'd like to take Marita to South Africa. I wouldn't go when there was apartheid. But I'd like to see Nelson Mandela.'

Kris and Marita married in 1976. 'We went to Paris after we got married. I never spoke French, but I loved Paris,' Kris recalls. As usual, it is almost impossible for him to reminisce without reverting to a business opportunity. 'I went there one other time, went to La Coupole, the famous restaurant on boulevard Montparnasse. I'd taken someone there, a business contact, and he ordered something fancy. I just wanted something I knew. I saw this thing on the menu called *Pied au Porc*. I thought that meant pork pie, so I ordered it. The waiter came up with a big tray, and it had two pig trotters on it. I tried to send it back: that wasn't what I ordered. But he explained to me. I was shocked. Here was this expensive dish, and I was selling pig trotters in Africa for two shillings each at the time. It was done in white wine, with butterbeans – it was delicious. I took the recipe home with me. Dorothy from Jamaica was our housekeeper at the time. She was a wonderful cook, and she used to do it after that.'

But Kris has changed over the years. *Now*, whenever he finishes a story about a business deal, he will always turn back to his wife.

'Between you and me, and God,' Kris says, looking up at the neon lights, 'I didn't expect her to stay with me. She was beautiful, educated, speaks six languages. I thought she would move on. But she didn't. "You're the man I married," she said. "I agreed till death us do part." Not one in a million women would have stayed through all this.'

He is reflective again. I wonder if this unburdening – rare for him – is provoked by his most recent close encounter with death. 'Perhaps I can fool you, and perhaps you can fool me, but we can't fool God. And I have to be honest. If this happened to Marita back in 1986, would I have stuck by her like she did me? The straight answer is no. I would have paid whatever it took, given her money. But I'd not have stuck by her all these years. Now, it's different, and that's one thing I've learned. Now, if she needed a heart transplant, I'd give her mine. Not a second thought. May God take me home before her – that's all I want. Don't leave me on this Earth without her.'

Kris asks me to pass a message along to Marita. 'I love you till the day I die. I've been crying for you until today, when I learned that you were okay. I miss your voice every night, but I look forward to being out of here soon, so I can see you every Saturday.'

I ask Kris what keeps him going, when he can't do anything in the hospital. He responds by quoting Psalm 23 – the entire thing from memory. 'Surely goodness and mercy and love shall follow me all the days of my life,' he intones. I look at the grubby wall again, and wonder.

We talk about how things have changed for him since we met back in 1994. 'Well,' he begins, with slight hesitation. He has been happier talking about his business ventures, past and future. 'I suppose you could say I've lost my hair. Right now I feel like I've lost my brain. Here in this hospital bed I'm ruined completely.' He pauses briefly again, before the true Kris reappears. 'But I'll get it back. I'll get it back. I'm not afraid of this. They've tried to kill me for twenty-five years. I can't allow them to finish killing me.'

I tell him I have to leave soon. He looks up at me. 'When you get up in the morning, just remember me and Marita. Remember we're suffering.'

He wants to return to the South Unit, at the prison, where there is a three-mile concrete track. Kris is already planning how he will use his wheelchair as part of his rehabilitation. On a good day he hopes for eight hours outside, even in the South Florida heat. He describes the regime he has in mind. Perhaps a mile in the chair, to strengthen his arms; followed by a mile behind the chair, using it as a walker; a mile in the chair; followed by a mile behind the chair.

'I can't allow them to finish killing me,' he says again. 'I want to be the best bloody wheelchair man in the whole place.'

Acknowledgements

First I must acknowledge that this book is about a case in which I have thus far failed. Kris Maharaj remains in prison, and while I've tried to show how the system is designed to let people like Kris down, what matters most to me is that Kris is freed before he dies.

Therefore, in acknowledging failure, I must also ask for help. First and foremost for the help of those who are yet to come forward and tell us what really happened in this case. Justice for Kris Maharaj will never be achieved if we don't hear from you. You may have heard someone talking about the case. You may have access to the records that with a few keystrokes would show the historical connections behind the murder. You may know the people described in these pages. It's not too late and it won't be while Kris is alive. Everyone now knows that Miami was riddled with Colombian cartel corruption in the 1980s, but we are not asking you to bring down any institutions – legal or otherwise – with the information you may have. We just need to know who knew what when the Moo Youngs were murdered.

Anyone who has information that may relate to the case in some way, however seemingly distant, can write to me at clive@reprieve.org.uk, or contact me at Reprieve, PO Box 52742, London EC4P 4WS; phone: +44 (0)20 7353 4640.

The case also needs funding. Kris is in prison in part because we have never had the money needed for a full investigation. This case spans continents. We need cash for airfares, petrol, accommodation, copies of old files that may contain the key to the case – the list goes on and on. To date, the investigation and litigation has cost tens of thousands of pounds in direct costs, as well as tens of thousands of hours of pro bono labour. Yet the battle is far from over.

I must also acknowledge that the publication of this book is going to magnify the pain experienced by the victims' family. They have been told that Kris Maharaj killed Derrick and Duane Moo Young, and they believe this. The justice system left them awaiting the 'closure' of an execution for many years, and now all they are told to hope for is that Kris never leaves prison. This book may stir up more questions, and dredge up additional anguish for the family. For this, I am truly sorry, but I must also beg the family to consider, in the light of evidence presented in these pages, whether their certainty that the right person is in prison for this crime is not misplaced, and whether they remember anything about Derrick and Duane's business activities in the months before they were killed that might suggest someone other than Kris Maharaj had a motive to see them murdered.

With these grim but necessary acknowledgements made, there comes the happier task of recognising the extraordinary work of Kris' dedicated but entirely *ad hoc* defence team.

For reasons of space, the impression this book leaves is that I somehow did all of the work on Kris' case myself. But I want to undo that impression here, as it is false. It has been a challenge to find a sufficiently clear narrative in the maelstrom of facts that surround the murder of the Moo Youngs to make a readable book, and it would have been too distracting for the reader to introduce each person who has worked on this case at the appropriate moment in the text. But these people are legion. And if you have worked on this case but are not listed here, please forgive me; a quarter of a century is a long time …

The state has never provided Kris Maharaj with the resources he needs to bring his claim of innocence fairly before the courts, and he has never had more than the part-time assistance of a motley crew of over-worked volunteers, but they have all done their damnedest to make the courts see that a terrible mistake has occurred.

White-collar criminal defence lawyer Ben Kuehne, his law partner Susan Dimitrovsky and others in Ben's law firm have been lynchpins in this case. Ben signed on to help Kris for a reduced fee on one element of the appeal eighteen years ago, and has remained loyal to Kris' cause ever after, never being paid again.

The UK law firm Freshfields Bruckhaus Deringer has acted as British liaison on the case for almost as long. I'll mention by name Paul Lomas, Clarissa O'Callaghan, Malindi Durrant, Florence Brocklesby, Patrick Doris, Peter Turner and Mark Boyle but there were many others at the firm who worked on this case on a purely pro bono basis. Most recently, Paul and Clarissa had the task of pleading for clemency for Kris in Tallahassee; tragically, their plea was rejected by an unreceptive governor and his panel.

I was director of the Louisiana Crisis Assistance Center in New Orleans for eleven years, and during that period many of the staff and volunteers there dedicated their 'spare' time and effort to this case. Staff members and volunteers Richard Bourke, Frieda Brown, Chris Eades, Joe Hingston, Malkia Johnson, 'Mwalimu Johnson, 'Mlinata Johnson, Shauneen Lambe, Simone Leijon, Dale Long, Beth O'Reilly, Lynne Overman, Gary Proctor, Bart Stapert and Kim Watts all somehow squeezed time for Kris into their already full caseloads, poring over the documentary evidence, tracking down witnesses and records, working overnight to get exhibits ready for hearings, liaising with British Government officials and generally keeping alive a man who the State of Florida would much rather have seen executed.

Ron Petrillo, the investigator originally hired by Kris' trial lawyer, has refused to let this case die, and has made himself available to every subsequent investigator, lawyer and journalist who has attempted to retrace his footsteps. He remains convinced to this day that the wrong person is in prison for this crime. Another South Florida private investigator with an Achilles heel for wrongful conviction cases has provided vital local advice and assistance on Kris' case more recently, at considerable cost to his solo practice.

Peter Bottomley MP has been the most dedicated of the British parliamentarians to support Kris, though a hundred others signed onto Kris' brief before the Florida Supreme Court. Barristers have come out from the UK to Florida to help on the case, including Geoffrey Robertson QC and Philip Sapsford QC. And I am grateful to various journalists who have brought the case to public attention, including (but not limited to) Tim Samuels and Ian Katz.

Since I came back to the UK in 2004 to work with the charity Reprieve (www.reprieve.org.uk), staff on the death-penalty team there have all pitched in to support Kris and Marita, including Clare Algar, Marc Callcutt, Hayley Ichilcik, Fatou Kane, Zachary Katznelson, Caroline Morten, and others, operating on a shoestring budget but achieving results that are even more disturbing for those who think the Florida criminal justice system always gets it right.

Other friends, troubled by Kris' story, have helped out in various ways, including Sue Carpenter, Ben Rich (and his colleagues at Luther Pendragon), as well as Kris' old friends Thelma and Tom Wade. I am particularly grateful to the two anonymous benefactors who have helped Marita survive, and support her husband, under particularly dire circumstances.

I also wish to thank the many consular officials at the Foreign & Commonwealth Office (FCO) who have had contact with Kris and Marita over the years. When this case began, the UK had a rather lacklustre policy on helping Britons facing the death penalty – and Kris suffered specifically because of such a lack of support. However, much has changed, and today's FCO is vastly more proactive. This has been a very positive evolution, which has received too little recognition; long may it continue to develop.

When it comes to the book, my thanks to my agent, Patrick Walsh, for his constant encouragement, along with everyone at Conville Walsh; and to Rebecca Carter, whose vigour with the red pen is the kind of editing I have often longed for (and always needed). Also to others who have worked with the team at Random House, including: Sue Amaradivakara, Liz Foley, Sinead Martin, Ellie Steel, Amanda Telfer and Simon Wilkes.

A thank you to my mother, Jean, who proofread the book, and to my wife, Emily Bolton, who has worked on the case for many years, and has also helped shape both the litigation and the writing.

Notes

1
The Case

1   This version of the case is taken essentially verbatim from the opening statement of the prosecution in the trial. *State v. Maharaj*, Transcript at 2151–76. This was a much more coherent presentation of the prosecution case than the closing argument, which was a response to the defence closing and therefore rambled, and would not have been comprehensible to anyone who had not heard the case. I have added minor matters necessary to a full understanding of the case (e.g., the location of the Dupont Plaza Hotel – in Miami), for those to whom this would not be immediately obvious. And I have done what all trial lawyers wish the court reporter would do – clarified a few places where the speaker was incoherent.

2   Joanne Green, 'British Ex-Millionaire Fights for Freedom: Krishna Maharaj went from the high life to a life sentence – for a crime he might not have committed', *Miami Times* (Sep. 27th, 2007), http://www.miaminewtimes.com/2007-09-27/news/british-ex-millionaire-fights-for-freedom/.

2

The Execution

1   As a result of litigation, Georgia has since changed its method of execution to lethal injection. Plenty of problems have arisen with respect to this 'kinder, gentler' form of execution as well. For details, see the Reprieve website. www.reprieve.org.uk.

2   Various articles on the subject subsequently came out. See, e.g., 'Chefs Choose their Last Suppers', *Washington Post* (April 2006). Subsequently Melanie Dunea produced a book on the subject: Dunea, *My Last Supper: 50 Great Chefs and Their Final Meals – Portraits, Interviews and Recipes* (2007).

3   Compare this to the electric-chair eloquence that was expected of him. See http://www.corsinet.com/braincandy/dying2.html. In 1977 the first person executed in the modern era, Gary Gilmore, said, 'Let's do it!' In 1987 Jimmy Glass told his Louisiana executioners, 'I'd rather be fishing.' Other statements that satisfied the media included the final words of George Appel, electrocuted by New York in 1928 ('Well, gentlemen, you are about to see a baked apple'); similar bravado from James French, electrocuted by Oklahoma in 1966 ('How about this for a headline for tomorrow's paper? French fries'); Thomas J. Grasso, executed by Oklahoma in 1995 ('I did not get my Spaghetti-O's, I got spaghetti. I want the press to know this'); and so forth. In Georgia the prison taped the final statements of each prisoner who made one and, along with a description of the execution from the 'command post', they are posted on the internet. http://soundportraits.org/on-air/execution_tapes/last_words.php.

4   Ironically, one claim that we had raised to try and prevent Nicky's execution this time around was the cruelty of the use of electrocution. Filing the claim was not an easy choice, because it meant that Nicky would have to read in detail what the State of Georgia had in store for him. The federal Court of Appeals summarily dismissed the issue, stating that '[t]he contention that death by electrocution violates the Eighth Amendment is frivolous'. *Ingram v. Ault*, 50 F.3d 898 (11th Cir. 1995), quoting *Johnson v. Kemp*, 759 F.2d 1510 (11th Cir. 1985). Much later everyone would agree that electrocution, along with the gas chamber and various other such forms of execution, was indeed a cruel and unusual punishment and would turn to lethal injection. But Nicky's death would be just one additional cruelty before these later decisions would take effect.

5   This book is not the place to attempt to describe Nicky's sad life, and

the tragic and senseless death of J.C. Sawyer. Briefly, Nicky was accused of entering the home of J.C. and Mary Sawyer in Cobb County, marching them out into the woods and shooting them both. J.C. died instantly; Mary feigned death, and fortunately survived. Nicky, who was just nineteen, was an alcoholic, and claimed that he could remember nothing of the evening. Another person implicated in the crime testified against him and escaped punishment.

3

The Mission

1   An apologist for the lie detector would either say this is not possible or label me as part of the 'sociopathic segment of the population', capable of lying without emotion. See 'How Accurate is a Polygraph', at http://www.truthorlie.com/beatpoly.html (accessed Sep. 7th, 2010). ('How can you beat a polygraph? You can't. If the examinee KNOWS they are lying [*sic*], the polygraph will detect the lie. Unless the examinee is part of that tiny sociopathic segment of the population that can tell a lie *and honestly believe it*, they cannot beat the polygraph. Most *experienced* polygraph examiners can detect deception') (emphasis in the original). However, this is nonsense. I am a hopeless liar. Others agree that the polygraph can quite readily be fooled. See Anti-Polygraph.Org, at http://antipolygraph.org/ (accessed Sep. 7th, 2010). ('Liars can beat the test by covertly augmenting their physiological reactions to the "control" questions. This can be done, for example, by doing mental arithmetic, thinking exciting thoughts, altering one's breathing pattern, or simply biting the side of the tongue. Truthful persons can also use these techniques to protect themselves against the risk of a false positive outcome. Although polygraphers frequently claim they can detect such countermeasures, no polygrapher has ever demonstrated any ability to do so, and peer-reviewed research suggests that they can't.')

4

The Defendant

1   Actually, in Kris' case, various steps had already gone by – as discussed in more detail in Chapter 14. After the initial trial, the Florida Supreme Court had sent the case for a hearing on new evidence before

the appeal took place, but no lawyer had appeared on Kris' behalf, and the ninety days allowed for the so-called *coram nobis* writ had simply expired. The court then denied his direct appeal, and the US Supreme Court in Washington refused to hear the case (denying *certiorari*, as it is called). See *Maharaj v. Florida*, 506 US 1072, 113 S. Ct. 1029, 122 L. Ed. 2d 174 (1993). Represented by new counsel, Kris had filed his application for a fresh trial – called a Rule 3.850 Petition in Florida, after the section of the criminal code that authorises it – again confident that he would soon be home. A new judge denied him a hearing and affirmed his conviction. This was now on appeal to the Florida Supreme Court.

2   See *Maharaj v. State*, 597 So. 2d 786 (Fla. 1992).

3   In 1994, for example, the Supreme Court granted review in the cases of eighty-three of 2,151 people who were able to pay their lawyers (3.9 per cent), and only ten of 4,979 who had no money (*in forma pauperis*, or pauper cases, as they are called) (0.2 per cent). Timothy Bishop & Jeffrey Sarles of Mayer Brown, 'Petitioning and Opposing Certiorari in the US Supreme Court' (1999), at http://library.findlaw.com/1999/Jan/1/241457.html. Even after the case is granted, the chances of winning are no better (and often worse) than fifty:fifty. Thus the odds of winning are perhaps one in 1,000.

4   When I first took on Kris Maharaj's appeals, I had never won at this stage of a case. One can go back to the state Supreme Court, and then try one's luck with the Supreme Court in Washington at this point, but it's pretty hopeless: only one capital defendant has won a US Supreme Court writ in state habeas in twenty years. Because I am such an optimist I always tried it, and was fortunate enough to win that case – *Johnson v. Mississippi*, 486 US 578, 108 S. Ct. 1981, 100 L. Ed. 2d 575 (1988) (holding that the Eighth Amendment requires re-examination of the Mississippi death sentence where one factor considered aggravation was a prior New York conviction, which was subsequently invalidated by the New York Court of Appeals).

5   Since they don't seem to update the photos very often, the Florida Department of Corrections photograph of Kris reflects the way he looked when I first met him. See http://www.dc.state.fl.us/ActiveInmates/Detail.asp?Bookmark=1&From=list&SessionID=690933893 (as accessed, Aug. 2010).

6   His record showed a daily pharmaceutical intake that included 10mg Glucotrol, 5mg Altace, 850mg Glucophage, 25mg Atenolol, 10mg Norvasc, 10mg Lipitor, 325mg Xaspirin, 500mg Acetaminop, 4mg Cardura. See Tim Samuels, 'Killing Time', *The Guardian* (Aug. 4th, 2001), http://www.guardian.co.uk/Archive/Article/0,4273,4232492,00.html.

7   See Florida Department of Corrections website, 'Death Row Fact Sheet:

The Daily Routine of Death Row Inmates', at http://www.dc.state.fl.us/oth/deathrow/#Routine (accessed Aug. 8th, 2010) ('Inmates may receive mail every day except holidays and weekends. They may have cigarettes, snacks, radios and 13" televisions in their cells. They do not have cable television or air-conditioning and they are not allowed to be with each other in a common room. They can watch church services on closed circuit television. While on Death Watch, inmates may have radios and televisions positioned outside their cell bars.')

8   My longer conversations came when he volunteered to be a witness for Kris much later. This was in itself an extraordinary statement about a Death Row prisoner, as guards are reticent about testifying – if they do it for one person, they get pressure to do it for any number. But in Kris' case we were spoiled for choice. In the end, four senior Death Row guards voluntarily drove 360 miles together down to Miami to say their piece in court. All believed in the death penalty, but none did for Kris.

9   See Florida Department of Corrections, Execution List (1976–present), http://www.dc.state.fl.us/oth/deathrow/execlist.html (accessed Aug. 7th, 2010). That means Guthrie was involved in the deaths of twenty-nine men, including David Raulerson, who Steve Bright represented with very limited help from me, and Jesse Tafaro, whose mother used to ride up with Marita Maharaj from Fort Lauderdale for prison visits. Mrs Tafaro had become Marita's good friend.

10   When I write about 'criminal defendants' generally, I will use the male gender for simplicity's sake, since, while there are roughly 200,000 women in American prisons and jails, there are roughly 2.2 million men.

11   Ken Payne's rise as a window-cleaner-turned-racehorse-trainer was sadly the precursor to an equally rapid fall. See Gary Owen, 'Where are they now? Ken Payne', Daily Record (Aug. 30th, 2003), http://www.highbeam.com/doc/1G1-107088188.html (after a few years of the champagne lifestyle, in 1976 Payne's three-year-old son was tragically killed in a farming accident. Payne declared bankruptcy owing £250,000 – an extraordinary amount for that time – and then attempted suicide).

12   'The Golden Age of Grunt'n'Groan', The Independent (Feb. 18th, 2006), http://www.independent.co.uk/news/media/the-golden-age-of-gruntngroan-466931.html.

13   See http://www.lordstaverners.org/.

14   There are many people who must be given credit for a great deal of work that has been done on Kris' case. When I first took on Kris' appeal, I had just left my job in Atlanta to set up a new and very tenuous charity in New Orleans called the Louisiana Crisis Assistance Center (LCAC), devoted primarily to capital trials. The staff there gradually

grew to twenty-three, along with a large number of Reprieve volunteers from Britain and Australia, as well as the US. Since 2004, when I left New Orleans to return to Britain, I have worked at Reprieve with a similarly dedicated crew of lawyers, investigators and volunteers. Over the last two decades many of these people have devoted time to Kris' case. Furthermore, all along I have worked with Ben Kuehne, who was originally retained for Kris' post-conviction appeal in 1994. Since the funds ran out (shortly thereafter), Ben has represented Kris pro bono, along with others in his Miami law office. In the UK the law firm of Freshfields Bruckhaus Deringer has also put in countless hours of pro bono work.

15   The list of people who had benefited from Kris' generosity was a long one. For example, Clive Brittain was perhaps the most successful flat-racing trainer of his generation. Kris spontaneously helped him when he started out training, and gave Brittain his first chance at training a Classics horse. Brittain had even more to say about Kris' generosity towards his stable lads, and his concern for the jockeys who were injured. Tom and Thelma Wade have been among Kris' firmest friends since the Sixties, when they met – as usual – at the racetrack. Before his retirement, Tom was a doctor, his clientele drawn mainly from the Middle East. The Wades have continued to back Kris throughout his imprisonment. Kris was often a dinner guest at the Wades' Harley Street home. Peter Bottomley MP, became one of Kris' advocates, giving up his place at the funeral of Princess Diana to come over to the US and be a witness for him. And Leslie Hall had suffered a serious car accident, and been told by her doctor that she would never ride again. She sat next to Kris at a dinner party at the Wades' house one evening, and when he heard her story, he promised to set her up with board and lodging to ride his horses. 'I thought it very unlikely that he would do all this for me, someone he had barely met,' she said, 'but that was to underestimate Kris Maharaj. He was a man of his word.' Thanks to him, Leslie achieved her dream to ride in a professional race. And so it went on and on.

16   Kris' battle is discussed in a book on the subject. See Gordon Myers, *Banana Wars: The Price of Free Trade: A Caribbean Perspective* (2004), reviewed at http://www.allbusiness.com/government/employment-regulations/3993242-1.html.

17   'Cockfield defeated in Green Bananas trade battle', *Daily Telegraph*, at 3 (Saturday, March 5th, 1983).

18   Surprisingly, perhaps, Britain has been the largest foreign investor in the US consistently since 1803 (when it took over from the Dutch). See 'Foreign Investment in the US', *US History Encyclopedia*, http://www.answers.com/topic/foreign-investment-in-the-united-states. During

the 1980s British investment in the US rose from $11.3 billion to a staggering $119.1 billion. Marvin H. Kosters & Allan H. Meltzer, *International Competitiveness in Financial Circles* (1991), at 355–6.

19   There are a number of articles about Kris' life from which I have drawn, in addition to recapping the history with Kris in person. See Tim Samuels, 'Killing Time', *The Guardian* (Aug. 4th, 2001), http://www.guardian.co.uk/Archive/Article/0,4273,4232492,00.html; Joanne Green, 'British Ex-Millionaire Fights for Freedom: Krishna Maharaj went from the high life to a life sentence – for a crime he might not have committed', *Miami Times* (Sep. 27th, 2007), http://www.miaminewtimes.com/2007-09-27/news/british-ex-millionaire-fights-for-freedom/; BBC *Newsnight*, 'Krishna Maharaj's Death Row Diary' (Oct. 13th, 2004), http://news.bbc.co.uk/1/hi/programmes/newsnight/3740328.stm; Dana Canedy, 'Britons Testify To Spare Life Of Millionaire', *New York Times* (March 26th, 2002), http://query.nytimes.com/gst/fullpage.html?res=9400E1DA123BF935A15750C0A9649C8B63#; Tim Samuels, 'Murder trial of British businessman in America was "riddled with [mistakes]"', *The Independent* (Oct. 13th, 2004), http://findarticles.com/p/articles/mi_qn4158/is_20041013/ai_n12815774; David Adams, 'British rally to save man on Death Row', *St Petersburg Times* (Sep. 10th, 1997), http://pqasb.pqarchiver.com/sptimes/access/14097853.html?FMT=FT&dids=14097853:14097853&FMTS=ABS:FT&type=current&date=Sep+10%2C+1997&author=DAVID+ADAMS&pub=St.+Petersburg+Times&desc=British+rally+to+save+man+on+death+row.

5

The Witness

1   See, e.g., *United States v. Kincade*, 379 F.3d 813, 838 (9th Cir. 1994) ('In our system of government, courts base decisions … on concretely particularized facts developed in the cauldron of the adversary process'); Robert Z. Dobrisch, 'A Lawyer's Considerations in Selecting a Mental Health Expert', reproduced in Linda Gunsberg & Paul Hymowitz, eds, *A Handbook of Divorce & Custody* (2005) ('Our system of justice is called the adversary system. Rather than determining the outcome of a controversy by ordeal or by battle, we do so by pitting lawyer against lawyer, trusting that, through the cauldron of negotiation or litigation, the truth will out').

2   Wigmore was a famous American legal scholar. Although he published it in 1904, his treatise on evidence is still considered an authority. See

generally W.R. Roalfe, *John Henry Wigmore, Scholar and Reformer*, (1977); *Kentucky v. Stincer*, 482 US 730, 736 (1987) ('The opportunity for cross-examination … is critical to the integrity of the fact-finding process. Cross-examination is "the principal means by which the believability of a witness and the trust of his testimony are tested"').

3   Jules Epstein, 'The Great Engine that Couldn't: Science, Mistaken Identifications, and the Limits of Cross-Examination', 36 *Stetson Law Review* 727 (2007).

4   See http://www.glossophobia.com/ ('As many as 75% people have glossophobia. Statistically, far more of us claim that we would prefer death to giving a speech; even comedian Jerry Seinfeld used to joke that at a funeral, most people would rather be lying in the casket than delivering the eulogy'); Peter Fisher, 'Public Speaking – a Greater Fear than Death?', http://ezinearticles.com/?Public-Speaking---A-Greater-Fear-Than-Death?&id=620521 (accessed (Nov. 27th, 2010) ('According to studies, public speaking is a bigger fear than death. Fear of public speaking is reported to be the number one fear of American adults, with many people experiencing tremendous suffering because of it').

5   For anyone who thinks these cases have happy endings, the jurors acquitted Smitty of the Skyway Bridge homicide, but still convicted him of enough crimes to send him to prison for life. Thus they credited the testimony of even 'Sick Quick' Holley when it came to various other offences.

6   *Maharaj Trial Transcript*, at 2730 *et seq.*

7   Det. Buhrmaster's description of his unrecorded conversation with Kris Maharaj was inculpatory by circumstantial implication – Kris' alleged denial that he was in Room 1215, when his fingerprints were found there.

8   *Second Deposition of Neville Butler*, at 9–10 (March 30th, 1987, 14.15 p.m.) (108911-983); see also *id.* ('He felt all along that I may have been part of it, but after meeting with me and getting to know me that three or four weeks, he was satisfied that I had no participation in the extortion.')

9   Butler's story leapt from one version to the next throughout his testimony. At trial, Butler said that Kris did not accuse him of being involved in the extortion. 'He never did express concern that I made … knew anything about it,' Butler told the jury, directly contradicting his earlier story. But later he changed again: 'And indeed at some time later on, he said to me he thought I was involved in … with exposing us … because in fact, my name was the one being used in Trinidad as having been behind the extortion. He told me that on a number of occasions.' *Maharaj Trial Transcript*, at 2759. He had been similarly inconsistent in his pre-trial deposition, where somehow

his involvement hinged on whether the name Butler was easier to remember than Carberry. See *Second Deposition of Neville Butler*, at 12 (March 30th, 1987, 14.15 p.m.) (108911-983). ('He never said that he knew that I contributed. But the fact that my name was much more easier to remember than Carberry, and I believe his people in Trinidad told him Butler was suppose to come, and he sort of tied Butler because he know I worked for the *Echo* and the assumption was drawn at that point that I did all the talking on the telephone or I wrote the articles.') Bizarrely, in his deposition, Butler had admitted that he actually had been involved in the extortion: 'Calls had been made from my home.' *Second Deposition of Neville Butler*, at 11 (March 30th, 1987, 14.15 p.m.) (108911-983). Carberry had called a man named Ramsook, and it involved bringing as much as $3 million out of the country. Supposedly, Kris complained that '[t]hey had extorted from his uncle [Ramsook] $160,000 using my name and that it would be in my best interest to assist him to set up this meeting.' *Id.*, at 9. It was all very muddled, something that Kris' lawyer should have hammered home to the jury.

10 *Maharaj Trial Transcript*, at 2755.

11 Even at trial, Butler was not able to maintain consistency about who Kris Maharaj supposedly wanted to meet – Moo Young or Carberry. At one point he testified: 'He kept saying, well, Carberry is involved in it and I think I would like to meet with him, and if you would help me set up – he couldn't talk to me,' Butler explained. 'He said that, "I will have evidence, I will have documents to prove where he received the money, because the money was gotten from some bank." I think he mentioned the Landmark Bank, and this was the story that he gave me.' *Maharaj Trial Transcript*, at 2756.

12 Butler was confused on this point. He went on to say he had already talked to Derrick Moo Young about some extortions, and Derrick was apparently the one to tell him that his name was linked with the crime: 'Before he even suggested that, I tried to speak with Mr Moo Young and became very concerned what he told me about my name being used in Trinidad as a person who is extorting money from his relatives. The reason I became very concerned, before I came to the United States, I was working with the Prime Minister in Trinidad and Tobago and I was publishing articles and well known and the president and everyone know who I was. And this would be a calamity as far as my name was concerned.' *Maharaj Trial Transcript*, at 2759.

13 *Maharaj Trial Transcript*, at 2756.

14 *Maharaj Trial Transcript*, at 2758–9. Although Hendon did not discuss this at trial, Butler had previously said that Dames wanted to get some restaurant equipment. See *Initial Deposition of Neville Butler*, at

45 (Jan. 13th, 1987, 15.30–18.30) (108736-860) ('We spoke of a specific project, the supplying of items that Eddie Dames may be interested in'). See also *Second Deposition of Neville Butler*, at 17–18 (March 30th, 1987, 14.15 p.m.) (108911-983) (Butler says he spoke to Derrick about restaurant equipment and property investment for his friend from Nassau, not about drugs).

15   *Maharaj Trial Transcript*, at 2763.

16   Detective Buhrmaster had made a statement to this effect himself. 'Sometime prior to October 15, 1986,' Buhrmaster explained, 'a man named Dames … had attempted to contact the Moo Youngs to arrange for shipment of equipment he had purchased in the Florida area …' *Maharaj 3.850 Clerk Tr. 2446*. Shaula Nagel had likewise told Buhrmaster that 'her father had mentioned that he received several messages from a Mr Dames, who he did not know, and did not bother returning the calls.' *Id.*, at 2453; *Maharaj 3.850 Exhibit OC*, at 9.

17   *Maharaj Trial Transcript*, at 2708.

18   In her initial statement Rivero seemed very certain – indeed, 100 per cent certain. *Maharaj Record No. 044_105518-525*, at 524 (initial sworn statement of Arlene Rivero to John Buhrmaster, March 3rd, 1987) (Q. 'You are one hundred percent sure that this was in fact the man?' A. 'Yes.'). She had been shown only one photograph alone, and had signed the back of it attesting that it was the person. Prior to making the identification, she gave no description of the person – age, height, weight, unique features, and so forth. In other words, it was about as suggestive an identification as one can imagine, and Eric Hendon should have asked the court to exclude it from the trial.

19   *Maharaj Trial Transcript*, at 2721. She said the police identification happened 'a couple of months later …' *Id.* She was off even on this. The interview was actually four and a half months later. *Maharaj Record No. 044_105518-525* (initial sworn statement of Arlene Rivero to John Buhrmaster, March 3rd, 1987).

20   *Maharaj Trial Transcript*, at 2722.

21   *Maharaj Trial Transcript*, at 2724. Rivero testified that the person was five-eight, five-ten or taller, thereby including a large proportion of the population. Her colleague, Inez Vargas, put the man's height at five-five, *Maharaj Trial Transcript*, at 2658 – far from Kris Maharaj, but close to Neville Butler. Vargas was another witness who identified Kris as the person who made the reservation. Her identification was much more equivocal from the beginning – she said only, 'I think that he was the one that made the reservation.' *Maharaj Record No. 044_105542-554*, at 549 (initial sworn statement of Inez Vargas to John Buhrmaster, March 3rd, 1987). Again, Buhrmaster had shown her a solitary photo, and had taken no prior description of the individual

beforehand. Such suggestive identification procedures are generally condemned, but Hendon did not bring any challenge pre-trial. *United States v. Wade*, 388 US 218, 228–9 (1967) (identification evidence is 'proverbially untrustworthy' and mistaken eyewitness identifications 'account for more miscarriages of justice than any other single factor'; unreliable IDs should be excluded by the trial judge). Intriguingly, Detective Buhrmaster asked both Rivera and Vargas whether anyone paid them to make sure that nobody else took rooms on the twelfth floor, based on information he had apparently received. *Id.,*.at 105553. This information has never been turned over to the defence, but it would clearly be helpful, as it would explain that whoever wanted to use Room 1215 wanted nobody snooping around. Of course, one room on the floor was permanently occupied – the room across the hall, which was registered to Jaime Vallejo Mejia, from Colombia.

22   In his first police statement Butler told Buhrmaster he got the room. See *Initial Police Statement of Neville Butler*, at 4 (Oct. 17th, 1986, 00.50 –01.30) (118882-99) (18 pages) (Q. 'When did you get that room?' A. 'The morning he was due to arrive.' Q. 'And that was Wednesday?' A.'Wednesday, yes.'). He repeated this in his first deposition. *Initial Deposition of Neville Butler*, at 9 (Jan. 13th, 1987, 15.30–18.30) (108736-860).

23   *Second Deposition of Neville Butler*, at 19 (March 30th, 1987, 14.15 p.m.) (108911-983).

24   *Second Deposition of Neville Butler*, at 19–20 (March 30th, 1987, 14.15 p.m.) (108911).

25   By the time of trial the prosecutors had elaborated on this story. To cover for all the times Butler said he had made the reservation, they had now led Butler to say that he did not even know that Maharaj had already done it. This time it was John Kastrenakes who was asking the questions – or, rather, telling Butler what might have happened: 'Did you know [Maharaj] had already registered into the room in the name of Eddie Dames?' Kastrenakes asked. 'No, I was not aware of that,' said Butler. *Maharaj Trial Transcript*, at 27. Kastrenakes drew out of the witness that Kris was in the hotel at the time Butler paid for the room. *Second Deposition of Neville Butler*, at 24–25 (March 30th, 1987, 14.15 p.m.) (108911-983). But Butler could not keep his story straight. He slipped up and said once again at trial that he made the reserva-tion. *Maharaj Trial Transcript*, at 2767. When the trial was over, and he had again lost his prompter, he reverted to his original story – that he reserved the room. In 1995 he repeated that 'I had booked a room in his [Dames'] name.' *Maharaj 3.850 Exhibit HP*, at 6 (1995 Channel 4 interview with Neville Butler).

26   *Second Deposition of Neville Butler*, at 23 (March 30th, 1987, 14.15 p.m.)

(108911-983). This was a fact that Hendon failed to bring out at trial. Back in 1986 few people carried hundred-dollar bills with them. I am not sure I have ever seen one, and I certainly had not then.

27 *Maharaj File No. 044_124776.*

28 Butler had insisted that he paid more than $55 per night. *Initial Deposition of Neville Butler*, at 10 (Jan. 13th, 1987, 15.30–18.30) (108736-860).

29 There is another – relatively inconsequential, but telling – example of Butler changing his story to fit the evidence. He had previously said that they had secured a rental car when Dames arrived, but now the prosecution had checked out the rental agreement (*State's Exhibit 100*) and it showed that the rental car was taken much later in the day – so Butler's story duly changed to fit the corroborating proof. *Maharaj Trial Transcript*, at 2774–5.

30 *Maharaj 3.850 Exhibit ICF.*

31 *Maharaj Trial Transcript*, at 2780.

32 The jurors would not have noticed, but Butler had given the wrong Moo Young number. 'On the newspaper there is written in blue ink on a complimentary copy of the DuPont Plaza, and *USA Today*, Exhibit Number 42, there is a number written in blue ink, 434-3648,' Kastrenakes interrupted again, smoothly. 'My question is, is that your handwriting?' Butler said it was, and that it was the Moo Young number. *Maharaj Trial Transcript*, at 2782–3.

33 *Maharaj Trial Transcript*, at 2803. It did not make much sense that Derrick would only now be recognising Butler – in setting up the Dames meeting, Butler would have clearly explained who he was and how they had previously met.

34 *Maharaj Trial Transcript*, at 2804–5.

35 Even Patton's guns – originally a pair of Colt Revolvers – were not actually white, but had white ivory handles. He carried two because, in his first taste of violence in 1914, in a punitive foray into Mexico chasing Pancho Villa, he had emptied the only handgun he carried, and had never again wanted to be without a backup. He gave one of his pair of Peacemakers away to a Hollywood star who came to the front in the Second World War, and thereafter substituted a Smith & Wesson .357 Magnum. See Masaad Ayoob, 'Why Patton Carried Two Guns' (*Guns Magazine*, Aug. 2003), at http://findarticles.com/p/articles/mi_m0BQY/is_8_49/ai_103381587/ (accessed Oct. 6th, 2010).

36 *Initial Police Statement of Neville Butler*, at 12 (Oct. 17th, 1986, 00.50–01.30) (118882-99) (18 pages).

37 *Initial Deposition of Neville Butler*, at 110 (Jan. 13th, 1987, 15.30–18.30) (108736-860) (even though he varies the amount of time he says that Kris may have had the gun tucked into his belt, Butler admits that he was with Kris, with the gun visible for at least an hour).

38   *Maharaj Trial Transcript*, at 2805.

39   *Maharaj Trial Transcript*, at 2806.

40   At the first deposition, frustratingly, Hendon had noticed this and rubbed in the folly of Butler's effort to explain the change away: Q. 'My question to you is what colour was the gun?' A. 'Silver or white or something like that was what I saw.' Q. 'Do you recall telling Detective Buhrmaster that the gun was white?' A. 'Well, I am not familiar with guns. I may have said that.' Q. 'Colour has nothing to do with guns. I am asking do you recall telling him that the gun was white? ...' *Maharaj 3.850 Tr. 1455, Initial Deposition of Neville Butler*, at 106 (Jan. 13th, 1987, 15.30–18.30) (108736-860). He forgot to do it at trial.

41   When he first talked to Detective Buhrmaster, Butler described Kris Maharaj confronting Derrick and Duane Moo Young over money, bandying about various large but uncertain sums. His original sworn statement was: 'I can only hazard guesses. That one had to do with moneys that apparently Moo Young spent that was belonging to people who Maraj [*sic*] introduced to him; or else some sums of money he claims, Maraj claims, was extorted from Maraj's family.' *Maharaj 3.850 Exhibit FCW*, at 6, *Statement of Neville Butler* (Oct. 17th, 1986, 00.50 a.m.). By the time of his second deposition Butler had settled on a rather precise amount that was in dispute – $160,000. *Maharaj Trial Transcript*, at 2806, 3124. This number cropped up for the first time in Butler's second deposition, after he had changed his story. *Second Deposition of Neville Butler*, at 38–9 (March 30th, 1987, 14.15 p.m.) (108911-983) (there were to be two cheques written to cover the $160,000 and Butler was to take them to Fort Lauderdale to be certified). Eslee Carberry and the *Echo* had published an article in July 1986, three months before the murders, entitled 'The Echo will not be Bought', which made vague allegations of bribery in precisely that amount – $160,000. *Maharaj Trial Transcript*, at 2753. See 'Echo Will not be Bought', *Caribbean Echo* (July 25th, 1986) (alleging that a 'prominent Ft Lauderdale' businessman had taken $160,000 'hush' money). Yet the evidence strongly suggests that Butler made this up. First, the dispute between Kris and the Moo Youngs was laid out in the civil litigation that Kris had brought against them, and the sum at issue was more than $400,000. But, more important, it was clear that the figure in the paper ($160,000) was itself a mistake. I later found records that were in the prosecution's hands, but that had not been turned over to the defence. A payment of $150,000 (not $160,000, as alleged in the paper) was made by bank transfer on July 21st, 1986, to a Moo Young account from a Sun Bank Miami account in the name of Hance and Sam Persad. Thus, the number that Butler came up with for his testimony was the same erroneous number as had been

published in the paper – which is where he clearly got it from, and which was then used to 'corroborate' his story.

42 *Maharaj 3.850 Exhibit HP*, at 15 (1995 Channel 4 interview with Neville Butler) ('Well, I can't understand why nobody heard with all these gun shots going off, but apparently the hotel room is very airtight, you know, soundproof. However, nobody knocked on the door or anything of that sort'); *Maharaj 3.850 Exhibit HP*, at 39 (1995 Channel 4 interview with Neville Butler) ('They were loud, they were loud shots so if there was anybody within earshot they ought to have heard it …'); *Maharaj 3.850 Exhibit HP*, at 40 (1995 Channel 4 interview with Neville Butler) ('I can't imagine anybody can hear argument and not hear gunshots').

43 *Maharaj Trial Transcript*, at 2814. See also *Maharaj 3.850 Exhibit FCW*, at 14, *Statement of Neville Butler* (Oct. 17th, 1986, 00.50 a.m.) (in his first statement, Butler told Buhrmaster that none of the shots had been muffled: Q. 'Any of the shots sound different to you, like the sounds being muffled?' A. 'No.' Q. 'All the shots downstairs sounded pretty much the same?' A. 'All the same.' Q. 'How about the shots [*sic*] upstairs?' A. 'The shots [*sic*] upstairs may be a little muffled. It's only because it's upstairs it sounded a lesser noise to me').

44 *Maharaj 3.850 Exhibit FCW*, at 13–14, *Statement of Neville Butler* (Oct. 17th, 1986, 00.50 a.m.) (118882-99) (A. [by Butler] 'He had a pillow partly as part of whatever he had in his bag and—' Q. 'Are you saying that you thought he brought the pillow with him?' A. 'Yes. As he walked around, all the time it was in his left arm. I cannot say whether he used it when he was firing or not.')

45 Prosecution copy of *Initial Police Statement of Neville Butler*, at 14 (Oct. 17th, 1986, 00.50–01.30) (124767).

46 In his first deposition, prosecutor Paul Ridge led Butler into the prosecution backup theory on this issue – that there were two pillows, one left at the scene and one apparently taken away – which was the best they could do to neutralise his obvious mistake. See *Initial Deposition (Part 2) of Neville Butler*, at 39–40 (Jan. 16th, 1987, 08.00 a.m.) (108861-910) (Q. [by Ridge] 'I will ask you do you recognise the pillow contained in these photographs?' A. [by Butler] 'This doesn't appear to be the pillow.' Q. 'Why do you say that?' A. 'Because of the colour.' Q. 'The pillow you saw appeared to be brownish in colour?' A. 'Yes.' Q. 'Could you be mistaken as to the colour?' A. 'I could be, but it is very doubtful').

47 More recently Butler reverted to his original story. When I cross-examined him in 2002, Judge Bagley barred me from questioning him about most issues, but because Butler had mentioned the pillow in passing, I was allowed to ask him questions about it. Despite

being shown a picture of the sofa in the room with pillows similar to the one he had identified, he continued to insist under oath that Kris had brought with him to the room the pillow that had been used as a silencer.

48 *Maharaj Trial Transcript*, at 2804.

49 The prosecution went on to argue that the print technician did not tell Detective Buhrmaster which of Maharaj's prints had been matched until four days after Butler gave his initial statement, so the witness had to be telling the truth. *Maharaj Trial Transcript*, at 3185.

50 *Maharaj Trial Transcript*, at 2821, 2824.

51 *Maharaj Trial Transcript*, at 2826.

52 *Initial Police Statement of Neville Butler*, at 12 (Oct. 17th, 1986, 00.50–01.30) (118882-99) (18 pages).

53 'The next thing I heard was boom!' Butler now describes it. 'He shot the boy in the back of the head.' *Maharaj 3.850 Exhibit HP*, at 19 (1995 Channel 4 interview with Neville Butler). How would he know that the bullet was in the back of the head, if he were in the downstairs room where he could not see?

54 *Initial Police Statement of Neville Butler*, at 13 (Oct. 17th, 1986, 00.50–01.30) (118882-99) (18 pages)

55 When asked why he did not run, Butler replied, 'Very simply, sir. I cannot move faster than a bullet.' *Maharaj Trial Transcript*, at 3079. But this was fatuous. He would have been out of the room long before anyone could have fired a bullet at him. His further effort to pretend that he feared waiting for the lift was equally unconvincing – he could have gone down the emergency stairs. *Maharaj Trial Transcript*, at 3790 ('If I may explain, there is an elevator. We are on the twelfth floor. I have no idea whether the elevator is on the ground floor or what have you. I am go – trying to run away, stick my finger on the elevator button, and have to wait two or three minutes to run away from a bullet.').

56 *Maharaj Trial Transcript*, at 2824.

57 *Maharaj Trial Transcript*, at 2825.

58 *Maharaj Trial Transcript*, at 2825.

59 Some years later Butler was asked by a television crew why he had not been killed. See Channel 4 Interview with Neville Butler, at 102400-01 (1995) (102315-407) (Q. 'Why didn't Kris kill you? You'd witnessed what had happened. You'd witnessed a double murder, why didn't he kill you?' A. 'Because I believe in God, and I believe that if your heart is clean and your mind is clear and you're doing what is right and you feel you're above reproach, what you're doing, God takes care of you. And I am firmly – I firmly believe that').

60 *Maharaj Trial Transcript*, at 2829. ('It had to have been about three

hours. It seemed like we were sitting there for – Dames was coming and I was hoping that he would come as soon as possible'). Earlier, Butler had said that, after leaving the room, he and Mr Maharaj left to go to Mr Maharaj's Chevy Impala: 'I think an '83 or '84 … Dark blue; vinyl top.' *Maharaj 3.850 Exhibit FCW*, at 14, *Statement of Neville Butler* (Oct. 17th, 1986, 00.50 a.m.). The car was parked downstairs and they did not move until 3 p.m. *Maharaj 3.850 Exhibit FCW*, at 15, *Statement of Neville Butler* (Oct. 17th, 1986, 00.50 a.m.). See also *Second Deposition of Neville Butler*, at 50 (March 30th, 1987, 14.15 p.m.) (108911-983) (Hendon: 'How long before you saw Eddie?' Butler: 'Had to be a couple of hours. Seems like we were there a long time. Had to be a couple of hours we were sitting out there').

61   *Maharaj Trial Transcript*, at 2842.

62   *Maharaj Trial Transcript*, at 2839. See also *Second Deposition of Neville Butler*, at 67–8 (March 30th, 1987, 14.15 p.m.) (108911-983) ('In no uncertain terms,' interjected Paul Ridge. 'Mr Butler has absolutely not been promised any immunity from prosecution for the perjury or the alleged perjury in this case. We made that clear to him in no uncertain terms. At this moment he does not know whether or not he will be arrested for the murder or whether or not he will be arrested for any possible perjury in this case').

63   In many states, for reasons that are difficult to comprehend, defence counsel may have only a very general sense of what the government's star witness is going to say. Most southern states do not require the prosecution to turn over previous statements of witnesses, and even the federal courts only require disclosure once the witness has testified and before cross-examination (i.e., not just mid-trial, but in the middle of the witness' testimony). Florida is one of the few states that allow the defence to take statements from all of the witnesses. Butler gave several sworn versions of his story before the actual trial. On the night after the murder he gave a lengthy taped statement to Detective Buhrmaster. In January 1987, over two days, he was questioned by Kris' lawyer, Eric Hendon, in a deposition. As a result of the changes in his story, Hendon deposed him again for much of a third day. Finally, a year after the crime, he testified to the jury over two days.

64   *Maharaj Trial Transcript*, at 3126.

65   There is a different standard of practice on either side of the Atlantic on this, and again between state and federal court in the US itself. See Richard C. Wyrick, 'The Ethics of Witness Coaching', 17 *Cardozo Law Review* 1, 5 (Sep. 1995) ('Comparison of American and English practice'). In Britain there is a strong sense that barristers should not prepare a witness, and this is sometimes posited as evidence that the process is less subject to manipulation. Yet solicitors do it every

day, and in some ways they 'prep' their case far more extensively and directly than their American counterparts. Indeed, rather than all the depositions that take place in US practice – where the other party's lawyers get to ask the witness essentially what they like – in the UK the lawyers exchange witness statements, which are specifically prepared by the lawyers. *Id.* at 7.

66   One of the very few legal ethicists to have addressed the issue is Professor Monroe Freedman of Hofstra University Law School. See Ralph J. Temple, 'Monroe Freedman and Legal Ethics: A Prophet in his own Time', 13 *Journal of the Legal Profession* 233, 237 n.22 (noting that Monroe Freedman was 'the first to analyze the ethical issues in preparing witnesses'),   http://www.law.ua.edu/pubs/jlp/files/issues_files/vol13/vol13art10.pdf, citing Freedman, 'Counseling the Client: Refreshing Recollection or Prompting Perjury?', *Litigation* 2, 35 (Spring 1976). Monroe is a firm advocate of the adversarial system and tends to view the world from that perspective: in other words, the defence lawyer cannot be prevented from pursuing a course of action, routinely taken by the prosecution, if there is to be any hope of the truth coming out. Nevertheless, despite his raising these issues for the first time many years ago, it remains true that 'little is said about what an attorney should not do when preparing a witness, except for the obvious warning to avoid suborning perjury. Tension exists between an attorney's ethical duty to proffer only truthful evidence and an attorney's duty to represent his client zealously, because under the latter an attorney's allegiance is to the client, not the truth.' Liisa Salmi, 'Don't Walk the Line: Ethical Considerations in Preparing Witnesses for Deposition and Trial', 18 *Review of Litigation* 135 (1999) (footnotes omitted). In one case, the US Equal Employment Opportunity Commission (EEOC) gave advice to witnesses in a sexual-harassment case. They put it in writing, so that the other side would know what was said: 'The letter included "memory joggers" that advised the women: "Try to remember whether or not you have experienced or observed" various incidents, such as "sexual jokes," "unwelcome touching" and "circulation of pornographic photographs."' The defendant corporation, Mitsubishi, complained that this letter was unethical, but the judge disagreed, ruling that 'suggesting subject matters to focus on in telling [the client's] story is surely what every competent lawyer, including the Mitsubishi lawyers, does to prepare clients ... for a deposition.' 'Why the Fine Line between preparing witnesses and suborning perjury is more than an affair of state for Lawyers', *ABA Journal*, 52, at 56 (May 1998).

67   W. William Hodes, 'Seeking the Truth versus Telling the Truth at the Boundaries of the Law: Misdirection, Lying, and Lying with an Expla-

nation', 44 *South Texas Law Review* 53, 65 (2002–3) (addressing 'yet another intractable boundary-line dilemma: insufficient preparation of a witness is malpractice, while preparing "too well" can degenerate into subornation of perjury').

68   While the academicians debate the ethical issues at great length, they rarely cite any instance where a lawyer has been sanctioned for coaching a witness. See Richard C. Wyrick, 'The Ethics of Witness Coaching', 17 *Cardozo Law Review* 1, n.20 (Sep. 1995) (discussing many hypotheticals, but citing no real-world examples of sanctions). Professor Hodes details his own experience as an expert witness with respect to the Baron & Budd asbestos memorandum, where the lawyers had written a detailed memo that was used to go over the testimony of each witness. Professor Hodes vigorously defended the ethics of counselling witnesses on what they might say – indeed, he notes that he was himself prepped (or, to use his quaint term, horseshedded) by the lawyers representing the authors of the memo. Hodes, *The Professional Duty to Horseshed Witnesses Zealously, Within the Bounds of the Law*, 30 *Texas Tech Law Review* 1343 (1999). The Baron & Budd lawyers were not sanctioned for what they did. See 'Baron & Budd Asbestos Memo', http://www.ask.com/wiki/Baron_&_Budd_asbestos_memo. Indeed, Hodes describes accepted US practice as being far over any line that most people would think acceptable in a justice system that seeks the truth. See W. William Hodes, 'Seeking the Truth versus Telling the Truth at the Boundaries of the Law: Misdirection, Lying, and Lying with an Explanation', 44 *South Texas Law Review* 53, 78 (2002–3) ('the boundary lines … are relatively well defined, relatively stable, and drawn in about the right place. In criminal cases almost certainly, and probably in many civil cases as well, it ought to be open to lawyers to make misleading arguments during litigation, so long as the underlying evidence presented in court is factual. But actively contaminating the proceedings with evidence that is known to be false has always been forbidden, and should always remain forbidden').

69   While the civil litigation brought against him by Paula Jones in Arkansas resulted in dismissal, Clinton was nevertheless held in contempt of court, and referred to the Arkansas bar association, for giving intentionally misleading or false answers to various questions on deposition concerning his sexual relations with Monica Lewinsky. *Jones v. Clinton*, 36 F. Supp. 2d 1118, 1135 (E.D. Ark. 1999) ('the Court will refer this matter to the Arkansas Supreme Court's Committee on Professional Conduct for review and any action it deems appropriate'). Clinton was suspended from practice for five years by the Arkansas bar. See http://archives.cnn.com/2001/LAW/10/01/scotus.clinton/.

70   There were various suggestions in the Clinton case that witnesses had

been leaned on, heavily, in order to say one thing or the other. For example, there was a 'Talking Points' memo that had been prepared, presumably by someone in the White House, that seemed to give instructions to one potential witness concerning what she should say about former White House aide Kathleen Willey, who accused Clinton of sexual harassment. The memo said: 'You never saw [Willey] go into the oval office, or come out of the oval office. You have never observed the President behaving inappropriately with anybody.' This could be read in two ways: one, that it was merely a reflection of an earlier interview; and two, that it was basically telling the witness what to say. The ABA article concludes that '[t]he difference between preparing a witness and suborning perjury is in the eye of the opponent.' 'Why the Fine Line between preparing witnesses and suborning perjury is more than an affair of state for Lawyers', *ABA Journal*, 52, 53 (May 1998).

71   Of course, the Clinton example is ultimately inapposite in the sense that the lawyer being punished (Clinton) was the witness, the actual perpetrator of the misconduct, rather than the lawyer representing him, who may have provoked the lie. Richard C. Wyrick, 'The Ethics of Witness Coaching', 17 *Cardozo Law Review* 1, n.72 (Sep. 1995) ('Paraphrasing Lord Coke, Thomas Wood explained that under the perjury statute of Elizabeth the First's time, "[a] greater Penalty is inflicted on Subornation of Perjury than on the perjury itself. For the author sins more than the actor." Thomas Wood, *An Institute of the Laws of England*, 414 (1979) (3rd edn 1724). See Edward Coke, *The Third Part of the Institutes of the Laws of England*, 166–7 (1979) (1628)').

72   'How Accurate is a Polygraph', at http://www.truthorlie.com/accu rate.html (accessed Sep. 7th, 2010) ('While the polygraph technique is highly accurate, it is not infallible and errors can occur. According to the American Polygraph Association over 250 studies have been conducted on the accuracy of polygraph testing during the past 25 years. Recent research reveals that the accuracy of the new computerized polygraph system is close to 100%').

73   *Maharaj Trial Record, RA 103–9* (Jan 30th, 1987) (Polygraph of Krishna Maharaj by George B. Slattery, Slattery Associates Inc.). There was (and could be) no disagreement to this fact, as Eric Hendon had given a copy of the report to the prosecution at the time of trial.

74   *Maharaj Trial Transcript*, at 604–5; *Maharaj 3.850 Exhibit K* (Letter of John Kastrenakes to Eric Hendon, Feb. 9th, 1987).

75   *Maharaj 3.850 Exhibit L (RA 114)* (Letter of John Kastrenakes to Eric Hendon, March 20th, 1987). Since the defence was not paying, apparently the state took the position that the defence should not be allowed a copy of the report. This was to have significant consequences.

76   Hendon certainly was not suspicious. He testified that the prosecutors

told him orally (*3.850 Tr. 247*) and by letter (*3.850 Tr. 384*) that Butler had passed his test.

77   *Maharaj Trial Transcript*, at 908–9.

78   *Maharaj Trial Transcript*, at 4435–6.

79   There are exceptions even then. The state is allowed to claim exemptions for various materials, including the prosecutors' own work product, various information about informants, and so forth.

80   *Dudley Dickson report on polygraph of Neville Butler* (March 2nd, 1987).

81   *Dudley Dickson report on polygraph of Neville Butler*, at 3 (March 2nd, 1987).

82   *Dudley Dickson report on polygraph of Neville Butler*, at 1 (March 2nd, 1987).

83   And so it went on. The other questions asked by Dickson of Neville Butler included:

> Did Maharaj ask you to arrange a meeting between himself and Derrick Moo Young?
> Yes.
> On October 16, 1986, did you personally arrange the meeting between Derrick Moo Young and Kris Maharaj?
> Yes.
> Other than what you have explained was anyone else present when the Moo Youngs were shot?
> No.

Dudley Dickson report on polygraph of Neville Butler, at 2 (March 2nd, 1987). On each of these, Butler's replies were scored by Dickson as being without deception. Likewise, the other questions on the Slattery–Maharaj polygraph were as follows:

> Regarding the shooting deaths of Derrick and Duane Moo Young; at the time they were shot and killed were you in Room number 1215 of the DuPont Plaza Hotel?
> No.
> Regarding the shooting deaths of Derrick and Duane Moo Young; do you know for sure who killed them?
> No.

He asked the same questions three times, in different sequences. 'It was the opinion of this examiner that Mr Maharaj did truthfully answer those questions.' See *George Slattery report on polygraph of Krishna Maharaj*, at 4 (Jan. 30th, 1987).

84   I am assuming that this was either ASA Kastrenakes or ASA Ridge, since the copy provided to me came from their file and did not appear in the file of the police.

85   *Maharaj 3.850 Exhibit FCW*, at 6, 8, *Statement of Neville Butler* (Oct. 17th, 1986, 00.50 a.m.).

86   Channel 4 interview with Neville Butler at 102366–67 (1995) (102315–407).

6

The Prosecutor

1   *Berger v. United States*, 295 US 78, 88, 55 S. Ct. 629, 79 L. Ed. 1314 (1935).

2   *Maharaj 3.850 Exhibit HD*, Channel 4 interview with John Kastrenakes, at 40.

3   *Maharaj 3.850 Exhibit HD*, Channel 4 interview with John Kastrenakes, at 18.

4   *Maharaj 3.850 Exhibit HD*, Channel 4 interview with John Kastrenakes, at 12–13.

5   *Maharaj 3.850 Exhibit HD*, Channel 4 interview with John Kastrenakes, at 13.

6   *Maharaj 3.850 Exhibit HD*, Channel 4 interview with John Kastrenakes, at 46–7.

7   *Maharaj 3.850 Exhibit HD*, Channel 4 interview with John Kastrenakes, at 45–6.

8   I should underline that this is not actually the legal test: evidence does not have to prove the suspect innocent, but rather be of material assistance to his defence, in any number of ways. For example, a suspect may actually have committed a homicide, but evidence of provocation might reduce the crime from murder to manslaughter. However, prosecutors routinely mischaracterise the test.

9   John Kastrenakes made it clear that this was, indeed, his view. *Maharaj 3.850 Exhibit HD*, Channel 4 interview with John Kastrenakes, at 66 (speaking to the Channel 4 interviewer, he complained that all prisoners on Death Row allege that their lawyer failed them, but: 'The truth of the matter is that Eric Hendon did an effective job, his client was just guilty').

10   At least this was true until, as a judge, he found himself at odds with an office of the law. He had been pulled over by an officer from the Florida Highway Patrol (FHP) late one night – much as Kris Maharaj alleged that he had been stopped twenty-four years before, when

money and the gun were taken from him. Judge Kastrenakes was accused of driving the wrong way in a one-way parking lot and of lacking proof of insurance. The trooper said the judge tried to pull rank on her, flashing his judicial badge; he said that she was a liar and this never happened. As a result of this belated personal experience, Kastrenakes said that he 'would always have doubts when a trooper appears in his courtroom'. See Michael Laforgia, 'Prosecutor: Judge Kastrenakes biased against FHP', *Palm Beach Post*, Feb. 27th, 2010, at http://www.palmbeachpost.com/news/prosecutor-judge-kastre nakes-biased-against-fhp-297471.html (accessed Jan. 18th, 2011).

11   *Maharaj 3.850 Exhibit HD*, Channel 4 interview with John Kastrenakes, at 35–6.

12   *Maharaj 3.850 Exhibit HD*, Channel 4 interview with John Kastrenakes, at 36.

13   *Maharaj 3.850 Exhibit HD*, Channel 4 interview with John Kaṣtrenakes, at 37; see also *id.*, at 1 ('In this case, the right verdict was the guilty verdict').

14   *Maharaj 3.850 Exhibit HD*, Channel 4 interview with John Kastrenakes, at 48. He feels that the process of appeals in capital cases should be radically cut back. *Maharaj 3.850 Exhibit HD*, Channel 4 interview with John Kastrenakes, at 51 ('There is a movement afoot to reduce the federal processes and reviewing ad nauseam, litigation, and, er, as a taxpayer I would be in favour of that …').

15   *Maharaj 3.850 Exhibit HD*, Channel 4 interview with John Kastrenakes, at 44.

16   I am referring primarily here to state courts. Federal cases represent fewer than 5 per cent of criminal prosecutions, so prosecutions in state court by local prosecutors represent the overwhelming majority of cases. Of the sentences of death imposed in US courts, something under 2 per cent – in 2010, just fifty-nine out of 3,268 – had been imposed in federal court, with an additional eight in military courts. See 'Death Row Winter 2010', NAACP Legal Defense Fund, at 36, http://naacpldf.org/files/publications/DRUSA_Winter_2010.pdf.

17   Ric Simmons, 'Election of Local Prosecutors', the blog 'Election Law at Moritz', http://moritzlaw.osu.edu/electionlaw/ebook/part7/elections _prosecutors.html, citing Bureau of Justice Statistics Bulletin, *Prosecutors in State Courts, 2001*, US Department of Justice, July 1st, 2002, at 1 (2,341 local offices). There are an additional 6 million misdemeanours, which can also carry prison sentences up to one year.

18   Simmons, 'Election of Local Prosecutors', at 2. More than half of the states elect prosecutors by county; some are elected by judicial district (which may include several counties or, in Louisiana, several parishes). Notably, also, the Attorneys General for the states are elected: 'The

Attorney General is popularly elected in 43 states, and is appointed by the governor in five states (Alaska, Hawaii, New Hampshire, New Jersey and Wyoming) and in the five jurisdictions of American Samoa, Guam, the Northern Mariana Islands, Puerto Rico and the Virgin Islands. In Maine, the Attorney General is selected by secret ballot of the legislature, and in Tennessee, by the state Supreme Court. In the District of Columbia, the Mayor appoints the Corporation Counsel whose powers and duties are similar to those of the Attorneys General of the states and jurisdictions.' See National Association of Attorneys General website, http://www.naag.org/how_does_one_become_an_ attorney_general.php. The Attorneys General are normally responsible for the appellate litigation in the state. Thus, when Kris Maharaj's case was on appeal, the work was generally done by the Office of the Attorney General rather than the Office of the State Attorney (called, in many states, the District Attorney).

19   In the federal system the Attorney General is appointed by the President, which better reflects the US division between an elected legislature and a generally appointed executive. This distinction has been lost in the UK, and the current proposal to start electing local police chiefs reflects the government's failure to appreciate a sensible and practical distinction.

20   Simmons, 'Election of Local Prosecutors', citing Abbe Smith, 'Can You be a Good Person and a Good Prosecutor?', 14 Georgia Journal of Legal Ethics 355, 389 (2001).

21   One notable exception to this rule has been the recent election in Dallas County. Craig Watkins ran for office promising to clean up the ethics of the office and review doubtful convictions. See website of the Dallas County District Attorney, http://www.dallasda.com/ (accessed Oct. 31st, 2010) ('Committed to the concept of "doing the right thing," our talented and diverse staff prides itself on seeking justice not on high conviction rates'). Watkins had even called for jail time for unethical prosecutors who secure convictions against the innocent. Jennifer Emily & Steve McGonigle, 'Dallas County district attorney wanted unethical prosecutors punished', Dallas News (May 4th, 2008), http:// www.dallasnews.com/sharedcontent/dws/news/localnews/stories/ DN-misconduct_04met.ART0.State.Edition2.46518c2.html (accessed Oct. 31st, 2010) ('The Dallas County district attorney who has built a national reputation on freeing the wrongfully convicted says prosecutors who intentionally withhold evidence should themselves face harsh sanctions – possibly even jail time. "Something should be done," said Craig Watkins, whose jurisdiction leads the nation in the number of DNA exonerations. "If the harm is a great harm, yes, it should be criminalized"'). I have some familiarity with the office,

since I have worked on two capital cases from there, and while I have no doubt of Watkins' good intentions, the general mindset of the assistant prosecutors who are on the Dallas front line remains similar to the one discussed in this chapter. The transformation of an organisational culture is not easily achieved, and whether Watkins will be DA long enough to achieve it remains to be seen.

22   Kenneth Bresler, ' "I Never Lost a Trial": When Prosecutors Keep Score of Criminal Convictions', 9 *Georgia Journal of Legal Ethics* 537, 541 n.18 (1996); Catherine Ferguson-Gilbert, 'It is not whether you win or lose it's how you play the game: Is the win–loss scorekeeping mentality doing justice for prosecutors', 38 *California Western Law Review* 283 (2001).

23   Mike Tolson & Steve Brewer, 'Harris County is a Pipeline to Death Row', at 1 (*Houston Chronicle*, Feb. 21st, 2001) (District Attorney of Harris County, Texas, campaigned on his record of having put fourteen murderers on Death Row 'where they belong'); Daniel S. Medwed, 'The Zeal Deal: Prosecutorial Resistance to Post-Conviction Claims of Innocence', 84 *Boston University Law Review* 125 (2004) (abstract: 'there are a series of political incentives for prosecutors to resist post-conviction innocence claims, even potentially meritorious ones, with zeal. Candidates vying for the office of chief prosecutor typically campaign on a general tough-on-crime platform, strewn with references to their overall win–loss record and reminders about specific successes in high-profile cases. Appearing "soft" on criminals, such as by accepting the possible validity of a prisoner's innocence claim, detracts from that tough-on-crime rhetoric and is largely an anathema to prosecutors').

24   I should emphasise that any rule that pretends to be one-size-fits-all is obviously not accurate. I have come across very fine, principled prose-cutors over the years; at the other end of the scale, I have encountered a small group of prosecutors who are blatantly corrupt. Neither of these groups is the main focus of this chapter; rather, it is the large mid-section who are very principled, but whose personalities simply fit a law-and-order profile. Without intending it, these are the people who impose their biases on a process in such a way as to ensure the conviction of the innocent.

25   See Daniel S. Medwed, 'The Zeal Deal: Prosecutorial Resistance to Post-Conviction Claims of Innocence', 84 *Boston University Law Review* 125, 140 (2004).

26   See George T. Felkenes, 'The Prosecutor: A Look at Reality', 7 *South-western University Law Review* 98, 112 (1975) (more than 50 per cent of prosecutors surveyed did not presume that a man is innocent until proven guilty, and many believed that guilt was determined by the

screening processes of the police and prosecutor prior to trial).

27 See, e.g., Medwed, 'The Zeal Deal', at 138 ('one study demonstrated that assistant district attorneys articulating a primary focus on convictions had, on average, roughly twice as much experience as those who displayed a deep concern for justice'), citing Felkenes, 'The Prosecutor: A Look at Reality', at 111. See also H. Richard Uviller, 'The Neutral Prosecutor: The Obligation of Dispassion in a Passionate Pursuit', 68 *Fordham Law Review* 1695, 1702 (2000) ('even the best of the prosecutors – young, idealistic, energetic, dedicated to the interests of justice – are easily caught up in the hunt mentality of an aggressive office ... I know that the earnest effort to do justice is easily corrupted by the institutional ethic of combat'). I had the privilege of being taught by Professor Uviller at Columbia Law School and, as a former prosecutor, he knew whereof he spoke.

28 See Abbe Smith, 'Can You Be a Good Person and a Good Prosecutor?', 14 *Georgia Journal of Legal Ethics* 355, 384 (2001) ('Notwithstanding the legal presumption of innocence, the cultural and institutional presumption in most prosecutor offices is that everybody is guilty').

29 This is not as simple an issue as may first appear. There are many shades of culpability. If a killing happened when the perpetrator was provoked, it may be deemed manslaughter; if it was a moment of panic, there might not have been specific intent to kill (the active desire that a death should take place). After immersing myself in the facts, it has generally seemed to me that a partial defence is often closest to the truth. But if my experience is anything to go by, the defendant will probably be found guilty regardless.

30 Bill Foster went forward and prosecuted John for the death penalty, and John was sentenced to die. It was small wonder: Bill was well attuned to the local jurors. I was wet behind the ears. I was immensely grateful when, some months later, we got the case reversed on appeal. *Pope v. State*, 256 Ga. 195, 345 S.E.2d 831 (1986). On retrial, thankfully Bill agreed to a plea and John was sentenced to life. I had hoped to go back to visit my first client before leaving the US in 2004, but when I called over to make arrangements for a visit, I was sorry to learn that he had died in prison.

31 For more on the issue of 'objectivity', see the end of Chapter 13 on judges.

32 They have sometimes pointed to an ethical rule that, they think, forbids them from taking such a step: if they speak to the accused and learn something that makes them a witness, they are forbidden from being both the advocate and the witness. See, e.g., *United States v. Hosford*, 782 F.2d 936 (11th Cir. 1986) ('it is clear that a prosecutor must not act as both prosecutor and witness'). This might be seen as another

rule that prevents the prosecutor from behaving as a human being. However, it is readily soluble: there can be another person in the room as well, who could be the witness if necessary.

33   Some prosecutors' offices have 'screening' procedures that are designed to eliminate bad cases before they reach court, and no doubt they play an important role. Indeed, when they were willing, we used to work closely with the Office of the District Attorney in Orleans Parish to ensure that this happened in potentially capital cases. Such cooperation as we briefly enjoyed is rare, and the problem becomes greater at the next stage of the process – once the trial has been set in motion – and then again when someone has been convicted and sent to prison. It is not the case (obviously) that prosecutors never admit mistakes; my thesis is that prosecutors are selected, and self-select, from a group with attitudes that make such a decision far less likely – and if we are serious about remedying mistakes, then we need to recognise this and take affirmative steps to put a very different institutional culture in place.

34   In addition to the videotape and the various witnesses, 'two recreation department supervisors, Cousin's coach, and an opposing team's player testified that the game had started late and ended late, and the coach testified that he dropped Cousin off at his house at approximately 10.45 p.m.' *Cousin v. Small*, 325 F.3d 627, 629 (5th Cir. 2003). This was well after the murder took place.

35   The Louisiana Supreme Court later characterised these statements as 'obviously exculpatory' and held that they should have been turned over. *State v. Cousin*, No. 96-KA-2973 (La. 4/14/98), 710 So.2d 1065 ('[t]he prosecutor did not disclose this obviously exculpatory statement to the defense prior to the trial, as required by *Brady v. Maryland*, 373 US 83 (1963), and *Kyles v. Whitley*, 514 US 419 (1995)'). However, I suspect Jordan thought his witness was telling the truth now, rather than in the earlier versions, so he did not think the statements credible.

36   *Complaint*, at 32–3, in *Cousin v. Small et al.*, No. 00069, Section R, Mag. 2 (US Dist. Ct. S. D. La.).

37   Small's colleague Detective Mims received this Crime Stopper tip: 'The form was dated 3-10-95 and the anonymous caller named Antonio Harper, Derrick Smith and a subject known only as "Brandon" as being the subjects responsible for the robbery/murder which occurred in the 1300 block of Dauphine.' This lead fit snugly with the evidence that had been developed on the night of the crime. Jonathan Webb, an eyewitness whose name was kept from the defence by the defendants, watched the killers leave in their car and, because he was a birdwatcher by habit, used his binoculars. Within minutes of the crime, he had

called in the licence plate of the rapidly departing vehicle. The police ran a printout for BVG456 at 11.39 p.m. on the night of the crime – less than two hours after the murder. This gave the police the name Christell B. Baham. The car was a red 1989 Ford four-door. Her address was listed as 945 Trianan Square, Apt. B, Gretna, La. 70056. Based on other evidence, on March 13th, 1995, at 10.50 p.m., Detectives Mims, Zenon and Lawless went to 3244 Desaix Street to find Antonio Harper. Det. Mims noted in his report *that parked outside the address was the car he had tried to find earlier in the week: a red Ford Escort registered to Christell Baham with plate # BVG456.* Baham, he learned, was the mother of Derrick Smith. In other words, the police put together a compelling case against three other suspects soon after the crime – but none of this was disclosed to Shareef's trial lawyers, because Det. Small had already decided that Shareef was the killer.

38 See generally *Complaint* in *Cousin v. Small et al.*, No. 00069, Section R, Mag. 2 (US Dist. Ct. S. D. La.).

39 *Complaint*, at 34, in *Cousin v. Small et al.*, No. 00069, Section R, Mag. 2 (US Dist. Ct. S. D. La.).

40 *Complaint*, at paras. 170–1, 175, in *Cousin v. Small et al.*, No. 00069, Section R, Mag. 2 (US Dist. Ct. S. D. La.); *In Re Roger W. Jordan Jr.*, at n.10 (La. 06/29/12005), 913 So.2d 775 (Johnson, J., concurring and dissenting).

41 At the hearing on the Motion for a New Trial, both trial prosecutors admitted that they had secreted defence witnesses to the DA's office. See *Complaint*, at paras. 171, 175. Shareef's defence attorney at trial testified that he had specifically asked one of them during the trial if he knew where one of the witnesses was, and the prosecutor stated, 'No, I don't know where he is.' *Cousin Motion for a New Trial Transcript*, at 86.

42 Shareef had also been charged with four armed robberies and entered a guilty plea when his lawyer insisted that he was looking at ninety-nine years himself. Shareef was no angel, which is ultimately the explanation for the way in which Det. Small put together the murder case against him. But neither was he the one-lad crime wave portrayed by the prosecution: when we subsequently investigated the robbery cases it was clear that, while he got in with a bad crowd, Shareef never used a weapon himself. He was sentenced to twenty years for those offences, which might be deemed extremely harsh for a juvenile first-offender, by any standards.

43 *Cousin v. Small*, 325 F.3d 627, 634 (5th Cir. 2003).

44 *Cousin v. Small*, 325 F.3d 627, 634 (5th Cir. 2003).

45 Sad to say, life in prison for a juvenile was not uncommon at the time in the US, and remains available as a sentence today. 'No Way Out',

New York Times (Nov. 22nd, 2005), http://www.justicebehindthewalls.
net/news.asp?nid=67 (accessed Nov. 1st, 2010); outside the US, only
three countries had any juveniles serving life without parole: seven in
Israel, four in South Africa and one in Tanzania). Thankfully, in *Graham v. Florida*, 130 S.Ct. 2011 (2010), the Supreme Court decreed that
life *without parole* was an unconstitutional punishment for juveniles who commit a crime less than murder. On the other hand, it is
still possible for a juvenile to be sentenced to life without parole for
murder, or life with the possibility of parole for a lesser offence.

46   *Cousin v. Small*, 325 F.3d 627, 634 (5th Cir. 2003).

47   Rowell said the earlier statement was false, but admitted that he had
made it. He said he had only implicated Shareef to save himself from
some criminal charges. Thus, legally, he could not be 'impeached'
with the substance of the prior statement, since he had not denied
making the statement. While this is black-letter evidence law, the
prosecutor went through the entire statement with Rowell, and then
argued to the jury that the prior statement was evidence of Shareef's
guilt. *State v. Cousin*, No. 96-KA-2973 (La. 4/14/98), 710 So.2d, at 1065.
Jordan admitted that this was not allowed. *State v. Cousin*, 710 So.2d,
at 1072 (reversing in part 'because of [Roger Jordan] the prosecutor's
flagrant misuse of that evidence for purposes that the prosecutor
himself admitted was an improper use of that evidence'). While there
were a number of other highly prejudicial issues, the Supreme Court
chose only to address the one.

48   As noted above, Shareef did not go free. Prior to his capital trial, he had
pleaded guilty to the charges of armed robbery and received a twenty-
year sentence.

49   *In Re Roger W. Jordan Jr.*, at n.8 (La. 06/29/12005), 913 So.2d 775 (Johnson, J., concurring and dissenting) ('Even after the dismissal of the
charges … Jordan continued to insist on the guilt of [Shareef Cous-
in]').

50   I believe Jordan took steps that are profoundly wrong, and the anti-
thesis of what the judicial system purports to mandate. But what he
actually did is rather human and sadly typical of how the system operates in the real world. Jordan believed that he never made mistakes.
He believed that essentially everyone brought to trial – particularly
on his watch – was inevitably guilty, and that slippery defence lawyers
were trying to help them avoid their just desserts. And he shared the
very human weakness of being unable to accept that he had made a
mistake in a case as important as Shareef's.

51   The lack of compensation may be slowly changing. Even Louisiana has
now enacted rules governing what a prisoner may be paid for a wrongful
conviction, although it remains very low – roughly $10,000 for every

year spent in prison, with no differential for those who faced execution for that time. La. Rev. Stat. 15:572.8(c)(3) (Compensation for wrongful conviction and imprisonment) ('Compensation shall be calculated at a rate of fifteen thousand dollars per year incarcerated not to exceed a maximum total amount of one hundred fifty thousand dollars'). When one considers that the average income for those outside prison is double that figure, it is a fairly derisory amount, albeit an improvement over the past. In any event, this does nothing to deter prosecutors from future misconduct, since they do not have to contribute in any way to the compensation. Indeed, the new state schemes effectively provide prosecutors who send innocent people to Death Row with a kind of insurance policy against being held responsible.

52   The British are not quite as extreme on this point, but generally insist, for example, that a prisoner must show being more than 'merely' the victim of an unsafe conviction, before receiving compensation; they apply the rule that it counts against a prisoner's chances of early parole if he refuses to admit his guilt; and they insist that any compensation paid to a prisoner who has been exonerated be offset by a charge for 'three hots and a cot' (three meals and a bed in prison) for the time he spent at Her Majesty's pleasure.

53   The 'logic' underlying this attitude can be seen partially in the varying burdens of proof. When someone is acquitted, in theory this means only that the prosecution did not prove *beyond a reasonable doubt* (BARD) that he was guilty. Thus, if proof BARD means that you have to be 99 per cent sure, then an acquittal may mean that you were actually 98 per cent sure of guilt, and this is certainly not proof of his innocence. Yet this logic obscures two facts: one, that jurors tend not to think that way, and tend to hold the prosecution to a rather lower standard. In other words, the fact that you are acquitted is rather strong evidence of innocence. But the second, and far more important, factor is that our criminal justice system is founded on the idea that if you are not proven guilty then you are *innocent* – or it has been, until the abhorrent introduction of 'Control Orders' for people who cannot be shown guilty of any crime. In any event, the perceived gulf between acquittal and innocence is bridged in other perfectly satisfactory ways: O.J. Simpson, for example, was found not guilty of double homicide under the reasonable-doubt standard, but was then found culpable in a civil action brought by the victims' survivors, where the burden of proving his involvement only had to be proven by a preponderance of the evidence (51:49 per cent).

54   On the morning I was writing this (November 2nd, 2010) Lord Faulkener was being interviewed on the *Today* programme on Radio 4 about the Coalition Government's belated decision to obey the

ruling of the European Court of Human Rights (ECHR) and restore the vote to certain prisoners. Lord Faulkener agreed that the right to vote was a fundamental human right, but nevertheless argued – on the radio, as he did in the courts – that those who commit crimes somehow forfeit this right. What he notably failed to identify was where in the Tablets that Moses brought down from Mount Sinai this 'rule' is identified. Prisoners are one despised group of the population who need protection from populist discrimination more than most: they need the right to contact the media more than most people; they need the right to complain to politicians; and so forth. So why should they not be allowed to vote? What would we think if the government said that, by committing a crime, the prisoner had forfeited his right to medical treatment?

55   *Cousin v. Small*, 325 F.3d 627, 634 (5th Cir. 2003).

56   *Cousin v. Small*, 325 F.3d 627, 631 (5th Cir. 2003) (noting that there is no official codification of the 'doctrine', but quoting the Supreme Court for the assertion that Congress must clearly have intended to adopt such a rule, as it existed in the common law, as developed by the courts), quoting *Kalina v. Fletcher*, 424 US 118, 123 (1997). See also *Imbler v. Pachtman*, 424 US 409 (1976) (the seminal Supreme Court decision recognising this immunity).

57   *In Re Roger W. Jordan Jr.*, (La. 06/29/2005), 913 So.2d 775. The only case cited is *In Re Burns*, 2001–1080 (La. 11/28/01), 800 So.2d 833, a case with which I am very familiar, since it happened when I was spending a great deal of time in the same courthouse. Indeed, it involved misconduct by the *same* prosecutor's office as Shareef's, and a finding by the trial judge that an assistant district attorney had actually planted evidence, in addition to failing to notify the defence of hugely important evidence in the case. While it may be the only case where a prosecutor had been convicted of contempt, the conviction was in large part reversed, the Supreme Court finding the proof that the evidence had been planted to be insufficient, and ordering only a $500 fine on the failure to notify the defence of the evidence.

58   *In Re Roger W. Jordan Jr.*, Slip Op. at 10 & n.17 (La. 06/29/2005), 913 So.2d 775.

59   *In Re Roger W. Jordan*, No. 57,734 (La. Oct. 8th, 1979).

60   'Neither are [prosecutors] realistically subject to criminal sanctions,' the Louisiana Supreme Court acknowledged in Roger Jordan's case. *In Re Roger W. Jordan Jr.*, (La. 06/29/2005), 913 So.2d 775.

61   'Our research reveals only one instance in which a judge held a prosecutor in contempt of court for failing to disclose evidence,' the Louisiana Supreme Court observed. *In Re Roger W. Jordan Jr.*, (La. 06/29/2005), 913 So.2d 775.

62 Ben Kuehne is a very fine lawyer in private practice, perhaps best known for his involvement in the case where Al Gore and the Democratic Party were pitted against the Republicans in the famous Florida 'hanging chads' litigation that ultimately resolved the presidential election in 2000. George W. Bush prevailed in a narrow and ideological decision in the Supreme Court. *Bush v. Gore*, 531 US 98 (2000). In Kris' case, Ben had originally been hired, at a very cut-rate fee, to do Kris' state habeas corpus appeal after Judge Glick denied a hearing. Those funds ran out very rapidly, and for the next eighteen years – and counting – Ben has represented Kris without charge, and I have had the genuine pleasure of working with him.

63 The central allegation did not even involve fees that would be paid to Ben, but rather his investigation into the validity of fees that were being paid to another lawyer, and his determination that the lawyer could agree to be retained without fear of violating the law. After the federal judge threw out most of the case, the government took it on appeal to the Eleventh Circuit in Atlanta, where they lost again. Ultimately they dismissed the charges. Jennifer Forsyth, 'DOJ Gives Miami Lawyer Ben Kuehne Happy Thanksgiving, Drops Charges' (Nov. 26th, 2009), http://blogs.wsj.com/law/2009/11/26/doj-gives-miami-lawyer-ben-kuehne-happy-thanksgiving-drops-charges/.

64 The charge and my ultimate acquittal are detailed in the court record of *State of Louisiana v. Marcel O'Connor*, No. 07-98-62 (19th JDC, East Baton Rouge).

7
The Police

1 See http://www.crimestoppersonline.com/CSOflashpop.php; http://www.crimestoppers-uk.org/giving-information. In the US the local Crime Stoppers organisations may vary in their precise rules. See generally http://www.crimestopusa.com/.

2 All of this (and much more) was laid out in our complaint when we later sued Small. See generally *Complaint* filed in *Cousin v. Small et al.*, No. 00069, Section R, Mag. 2 (US Dist. Ct. S. D. La.).

3 In the Vietnam war, 58,148 Americans were killed out of 2.59 million who served, or one in forty-five. See http://www.vietnam-war.info/facts/. However, the war lasted much longer than one year – fifteen years is a reasonable approximation. US advisers began arriving in Vietnam in the 1950s, although combat troops did not arrive in earnest until around 1960. Given the timeframe, if each person averaged two

years in Vietnam, the death rate would have been virtually identical to the St Thomas Projects.

4   The term derives from the 'Thin Red Line', which originally described the line of British soldiers who faced down the charging Russian Hussars at the Battle of Balaclava in the Crimea in 1854. It later became a general term used for supposed British sangfroid in battle. The 'Thin Blue Line' was therefore adopted by the police to describe their role in protecting society from an overwhelming threat. The title was taken from the film describing Randall Adams' false conviction, which led to him spending years on Texas' Death Row. See Randall Adams, 'Journey of Hope', http://www.journeyofhope.org/old_site/People/randall_dale_adams.htm.

5   *Serpico* was a 1973 film starring Al Pacino as Frank Serpico. Based on the true story of a New York police officer, it traces his efforts to expose corruption in the NYPD, starting and ending with the moment when he was shot on patrol, due to his fellow officers' refusal to come to his aid. He barely survived, and received hate-mail from other police while he recuperated. He testified before the Knapp Commission on police corruption, which was set up in large part because of his very public allegations. See Martin Arnold, 'Serpico's Lonely Journey to Knapp Witness Stand', *New York Times* (Dec. 15th, 1971). The Commission identified two categories of corrupt police: 'Grass Eaters' described officers who 'accept gratuities and solicit five, ten, twenty dollar payments from contractors, tow-truck operators, gamblers, and the like but do not pursue corruption payments'. Grass-eating was a rite of passage for many police, to prove their loyalty to the brotherhood, and was treated like a job incentive. 'Meat Eaters' were officers who 'spend a good deal of time aggressively looking for situations they can exploit for financial gain'. An example of this is shaking down pimps and drug dealers for money, because not only does the officer profit from it, but he or she can neutralise their guilt by convincing themselves that the victim deserves it. They justify taking advantage of criminals because they are considered the dregs of society. See generally http://en.wikipedia.org/wiki/Knapp_Commission.

6   Much too late Kris had mentioned in his penalty-phase testimony that a police officer testified in a pre-trial deposition to the fact that he – Kris – had told Buhrmaster that he was present in Room 1215 that morning. But Hendon had failed to call the officer at the culpability phase of the trial, or even to point out this prior statement under oath.

7   See *Maharaj 3.850 Exhibit P, Tr. 114*. At a subsequent hearing on this issue, with his superior officer accused of perjury, Romero tried to wriggle out of what he had said. However, at the time, the question and his answer could not have been clearer.

8   *Maharaj 3.850 Clerk Tr. 2021.*

9   At a later hearing there was no denial from the state that this note was valid, and there can be no debate what the consequences of this would have been. Any statement would indubitably have to be suppressed. See *Edwards v. Arizona*, 451 US 47 (1981). The only question was what time any statements were made. Naturally, when this note came to light, Buhrmaster tried to suggest that anything he quoted from Kris at trial had been said before midnight. However, given the time of arrest at the Denny's Diner, this timeframe was almost impossible. Regardless, the intentional suppression of this information reflected very badly on the integrity of the process.

   Soon I came across another similar note. Kris was supposed, additionally, to have said: 'That's all I have to say about today's activities.' This was scratched out and replaced with: 'That's all he was able to tell me about the day's activities.' The difference was critical: the first was an assertion of the right to remain silent, which would have barred the police from asking further questions; the second was not. See *Maharaj 3.850 Clerk Tr. 2034*. At the hearing the prosecution tried to make out that this was a change they would have made, rather than Buhrmaster himself, in order to prevent the detective from commenting on the accused's assertion of his rights. It is true that in *Griffin v. California*, 380 US 609 (1965), the Supreme Court laid down the rule that no comment may be made on the accused's assertion of his right to remain silent, and not to testify. The theory of *Griffin* was then expanded to include a prohibition against commenting on the defendant's refusal to talk to the police. So the prosecutors would have wanted Buhrmaster not to mention this before the jury. But again the crucial issue, from the defence perspective, is that the notes had not been turned over to Hendon, so he did not know there was independent proof that Kris had asserted his rights.

10   When later confronted with this, Buhrmaster said he had originally given the briefcase back to the family but, after Petrillo's request, he retrieved it. If it had been true, and he handed over such a treasure trove without making a copy of it, then he was highly irresponsible. He would also have been under a clear duty to correct his statement to the defence investigator.

11   *Maharaj 3.850 Exhibit FAO.* Illustrating the degree to which the Moo Youngs and Carberry were acting hand-in-glove, in the same batch of documents I came across a copy of the KDM International Articles of Incorporation, presumably received from Derrick, which Carberry used as the prototype for his own new corporation, Harlom View Tours & Travel. *Maharaj 3.850 Exhibit FAO.*

12   The Maharaj and Moo Young families lived adjacent to each other – a

decision that had been made in happier days. Kris and Marita Maharaj lived at 4951 SW 193rd Lane, in Fort Lauderdale; the Moo Youngs in 4901 SW 193rd Lane. The one-number difference would be easily explained as a typographical mistake to any attentive bank teller.

13   *Maharaj 3.850 Exhibit FAB.*

14   I had already found evidence in the briefcase materials to identify plenty of others who had been ripped off by Derrick and Duane. Derrick had been a signatory on a number of bank accounts belonging to Trinidadians who were moving funds out of the country to the US to finance their holidays. The procedure was simple: they would purport to buy something from the US at double its real price. When they sent the payment, half would go towards the purchase, the other half into their US bank account. There was nothing illegal about this in the US, but it violated Trinidadian money-export laws. Derrick must have realised that these accounts were easy pickings, as nobody was in a position to complain if he embezzled the money. If he signed cheques to himself, he was committing no crime in the US, as he was an authorised signatory. If their money mysteriously disappeared, the victims were in no position to sue, since any civil lawsuit would soon be copied to the Trinidad authorities, and those suing would land themselves in trouble back home. The briefcase reflected how Derrick skimmed $3,500 off one savings account, $5,000 from another, $23,000 from another and $38,855 from a fourth. Derrick was tens of thousands of dollars better off, and he must have thought himself untouchable.

15   *Maharaj 3.850 Exhibit NJ*, at 6.

16   At the time the company was established, in 1986, it was still six years before Noriega would be convicted in federal court in Miami on charges of cocaine trafficking, racketeering and money-laundering.

17   *Maharaj 3.850 Exhibit NJ*, at 14.

18   I read up more about it that evening, after I had returned to a computer with Internet access. Keyman insurance would provide cover if someone in the company were to die or be incapacitated. See http://www.investorprofit.com/insurance/insure-10.html ('Keyman Insurance represents a group of insurance plans all designed to financially protect business from the effects of prolonged illness or even death of staff who are central to the prosperity of the business. The insurance can't replace people but it can provide cash to buy time and cover the costs of temporary staff, recruitment, loss of profits or provide a cash injection').

19   See *Maharaj 3.850 Exhibits U(1), U(2), U(3) (RA 137, 138, 139–40), & AA, AB & AC.*

20   The corporation website suggested that Cargill had 61,000 employees in fifty-five countries even in 1986. In the decades since its founda-

tion in 1865 the company had grown from a single grain warehouse in Conover, Iowa, to profits of $2.34 *billion* on revenues of $88.3 billion.

21 *Maharaj 3.850 Exhibits OAG, OAL, OCS, OCT*, at B000539, 546, 562, 570, 571, 572, 573, 575, 576, 580, 581.

22 *Maharaj Exhibit OCY*, at B002196.

23 In April 1986 Gordon Daskowski supposedly wrote to Dr W.C. Bryant regarding $134,872,546.66 worth of gemstones in the possession of the LA Church Loan Corporation. *Maharaj 3.850 Exhibit OCY*, at B002193. The Moo Youngs had all the gemstone documents in their files, indicating a supposed effort to use them as collateral for other transactions.

24 *Maharaj 3.850 Exhibit OCY*, at B002195.

25 The references in the handwritten notes reflected dealings in Panama, Paraguay and Trinidad (*3.850 Clerk Tr. 2272*) as well as Costa Rica (*3.850 Clerk Tr. 2281*). They included:

- A note concerning how 'Duane [would be] M[oo] Y[oung] agent for Panama Co with 100m … to invest _ % fee advance $100,000 …' (*3.850 Clerk Tr. 2215*)
- A memo about the Moo Youngs' effort to induce Dr Richard Hayes, then Minister of Finance for the Government of Barbados, into paying for a loan, using Dr E.E. Ward as the go-between. (*3.850 Clerk Tr. 2267*) This was later turned into the letter that proposed the movement of $100 million to Barbados.
- A draft of a letter from Derrick Moo Young offering $100 million to someone unknown, from Cargil International. (*3.850 Clerk Tr. 2270*)
- A draft letter regarding the 'difficulty [of] getting US $ funds out of Mexico but [saying it is] not impossible. To avoid any exchange control problems in Mexico … must instruct foreign bank to pay to Cargil 2% commission …' (*3.850 Clerk Tr. 2276*)
- A draft memo written by Derrick Moo Young about the requirements to receive a $250 million loan from Cargil International (Panama). (*3.850 Clerk Tr. 2274*) The Moo Youngs expected to net 6 per cent, or $15 million, from lending this money.
- A draft of the letter to Amer Edoo concerning a loan of $250 million to Trinidad. (*3.850 Clerk Tr. 2276*) This includes the signature 'S. Scott'.

26 A June 6th, 1986, letter from Derrick Moo Young, written on behalf of Cargil International to Dr W.C. Bryant, represents that Cargil has $5 billion in yen bonds. *Maharaj 3.850 Clerk Tr. 4947*.

27 According to UN data for 1986, the GDP of the following countries

amounted to less money than the Moo Youngs purported to have available for loans: Bahrain, Belize, Bermuda, Bhutan, Botswana, British Virgin Islands, Cayman Islands, Cyprus, Dominica, Estonia, Fiji, French Guiana, Gambia, Grenada, Guyana, Jordan, Latvia, Liberia, Malta, Netherlands Antilles, Oman, Panama, Papua New Guinea, Peru, St Vincent, Seychelles, Solomon Islands, Suriname, Swaziland, Turkey, Uruguay and Yugoslavia. See http://data.un.org/Data.aspx?q=1986+gross+national+product&d=SNA&f=group_code%3a103%3bitem_code%3a8%3bfiscal_year%3a1986.

28   *Maharaj 3.850 Exhibits OAY, OAZ*. In the month of September someone got careless and allowed the account to rise briefly to $66,688.23. *Maharaj 3.850 Exhibit OBE*.

29   Of course the formulation of the question here is important: is the best (or 'fittest') police officer the one who arrests the most guilty people or the one who arrests the fewest innocent ones?

30   Taiping Ho, 'The Interrelationships of Psychological Testing, Psychologists' Recommendations, and Police Departments' Recruitment Decisions', 4 *Police Quarterly* 318–42 (2001) ('This study's results showed that the applicant's general intelligence and police-oriented vocational profiling in a variety of social activities or interests demonstrated a significant effect on psychological assessment and hiring recommendation in terms of the applicants' fitness for being a police officer').

31   There are interesting (albeit mainly anecdotal) discussions concerning the psychological testing of officers, indicating that those rejected for police jobs include people with a problem with authority figures. See, e.g., http://forums.officer.com/forums/showthread.php?t=56663 (accessed Sep. 12th, 2008) (applicant apparently failed because of MMPI (Minnesota Multiphasic Personality Inventory) results 'in the areas of respect of authority figures').

32   Zhao, He & Zovrich, 'Individual Value Preferences Among American Police Officers: The Rokeach Theory of Human Values Revisited', 21 Policing 22–37 (1998), http://www.ncjrs.gov/App/Publications/abstract.aspx?ID=173168.

33   Teahan, Adams & Podany, 'A Comparison of the Value Structure of the British and US Police', 26 *International Journal of Social Psychiatry* 246–54 (1980).

34   This term has applied with more or less force to different police recruits. See, e.g., Smith, Locke & Walker, 'Authoritarianism in Police College Students and Non-Police College Students', 59 *Journal of Criminal Law, Criminology & Police Science* 440 (1968).

35   Teahan, Adams & Podany, 'A Comparison of the Value Structure of the British and US Police', 26 *International Journal of Social Psychiatry*

246–54 (1980) (questioning 'whether the characteristics found are due to the kind of men attracted to police work, or whether, instead, they result from the occupational stress of the work itself').

36 A typical description of the job of an officer, taken from an official federal government website, can be found at: http://www.bls.gov/oco/ocos160.htm#nature; see also Legal-Criminal-Justice-Schools.com, http://www.legal-criminal-justice-schools.com/Criminal-Justice-Degrees/Police-Officer-Career.html#forms ('In local, state and federal police related departments a police officer's career description includes maintaining law and order, collecting evidence and conducting investigations').

8
The Expert

1 Sadly this comes from a real case in New Orleans, Louisiana. *Ladner v. Higgins*, 71 So.2d 242, 244 (La. App. 1954). The appellate judges introduced this quote, rather incredulously, with the following observation: 'of vast significance in our judicial determination of the serious medical issues involved herein, we find these pearls of wisdom emanating from the mouth of one whose testimony was being adduced to assist the court and whom we must presume, from the very nature of his profession, has accepted the Hippocratic Oath which, as we all know, is the foundation of medical ethics'. *Id.* It must be said, in Dr Unsworth's favour, that he spoke more openly than some experts.

2 See *Maharaj v. State Trial Transcript*, at 3264–72. Obviously, he 'found out' it was Kris when another police officer told him. However, Eric Hendon never asked him this.

3 See *Maharaj v. State Trial Transcript*, at 3382–9.

4 See *Maharaj v. State Trial Transcript*, at 3303–82.

5 See generally Jenny Uglow, 'The Other Side of Science', *New York Review of Books*, at 31 (June 24th, 2010), reviewing Steven Shapin, *Never Pure: Historical Studies of Science as if it was Produced by People with Bodies, Situated in Time, Space, Culture, and Society, and Struggling for Credibility and Authority* (2010). Shapin describes how the scientist of the seventeenth century gradually lost his original status as the educator of the people as he moved through the nineteenth century and into the twentieth. Scientists started to make a living out of plying their trade. Some critics became 'alert to the independence or bias of "experts" and the communities that support them'. *Id.*, at 30. However, for many, the original unquestioning respect for science remained.

6   A scientist is a researcher committed to the scientific method, which
     is 'an organized approach to problem-solving that includes ... testing
     data objectively, interpreting results, and stating conclusions that can
     later be evaluated independently by others'. *Academic Press Dictionary
     of Science and Technology 1926* (1992). To ensure objectivity, scientists
     frequently design 'blind' tests to ascertain whether a given result is
     produced by the expected combination of indicators or by the chance
     intervention of a contaminant. *Hammond Barnhart Dictionary of Sci-
     ence* 72 (1st edn 1986). The scientific method has four essential steps:
     1 Observation and description of a phenomenon. 2 Formulation of
     an hypothesis to explain the phenomenon. In physics, the hypothesis
     often takes the form of a causal mechanism. 3 Use of the hypothesis
     to predict other phenomena, or to predict the results of subsequent
     observations. 4 Performance of experimental tests on the predic-
     tions by several independent experimenters and properly performed
     experiments, preferably in different locations. If the experiments bear
     out the hypothesis, it may achieve the status of a theory. If the experi-
     ments do not bear out the hypothesis, it must be rejected or modified.
     What is key in the description of the scientific method is the predic-
     tive power of the theory, as tested by experiment. It is often said in
     science that theories can never be proved, only disproved. There is
     always the possibility that a new observation or a new experiment will
     conflict with a long-standing theory. See, generally, http://teacher.pas.
     rochester.edu/phy_labs/appendixe/appendixe.html (for a good intro-
     duction to the scientific method).

7   The many ways in which these results can be fudged are discussed
     in entertaining detail by Dr Ben Goldacre in his book *Bad Science*
     (2009).

8   I shall, for the most part, do away with the inverted commas around
     'forensic science', but please continue to imagine them there – as, with
     so much of 'forensic science', there has been no proof that it is science
     at all.

9   See generally *Handbook of Forensic Science* (1981).

10   More recently, after being thoroughly embarrassed in court, hair
     analysts have taken to referring to European Origin, African Origin
     and Asian Origin. See generally http://www.enotes.com/forensic-
     science/hair-analysis (accessed Aug. 2nd, 2010). However, even here
     the definition is fairly meaningless, just as it is in many of these racial
     definitions: if an individual has one grandparent each from England,
     Russia, Thailand and Ghana, how do we categorise him?

11   With an apology I refer those with more than a passing interest to
     a lengthy article I co-authored on the issue. See Stafford Smith &
     Goldman, 'Forensic Hair Comparison Analysis: Nineteenth Century

Science or Twentieth Century Snake Oil?', 27 *Columbia Human Rights Law Review* 227 (1996).

12   See *Bevill v. State*, 556 So. 2d 699 (Miss. 1990).

13   Jack was a very colourful and successful criminal defence lawyer, with only one southern hangover in his otherwise very liberal beliefs: he insisted on carrying his automatic pistol wherever he went. To keep costs down, since we were not being paid for the case, we shared a motel room when preparing for trial, and nothing I could do would persuade him to remove the gun from under his pillow. He insisted that he would whip it out and take care of any prosecutor who might decide to take us out. As a result, if I needed to get up in the middle of the night, it was with great trepidation.

14   See *Bevill v. State*, 556 So. 2d 699, 707 (Miss. 1990).

15   See, e.g., *Allen v. Secretary, Florida Department of Corrections*, 2010 US App. LEXIS 14570 (July 2010) (affirming death sentence; relevant hair could have been one victim's); *Duckett v. McDonough*, 2010 US Dist. LEXIS 38440 (M.D. Fla. March 25th, 2010) (death sentence affirmed, against challenge that the state had searched out a hair expert who would testify unfavourably to the defendant); *West v. Ricks*, 2010 US Dist. LEXIS 1119 (W.D.Ct. Jan. 7th, 2010) (life sentence in a capital case affirmed against challenge on the use of hair analysis); *Manning v. Epps*, 695 F. Supp. 2d 323 (N.D. Miss. 2009) (death sentence affirmed); *Blankenship v. Hall*, 542 F.3d 1253 (11th Cir. 2008) (death sentence affirmed); *Storey v. Roper*, 2008 US Dist. LEXIS 46662 (E.D.Mo. 2008) (death sentence affirmed); *Green v. Quarterman*, 2008 US Dist. LEXIS 11459 (S.D.Tx. 2008) (death sentence affirmed); *Berryman v. Ayers*, 2007 US Dist. LEXIS 51738 (E.D. Ca. 2007) (rejecting challenge to hair analysis in capital case; conviction upheld); *Thomas v. Beard*, 388 F. Supp. 2d 489 (E.D. Pa. 2005) (conviction upheld; sentence reversed on other grounds), *death sentence reinstated*, *Thomas v. Horn*, 570 F.3d 105 (3d Cir. 2009); *Bryan v. Mullin*, 100 Fed. Appx. 783, 2004 US App. LEXIS 11172 (10th Cir. 2004) (motion for stay of execution denied, death sentence affirmed; noting that since 'the evidence relied upon by Bryan to assert the unreliability of the bullet comparison and the hair analysis did not exist until well after the completion of Bryan's direct appeal', the state was not in a position to ensure its accuracy at trial); *Bagwell v. Cockrell*, 2003 US Dist. LEXIS 16107 (W.D.Tx. 2003) (affirming death sentence and vacating stay of execution); *Crawford v. Head*, 311 F.3d 1288 (11th Cir. 2002) (death sentence affirmed); *Smith v. Massey*, 235 F.3d 1259 (10th Cir. 2000) (death sentence affirmed); *Barnabei v. Angelone*, 214 F.3d 463 (4th Cir. 2000) (death sentence affirmed); *Dowthitt v. Johnson*, 180 F. Supp. 2d 832 (S.D.Tx. 2000) (death sentence affirmed). Notably the courts may

seem more willing to question the honesty of the police than the reliability of forensic science. See *Moore v. Gibson*, 195 F.3d 1152 (10th Cir. 1999) (death sentence and conviction affirmed with respect to hair analysis, but reversed for hearing with respect to allegations that the police corruptly planted evidence).

16   See B.D. Gaudette & E.S. Keeping, 'An Attempt at Determining Probabilities in Human Scalp Hair Comparison', 19 *Journal of Forensic Science* 599 (1974); B.D. Gaudette, 'Probabilities and Human Pubic Hair Comparisons', 21 *Journal of Forensic Science* 514 (1976). Since even hair analysts agree that scalp hair and pubic hair are very different, this really meant that only one study had been done on either, and none on the key evidence in Randy's case – chest hair. Gaudette published a subsequent article further discussing his own studies. B.D. Gaudette, 'Some Further Thoughts on Probabilities in Human Hair Comparisons', 23 *Journal of Forensic Science* 758 (1978). Two other hair analysts published a later review of these materials. Ray A. Wickenheiser & David G. Hepworth, 'Further Evaluation of Probabilities in Human Scalp Hair Comparisons', 35 *Journal of Forensic Science* 1323 (1990).

17   The probability of a false match with scalp hair, he said, was even lower – one in 4,500. He did not test chest hairs.

18   To be more precise, the actual number he came up with was one in 65,000,000,000,000,000,000,000,000,000 of a false match. Given that the population of the world was roughly 6,000,000,000, clearly Randy Bevill had to be the perpetrator.

19   Mark Twain, *Life on the Mississippi* (1874), quoted in Darrell Huff, *How to Lie with Statistics*, 142 (6th edn 1954). Twain may have been a mile or two off, but he was close: the lower Mississippi (that portion of the great river south of Cairo, Illinois) is just under 1,000 miles long. In 700 years, if it continued to shorten at a continuous rate of 1.375 (242/176) miles per year, it would shorten by a further 962 miles.

20   I also phoned the Royal Canadian Mounted Police (RCMP) to see whether I could get a copy from them, but they said that the original materials had been destroyed.

21   There were many hairs found at the scene, and taken from Randy Bevill. Joe Andrews found two pubic hair 'matches' in a sample size where, under a correct analysis, we would expect to find 1.4 false matches. In other words, making the assumption that he did his work studiously, he found roughly what we would expect to see if the evidence meant nothing.

22   Andrews said that when he looked down the microscope he saw two hairs that matched in every respect. I had him go through packs of cards, and explained that he would never call a match if he saw a Queen of Hearts and a King of Spades, or even a Queen of Hearts

from one pack (a regular one) and a Queen of Hearts from another (a Mutant Ninja Turtle pack). Rather, he would only call a match if they were two Queens of Hearts that were similar in every respect. He agreed that two Queens that I had pasted on to a piece of polystyrene board depicted the kind of similarity that he saw. He followed willingly down this path, as it overstated what he really did to a significant degree. Finally, though, I asked him to remove from the polystyrene board the cards that he had confidently called a match. He smelled a rat and resisted my efforts to have him take the cards off, but Judge Russell ordered him to do as he was asked. Of course, the seemingly identical Queens of Hearts came from obviously different packs – one blue and one red. This made the point that he had called as a match two 'hairs' that came from different 'heads'.

23   In the retrial Randy was acquitted of capital murder, but convicted of the lesser crime of simple murder. Given his prior history, he was sentenced to life imprisonment. Very rarely does a prisoner receive two reversals of a conviction, and Randy did not, despite Jack's efforts and my own. He is therefore still incarcerated at Parchman Penitentiary, in the Mississippi Delta.

24   *Williamson v. Reynolds*, 904 F. Supp. 1529, 1554–8 (E.D. Okla. 1995), *aff'd Williamson v. Ward*, 110 F.3d 1508 (10th Cir. 1997). The Court of Appeals refused to ratify Judge Seay's finding that the hair analysis should have been excluded as a matter of law. The court held that while it did not 'review the merits of the court's ruling [in that respect], we note that some of the authorities it cited view hair analysis as highly subjective and unreliable. It is undisputed that hair analysis ... is not conclusive.' *Id.*, at 1520.

25   Gore was sentenced to death, but the case was reversed on appeal, and he ultimately received life imprisonment. Williamson's freedom was short-lived. He received compensation from the State of Oklahoma, but was dead within a year from liver disease. John Grisham wrote a book about the case: *An Innocent Man* (2006).

26   See Houck, 'Hair Bibliography for the Forensic Scientist' (Jan. 2002), at http://www.fbi.gov/hq/lab/fsc/backissu/jan2002/houck.htm.

27   See Houck, 'Hair Bibliography', quoting P. L. Kirk & J. I. Thornton, *Crime Investigation* (1994) at 143.

28   Houck is also a member of the Forensic and Investigative Science Faculty and Staff at the University of West Virginia, where we can find a brief biography. See http://forensics.wvu.edu/faculty_staff.

29   It is important to be clear what is meant here by 'bogus': the result in *Williamson* showed that the evidence was wholly false. However, a purported science is also bogus if it is unproven, yet presented as proven. This is ultimately the flaw in hair analysis – whether there is

anything to the process or not, it has not been validated.

30   There are, of course, other problems with the crime laboratories that do this work. Many of their flaws – low standards of competency among staff, low salaries that do not attract better staff, inadequate budgets for the caseloads, pressure to produce results too rapidly, and so forth – are detailed in Craig Cooley's article, 'Forensic Science and Capital Punishment Reform: An "Intellectually Honest" Assessment', 17 *George Mason University Civil Rights Law Journal* 299 (2007). Indeed, there has been another capital case where hair analysis was brought directly into question: see *Miller v. Anderson*, 162 F. Supp. 2d 1057 (N.D. Ind. 2000) (affirming the conviction), *rev'd Miller v. Anderson*, 255 F.3d 455, 457 (7th Cir. 2001) (Judge Posner, a renowned and conservative judge, writing an opinion reversing both the conviction and the death sentence). Notably, of course, in *Miller* the original hair analysis was disputed by another hair expert, rather than some kind of independent scientific method. It must, then, go down as an example of a more experienced expert challenging the competence of the original expert, rather than anyone challenging the reliability of the 'science' itself.

31   There is nowhere in the criminal law where the hubris of pseudo-science is more dangerous than in the notion of 'shaken baby syndrome' (SBS). I have represented a number of prisoners over the years who have been charged with such offences. The issue is worthy of a book to itself, and cannot be addressed properly here. Suffice it to say that when pseudo-science is presented by neurologists ('brain surgeons') as a medical diagnosis that proves the defendant guilty, the danger of a wrongful conviction is frightening.

32   See, generally, Solomon Moore, 'Science Found Wanting in Nation's Crime Labs', *New York Times* (Feb. 4th, 2009).

33   Craig Cooley, 'Forensic Science and Capital Punishment Reform: An "Intellectually Honest" Assessment', 17 *George Mason University Civil Rights Law Journal* 299, n. 200–2 (2007). The rather greater, but still small proportion (12 per cent) of exonerations where DNA was implicated is probably a reflection of the fact that it is much harder to secure an exoneration without a much-touted DNA result.

34   One example of the prosecutor's statistical fallacy is the notion that, if the odds of a chance match to a DNA profile are one in a billion, then the odds that the accused is innocent are one in a billion. In truth, even accepting the demographic DNA data, the likelihood of a mistake by a technician (which might be one in 100 or even one in ten) easily swamps the mind-boggling number that the prosecution would rather tout to the jury. Indeed, there are many other flaws in these statistics. Some are succinctly discussed in the Wikipedia entry

on the 'prosecutor's fallacy'. See http://en.wikipedia.org/wiki/Prosecutor's_fallacy (accessed Aug. 5th, 2010).

35   The Second Amendment to the US Constitution protects the right to bear arms. See US CONST. amend. II ('A well regulated militia, being necessary to the security of a free state, the right of the people to keep and bear arms, shall not be infringed').

36   See 'FBI Crime Statistics, Expanded Homicide Data Table 7' (2005), available at http://www.fbi.gov/ucr/05cius/offenses/expanded_infor mation/data/shrtable_07.html (10,100 homicides committed with guns in 2005, of which 74.6 per cent were with a handgun; two-thirds of homicides committed with a gun as compared to all other methods combined).

37   See Center for Disease Control, 'Suicide and Self-Inflicted Injury', at http://www.cdc.gov/nchs/fastats/suicide.htm (17,352 suicides with firearms in 2004); see also Kellerman *et al.*, 'Suicide in the home in relation to gun ownership', 327 *New England Journal of Medicine* 467 (Aug. 13th, 1992) (quantifying the intuitively obvious link between gun ownership and the use of guns in suicide, and suggesting that gun owners consider this link in the light of other perceived 'benefits' of having guns in the home).

38   See Center for Disease Control, National Center for Injury Prevention and Control, at http://webappa.cdc.gov/sasweb/ncipc/nfirates2000. html (75,685 such injuries recorded in one year, including 23,237 accidental firearm injuries). Almost a million crimes a year are committed with guns, yet Americans have a weapon to hand to protect themselves against such crimes in fewer than one in 100 of these assaults, and a large number of such acts of self-defence involve police officers.

39   *District of Columbia v. Heller*, 128 S. Ct. 2783 (2008) (the court declared, by a vote of 5:4, that the Washington DC ordinance barring possession of guns in the home violated the Second Amendment); *McDonald v. Chicago*, 130 S. Ct. 3020 (2010) (again narrowly upholding, by 5:4, Chicago residents' challenge to gun prohibitions, on the grounds that it 'left them vulnerable to criminals').

40   See Florida Statutes §§790.001(17), 790.06, 790.253 (Licence to carry concealed weapon or firearm, limited concealed carry rights, etc.), http://www.flsenate.gov/statutes/index.cfm?App_mode=Display_ Statute&URL=Cho790/cho790.htm.

41   Jonathan Hamilton & David Burch, 'Gun Ownership – It's the Law in Kennesaw', *Marietta Daily Journal* (March 14th, 2001).

42   See BBC World Service, http://www.bbc.co.uk/worldservice/people/ features/ihavearightto/four_b/casestudy_art29.shtml ('The United States has the largest number of guns in private hands of any country in the world with 60 million people owning a combined arsenal of

over 200 million firearms'). Taking into account the arsenal owned by the military, there is probably at least one gun available for each of the 300 million Americans.

43   Cook & Ludwick, 'Guns in America: National Survey on Private Ownership and Use of Firearms', at Table 4A, US Department of Justice, National Institute of Justice (1997), at http://www.ncjrs.gov/pdffiles/165476.pdf (1994 data).

44   Of course a foreign perpetrator could have brought his own gun with him, but that seems unlikely – particularly given the ease with which someone could buy a gun in Florida. It seems likely that the weapon used was not a rifle, although that is not impossible. Only a semi- or an automatic would eject the shell casings, so if it were a revolver, the perpetrator would have to take the used casings out while reloading and leave them in the room – again, not impossible, but perhaps unlikely. Quirk would say that he could rule this out by demonstrating the markings on the casing made by the extractor mechanism on the gun, but again that presupposes that his 'tool mark' testimony validly excludes the alternative explanation.

45   See http://en.wikipedia.org/wiki/Ballistic_fingerprinting. This story seems improbable, since Holmes was elevated to the Supreme Court that year, and he had previously been Chief Justice on the Massachusetts Supreme Judicial Court.

46   See http://en.wikipedia.org/wiki/Ballistic_fingerprinting.

47   *United States v. Glynn*, 578 F.Supp.2d 567 (S.D.N.Y. Sep. 22nd, 2008). See also Dr Adina Schwartz, 'A Systemic Challenge to the Reliability and Admissibility of Firearms and Toolmark Identification', 6 *Columbia Science and Technology Law Review* 1–42; National Research Council report ('Ultimately, as firearms identification is currently practiced … the decision of what does or does not constitute a match comes down to a subjective determination based on intuition and experience').

48   *United States v. Glynn*, 578 F.Supp.2d 567, 569 (S.D.N.Y. Sep. 22nd, 2008), quoting *United States v. Hicks*, 389 F.3d 514, 526 (5th Cir. 2004) ('the matching of spent shell casings to the weapon that fired them has been a recognized method of ballistics testing in this circuit for decades'); *United States v. Foster*, 300 F.Supp.2d 375, 377 n.1 (D.Md. 2004) ('Ballistics evidence has been accepted in criminal cases for many years').

49   *United States v. Glynn*, 578 F.Supp.2d 567, 572 (S.D.N.Y. Sep. 22nd, 2008).

50   Before staring at the websites of various gun enthusiasts made me lose the will to live, I learned that the Browning 9mm is itself a very famous and widely circulated pistol, seemingly more common than the Smith

& Wesson described by Quirk. See http://www.browning.com/prod
ucts/catalog/family.asp?webflag_=007B&catalog_=B&content=Hi-
Power-Pistols. Millions of them have been made. While I have not
been able to find precise numbers for the whole period, 251,000 were
manufactured between 1954 and 1969. See 'Browning Hi-Power Dates
of Manufacture', at http://www.hipowersandhandguns.com/Hi%20P
ower%20Dates%20of%20Manufacture.htm. Even before that, more
than 300,000 had been made for the German military in the Second
World War, and many could have found their way back to the US. See
http://www.handgunsmag.com/featured_handguns/browning_hi_
power/. Again, the Sig-Sauer is a hugely popular pistol, used by the
US military and numerous American law-enforcement and military
agencies. See generally http://www.sigsauer.com/Products/ShowCat
alogProduct.aspx?categoryid=7. I could not find precise numbers on
sales, but this seemed to be an intensely popular gun in the trade and
was described as selling out the moment a dealer gets some in. http://
gunner777.wordpress.com/category/sig-sauer-pistols/.

51 *Chavez v. State*, 2002 Fla. LEXIS 1150, at *28 (Fla. 2002) (Quirk testified: 'My conclusion is that this bullet was fired in this weapon to the
exclusion of all other weapons in the world. This is the gun that fired
this bullet'). Chavez remains on Death Row. See *Chavez v. State*, 12 So.
3d 19 (Fla. 2009).

52 *Brief of Appellee in Griffin v. State*, Fla. S. Ct. No. 77,843, at 16 (filed June
11th, 1993), http://www.law.fsu.edu/library/flsupct/77843/77843brief.
pdf ('Thomas Quirk, a firearms examiner, had made shoe impressions from the sneakers taken from Griffin. He concluded that shoe
impressions lifted from the Holiday Inn balcony were those of Griffin.
Quirk also determined that shots fired into Officer Martin's vest and
shirt were from a .357 Magnum ... the gun which Griffin had stolen
from Pasco and used to shoot Martin'). Griffin remains on Death Row
today, *Griffin v. McNeil*, 2009 US Dist. LEXIS 81824 (S.D. Fla. Aug.
20th, 2009).

53 *Riechmann v. State*, 581 So. 2d 133, 136 (Fla. 1991) ('The expert also testified that the bullet that killed Kischnick could have been fired from
any of three makes of guns. Riechmann owned two of those three
makes of weapons').

54 See *Brief of Appellant, Riechmann v. State*, S. Ct. Fla. No. SC37-060, at 22
(filed March 15th, 2005), available at http://www.law.fsu.edu/library/
flsupct/sc03-760/03-760amd-ini.pdf. Riechmann's challenge to his
appeal was rejected and he remains on Death Row today. *Riechmann
v. State*, 966 So. 2d 298 (Fla. 2007).

55 See *Exhibit IAF*, at 4 (attached to the petition for a writ of habeas
corpus).

56   Finally, there was a third line to the note: 'Subsequent to arrest, "Don't
      you remember. I told you in July that the gun was stolen."' Again
      this needed some explanation. Kris made this statement to Buzzo,
      in Buhrmaster's presence. Buzzo had confirmed that he did, indeed,
      remember Kris saying this. Small wonder, perhaps, that Buzzo was
      one police officer whom the prosecution did not call as a witness;
      sadly, Eric Hendon never spoke with him and by the time I took over
      the case, Buzzo had died.
57   *Maharaj v. State, 3.850 Clerk Tr. 2171.*

9

The Defence Lawyer

1   Statement of Tino Geddes (Oct. 23rd, 1986, 14.54 p.m.), File 044-
      103101-106.
2   Statement of Arthur McKenzie (Oct. 23rd, 1986, 15.15 p.m.), File 044-
      101625-28. Again, some years later, we called him as a witness and
      he testified consistently with his statement. Testimony of Arthur
      McKenzie, *Maharaj 3.850 Hearing Tr.*, at 836.
3   Statement of George Bell (Oct. 24th, 1986, 19.17 p.m.), File 044-101579-
      85.
4   Bizarrely, Judge Bagley, who was sitting on Kris' post-conviction hear-
      ing, would not allow George Bell to testify, based on the prosecution's
      objection that Hendon had specifically withdrawn him as a witness
      at the trial. *Maharaj 3.850 Hearing Tr.*, at 861. The issue before Judge
      Bagley was whether Hendon had acted appropriately in making this
      decision – so of course his testimony was relevant.
5   Statement of Douglas Scott (Oct. 29th, 1986, 14.35 p.m.), File 044-
      101620-24.
6   Testimony of Douglas Scott, *Maharaj 3.850 Hearing Tr.*, at 848–9.
7   Indeed, Ramkissoon had seen Kris the day before – the Wednesday
      – clean-shaven, which specifically corroborated Kris' statement that
      he had shaved on the 15th and not, as the prosecution suggested, on
      the 16th (which they alleged was his effort to disguise his appearance).
      Statement of Gangabissoon Ramkissoon, at 3 (Nov. 5th, 1986), File
      044-101612-618.
8   See generally Statement of Gangabissoon Ramkissoon (Nov. 5th, 1986),
      File 044-101612–618. Ramkissoon knew Kris very well, and would have
      been able to provide other important testimony. He had been present
      when two women from Trinidad were meeting Kris about Derrick
      Moo Young ripping them off for a total of $135,000, and Kris' response

was not to get angry – he had the money, so he reimbursed them what they had lost and tried to settle matters peacefully. *Id.*, at 5. Indeed, as many other witnesses could have confirmed, rather than killing Derrick over this, Kris simply brought a suit to get the money back.

9   Statement of Ronald Kisch (Oct. 23rd, 1986, 21.11 p.m.), File 044-101597-600.

10   The three investigators were Ron Petrillo, Kenneth Holley and Bill Danforth.

11   This witness was Dr Marianne Cook, a psychologist, who had had a conversation with Kris that day. She, too, had been shocked when Kris was arrested as she clearly remembered seeing him the day before – although the defence investigators did not track her down at the time. We ended up not calling her because of some choice things that she said about law enforcement during her deposition. *Maharaj 3.850 Hearing Tr.*, at 942–7. Still, I believed her, certainly given what all the other witnesses were saying.

12   Interview of John Kastrenakes, Channel 4, at 20.

13   Testimony of Eric Hendon, *Maharaj 3.850 Hearing Tr.*, at 331.

14   Testimony of Eric Hendon, *Maharaj 3.850 Hearing Tr.*, at 332.

15   Testimony of Eric Hendon, *Maharaj 3.850 Hearing Tr.*, at 331. The Notice of Alibi (along with the various statements of the witnesses) was indeed filed on the prosecution. See *Maharaj 3.850 Exhibit B.* The state did not begin to see a way past the alibi until much later, when Tino Geddes changed his sworn testimony. This was shortly after Neville Butler had changed his testimony as well. Surely Eric Hendon should have been wondering to himself why all these sea changes were taking place in a capital case, where the witnesses were altering testimony that had been given under oath, under the penalties of perjury?

16   Space does not allow me a full analysis of Geddes' testimony here, because it would add another 30,000 words, but for those who are interested, there is a thorough analysis at www.injusticebook.co.uk

17   Jack P. Friedman, 'Criminal Procedure – Alibi Instructions and Due Process of Law', 20 *Western New England Law Review* 342 (1988), http://digitalcommons.law.wnec.edu/cgi/viewcontent.cgi?article=1260&context=lawreview (accessed Nov. 28th, 2010) ('An "alibi instruction" informs the jury that the prosecution has the burden of disproving the defendant's alibi beyond a reasonable doubt and that the defendant does not have the burden of proving the alibi'). British law is similar to this. See 'Crown Court Bench Book: Directing the Jury', at 289–92 (March 2010), http://www.judiciary.gov.uk/NR/rdonlyres/BE25EBB6-AAD2-4ACD-8115-28D3BF613164/0/benchbook_criminal_2010.pdf ('The first requirement of the direction to the jury is that they understand there is no burden on the defendant to prove that he was

elsewhere. The prosecution must prove its case and that includes the need to prove that the defendant committed the offence'). Alibi is described as being a 'defence', though it is not really: it is merely putting the government to its full burden of proof. As with so many matters, the instruction that a jury must be given may seem clear to a judicial mind parsing the words, but it is actually fairly opaque to a juror who is listening to some interminable jury instructions. The judge is advised to tell the jury as follows:

> If you conclude that the defendant's alibi is true or may be true, then he cannot have participated in the attack on V and you must find him not guilty. If, on the other hand, you are sure, having considered the evidence carefully, that the defendant's alibi is false, that is a finding of fact which you are entitled to take into account when judging whether he is guilty. But do not jump to the conclusion that because the alibi put forward is false the defendant must be guilty. You should bear in mind that sometimes an alibi is invented because the defendant thinks it is easier than telling the truth. The main question for you to answer is: are we sure that A and B have correctly identified the defendant as the man who wounded V?

Id., at 291. While this is logically correct, and could be justified in front of a class of law students, it is nevertheless the type of hyper-technical language that is liable to send jurors down all kinds of rabbit holes. They are never told that they must disbelieve the alibi beyond a reasonable doubt and, if they have any reasonable doubt about its truth, they must acquit. When they hear that they can hold it against the accused if they disbelieve the alibi, they are likely to hear this to the exclusion of other instructions.

18   See *Memo of Bart Stapert interview with Eric Hendon* (July 31st, 1995) (on file).

19   Testimony of Eric Hendon, *Maharaj 3.850 Hearing Tr.*, at 332. Even if one accepts Hendon at his word on this, it would still mean little. It is the lawyer's task to persuade witnesses how important their role is – Kris' life was at stake.

20   Testimony of Eric Hendon, *Maharaj 3.850 Hearing Tr.*, at 332.

21   It was all the worse that Hendon turned over the alibi statements to the prosecution without talking to the witnesses. Indeed, the prosecution immediately had them all interviewed, and could find no cracks in the alibi – itself a highly significant fact.

22   Hendon was an Assistant State Attorney (prosecutor); then an Assistant Public Defender; at the time of Kris' trial he was in private practice; he then went back to the PD's office; and ultimately became a

county-court judge, which is the step down from the Circuit Court where Kris was tried. He was initially appointed by Republican governor Jeb Bush in 1999, but was then unseated in the first election he had to face, in 2002. This was, according to various commentators, because his opponent looked around to find the person she could most readily unseat and thought that the African American Hendon would be the easiest target. In what is almost a unique occurrence, he was then reappointed to a vacant seat, again by Governor Bush. He finally won an election to retain his seat in 2008. See generally http://business.highbeam.com/437111/article-1G1-147640561/taking-bench-again; http://findarticles.com/p/articles/mi_pwwi/is_20050229/ai_mark07991019/ ('Eric has been a tremendous asset to the state's criminal justice system,' Governor Bush said. 'His experience as an assistant state attorney, and his continued work as a public defender, will enable him to bring a diverse background to the bench that will benefit both the judicial community and the community at large'); http://www.miamidade.gov/elections/Library/run_for_office/handbook/county-court-judge.pdf; http://justicebuilding.blogspot.com/2008/03/denise-martinez-scanziani-responds.html (accessed Nov. 28th, 2010).

23   This is what Eric Hendon told Bart Stapert when they spoke on July 7th, 1995. See *Memo of Bart Stapert interview with Eric Hendon* (July 31st, 1995) (on file). Hendon said that the original contract with Robert Trachman had been $50,000, but Kris negotiated a lower payment to him. This would not have included the costs of the investigators and experts.

24   'ABA Guidelines for the Appointment and Performance of Defense Counsel in Death Penalty Cases' (rev. edn 2003), 31 *Hofstra Law Review* 913, 952 (2003) ('The defense team should consist of no fewer than two attorneys qualified in accordance with Guideline 5.1, an investigator, and a mitigation specialist'). The Guidelines refer to 'the four individuals constituting the smallest allowable team' in a capital case (*id.*, at 957), and yet here was Eric Hendon sailing totally solo.

25   Repellent though some might find it, a rate of several thousand dollars per hour is not unheard of in the law. See, e.g., Peter Lattman, 'Lerach's Enron Class-Action: the First $1 Billion Fee?', *Wall Street Journal* (June 1st, 2006) ('class-action king Bill Lerach could be on the verge of winning the first billion-dollar award of attorneys' fees in the history of American securities litigation. [...] According to the *Sun*, Lerach's deal reached with the university in 2002 entitles his firm to 8% of the first billion dollars recovered, 9% of the second billion, and 10% of all amounts above $2 billion. Although that works out to $690 million, more defendants are likely to settle before the trial scheduled for

October. The *Sun* did back-of-the-envelope calculations and concluded that at $1 billion, if the Lerach firm dedicated 20 lawyers to work 40 hours a week, 50 weeks a year for four years, the fee would work out to an hourly billing rate of $6,250 an hour'; if, of course, they worked far less time, their fee would have been far higher), http://blogs.wsj. com/law/2006/06/01/lerachs-enron-class-action-the-first-1-billion-fee/ (accessed Nov. 30th, 2010). This is not unique. Those in Britain who are so keen to adopt the US contingency-fee process would be well advised to study its excesses prior to going down that path. In a class action concerning Native American land rights, settled for $4 billion, the attorneys raked in $688 million dollars in fees. See 'Lawyer Fees questioned in Billion Dollar Class Action', *Lawyers Weekly* (June 10th, 2010), at http://www.lawyersweekly.com.au/blogs/top_stories/ archive/2010/06/03/lawyer-fees-questioned-in-billion-dollar-class-action.aspx (accessed Nov. 30th, 2010). See also Frank Nelson, 'When the Wheels of Justice Grind Out ... Coupons: Critics draw attention to massive class actions that compensate attorneys well but recompense the afflicted with little or nothing of value', Miller-McCune (Aug. 3rd, 2010) ('a case brought against Motorola and other headset makers in 2006 claiming their Bluetooth products carried insufficient warning about potential damage to hearing. Under the settlement – since appealed – the plaintiffs receive nothing, their lawyers get $850,000 in fees and expenses, and the instruction manual was reworded'), at http://www.miller-mccune.com/legal-affairs/when-the-wheels-of-justice-grind-out-coupons-19788/ (accessed Nov. 30th, 2010); *id.* (in a 'settlement against the brokerage firm A.G. Edwards where the plaintiffs received about $24 worth of coupons toward mutual fund fees – to be used over three years – while their lawyers split $21 million in fees'). In 2004 Florida amended its constitution so that lawyers could 'only' take $75,000 in fees from the first $250,000 in any award, and 10 per cent of anything thereafter. *Fla. Const. Art. 1, SECTION 26. Claimant's right to fair compensation* ('(a) Article I, Section 26 is created to read "Claimant's right to fair compensation." In any medical liability claim involving a contingency fee, the claimant is entitled to receive no less than 70% of the first $250,000.00 in all damages received by the claimant, exclusive of reasonable and customary costs, whether received by judgment, settlement, or otherwise, and regardless of the number of defendants. The claimant is entitled to 90% of all damages in excess of $250,000.00, exclusive of reasonable and customary costs and regardless of the number of defendants'), at http://www.flsenate. gov/Statutes/index.cfm?Mode=Constitution&Submenu=3#A01S26 (accessed Nov. 30th, 2010).

26   Hendon's original letter to the prosecutors asked for only fifteen min-

utes (*Maharaj 3.850 Exhibit DH*), but they replied saying he would need much more than this.

27   Ellen Rosen, 'For New Lawyers, the Going Rate Has Gone Up', *New York Times* (Sep. 1st, 2006) ($145,000 in 2006), http://www.nytimes.com/2006/09/01/business/01legal.html?_r=1&adxnnl=1&adxnnlx=1221815274-Ug4LGRQaoUYzoOhXdUVsoQ&oref=slogin.

28   Dominic Carman, 'Are top lawyers worth their huge fees?', *The Sunday Times* (July 13th, 2008), http://business.timesonline.co.uk/tol/business/law/article4303609.ece. (In the UK, 'There are almost 150,000 practising lawyers in England and Wales – up from 91,000 a decade ago. Last year, the top 100 City law firms employed 46,000 lawyers, generating £12.25 billion in revenues and £4.2 billion in profit. This year, at least 800 lawyers will earn £1m or more. They remain largely an Oxbridge elite – over 60% of the top players went to either Oxford or Cambridge, and nearly all were privately educated.') (As a pound is closer to $1.60 these days, £1 million translates as rather less than $2 million.)

29   Nationwide, a lawyer immediately out of law school expects to be paid $151 per hour, ranging up to $224 after twenty years of practice. See Pay Scale, 'Hourly Billing Rate Survey Report for Job: Attorney / Lawyer' (accessed Sep. 18th, 2008), http://www.payscale.com/research/US/Job=Attorney_%2f_Lawyer/Billing_Rate.

30   By 2005 the highest-paid lawyers in New York were asking *one thousand dollars* per hour. Andy Soltis, 'Lawyer Rai$es The Bar – First-Ever 1g/Hr. Fee', *New York Post*, at 23 (Dec. 13th, 2005); see also Pay Scale, 'Hourly Billing Rate Survey Report for Job: Attorney / Lawyer' (accessed Sep. 18th, 2008), http://www.payscale.com/research/US/Job=Attorney_%2f_Lawyer/Billing_Rate.

31   Jonathan D. Glater, 'Partnerships More Elusive At Law Firms, Survey Shows', *New York Times* (March 1st, 2005), http://query.nytimes.com/gst/fullpage.html?res=9A0DE7DF123DF932A35750C0A9639C8B63 ('Lawyers – both partners and associates – on average billed about 1,750 hours each last year').

32   This would be around eighty years' worth of the average American's salary. The median income for Americans over eighteen years old is something over $25,000. See US Census Annual Demographic Survey, March 2006, http://pubdb3.census.gov/macro/032006/perinc/new02_001.htm (median income $25,149). At $1,000 per hour, most Americans, then, if they gave up eating and had nowhere to live, could afford to pay for about twenty-five hours of top-notch corporate legal assistance each year. As discussed in greater detail later, there must be at least two lawyers working each case, and each is likely to average around 1,000 hours, hence the $2 million figure.

33   The short answer, in my opinion, is that no case should cost $2 million in legal fees. But many cases cost far more than that, the overwhelming majority of which are corporate disputes over money – and the issue here is how we value truth for the defendant in a criminal case, as contrasted to truth for a corporation. If you are an indigent, probably black, person accused of a capital crime, there is no chance your defence will cost anything like as much.

34   *Martinez-Macias v. Collins*, 979 F.2d 1067 (5th Cir. 1992).

35   *Martinez-Macias v. Collins*, 810 F. Supp. 782, 786–7, 796–813 (W.D. Tex. 1991), *aff'd*, 979 F.2d 1067 (5th Cir. 1992).

36   Gordon Dickinson, 'Man Freed in Machete Murder Case', *El Paso Times*, June 24th, 1993, at 1.

37   *Wilson v. State*, 574 So. 2d 1338, 1340 (Miss. 1990); *Pruett v. State*, 574 So. 2d 1342 (Miss. 1990). All of the lawyers in these two cases received less than the minimum wage. The two attorneys for Mr Wilson documented 779.2 and 562 hours and the two attorneys for Mr Pruett documented 449.5 and 482.5 hours. Thus, the rates ranged from $1.28 per hour to $2.22 per hour. *Id.*, at 1348 n.7 (Anderson, J., dissenting).

38   US Department of Labor, Employment Standards Division, Fair Labor Standards Act, http://www.dol.gov/esa/whd/flsa/.

39   By the time one has paid administrative staff, paralegals and others, as well as the rent, it costs more than $25 for every hour an office remains open, so this is still a losing proposition – even if the State of Mississippi were inclined to pay for every hour one works. Long ago I wrote something on this. See Anthony Paduano & Clive Stafford Smith, 'The Unconscionability of Sub-Minimum Wages Paid Appointed Counsel in Capital Cases', 43 *Rutgers Law Review*. 281 (1991). So have many others. Louis D. Bilionis and Richard D. Rosen, 'Lawyers, Arbitrariness and the Eighth Amendment', 75 *Texas Law Review* 1301 (1997); Michael D. Moore, 'Analysis of State Indigent Defense Systems and their Application to Death-Eligible Defendants', 37 *William and Mary Law Review* 1617 (1996); Norman Lefstein, 'Reform of Defense Representation in Capital Cases: the Indiana Experience and its Implications for the Nation', 29 *Indiana Law Review* 495 (1996); Douglas W. Vick, 'Poorhouse Justice: Underfunded Indigent Defense Services and Arbitrary Death Sentences', 43 *Buffalo Law Review* 329 (1995); Ruth E. Friedman & Bryan A. Stevenson, 'Solving Alabama's Capital Defense Problems: It's a Dollars and Sense Thing', 44 *Alabama Law Review* 1 (1992); Albert L. Vreeland, II, 'The Breath of the Unfee'd Lawyer: Statutory Fee Limitations and Ineffective Assistance of Counsel in Capital Litigation', 90 *Michigan Law Review* 626 (1991).

40   Neither is this an issue that may be relegated to the 1980s. In November 2010 the Iowa Supreme Court struck down the $1,500 fee cap that

was applicable in all felony appeals. The court did its simple arithmetic: if the appellate lawyer did the maximum number of cases permitted each year (twenty-five) and received the maximum amount
($1,500), she would be paid $37,500. Since the average amount it
costs to run a law office in Iowa is $70,000 per year, she would lose
$32,500 before considering what she might pay herself in salary. The
lawyers in the relevant appeals kept time sheets, and they were being
paid between $12.27 and $12.56 per hour for their work. *Simmons v.
State Public Defender*, No. 07-0870, at http://www.iowacourts.gov/
Supreme_Court/Recent_Opinions/20101124/07-0870.pdf (accessed
Nov. 30th, 2010).

41   See Thomas L. Jones, 'The OJ Simpson Murder Trial', http://www.trutv.
com/library/crime/notorious_murders/famous/simpson/index_1.
html. Of this, the prosecution spent $4 million, using as many as nine
lawyers in court. The county spent $3 million, mainly on jurors. 'O.J.
Simpson double murder trial cost taxpayers in Los Angeles County $9
million', *Jet Magazine* (Dec. 25th, 1995). The precise cost of the defence
has never been made known, but it was certainly considerably more
than the prosecution, with as many as eleven lawyers appearing in
court for Simpson.

42   Guerinot represented thirty-eight clients charged with capital murder
in a capital career spanning from 1980 to 2003. Out of these, twenty
received the death penalty. Of the other eighteen cases, three were
dismissed by the state for lack of evidence against the accused; five
pleaded guilty to life in prison; in six cases death was taken off the
table by the state and they were convicted and sentenced to life. The
rest (four) received life at trial. To set this in perspective, I have been
responsible for many more capital trials but, because I have had the
assistance of dedicated co-counsel and investigators who have spent
the time necessary to prepare, I am glad to say I have no clients on
Death Row from cases that have gone to trial. In other words, it is
entirely possible to prevail on almost all capital cases, with the proper
resources. It is a testament to Guerinot's ineptitude and lack of preparation that his record is so bad.

43   These states were (as of November 2010) Colorado (3), Connecticut
(10), Delaware (19), Idaho (17), Illinois (15), Indiana (15), Kansas (10),
Maryland (5), Montana (2), Nevada (11), New Hampshire (1), New
Mexico (2), South Dakota (3), Utah (10), Virginia (15), Washington
(9), Wyoming (1) and the fourteen states that have no Death Row at
all. The US military has eight people on Death Row.

44   See Lisa Olsen, 'Hundreds kept jailed for months pretrial; Lawyers
for the poor have high caseloads, but little oversight, analysis shows',
Houston Chronicle (Oct. 4th, 2009), http://www.chron.com/disp/

story.mpl/metropolitan/6650826.html?plckFindCommentKey=Com
mentKey:73f02b7c-0c09-4141-99f0-7fb297af8cfd. The American Bar
Association allows lawyers to have no more than 150 cases going at
any one time, which is itself an extraordinary number.

45   Ultimately, much of the work we did was incorporated into a report
by Michael M. Kurth, PhD, & Daryl V. Burckel, DBA & CPA, *Defending
the Indigent in Southwest Louisiana* (2002) (on file with the author),
whence I derive the facts in the following paragraphs, except where
noted. Each resident of Calcasieu Parish paid the equivalent of $6.65
per year towards the local indigent defence system, which worked out
at $110 per criminal case. The prosecution was at least four times bet-
ter off, though they also complained of a lack of funding. In 2001
the Calcasieu Parish District Attorney's Office had a budget of $4.2
million and a staff of eighty-eight employees, including twenty-one
attorneys – each with their own investigator and secretary – as well
as access to forensic testing, expert witnesses and of course the entire
police force. By comparison, the Public Defender Office (PDO) had
a budget of just $1.2 million and a staff of eighteen, including nine
staff attorneys, no assistants and just two investigators to cover all the
cases. Even excluding the work the police did on the cases, the prosecution was funded almost four times as well as the defence, with five
times the number of personnel.

46   Private lawyers were forty-one times as likely to visit their clients.

47   Report of Michael M. Kurth, PhD, & Daryl V. Burckel, DBA & CPA,
Defending the Indigent in Southwest Louisiana (2002) (on file with the
author). Of these, 7,459 civil cases were filed, seeking some form of
monetary damages, and twenty-two full trials were held. This means
that the civil litigant was twice as likely to be allowed a jury trial as the
criminal defendant.

48   Thanks to an enormous amount of work by various volunteers, we
conducted similar evaluations of the indigent defence systems in
other parishes – including Caddo, Orleans and Rapides – with similar
results.

49   What of Britain? In Britain, in 2010, the annual bill of £2 billion for
legal aid costs roughly £38 per head – a rather reasonable figure when
you consider that this essentially acts as an insurance premium for all
litigation that a citizen might face. The total includes £914 million for
civil, welfare, negligence, immigration, employment and family law.
See Afua Hirsch, 'Radical plans may reduce legal aid cases by 547,000',
The Guardian at 6 (Nov. 16th, 2010). The cost per resident of criminal
legal aid is closer to £20, again a very reasonable figure.

50   My own career rather painfully reflects this. I graduated from law
school in 1984, and I tried two capital cases in 1985 and 1986, when I

barely knew the way to the courthouse; both men – John Pope and Willie Gamble – were sentenced to death. It was not surprising and I should never have been allowed to represent them. I was totally incompetent. The only saving grace was that their death sentences were later reversed, and they avoided going back to Death Row. *Pope v. State*, 256 Ga. 195, 345 S.E.2d 831 (1986); *Gamble v. State*, 257 Ga. 325, 357 S.E.2d 792 (1987) (prosecutor's use of all state's ten strikes against black venirepersons – the term used for those called to jury duty, before they are selected – established prima-facie case). I avoided representing anyone else in a capital trial until 1993, when I had a great deal more experience as well as the ability to obtain more resources. After that time, I tried nineteen cases and the jury voted for the death penalty in only one – which was also reversed on appeal.

51 For an excellent discussion of this, see the article by my former colleague and mentor, Stephen B. Bright: 'Counsel For The Poor: The Death Penalty Not For The Worst Crime But For The Worst Lawyer', 103 *Yale Law Journal* 1835 (1994).

52 I must emphasise that the number of those exonerated does not accurately reflect the frequency of error. For reasons discussed later in this book, the appellate process is itself structurally organised to *avoid* identifying mistakes. Thus the likelihood of error is much greater than the figures reflect.

53 CNN, 'Illinois suspends death penalty' (Jan. 31st, 2000), http://archives.cnn.com/2000/US/01/31/illinois.executions.02/ (' "We have now freed more people than we have put to death under our system – 13 people have been exonerated and 12 have been put to death," [Gov.] Ryan told CNN. "There is a flaw in the system, without question, and it needs to be studied" ').

54 A judge in a Florida case took a defence lawyer in chambers during the penalty phase to explain what the phase of trial was about. The lawyer responded: 'I'm at a loss. I really don't know what to do in this type of proceeding. If I'd been through one, I would, but I've never handled one except this time.' *Douglas v. Wainwright*, 714 F.2d 1532, 1556 (11th Cir. 1983), *vacated and remanded*, 468 US 1206 (1984), *on remand*, 739 F.2d 531 (11th Cir. 1984), *and cert. denied*, 469 US 1208 (1985). An Alabama defence lawyer asked for time between the guilt and penalty phases so that he could read the state's death-penalty statute. Record at 1875–6, *State v. Smith*, 581 So. 2d 497 (Ala. Crim. App. 1990). See Stephen B. Bright, 'Counsel For The Poor: The Death Penalty Not For The Worst Crime But For The Worst Lawyer', 103 Yale Law Journal 1835, n.50 (1994).

55 See *Coleman v. Kemp*, 778 F.2d 1487, 1494, 1495, 1503, 1516, 1522 (11th Cir. 1985) (one attorney appointed to defend capital cases claimed the

appointment was 'the worst thing that's ever happened to me professionally'; another stayed on the case because '[t]o refuse would be contempt of court'), *cert. denied*, 476 US 1164 (1986).

56 Record Excerpts at 102, *Dungee v. Kemp* (11th Cir.) No. 85-8202 (defendant called 'nigger' by defence counsel), *decided sub nom. Isaacs v. Kemp*, 778 F.2d 1482 (11th Cir. 1985), *cert. denied*, 476 US 1164 (1986). Sadly, this was not a unique case. *Goodwin v. Balkcom*, 684 F.2d 794, 805 n.13 (11th Cir. 1982) (defendant called a 'little old nigger boy' in closing argument by defence counsel); *Ex parte Guzmon*, 730 S.W.2d 724, 736 (Tex. Crim. App. 1987) (Mexican client referred to as 'wet back' in front of all-white jury by defence counsel). It is also notable that none of the appellate decisions in George Dungee's case ever mentioned the lawyer's use of a racial slur – thus making it improbable anyone took meaningful steps to ensure it would not happen in future.

57 *People v. Garrison*, 254 Cal. Rptr. 257 (1986). Counsel, an alcoholic, was arrested en route to court one morning and found to have a blood alcohol level of 0.27. The court was unwilling to assume that the lawyer was incompetent, even when under the influence of alcohol at breakfast time.

58 Defence counsel was found to have slept during a capital trial in *Harrison v. Zant*, No. 88-V-1640, Order at 2 (Super. Ct. Butts County, Ga. Oct. 5, 1990), *aff'd*, 402 S.E.2d 518 (Ga. 1991). See also *Tippins v. Walker*, 77 F.3d 682, 685–90 (2d Cir. 1996) (finding Tippins' attorney 'repeatedly unconscious … when Tippins' interests were at stake'); *Javor v. United States*, 724 F.2d 831, 832–5 (9th Cir. 1984) (Javor's attorney slept through a substantial part of a two-week trial).

59 See Note, '*Burdine v. Johnson*: The Fifth Circuit Wakes Up, But the Supreme Court Refuses To Put the Sleeping Attorney Standard To Rest', 39 *Houston Law Review* 835 (2002).

60 The judge was in Houston (Harris County), Texas, famous for having more people on Death Row than any other jurisdiction in the country, and not too concerned about how they got there. John Makeig, 'Asleep on the Job; Slaying Trial Boring, Lawyer Said', *Houston Chronicle*, Aug. 14th, 1992, at A35.

61 See *Burdine v. Johnson*, 231 F.3d 950 (5th Cir. 2000), *vacated en banc*, 262 F.3d 336 (5th Cir. 2001), *cert. denied*, 122 S. Ct. 2347 (2002).

62 Ultimately common sense prevailed and Burdine received a new trial. BBC News, 'Texas "Sleeping Lawyer" Verdict Overturned' (Aug. 14th, 2001), http://news.bbc.co.uk/1/hi/world/americas/1490734.stm. He avoided the death sentence on his retrial.

63 *Burdine v. Johnson*, 87 F. Supp. 2d 711, 713 & n.2 (S.D. Tex. 2000).

64 *State v. Leatherwood*, 548 So. 2d 389 (Miss. 1989). On retrial, Leatherwood pleaded to time served (meaning that he was freed

immediately) to avoid the possibility of his facing another death sentence. Notwithstanding substantial evidence of innocence then, he went on the sex-offender registry. He is still on it, more than twenty years later. See http://www.homefacts.com/offender-detail/ MS375307/Alfred-Dale-Leatherwood.html.

65   There are many other stories like this. See *Bellamy v. Cogdell*, 952 F.2d 626 (2d Cir. 1991) (seventy-year-old counsel's representation inadequate because he had been found incompetent *per se* prior to the trial, and promised to secure second counsel, but nobody told the client); cf. *Waterhouse v. Rodriguez*, 848 F.2d 375 (2d Cir. 1988) (Robert Waterhouse, who I was helping to represent on his capital charges in Florida at the time, had a prior New York conviction that was upheld, notwithstanding the fact that his lawyer was in the middle of disbarment proceedings at the time of Robert's trial); or see *House v. Balkcom*, 725 F.2d 608, 612 (11th Cir. 1984), *cert. denied*, 469 US 870 (1984) (the court-appointed lawyer cross-examined a significant witness although he had not heard the man's direct testimony to the jury, because he had been outside parking his car).

66   Calvin narrowly avoided the death penalty, which meant that he was perhaps less fortunate than others. Without a death sentence he had no lawyer until the Innocence Project – New Orleans (http://www. ip-no.org/) offered to take his case.

67   I should point out that no court has found Hendon *legally* ineffective. When I speak of him being ineffective here, I mean that whatever the legal standard – and it is demonstrably itself an ineffectual one, if the goal is to remedy second-rate lawyering – and whatever his excuses, his work on Kris Maharaj's behalf was inadequate.

68   Petrillo later repeated this to a journalist. See Joanne Green, 'British Ex-Millionaire Fights for Freedom: Krishna Maharaj went from the high life to a life sentence – for a crime he might not have committed', *Miami New Times* (Sep. 27th, 2007), http://www.miaminewtimes.com/2007-09-27/news/british-ex-millionaire-fights-for-freedom/; Joanne Green, 'Justice Severed: Maharaj went from the high life to a life sentence – 20 years so far for a crime he may not have committed' (Sep. 27th, 2007) http://florida-issues.blogspot.com/2007_09_01_archive.html. This is consistent with what Ron told me when I first talked to him more than ten years before.

10

The Other Suspects

1   As an alternative, the court thought the jurors would have properly
considered the pages and pages of Carberry's newspaper for the limited purpose for which it might be legally admissible – to show that
Kris Maharaj had a motive for being angry at the Moo Youngs, who
were spreading around this muck against him. But the jurors had no
reason to think any of the articles were false, and the notion that they
could carefully delimit the relevance of the material for one purpose
alone, and otherwise ignore it, is the kind of unmitigated fiction that
gives the courts a bad name.

2   Judge Solomon had also found this aggravating circumstance to exist,
illustrating the fact that the judge had made the same mistake. This
was also deemed harmless.

3   In referring to the next round of appeals as habeas corpus, I am using
shorthand. Each state uses a different nomenclature, and Florida calls
these proceedings a 3.850 writ, after the section of the code that sets
out the procedure. However, the term habeas corpus is used by many
states and the federal courts for this kind of process and I shall use it
throughout the book.

4   The process had been a little more convoluted, as we will see later in
Chapter 14. However, nothing substantive happened before Ben was
retained (for a reduced fee with the last of Kris' money) and I joined
the case pro bono at the request of the British Consulate. This was
in 1994, and Ben has since helped for Kris for eighteen years without
further payment.

5   See generally Ethan A. Nadelmann, *Cops Across Borders: The Interna-
tionalization of U.S. Criminal Law Enforcement* (1993), at 277 & n.50
(discussing drug corruption in the Bahamas); Carl Hiaasen & Jim
McGee, 'A Nation for Sale: Corruption in the Bahamas', *Miami Herald*
(Sep. 23rd, 1984); *Drugs, Law Enforcement & Foreign Policy* (US Senate,
Dec. 1988), at 18.

6   Paul Eddy, *The Cocaine Wars – Murder, Money, Corruption, and the
World's most Valuable Commodity* (1988), at 189.

7   *Biography of Carlos Lehder*, www.mundoandino.com/Colombia/
Carlos-Lehder.

8   *Biography of Carlos Lehder*, www.mundoandino.com/Colombia/
Carlos-Lehder.

9   Eddy, *The Cocaine Wars*, at 163.

10   By 1984 the Medellin Cartel controlled 80 per cent of the world's

cocaine. However, they went too far even for their crooked supporters in the Colombian Government. Lehder was believed to have been at least partially behind the 1985 Palace of Justice siege, which resulted in the death of eleven Supreme Court judges and eighty-four others, as well as being responsible for the death of the Justice Minister, Rodrigo Lara, in 1984. After this time many of the Medellin Cartel fled to the protection of Manuel Noriega in Panama. Lehder mistrusted Noriega and went instead to Nicaragua, before returning to the Colombian jungle, where he was eventually caught and extradited to the US.

11   Eddy, *The Cocaine Wars*, at 174.

12   Eddy, *The Cocaine Wars*, at 175.

13   Alan A. Block, *Masters of Paradise: Organized Crime and the Internal Revenue Service of the Bahamas* (1998).

14   *Drugs, Law Enforcement & Foreign Policy* (US Senate, Dec. 1988), at 19, citing INCSR, Dept. of State, at 123 (March 1989) ('The United States has for more than three years sought extradition of Nigel Bowe, a Bahamian lawyer with strong ties to the PLP and the Bahamian government'; 'US law enforcement authorities believe Bowe has played a key role in organizing smuggling throughout the Caribbean …').

15   'Gran Jurado Estatal Encause a 11 en Pesquisa sobre Cocaina', *El Nuevo Herald* (Oct. 24th, 1986) (Nigel Bowe, Cabrera Sarmiento and nine other people indicted in Miami for bringing 7,304 pounds of cocaine over five years).

16   Lehder would be extradited in February 1987. *United States v. Lehder-Rivas*, 955 F.2d 1510 (11th Cir. 1992). He would be convicted the next year, and would complain bitterly on appeal that 'the district court erroneously admitted evidence of his views on Hitler … and impermissibly allowed comparisons between Lehder's organization and the Third Reich. The government introduced this evidence primarily to establish Lehder's motives. See Fed.R.Evid. 404(b). Lehder consciously imitated Hitler's "organizational genius" in structuring his smuggling operation.' Later he would strike a deal to testify against Manuel Noriega, in order to reduce his sentence from life to fifty years – since he is still in prison, this is a deal that he insists the US has not respected. *United States v. Lehder-Rivas*, 136 Fed.Appx. 324 (11th Cir. 2005).

17   See *United States v. Bowe*, 221 F.3d 1183 (11th Cir. 2000).

18   She subsequently secured a company profile generated by International Company Profile, 6–14 Underwood Street, London (reflecting a registered office at Bowe & MacKay Attorneys, Frederick House, PO Box 4839, Frederick Street, Nassau, Bahamas. Cargil was described as 'an offshore company which has its registered office care of a corporate services company who merely maintain the company's registered

office and file appropriate documents with the Authorities to comply with Bahamas law'. Each such profile cost £70, and with as many as fifty front companies to research, this was the kind of tool that was generally beyond our means, and had not even existed when we began the investigation into Kris' case in the 1990s.

19   When I looked into him, I learned that Hosein had an extraordinary background. His brothers had been convicted in one of the most high-profile murder cases in British legal history, where they allegedly conspired to kidnap Rupert Murdoch's wife, and got the wrong woman (Muriel McKay, the wife of a senior Murdoch executive, who had borrowed the Murdoch car). She never reappeared and a rumour persisted that the Hosein brothers had chopped her up and fed her to their pigs, though that was never proven. Adam testified on behalf of his brothers, and suggestions were made (again not substantiated) that he himself had been involved in the crime. This is further detailed in the online supplement to the book.

20   Joanne Green, 'British Ex-Millionaire Fights for Freedom: Krishna Maharaj went from the high life to a life sentence – for a crime he might not have committed', *Miami Times* (Sep. 27th, 2007), http://www.miaminewtimes.com/2007-09-27/news/british-ex-millionaire-fights-for-freedom/. There were other possible explanations, of course – one cushion had almost certainly been used to muffle a shot, and there had been indications that another cushion might also have been used.

21   Green, 'British Ex-Millionaire Fights for Freedom'.

22   Green, 'British Ex-Millionaire Fights for Freedom'.

23   Green, 'British Ex-Millionaire Fights for Freedom'.

24   There were other indicators of how important Hosein might be to the case. Joe Hingston, still on the investigation trail, talked to a witness who relayed some important hearsay: Hosein had confessed his own involvement in the murders to a third person, divulging gruesome details and confirming that Kris was innocent. This would obviously be crucial evidence, but the third person subsequently refused to discuss it. Hosein has never agreed to respond to these allegations despite various efforts we have made. It must be assumed that he would deny them and, without a full and fair trial at which all of the evidence might be aired, it would not be fair to draw any conclusions against him.

25   Francis Joseph, 'Ramesh Maharaj 25 Years Later', *Newsday* (April 16th, 2000), http://www.nalis.gov.tt/Biography/bio_RameshLawrence Maharaj_2.htm.

26   I first met Ramesh before he authorised these hangings, detailed by Mark Fineman, 'Triple Hanging Returns Death Penalty to Trinidad',

Los Angeles Times (June 5th, 1999), http://8.12.42.31/1999/jun/05/news/mn-44346; see also Larry Roberts, 'Trinidad Executed nine in four days', World Socialist Website (June 17th, 1999), http://www.wsws.org/articles/1999/jun1999/cari-j17.shtml ('government officials in the Caribbean islands … launched a campaign to have capital punishment reinstated. Attorney General for Trinidad and Tobago Ramesh Maharaj and Jamaican Security Minister K.D. Knight became the main spokespersons for this reactionary movement'). However, Ramesh had already moved sharply in favour of capital punishment, even advocating that Trinidad withdraw from the jurisdiction of the Privy Council.

27   *Drugs, Law Enforcement & Foreign Policy*, at 114–15, A Report prepared by the Subcommittee on Terrorism, Narcotics and International Operations of the Committee on Foreign Relations, US Senate (Dec. 1988) (money-laundering operations that began in the Caymans and the Bahamas shifted in the mid-1980s to Panama, due to US pressure on the banks in the former countries).

28   *Drugs, Law Enforcement & Foreign Policy*, at 3.

29   *Drugs, Law Enforcement & Foreign Policy*, at 116; *id.*, at 81 ('between 1979 and 1983, the PDF [Noriega's party] helped the Medellin cartel launder billions of dollars through Panama').

30   *Drugs, Law Enforcement & Foreign Policy*, at 90 ('between 1970 and 1987, Noriega's name appeared in more than 80 different DEA files').

31   He arrived there on April 10th, July 21st, August 20th, August 28th, September 8th, September 15th and September 26th, his stays varying from one to five nights. Note the rapid acceleration of the visits as the day of the murder – October 16th – approaches. It would seem that the 'business' being conducted in Panama was picking up.

32   See *Maharaj Exhibit OCY*.

33   *Drugs, Law Enforcement & Foreign Policy*, at 116.

11

The Jury

1   There is some debate as to the genesis of the term *voir dire*. In modern French it literally means, 'to see, to say', which is a good description of the process: observing the prospective jurors speak, and listening to what they have to say, is the key to the process. However, there is one school of thought that suggests that the term comes from old Anglo-Norman, where *voir* (or *voire*) derived from the Latin *verum* ('that which is true'), so the phrase would mean to speak truthfully.

2   A juror must also swear that they will not *always* impose a death sen-

tence, should the defendant be found guilty. However, the process operates to the detriment of the person on trial. Most defence lawyers are not good at rooting out and removing the 'automatic pro-death-penalty' jurors. Additionally, and paradoxically, as the American public generally becomes less strongly in favour of the death penalty – a shift that we have witnessed over the past twenty years – the elimination of jurors becomes increasingly damaging to the defendant: there are fewer people who will always vote for death, and more who have qualms about the death penalty. When the US was in a more liberal phase in the 1960s this meant that as many as 50 per cent of jurors would be removed from the case for their opposition to capital punishment. Thus, in the seminal case of *Witherspoon v. Illinois*, 391 US 510 (1968), 'the prosecution eliminated nearly half the venire of prospective jurors by challenging ... any venireman who expressed qualms about capital punishment'.

3   Kris' defence counsel, Eric Hendon, made only a very cursory effort on *voir dire*, and excluded no jurors who would automatically impose a death sentence.

4   The best available solution to these problems is to ensure that everyone in the *voir dire* process speaks out, which is possible under some circumstances. However, this is not possible in the federal system (where the judge conducts much, and sometimes all, of the *voir dire*) and in some state systems. For example, in Mississippi the questioning is sometimes done collectively – with 100 people in the courtroom. The chance of getting jurors to speak their minds openly in front of ninety-nine of their neighbours is zero.

5   *Turner v. Murray*, 476 US 28, 30–1 (1986). In *Turner*, the court held that a capital defendant accused of an interracial crime is entitled to have prospective jurors informed of the race of the victim and questioned on the issue of racial bias. But this ruling only applies to capital cases, only to interracial crimes, and only if deemed to have an impact on the penalty phase of the trial – in other words, Turner's conviction was left undisturbed by the refusal to allow this line of questioning. All three of these caveats would seem to be unjustifiable: an African American defendant is surely likely to suffer discrimination at the hands of a bigot, no matter whether his trial is capital or not, no matter whether the victim is white or not. And how was it that the court could conclude that bigotry only affected the sentence, rather than the conviction? Mind you, *Turner* was a step in the right direction, particularly when compared to the British system, where the racism of the juror would not be exposed in any case.

6   Racism is not always overt or even conscious. We all have a level of prejudice – meaning, as the word does, pre-judgement of those around

us. That does not mean everyone is evil, but these are the kinds of attitudes that are important to root out in jury selection, so that one can anticipate how a particular person will respond to the evidence.

7   Given my own experiences with US law enforcement in Los Angeles and elsewhere, I would question whether Fuhrman's racism would impel him to concoct evidence against Simpson more than his simple membership of the police force. (See Chapter 7, above.)

8   Matthew, Chapter 5, Verse vii jurors are just fine; most jurors who cite any verse in 2 Timothy, particularly such lines as Chapter 3, Verse xvi, are dangerous.

9   Either party may move to exclude an unlimited number of jurors who are biased because they already formed an opinion about the case. *Murphy v. Florida*, 421 US 794, 95 S. Ct. 2031, 2036 (1975) (the 'constitutional standard of fairness requires that a state defendant have a panel of impartial, indifferent jurors'); *Irvin v. Dowd*, 366 US 717, 81 S. Ct. 1639, 1641–2 (1961) ('In essence, the right to a jury trial guarantees to the criminally accused a fair trial by a panel of impartial, "indifferent" jurors ... "The theory of the law is that a juror who has formed an opinion cannot be impartial" '); *Edwards v. Griner*, 155 S.E.2d 789 (Ga. App. 1930) ('jurors should come to the consideration of a case free from even a suspicion of prejudgment').

10 See *State v. Monroe*, 366 So.2d 1345 (La. 1978) (it was unreasonable for the trial court to conclude that an assistant prosecutor could be impartial despite his manifestations that he could).

11 See *State v. Lee*, 292 N.C. 617, 234 S.E.2d 574, 578 (1977) (wife of police officer, friendly with most of the force, should have been excused); *State v. Guynn*, 48 P.2d 902, 904 (Utah 1935) ('[t]he juror was subject to challenge for implied bias ... because of his position as a deputy sheriff'); *Tate v. People*, 125 Colo. 527, 247 P.2d 665, 671 (1952) (error not to exclude special deputy sheriff who was not regularly employed but was paid for special services).

12 See *State v. Lee*, 559 So. 2d 1310, 1316 (La. 1990) (discussing the importance of questioning on respect for the Fifth Amendment right to remain silent, since a number of jurors are unwilling to accept that this should not be proof of guilt); *State v. Hallal*, 557 So. 2d 1388, 1390 (La. 1990) (when the juror 'never expressly state[s] that [he] could put aside' the opinion, the trial court errs when it denies a challenge to that juror).

13 See *United States v. McCorkle*, 248 F.2d 1, 8 (3rd Cir.), cert. denied, 355 US 873 (1957) (juror in armed-robbery trial significantly affected by personal robbery seven months earlier); *Sims v. United States*, 405 F.2d 1381, 1384 n.5 (D.C. Cir. 1968) (jurors related to cab drivers should be excluded from attempted robbery of cab driver trial).

14   After removing jurors for a clear reason come the peremptory challenges. A peremptory challenge is one that is made by one of the parties, for which they generally do not have to articulate a reason. Depending on the jurisdiction in the US, the parties have a variable number of such strikes. In many states the parties have an equal number, varying according to the seriousness of the case. See Miss. Code Ann. § 99-17-3 ('In capital cases the defendant and the state shall each be allowed twelve peremptory challenges. In cases not capital the accused and the state each shall be allowed six peremptory challenges; but all peremptory challenges by the state shall be made before the juror is presented to the prisoner. In all cases the accused shall have presented to him a full panel before being called upon to make his peremptory challenges'). In Georgia, the defence used to have twice as many challenges as the prosecution, but this has now been amended to make them equal. O.C.G.A. § 15-12-165 (2010) (nine challenges each in regular felony trials, fifteen each in capital cases). However, some states have very idiosyncratic rules. For example, in Alabama the jury is struck down from whatever number available to twelve. See 2006 Ala. Code § 12-16-100 (in a capital case, at least thirty-six qualified jurors must be presented to the two parties prior to striking; 'the names of those jurors who were challenged or excused for good reason, the district attorney shall be required first to strike from the strike list the name of one juror, and the defendant shall strike one, and they shall continue to strike off names alternately until only 12 jurors remain on the strike list'). In one capital case we began with 108 jurors who had been qualified, and each side struck forty-eight people, until only twelve remained. Such a process can be invidious as it makes it much easier to get rid of minority jurors. Indeed, in that same trial the prosecutor struck seventeen African American jurors in a row. When I pointed out to the judge that the probability of this happening by chance was one-in-10^{35} the judge demurred, saying: 'You say it's one in ten to the thirty-fifth, but you're wrong. I know the prosecutor, and I know the odds are one-in-one – he does it in every case.' I thought this slightly missed the point. But to be fair, the judge then disallowed a number of the prosecution strikes on grounds of racial discrimination, and the jury was reasonably representative.

15   It is unfair to say – as is sometimes proposed – that all jury selection is the pursuit of ignorant jurors. However, the manner of jury selection does mean that sometimes jurors who do express opinions are struck by the lawyers, leaving jurors who display a remarkable degree of ignorance. See, e.g., http://blog.thejurorinvestigates.com/2009/10/13/an-ignorant-jury-in-the-carla-hughes-trial.aspx ('The deliberating jury in the [Mississippi] murder trial of teacher Carla Hughes sent an

appallingly ignorant question out to the judge this morning: "Could the prosecution have called Carla Hughes to the stand?"', apparently in ignorance of the US constitutional right to remain silent).

16   See Sarah N. Conde, 'Capote in the Jury Box: Analyzing the Ethics of Jurors Writing Books', *Georgetown Journal of Legal Ethics* (Summer 2006) (discussing books written by jurors in three high-profile cases: 'The Menendez jury hung, and O.J. Simpson and Michael Jackson were both acquitted. Although those who argue jurors should not be permitted to publish books may have valid concerns, the fact is that in these three instances at least, none of the defendants appear to have "suffered" from those publication plans').

17   See John Schwattz, 'As Jurors Turn to Web, Mistrials Are Popping Up', *New York Times* (March 17th, 2009), http://www.nytimes.com/-2009/03/18/us/18juries.html?_r=1. The article describes two different phenomena: one involved nine out of twelve jurors who used Google in breaks in the trial to check out facts in a major federal drug trial in Florida. While this was leading them towards acquittal of the accused, it thoroughly perverted the trial, as the jurors skirted the judge's ruling on admissibility of evidence by simply reading it on the Internet. The second involved a juror who had just been on the panel that awarded $12 million against a building-materials company, Stoam Holdings, and who tweeted, 'So Johnathan, what did you do today? Oh nothing really, I just gave away TWELVE MILLION DOLLARS of somebody else's money.' This is a wholly different matter, as it would seem, from the message, that the jury had already voted and he was merely reporting the result – which would be entirely unobjectionable.

18   I would generally get other staff members to do the first interview in a case that I tried, since I hoped this would allow the jurors to be more honest in their criticism (which could be hugely beneficial, but might be harder to say to my face). However, with post-conviction cases, where I was not the trial lawyer, I would often do the interviews myself, as I found them such a fascinating insight into what really happens in the jury process.

19   It is perhaps a tribute to the general racism of the day that the Kent State shootings involving white students attracted so much more attention than the Jackson State shooting of black students.

20   These are 2009 figures. See *Mississippi County Briefing Sheets*, MSU Social Science, http://www.dafvm.msstate.edu/resources/09county-demographics.pdf (accessed Dec. 4th, 2010). When I went there (in 1985) the balance was slightly different, but the racial dynamics quite overt.

21   The NAACP is the National Association for the Advancement of Colored People. The organisation was founded more than a century ago,

on February 12th, 1909. It remains the largest grass-roots civil rights organisation in the US and has maintained its anachronistic name. See http://www.naacp.org/pages/our-mission (accessed Dec. 4th, 2010).

22   It was a long battle. With the help of the New York law firm Cahill, Gordon, we persuaded a New York court to throw out Sam's prior conviction that had been used at his penalty phase. Then the US Supreme Court ordered a new sentencing trial based on the Mississippi jury's consideration of the unconstitutional prior conviction. See *Johnson v. Mississippi*, 486 US 578 (1988) (Eighth Amendment requires re-examination of Mississippi death sentence where one factor considered aggravation was a prior New York conviction, which was subsequently invalidated by the New York Court of Appeals).

23   There was a very strong case to be made for Sam's innocence, but despite challenging his conviction for several years, he remained in the Mississippi State Penitentiary at Parchman Farm until he died, a few years later, from a terrible cancer that had gone untreated.

24   See *Brief of Amicus Curiae of Kathleen Hawk Norman in Support of Petitioner's Application for Supervisory Writs* in Orleans Parish Case Number 375-994. 'F', Hon. Dennis Waldron, Presiding, arguing that the jurors were 'deceived, duped, and denied critical evidence necessary to complete their civic responsibility' (on file with author).

25   *State v. Bright*, No. 03-1238 (La. App. 4 Cir. 9/9/03).

26   *State v. Bright*, 875 So.2d 37 (La. 2004).

27   Kathleen went on to devote her substantial energies to working as the chair of the Board of Innocence Project – New Orleans (IPNO), set up by my wife. IPNO gives free legal assistance to the many people wrongfully convicted and serving life sentences in Louisiana and Mississippi. Sadly, in 2008, Kathleen suffered an unexpected and massive heart attack, depriving the community of an invaluable advocate.

28   The way instructions on the law are given to the jury varies from state to state, but in every state the notion that these instructions are understood is an improbable one. The instructions are almost invariably read out by the judge. They tend to be phrased in legal language that some lawyers do not understand. This process can last up to an hour, in which time even the judge gets bored; the eyes of the jurors simply glaze over. At the end, some states do not allow the jurors to take a written copy back into the jury room with them, on the principle that if they do they might give undue weight to one instruction or another. How can the jurors possibly understand what they have been told when they are not even allowed to reread the instructions themselves? While I have been doing capital cases for a quarter of a century, I still read the instructions over more than once to be sure they are correct, or that I have not missed something significant. To believe that

a lay person with no legal training at all would understand this legal mumbo-jumbo, after one soporific reading in a warm courtroom, falls into the realm of fantasy.

29   The difference between the US and the UK is that such studies are possible in the US. See, e.g., Alan Reifman, Spencer M. Gusick, Phoebe C. Ellsworth, 'Real Jurors' Understanding of the Law in Real Cases', 16 *Law & Human Behavior* 539 (1992). In the UK there is absolutely no way to validate a naïve belief that the jurors understand their true function, because we won't allow anyone to ask them.

30   One study was conducted in Michigan, where the educational background of the jurors was much higher than in most of the cases I tried in the Deep South. See Alan Reifman, Spencer M. Gusick, Phoebe C. Ellsworth, 'Real Jurors' Understanding of the Law in Real Cases', 16 *Law & Human Behavior* 539, 546–7 (1992) (studying 224 real jurors in Michigan; 97 per cent had high-school diplomas; 53 per cent had finished college; 22 per cent had graduate degrees; 'Jurors were more often wrong than right in their answers to questions about their right to ignore irrelevant instructions, the difference between direct and circumstantial evidence, the fact that the prosecution had the burden of proof (less than a third of those who served on *criminal* juries got this right), the prohibition against inferring guilt if a defendant did not testify, and their freedom to reject expert testimony') (emphasis in original).

31   This is not his real name. For legal reasons, I cannot identify him.

32   Fla. Stat. § 90.607(2)(b).

33   As best I understand it, this means that jurors cannot testify to anything they think, only to what they see. *State v. Hamiliton*, 574 So.2d 124, 125 n.3 (Fla. 1991) ('the questions posed to the juror were constrained by the requirements of section 90.607(2)(b), Florida Statutes (1987), which prohibit inquiry into jurors' thought processes. [...] Thus, counsel below properly limited their inquiry solely to the observable events surrounding the presence of the magazines in the jury room'). *Id.*, at 128 n.8, quoting *McAllister Hotel Inc. v. Porte*, 123 So.2d 339, 344 (Fla. 1959), ('The law does not permit a juror to avoid his verdict for any reason which essentially inheres in the verdict itself, as that he "did not assent to the verdict; that he misunderstood the instructions of the Court; the statements of witnesses or pleadings in the case; that he was unduly influenced by the statements or otherwise of his fellow jurors, or mistaken in his calculations or judgment, or other matters resting alone in the juror's breast"').

34   *Tanner v. United States*, 483 US 107, 117 (1987) (insanity of a juror considered totally irrelevant, as an 'internal consideration'), citing *Sullivan v. Fogg*, 613 F.2d 465, 467 (2nd Cir. 1980). What the Supreme Court

meant by this is that anything that is deemed properly inside the jury room (generally the evidence that has been admitted, but in this case a mentally imbalanced juror) cannot be the basis for the reversal of a conviction, whereas anything that is improperly brought in (a dictionary to check out the meanings of words, the Bible to determine whether God would vouchsafe the death penalty, and so forth) can.

35   The rule was originally set out in *Remmer v. United States*, 347 US 227 (1954), where someone allegedly made a statement, in jest, to a juror that he could profit by bringing in a verdict in favour of the taxpayer, where the man was on trial for evading income taxes. The rule of this case has been applied in various others, often because the jurors felt the need to consult a book in order to understand what the judge meant by his instructions. See, e.g., *State v. Richards*, 466 S.E.2d 395 (1995) (juror improperly conducted independent research by seeking a definition of 'malice' in a dictionary during jury deliberations; reference to a dictionary during deliberations is misconduct); *Allers v. Riley*, 901 P.2d 600 (Mo. 1995) (jurors used dictionaries to define 'proximate cause' and 'prudent' in ways other than provided by state law); *Fulton v. Callahan*, 621 So.2d 1235 (Ala. 1993) (jurors' use of dictionary to define 'wantonness' and 'oppression'); *Jordan v. Brantley*, 589 So.2d 680 (Ala. 1991) (jury foreperson took a dictionary into the jury room for purpose of defining 'prudent' and 'reasonable'); *Glage v. Hawes Firearms*, 276 Cal. Rptr. 430 (Cal. Ct. App. 1990) (jurors used dictionary to define 'preponderance'); *Jones v. Sieve*, 249 Cal. Rptr. 821 (Cal. Ct. App. 1988) (jurors used a reference book to define 'terms that were subject to deliberation'). See also *McCray v. State*, 565 So.2d 673 (Ala. Crim. App. 1990) (jurors improperly read portions of the Alabama Pattern Jury Instructions, which led one juror to erroneously assert that the jury could not convict the defendant of the lesser included offence).

36   This may well be the right rule, if jurors get something wrong by consulting the dictionary. However, logic is wholly abandoned when the case may be reversed where one jury used a dictionary to understand a word better, yet it is not permissible to show that another jury did not try to understand a vital legal term and therefore got it totally wrong.

37   *Tanner v. United States*, 483 US 107, 118 (1987).

38   The juror's letter reads as follows (the spelling and grammar are her own):

Dear Mr Dioguardi,

Under the situation and such circumstance I hope that I have made the right decision. I talk to my friends Bertha and her husband Olive about this, Olive agree that I write to you. Bertha, however, was against it. Nevertheless, I felt I had to write you. I cannot omit what I have seen. When I saw the good within you and how hard your wife was trying; I prayed about it. One word appear before me *repent*. If you repent and run a clean business it is the good within you that will save you, and you will gain what you have lost. Before I continue I must explain something to you. I have eyes and ears that I can see things before it happen. I can tell you about other and what they are thinking and doing. If I am wrong about this it is the first time.

I would like to visit you. I would like to talk to you about what appear before me. I would like to do so when my eyes fully open. They are only partly open. I don't know at the present when they will open. Unfortunate, a curse was put upon them some years ago. I have some people working on them. Everything is being done that can be done. So we will have to wait. As I stated I cannot omit what appear before me, when I was on the jury bench. You feel that this is the end for you. However, it is not. Something appear before me that I must do. It is the good within you that I must use and within that good, you will gain what you have lost. If, however, I am wrong it is the first time.

Why, you let such a relationship exist between you and a man like Hellerman? When I think of the good that I saw within you it does not add up. Where did Hellerman get those fur coats? Does he have any for sail? Omit the question. I really can't afford one, and if I could I probably be afraid to wear it.

Why persecute your wife? Your mistake your guilty then take it out on her. The ordeal you put her through I wonder how she survive through it. One word appear before me brave. She is a brave girl. She love you. She never stop loving you not a single moment. Tell her to please be careful. From what I can see she is still in business. I suggest it is not wise at this time. I believe she is being watch.

That was a good lawyer you had. I entain to send him some custom as soon as my eyes open. Tell [your co-defendant] Ostrer I am praying for him.

Mr Dioguardi, I want to ask a favor of you please. I want you to look upon me as a woman and I look upon you as a man and not white man and black woman. Olive agree with me. Let's leave color out, *OK*.

I was told you will only have to serve one third of the time given. So relax this is not the end. Soon you will be free. When I call the Federal information center and the record room yesterday they all know you.

> They all seem to have it in for you. Its seated deep within them like a
> personal matter.
>
> Sincerely, Genena

The letter sheets were printed with the word 'LIBRA' and a picture
of a woman with scales. On the last page of the letter, under the picture,
the juror wrote, 'The sign Libra is the heavenly house of the zodiac
under which I was born.' See *United States v. Dioguardi*, 492 F.2d 70, 75
n.7 (2nd Cir. 1974).

39   *United States v. Dioguardi*, 492 F.2d 70 (2nd Cir. 1974), cited in *Tanner
     v. United States*, 483 US 107, 118 (1987).

40   *Tanner v. United States*, 483 US 107, 117 (1987) ('when faced with alle-
     gations that a juror was mentally incompetent, "courts have refused
     to set aside a verdict, or even to make further inquiry, unless there be
     proof of an adjudication of insanity or mental incompetence closely
     in advance ... of jury service," or proof of "a closely contemporaneous
     and independent post-trial adjudication of incompetency"'). Indeed,
     the court went on to cite various cases where insanity was considered
     totally irrelevant, as an 'internal consideration'. *Tanner*, 483 US at 117,
     citing *Sullivan v. Fogg*, 613 F.2d 465, 467 (2nd Cir. 1980).

41   The case was by no means open and shut. The first trial resulted in a
     hung jury, since the twelve jurors could not agree on guilt. *Tanner v.
     United States*, 483 US 107, 112 (1987). Only at the retrial, where all the
     drinking and drug-taking took place, did the jury convict.

42   *Tanner v. United States*, 483 US 107, 113 (1987) ('Mr Milbrath [defence
     counsel]: But, in any event, I've noticed over a period of several days
     that a couple of jurors in particular have been taking long naps during
     the trial'). The judge explicitly said he would not take responsibility
     for watching whether jurors were actually asleep during the trial, as
     he had other things to do: 'I'm not going to sit here and watch.' *Id.*, at
     142 (dissenting opinion) (quoting the trial record at 12-100-12-101).

43   *Tanner v. United States*, 483 US 107, 115 (1987). Hardy was the second
     juror to come forward unsolicited. Earlier, Juror Vera Asbul had des-
     cribed the same kind of conduct, although not in the same detail. *Id.*,
     at 113.

44   Even had Tanner been properly convicted, he could have faced a maxi-
     mum of five years on one statute and twenty on the other. 18 U.S.C.
     § 371 (conspiracy to defraud the government, maximum penalty of
     five years); 18 U.S.C. § 1341 (mail fraud maximum sentence generally
     twenty years).

45   If one of the jurors, over the course of the trial, gave or sold a total of
     five grams or more of cocaine to the other jurors in the courthouse,

this would be a felony under federal law, worth between five and forty years in prison. See 21 U.S.C. § 841(B) ('such person shall be sentenced to a term of imprisonment which may not be less than 5 years and not more than 40 years'). For simple possession, it would be worth five to twenty years if there were more than five grams of cocaine. 21 U.S.C. § 844 (a) ('a person convicted under this subsection for the possession of a mixture or substance which contains cocaine base shall be imprisoned not less than 5 years and not more than 20 years, and fined a minimum of $1,000, if the conviction is a first conviction under this subsection and the amount of the mixture or substance exceeds 5 grams'). Under state law (equally applicable to the federal courtroom in the State of Florida), sale or delivery of cocaine carries a fifteen-year sentence. Fla. Stat. § 893.13(1). Since the juror could be charged in both state and federal courts, and sentenced in both, he could be looking at thirty-five to fifty-five years in prison. He could arguably face another three years for drug paraphernalia. See 21 U.S.C. § 863. Under state law he would be more likely, since he brought it into the courtroom, to be charged with transportation of drug paraphernalia, Fla. Stat. § 893.147(4), for which he could receive five years. This would add eight years onto the sentence, leaving him exposed to at least forty-three years in prison, and perhaps as much as sixty-three years.

46   Under Florida law, personal use of cocaine, charged as simple possession, carries up to five years in Florida prison, Fla. Stat. § 893.13(2), with an additional year under federal law. 21 U.S.C. § 844. Each of the jurors who simply possessed marijuana would face one year in prison and $1,000 fine under federal law, 21 U.S.C. § 844(a), plus another year under state law. Fla. Stat. § 893.13(3).

47   Four of the Justices in *Tanner* felt that evidence of drug abuse and alcoholism was an outside influence that should have resulted in reversal. *Tanner v. United States*, 483 US 107, 140–1 (1987) ('I would nonetheless find the testimony of juror intoxication admissible under the Rule's "outside influence" exception. As a common-sense matter, drugs and alcohol *are* outside influences on jury members') (dissenting opinion) (emphasis in original; footnote omitted). At this point the view of the minority counts for nothing.

48   On remand from the Supreme Court, the Eleventh Circuit Court of Appeals held that neither criminal law was even applicable to either Tanner or his co-defendant, William Conover, so they both walked free. *United States v. Conover & Tanner*, 845 F.2d 256 (11th Cir. 1988).

49   *Tanner v. United States*, 483 US 107, 117 (1987), citing 8 J. Wigmore, Evidence § 2352, pp. 696–7 (J. McNaughton rev. edn 1961).

50   Again, this argument is based on cases that are a century old. For example, the US courts refused to look into compromises in a criminal

case whereby some jurors exchanged their convictions on one issue in return for concession by other jurors on another issue. *United States v. Dioguardi*, 492 F.2d 70, 79 n.11 (2nd Cir. 1974), quoting *McDonald v. Pless*, 238 US 264 (1915) ('If evidence thus secured could be thus used, the result would be to make what was intended to be a private deliberation, the constant subject of public investigation – to the destruction of all frankness and freedom of discussion and conference'). In the case of a compromise, there would have been a unanimous conviction on *no* issue (the jurors unanimously found guilt beyond a reasonable doubt on nothing), yet the courts find it unacceptable to consider this.

51   Tony Blair has written that the Freedom of Information Act (FOIA) was perhaps his biggest mistake in government:

> Freedom of Information. Three harmless words. I look at those words as I write them, and feel like shaking my head till it drops off my shoulders. You idiot. You naive, foolish, irresponsible nincompoop. There is really no description of stupidity, no matter how vivid, that is adequate. I quake at the imbecility of it. Once I appreciated the full enormity of the blunder, I used to say – more than a little unfairly – to any civil servant who would listen: Where was Sir Humphrey when I needed him? We had legislated in the first throes of power. How could you, knowing what you know, have allowed us to do such a thing so utterly undermining of sensible government? […] The truth is that the FOI Act isn't used, for the most part, by 'the people'. It's used by journalists. For political leaders, it's like saying to someone who is hitting you over the head with a stick, 'Hey, try this instead', and handing them a mallet. The information is neither sought because the journalist is curious to know, nor given to bestow knowledge on 'the people'. It's used as a weapon.

Tony Blair, *A Journey* (2010). This is quite a turnaround since he spoke at the Campaign for Freedom of Information's 1996 Awards:

> it is not some isolated constitutional reform that we are proposing with a Freedom of Information Act. It is a change that is absolutely fundamental to how we see politics developing in this country over the next few years … information is power and any government's attitude about sharing information with the people actually says a great deal about how it views power itself and how it views the relationship between itself and the people who elected it.

'Speech by the Rt. Hon. Tony Blair MP, Leader of the Labour Party' at the Campaign for Freedom of Information's annual awards ceremony, March 25th, 1996, at http://www.cfoi.org.uk/blairawards.

html (accessed Dec. 2nd, 2010).

52   See Liebman & Fagan, *Summary of Central Findings,* 'A Broken System: Error Rates in Capital Cases 1973–1995', Columbia Law School (2000), http://www2.law.columbia.edu/instructionalservices/liebman/lieb man/Liebman%20Study/docs/1/section2.html. In Florida, where Kris Maharaj was tried, the figures were slightly more extreme: 73 per cent of cases did not survive review.

53   Proposals were made by the same authors as to how the problems could be addressed. See Liebman *et al., Final Technical Report, Getting to Death: Fairness and Efficiency in the Processing and Conclusion of Death Penalty Cases after Furman,* National Institute of Justice, US Dept. of Justice (2002), http://www.ncjrs.gov/pdffiles1/nij/grants/203935. pdf. The proposals suggested requiring 'proof beyond *any* doubt that the defendant committed the capital crime' before a death sentence could be imposed; making it clear that the alternative to death was life without parole; preventing judges from overriding a jury verdict of life; and so forth. *Id.,* at vii. None of the proposals have been adopted across the US, and the Supreme Court has explicitly determined that several are not constitutionally required.

54   The number of jury trials in Crown Court on criminal cases has remained relatively constant over several years, varying insignificantly between 2006 (9,569), 2007 (9,049), 2008 (9,076) and 2009 (9,196). See generally tables contained in the *Judicial & Court Statistics* (2009) http://www.justice.gov.uk/publications/docs/jcs-stats-2009-211010. pdf. Similarly, the number of verdicts where one or two jurors dissent from a conviction has remained constant, between 18 and 19 per cent – roughly one in five. *Id.,* Table 4.9. Six out of ten defendants in British criminal trials walk free, a remarkable rate, but the overwhelming majority of the acquittals – more than two-thirds – come from judges rather than jurors. Far fewer prisoners plead guilty in the UK (roughly 70 per cent) as compared to the US (over 90 per cent). Of those who enter a plea of not guilty, roughly 60 per cent are ultimately acquitted. *Id.,* Table 4.7. Contrary to the stereotype concerning devious defence lawyers manipulating the naïve jury, the overwhelming majority (at least 70 per cent each year) are discharged by the judge, or are the beneficiaries of a directed verdict of acquittal. *Id.,* Table 4.8. Of those who are convicted by jurors, roughly two-fifths subsequently prevail on appeal. A large percentage (varying from 37 to 42 per cent between 2006 and 2009) have their appeal allowed against the verdict (i.e., the conviction was flawed), and still more (45–7 per cent) prevail on their appeal against sentence. *Id.,* Table 4.10. What this tells us is that judges made their own decision in two-thirds of cases, taking the case away from the jury and ordering an acquittal. But in those cases that

went through to a jury verdict, the appellate courts reversed 40 per cent of cases, sometimes on issues that a lay person would find arcane and incomprehensible. The jury system is therefore 'breaking down' in at least four out of ten cases, in the sense that the appellate court reverses the conviction. There is little likelihood that jury misconduct, or outright juror loopiness, would result in the reversal of a greater proportion than this. Yet to allow the system to correct what is manifestly an injustice would serve the true purpose of the judicial system. Gradually, no doubt, if we paid the system more attention instead of rigorously ignoring its flaws, we would improve it.

55   Section 8 of the Contempt of Court Act 1981 ('Confidentiality of jury's deliberations') provides: '(1) Subject to subsection (2) below, it is a contempt of court to obtain, disclose or solicit any particulars of statements made, opinions expressed, arguments advanced or votes cast by members of a jury in the course of their deliberations in any legal proceedings. (2) This section does not apply to any disclosure of any particulars – (a) in the proceedings in question for the purpose of enabling the jury to arrive at their verdict, or in connection with the delivery of that verdict, or (b) in evidence in any subsequent proceedings for an offence alleged to have been committed in relation to the jury in the first mentioned proceedings, or to the publication of any particulars so disclosed. (3) Proceedings for a contempt of court under this section (other than Scottish proceedings) shall not be instituted except by or with the consent of the Attorney General or on the motion of a court having jurisdiction to deal with it.' See http://www.swarb.co.uk/acts/1981Contempt_of_CourtAct.shtml (accessed Dec. 1st, 2010).

56   I do not intend this statement to be taken as a documented fact. However, in the recent litigation we brought in the case of Binyam Mohamed, the British courts seemed significantly more inclined to reveal misconduct by the security services than they are to give details of the discussions of jurors.

57   I should emphasise that I count myself among advocates of the jury system. However, it must be seen as the least-bad option, which must constantly be improved, rather than as a panacea for society's disputes. Cf. Paul Reynolds, 'Still only two cheers for democracy', BBC (Oct. 8th, 2007) (Winston Churchill to Parliament in November 1947: 'Democracy is the worst form of government, except for all those other forms that have been tried from time to time').

58   For a discussion of how impossibly high the bar is set for the proof of innocence, see below, Chapter 14.

59   To give another example, in the context of censorship – may something be banned as pornography or is it covered by the First Amend-

ment's protection of free speech? – Justice Potter Stewart famously said he found hard-core pornography difficult to define, 'but I know it when I see it'. *Jacobellis v. Ohio*, 378 US 184 (1964) (Stewart, J., concurring) ('I shall not today attempt further to define the kinds of material I understand to be embraced within that shorthand description [hard-core pornography]; and perhaps I could never succeed in intelligibly doing so. But I know it when I see it, and the motion picture involved in this case is not that'). With respect, this is simply not good enough. The population at large cannot be governed by the unknown and unpredictable views of a judge who admits that he cannot define the parameters himself. Later the Supreme Court tried to set a more recognisable standard, which has its own flaws, but is at least an effort in the right direction. See *Miller v. California*, 413 US 15, 24–5 (1973) (the court, in an attempt to set such limits, devised a set of three criteria that must be met in order for a work to be legitimately subject to state regulation: whether the average person, applying contemporary community standards, would find that the work, taken as a whole, appeals to the prurient interest; whether the work depicts or describes, in a patently offensive way, sexual conduct or excretory functions specifically defined by applicable state law; and whether the work, taken as a whole, lacks serious literary, artistic, political, or scientific value).

60   The Florida pattern jury instruction on reasonable doubt goes as follows:

> Whenever the words 'reasonable doubt' are used you must consider the following: A reasonable doubt is not a mere possible doubt, a speculative, imaginary or forced doubt. Such a doubt must not influence you to return a verdict of not guilty if you have an abiding conviction of guilt. On the other hand, if, after carefully considering, comparing and weighing all the evidence, there is not an abiding conviction of guilt, or, if, having a conviction, it is one which is not stable but one which wavers and vacillates, then the charge is not proved beyond every reasonable doubt and you must find the defendant not guilty because the doubt is reasonable. It is to the evidence introduced in this trial, and to it alone, that you are to look for that proof. A reasonable doubt as to the guilt of the defendant may arise from the evidence, conflict in the evidence, or the lack of evidence. If you have a reasonable doubt, you should find the defendant not guilty. If you have no reasonable doubt, you should find the defendant guilty.

See http://www.floridasupremecourt.org/jury_instructions/instruct ions.shtml#.

61   See http://en.wikipedia.org/wiki/Prisons_in_the_United_States (2006 figures). Of course these numbers are affected by the fact that many of these prisoners would have entered a guilty plea – the general estimate is that 95 per cent of US cases are settled by a plea bargain. However, there is an argument that they cannot be discounted, as each person would have made an assessment of whether he or she would have been convicted at trial.

62   Many prisoners plead guilty to *avoid* the death penalty and – in a decision that I have never understood – this has been held not to be coercive. *North Carolina v. Alford*, 400 US 25 (1970) (the death penalty was only available after a jury trial; rather than risk this, although he claimed innocence on all charges, Alford pleaded guilty to second-degree murder; Alford appealed, claiming his plea was involuntary because it was principally motivated by fear of the death penalty; the Supreme Court held that a guilty plea that represents a voluntary and intelligent choice when considering the alternatives available to a defendant is not 'compelled' within the meaning of the Fifth Amendment just because it was entered to avoid the possibility of the death penalty); *Brady v. United States*, 397 US 742 (1970); cf. Kent S. Scheidegger, 'The Death Penalty and Plea Bargaining to Life Sentences' (Feb. 2009), at http://www.cjlf.org/papers/wpaper09-01.pdf (accessed Dec. 1st, 2010) (a con-servative Criminal Justice Legal Foundation paper which suggests that almost four times the proportion of people plead guilty when threatened with death than when the death penalty is not an option). Occasionally a prisoner is allowed to plead guilty in order to ensure that he *gets* the death penalty. See, e.g., *Chapman v. Commonwealth*, 2007 Ky. LEXIS 178 (Ky. 2007) (court rules that a competent defendant may plead guilty, forgo a jury trial and sentencing, and volunteer for the death penalty), reported at http://www.jaapl.org/cgi/content/full/36/3/409. Only a very small proportion of prisoners plead guilty and then contest the penalty phase, although it does happen – and used to more often when inexperienced lawyers thought that the remorse shown by a guilty plea would be important at the penalty phase.

63   See, e.g., Ben Ando, 'Making their minds up – or Not?', BBC News (March 23rd, 2009), at http://news.bbc.co.uk/1/hi/uk/7958322.stm (accessed Dec. 1st, 2010) ('Trevor Grove [author of *The Juryman's Tale*] believes most juries already work to this sort of level and said in his experience "juries do accept that about 95 per cent – pretty pretty sure – is good enough"').

12

The Laundry

1   Jeffrey Robinson, *The Laundrymen: Inside the World's Third Largest Business* (1994), at 224 ('At least three Colombian cartel members are purported to be among the five richest men in the world, surpassed only by the Sultan of Brunei and King Fahd of Saudi Arabia. Even their lieutenants are said to be worth more than the Queen of England').

2   'GM History 1980–1989', http://media.gm.com/corpcom/history/hist 05.htm.

3   Robinson, *The Laundrymen*, at 235 (in the 1980s the Cali Cartel was estimated to have annual profits of about $7 billion, more than three times that of General Motors).

4   *Drugs, Law Enforcement & Foreign Policy*, A Report prepared by the Subcommittee on Terrorism, Narcotics and International Operations of the Committee on Foreign Relations, US Senate (Dec. 1988), at 9.

5   Warren Strobel, 'US moves to extradite drug financier', *Washington Times* (Aug. 23rd, 1989) ('The Medellin cartel and a smaller one based in Cali are responsible for an estimated 80 percent of the cocaine imported to the United States'), in 'Noriega & Key Players in the Drug Trade, Part 1', at 82 of 127, http://historicaltextarchive.com/sections. php/sections.php?op=viewarticle&artid=114.

6   Misha Glenny, *McMafia: Crime without Frontiers* (2008), at 287–8.

7   Douglas Farah, 'Cali Drug Cartel avoids Crackdown, Powerful Traffickers operate differently from Medellin Rivals', *Washington Post*, A1 (Oct. 5th, 1989), in 'Noriega & Key Players in the Drug Trade, Part   1',   http://historicaltextarchive.com/sections.php/sections. php?op=viewarticle&artid=114.

8   'Noriega & Key Players in the Drug Trade, Part 1', at 4 of 127, http:// historicaltextarchive.com/sections.php/sections.php?artid= (Flavio Acosta was 'formerly commander of the Medellin Metro Police and considered to be in the traffickers' hip pocket. He never made an important narcotics arrest. Medellin police are known to frequently make multi-million peso bank deposits. Their arrest of Pablo Excobar in 1986 was a mistake').

9   Glenny, *McMafia*, at 290–1. See also *Drugs, Law Enforcement & Foreign Policy*, at 28 ('the Medellin Cartel … raised a 2,000 man army and equipped it with automatic weapons').

10 William R. Long, 'Colombia Drug Lords find fugitive life erodes Power', *Los Angeles Times* (Oct. 22nd, 1989), in 'Noriega & Key Players in the Drug Trade, Part 1', at 56 of 127, http://historicaltextarchive.com/

sections.php/sections.php?op=viewarticle&artid=114.

11   Glenny, *McMafia*, at 289.

12   See Al Capone, http://www.chicagohs.org/history/capone ('Frank
      Wilson from the IRS's Special Intelligence Unit was assigned to focus
      on Capone. Wilson accidentally found a cash receipts ledger that not
      only showed the operation's net profits for a gambling house, but also
      contained Capone's name; it was a record of Capone's income. Later
      Capone's own tax lawyer Lawrence P. Mattingly admitted in a letter
      to the government that Capone had an income. Wilson's ledger,
      Mattingly's letter and the coercion of witnesses were the main evidence
      used to convict Capone. In 1931 Capone was indicted for income tax
      evasion for the years 1925–29. He was also charged with the misde-
      meanor of failing to file tax returns for the years 1928 and 1929. The
      government charged that Capone owed $215,080.48 in taxes from his
      gambling profits. A third indictment was added, charging Capone with
      conspiracy to violate Prohibition laws from 1922–31. Capone plead-
      ed guilty to all three charges in the belief that he would be able to
      plea bargain. However, the judge who presided over the case, Judge
      James H. Wilkerson, would not make any deals. Capone changed his
      pleas to not guilty. Unable to bargain, he tried to bribe the jury but
      Wilkerson changed the jury panel at the last minute. The jury found
      Capone not guilty on eighteen of the twenty-three counts. Judge Wilk-
      erson sentenced him to a total of ten years in federal prison and one
      year in the county jail. In addition, Capone had to serve an earlier
      six-month contempt of court sentence for failing to appear in court.
      In May 1932, Capone was sent to Atlanta, the toughest of the feder-
      al prisons, to begin his eleven-year sentence. Even in prison Capone
      took control, obtaining special privileges from the authorities such
      as furnishing his cell with a mirror, typewriter, rugs, and a set of
      the Encyclopedia Britannica. Because word spread that Capone had
      taken over in Atlanta, he was sent to Alcatraz. There were no other
      outfit members in Alcatraz, and security was so tight that he had no
      knowledge of the outside world. He was unable to control anyone or
      anything and could not buy influence or friends. In an attempt to
      earn time off for good behavior, Capone became the ideal prisoner
      and refused to participate in prisoner rebellions or strikes. While at
      Alcatraz, he exhibited signs of syphilitic dementia. Capone spent
      the rest of his felony sentence in the hospital. On January 6, 1939, his
      prison term expired and he was transferred to Terminal Island, a Fed-
      eral Correctional Institution in California, to serve his one-year misde-
      meanor sentence. He was finally released on November 16, 1939 …').

13   Peter Ross, 'DEA scam hooks a Drug-Cartel money man', *Washington
      Post*, at A01 (Aug. 27th, 1989) ('The trade is so successful that its biggest

problem is not the threat of arrest or the seizures of drugs, but how to move vast amounts of money. Annual sales revenues are estimated at $100 billion, and almost all of it begins as cash. Managing that volume is extremely difficult, since federal law requires reporting of cash transactions or bank deposits in excess of $10,000. Some of the currency is used to purchase cars or small businesses, airplanes and real estate. But most of it must be converted into another form for return to the drug lords'); UPI, 'Anderson warns against powerful Medellin drug cartel' (Nov. 1st, 1988).

14 Robert Sherrill, 'Stalking International Drug Traffickers', *Washington Post*, at A04 (Jan. 6th, 1986) (review of James Mills, *The Underground Empire*, 1986) ('illegal drug dealers around the world earn a half-trillion dollars a year, and … for those who need imagery to grasp that figure, a half-trillion dollars would weigh more than the entire population of Washington DC').

15 Ross, 'DEA scam hooks a Drug-Cartel money man', at A01.

16 Eddy, *The Cocaine Wars*, at 34–6 (emphasis in original).

17 This process, along with many others, is described by Jeffrey Robinson in *The Laundrymen: Inside the World's Third Largest Business* (1994).

18 Robinson, *The Laundrymen*, at 264–74.

19 See http://www.wrestlingusa.com/Bryant%20Geneology%20site/group%20shots%20for%20wusa%20web%20site/wcbryant.html.

20 There is a Baptist Church Loan Corp that offers loans (as of 2008) from $25,000 to $5 million. http://www.baptistchurchloan.org/loaninfo.html.

21 According to Bryant, this was based at the Euclid Street Baptist Church, 1408 S. Euclid, Anaheim, California 92802. No corporate documents are available for the Los Angeles Church Loan Corporation (LACLC). It was, W.C. Bryant said, a non-profit, tax-exempt religious corporation founded in 1963.

22 *W.C. Bryant Deposition*, at 6, in *Shaula Ann Nagel and DMY International Inc. v. William Penn Life Insurance Company of New York*, No. 87–0786 CIV (S.D. Fla.) (taken on Oct. 31st, 1988).

23 *W.C. Bryant Deposition*, at 8, 10.

24 *W.C. Bryant Deposition*, at 10. Idle curiosity helped me put this in perspective with a quick check on the Internet: the year W.C. was born, the entire gross national product of the United States was a mere $12.68 billion. See http://www.infoplease.com/year/1918.html. According to W.C., his unlisted company was holding significantly more than that.

25 *W.C. Bryant Deposition*, at 17.

26 *W.C. Bryant Deposition*, at 18.

27 *W.C. Bryant Deposition*, at 19.

28 As of this writing, we still have not located any documents concerning

the Moo Youngs and Mexico. Our resources for such investigations are very limited, so this is not surprising, but it does make me wonder what remains out there.

29   *W.C. Bryant Deposition*, at 29 & *Exhibit 2*, in *Shaula Ann Nagel and DMY International Inc. v. William Penn Life Insurance Company of New York*, No. 87-0786 CIV (S.D. Fla.) (taken on October 31st, 1988).

30   Originally, W.C. said they were worth $500 million. In documents that Ver Ploeg had found, he put the second valuation at a very specific $94,488,614. *Id.*, at 29 & *Exhibit 2*. I located a third valuation, a letter in the Moo Youngs' briefcase from someone called Gordon Daskowski to Dr W.C. Bryant regarding two sets of gemstones worth $9,310,401.06 and $134,872,546.66 in the possession of the LA Church Loan Corporation (for a total of $144,182,947.72). *Maharaj Exh. OCY* at B002193. This reference to different sets of gems was consistent with the itemisation that was included in one of W.C. Bryant's documents. (see below). These hugely varied estimates gave me still more pause as to what was going on.

31   *W.C. Bryant Deposition*, at 8, 10.

32   *W.C. Bryant Deposition*, at 46 & *Exhibit 16*.

33   'The most famous of all Queensland sapphires is the 733 ct Black Star of Queensland. Found on Klondyke Ridge in 1935 by 14 year old Roy Spencer, it was allegedly used as a door stop for many years by his father Harry Spencer.' 'Mining Sapphire in Australia', http://www. gemselect.com/other-info/australian-sapphire.php. http://www.rom. on.ca/news/releases/public.php?mediakey=2k9td2lwct.

34   http://goliath.ecnext.com/coms2/summary_0199-841092_ITM (Dec. 11th, 2002) ('A Jewel of a Jewel: Legendary "Black Star of Queensland", Valued at $50 Million, has Commanding Appeal, World Class Status').

35   See Attachment to *Exhibit 2* of *W.C. Bryant Deposition* in *Nagel*.

36   There are various opinions on what the world's largest sapphire is, perhaps because of the variety of different types and the variation in purity. See 'Millennium Sapphire Set to Break World Record for Largest Sapphire Carving' (Jan. 8th, 2001) http://www.encyclopedia. com/doc/1G1-68866870.html (referring to the uncut weight: '[w]eighing in at 61,500 carats, the Millennium Sapphire is over 8,000 carats larger than the current record holder'); '"World's biggest sapphire" found', *The Nation* (Thailand) (Nov. 26th, 1999), http://www.encyc lopedia.com/doc/1P1-24115189.html ('the world's biggest sapphire, weighing 7.1 kilograms or 3,500 karats, will go on public display in Kanchanaburi where it was recently unearthed by a local'); 'The Biggest, the Best and the Most Gargantuan', http://www.tyler-adam. com/72.html (previously '[t]he largest Sapphire weighed 2,302 carats. It was found in Australia circa 1935, and was carved into the shape of

the head of President Abraham Lincoln. Another black star sapphire weighing 2,097 carats was carved into a bust of General Dwight D. Eisenhower, circa 1954'). No matter what the record, the church gems would have included sapphires among the largest ever found.

37   *W.C. Bryant Deposition*, at 12.

38   In the later 1980s, in the Japanese asset price bubble, some banks granted increasingly risky loans. DKB apparently financed yakuza (crime organisations) in order to invest in capital resources much more easily than its competitors. Loans to what are referred to as 'sōkaiya' amounted to 30 billion Japanese yen. After the bubble burst, the bad loans were poor value for money. A raid by Tokyo prosecutors in 1997 relating to the loans to 'sōkaiya' laid DKB open to public criticism. Kuniji Miyazaki, former president and the then chairman of DKB, faced severe pressure over a series of alleged misdeeds and committed suicide by hanging himself at his home. See generally http://en.wikipedia.org/wiki/Dai-Ichi_Kangyo_Bank.

39   *W.C. Bryant Deposition*, at 28 & *Exhibit 1*.

40   *W.C. Bryant Deposition*, at 49.

41   *W.C. Bryant Deposition*, at 30 & *Exhibit 3*.

42   *W.C. Bryant Deposition*, at *Exhibit 4*.

43   *W.C. Bryant Deposition*, at 53–4.

44   *W.C. Bryant Deposition*, at 39–40.

45   There were various such letters of credit. Some had the names whited out, and others had merely been marked through so that you could not read who the beneficiaries were. See, e.g., *W.C. Bryant Deposition*, at 32–3 & *Exhibit 6, 7*. One question was why the letter of credit that had been filled in was made out to both Cargil and Amer Enterprises. It seemed as if the Moo Youngs had got their hands on some (possibly genuine) letters of credit, whited out the names of the real beneficiaries, and then made up a substitute beneficiary with the same number of characters as the original – in other words, the name Cargil International was not long enough to fill the space, so they had to put both Cargil and Amer Enterprises in.

46   *W.C. Bryant Deposition*, at 33 & *Exhibit 8*.

47   The documents purported to come from Rex C. Jensen (VP) and Dennis L. Walker (President) of the International Bank of the South Pacific (Kingdom of Tonga), Fakafanua Centre, PO Box 1401, Nuku'Alofa, Tonga. *Maharaj 3.850 Exhibits T(2), FAP*.

48   *W.C. Bryant Deposition*, at 33–6.

49   *W.C. Bryant Deposition*, at 25.

50   R.T. Naylor, *The Wages of Crime: Black Markets, Illegal Finance, and the Underworld Economy* (2002), at 170 and via Google Books (accessed Dec. 16th, 2010). See also *United States v. Bell*, 27 F.Supp.2d 1191, 1196 (E.D.Ca.

1998) (case assessing tax liens on Glen D. Bell and his wife for $3.6 million plus interest; 'The beneficiary [of the property] was an apparent creation of Mr. Bell, known as the "International Bank of the South Pacific"'). Mr Bell, and his wife Jeanette, seem to have been very litigious. *United States v. Bell*, 80 A.F.T.R.2d (RTA) 6455 (E.D.Ca. 1997) (the earliest reported decision of the US efforts to collect on several million dollars' tax debt); *United States v. Bell*, 2002 US Dist.LEXIS 7487 (E.D.Ca. 2002) (IRS seeks ejectment from a property to satisfy the tax debt); *United States v. Bell*, 103 A.F.T.R.2d 932 (E.D.Ca. 2009) (litigation still ongoing over a million-dollar construction loan they took out in the mid-1980s).

51   *W.C. Bryant Deposition*, at 41–2 & *Exhibit 15*.

52   *W.C. Bryant Deposition*, at 45.

53   *W.C. Bryant Deposition*, at 49.

54   *W.C. Bryant Deposition*, at 39 & *Exhibit 13*.

55   *Maharaj Exhibit OCT*, at B000539, 581.

56   *Maharaj Exhibit OCT*, at B000538.

57   *Maharaj Exhibit OAL*, at 6000054. See http://www.yelp.com/biz/chinting-chinese-restaurant-placentia.

58   W.C. conceded that this happened, and said that Derrick came around October 7th–9th, 1986. *W.C. Bryant Deposition*, at 51. His memory of the meeting was remarkably accurate, but Ver Ploeg did not press him for details of what they discussed.

59   http://www.miaminewtimes.com/2007-09-27/news/british-ex-millionaire-fights-for-freedom/5.

60   http://en.wikipedia.org/wiki/Pereira,_Colombia.

61   Pereira has also long been in the area of influence of Carlos Mario Jiménez (alias Macaco). He was in partnership with Giorgio Sale, who was imprisoned in Italy. Macaco was one of fourteen so-called paramilitary leaders finally extradited to the US on drug charges in May 2008.

62   The address on his card was listed as All Leather Import & Export Inc., 100 S.E. 1st Street, #42, Miami, Fla. 33131.

63   See, e.g., Eddy, *The Cocaine Wars*, at 53 (as early as the 1970s Jorge Ochoa's 'import-export company', Sea-8 Trading Corporation of Miami, was bringing in cocaine from Colombia).

64   A leather company was such an archetype for drug dealers in the early 1980s that the DEA set up a sting operation using a phoney company called Green Ice, importing leather goods. Robinson, *The Laundrymen*, at 250.

65   Frustratingly, this was impossible during the early years of my involvement in Kris' case as well. When there was no Internet, the only way for the defence to check someone's criminal record was to search every courthouse in the US – dozens in each state, with fifty states and the federal government to cover. The prosecution, on the other hand,

had ready access to the NCIC (National Crime Information Center) computer. This imbalance was one reason for the prosecution's duty to reveal such information to the defence. This was another obligation that was ignored in Kris' case. It was only much later, when we were able to find Mejia's name on the Internet, that we were able to make the necessary connection.

66   Sworn Letter of Alexis Gomez, Personal Banking Officer, International Division, Florida National Bank (Oct. 15th, 1986) (File 044-132374).

67   Bank statements of All Leather Import & Export Inc. (File 044-132376-90).

68   All Leather Import & Export Inc., Profit & Loss Statement (December 31st, 1986) (File 044-132392). Interest income accounted for $3,805.19 of the income. In terms of profits on the actual export and import of leather goods, this was just $9,065.

69   There was something equally dubious about the initial incorporation of All Leather Import & Export Inc. in 1984 (File 044-132394-97). Mejia (here spelled Mejias) was the only director, notwithstanding Florida law (and the recitation in the incorporation documents themselves) that there 'shall never be less than two' directors (File 044-132395).

70   Memo to L.B. Schoenfeld, Chief, Bureau of Licensing, from T.P. Wheeler, Captain, District # 8 Miami, *Re All Leather Imports and Exports* (April 27th, 1988) (File 044-132367).

71   Perez, in turn, was very well connected, and was allegedly involved in the second-largest drug seizure that has ever taken place, worldwide. 'On 30 April 1983, 667 kilos of high purity cocaine was seized which had been found inside a small plane that had landed in Charallave, near Caracas. This plane came from Colombia and was owned by Lizardo Márquez Pérez, a retired military officer living in Estado Táchira. One of Márquez Pérez's partners was the Regional Commander of the Venezuelan army at the Colombian frontier, General Ital del Valle Alliegro, who later became Minister of Defence for Carlos A. Pérez in his second Presidency. This was the largest seizure of cocaine in Latin America and second in the world, surpassed only by the 800 kilos captured a few months earlier in Miami. Márquez Pérez fled to Medellin and was arrested in the USA on 10 November 1984 trying to cross the frontier with Nicaragua.' See Pedro Grima, *Narcotráfico S.A. La nueva ruta del Opio*, http://www.soberania.org/Articulos/articulo_314.htm.

72   Michael Abbell, 'Noriega & Key Players in the Drug Trade', http://historicaltextarchive.com/sections.php/sections.php?artid=114&op=viewarticle#.

73   'Noriega & Key Players in the Drug Trade, Part 1', at 81–2 of 127, http://historicaltextarchive.com/sections.php/sections.php?op=viewarticle&artid=114.

74   Pedro Grima, *Narcotráfico S.A. La nueva ruta del Opio*. Additionally on Ocando Paz, a report by Enrique Alberto Martín Cuervo (*Illegal Interferences with Civil Aviation – a summary of the Venezuelan history*), describes how in 1985 a plane belonging to Orlando Castro Yanez was stolen from Base Miranda, apparently with the intention of taking it to the USA and returning it to the then-fugitive Orlando Castro. After it took off, the ownership of the plane was transferred to Fogade because it had been confiscated from Castro's companies Latino-Americana-Progreso. The plane landed in Margarita and those on board were arrested on charges of drug trafficking, including Francisco Javier Ocando Paz.

75   'Florida Man Arraigned In Cash Transfer Scheme', *Daily Oklahoman* (Dec. 29th, 1987).

76   Appearance of Counsel in *United States v. Jaime Vallejo-Mejia*, No. M-89-160-C (W.D. Okla. May 4th, 1989) (File 044-132855).

77   See, e.g., *United States v. Acosta*, 881 F.2d 1039 (11th Cir. 1989) (del Corral case) (government took $6 million of a corrupt pharmacist's 'ill-gotten wealth' made by supplying the processing drugs to cocaine laboratories between 1979 and December 1986).

78   Bill of Information in *United States v. Jaime Vallejo-Mejia*, No. M-89-160-C (W.D. Okla. May 4, 1989) (File 044-132852).

79   Guilty plea form in *United States v. Jaime Vallejo-Mejia*, No. M-89-160-C (W.D. Okla. May 4th, 1989) (File 044-132857).

80   'Prosecutors Seek Alleged Drug Funds', *Tulsa World* (July 11th, 1989).

81   In total, they received more than $880,000. 'Distributed Assets to Law Agencies', *The Journal Record* (Oct. 27th, 1990) ('Tim Leonard, U.S. Attorney for the Western District of Oklahoma, distributed equal checks of $220,400 to the Oklahoma Bureau of Narcotic & Dangerous Drugs, the Oklahoma Sheriff's Department, the Oklahoma District Attorney's Task Force, and the Oklahoma City Police Department. The assets were seized from Francisco Javier Ocando-Paz, who was indicted in the Western District for violation of drug trafficking laws. The indictment was dismissed, and Ocando-Paz was deported to Venezuela, where he was expected to be prosecuted, Leonard said in a news release').

There was a footnote to the story: Mejia never did his community service because the US Embassy in Colombia sensibly refused to allow him a visa to re-enter the United States. *Letter of Manuel Fuente, counsel for Mejia, to Philip French, Department of State* (Sept. 20th, 1989) (File 044-132837). Being banned from the US upset Mejia considerably. He wrote to the Oklahoma magistrate about his treatment when he went to get a visa. 'I found myself in front of a person who didn't have the least consideration and respect toward me,' he complained in a

letter. 'He thought he was talking to a criminal or a delinquent …
when I expressed my admiration and respect for your country, he
had the impudence to suggest that he didn't believe the explanation
that I gave him relating to my case, and also that Colombians had a
bad prestige.' *Letter of Jaime Valejo Mejia to Hon. Robin J. Cauthorn,*
U.S. Magistrate (July 12th, 1989) (File 044-132839). Mejia submitted a
letter from the Pereira branch of the Colombia Red Cross, suggesting
that he be permitted to do his community service for them – in
between 'looking after his 85 year old mother'. *Letter of Yaneth Ch. De*
Jaramillo, President, Red Cross of Colombia, to Hon. Robin J. Cauthorn,
U.S. Magistrate (July 12th, 1989) (File 044-132840). But eventually his
lawyer worked out a deal where he was forgiven the 200 hours of
work. *Letter of Manuel Fuente to Maci Almon, US Probation Service*
(July 27th, 1989) (File 044-132842). In the end, then, he got off without
any punishment at all.

82   Eddy, *The Cocaine Wars*, at 291. When Mejia was purporting to run a
leather-goods concern in Miami, his compatriot Francisco Torres was
also operating an 'import-export business in Miami'. On November
22nd, 1983, Torres – a Medellin businessman – tried to buy 1,300 55–
gallon drums of ether in New Jersey. The company reported it to the
government, which then launched a sting operation. Torres candidly
told the FBI agents who posed as ether-dealers that it would be used
for processing cocaine. *Id.*, at 295–6.

83   Glenny, *McMafia*, at 288.

84   James Kelly, 'Trouble in Paradise', *Time* magazine (Nov. 23rd, 1983).

85   Eddy, *The Cocaine Wars*, at 231.

86   As the MDPD website explains, the Centac 26 bureau still exists. 'The
team, which eventually became the Specialized Investigations Squad,
has evolved through the years. The investigations have also expanded
to include organized crime, home invasions, complex murder cases,
police sting operations, and other acts of domestic street-style terrorism. Through the development of many confidential informants
and after numerous investigations, the squad has been credited with
not only convicting various previously "untouchable" criminals, but
also with the seizure of millions of dollars in cash and property.' See
Official MDPD website, http://www.miamidade.gov/mdpd/Bureaus
Divisions/bureau_Homicide_detailed.asp. If the squad would like to
help us solve a 1986 double–homicide, we would like to hear from
them …

87   Eddy, *The Cocaine Wars*, at 71, 92, 201.

88   Eddy, *The Cocaine Wars*, at 194 *et seq.*, 235 *et seq.*, 243, 256, 280.

89   Eddy, *The Cocaine Wars*, at 243, 256. At their first trial the jury could not
agree on a verdict. This was mainly thanks to the best narco-defence

376 Notes to pp. 198–202

lawyers money could buy – the same people who would normally line up for the cartel. The legal teams had been paid at least $1.6 million in legal fees. *Id.*, at 281.This seemed to me to be circumstantial evidence against them: police officers could not possibly afford to pay this kind of fee – unless they were guilty. Eventually, with most of their profits now in the pockets of their attorneys, their united front cracked and they started pointing fingers at each other. The prosecution went on to secure some convictions.

90 Eddy, *The Cocaine Wars*, at 202.

13
The Judge

1   While this is not covered in the print edition of the book, huge holes had been punched in the testimony – always of dubious relevance – of Eslee Carberry, the publisher of the *Caribbean Echo*, and Tino Geddes. Carberry had been chased from one state to the next by criminal charges, and then deported from the US. Geddes had been friends since boyhood with the Shower Posse, Jamaica's drugs gang, and had more recently been in trouble for his close links to them. There was no significant witness against Kris who had not been seriously discredited.

2   *Maharaj 3.850 Tr.* 224.

3   *Maharaj v. Moore, Petition for Habeas Corpus*, at 18–19, Civ. No. 01-3053-CIV-HUCK\BROWN (S.D. Fla.) ('Several months before the trial, Judge Howard Gross sent [a prosecutor] as his go-between (she was not the first) to solicit a bribe from Mr Maharaj to fix his case. Mr Maharaj indignantly refused, and reported the incident to his attorney who, in turn, informed the state. Although Paul Ridge and John Kastrenakes, who prosecuted Mr Maharaj, worked with [this prosecutor], they did nothing about it, presumably because they did not believe the judge would be soliciting bribes, or anyone would be doing it for him. Meanwhile, his bribery spurned, Judge Gross became increasingly hostile to the defense').

4   *Maharaj 3.850 Tr.* 225.

5   *Maharaj 3.850 Tr.* 229.

6   Hendon did not discuss with Kris the fact that he might seek recusal of either the judge or the State's Attorney's Office; he did not seek any hearing or inquiry into the contact between his client and the prosecutor who allegedly solicited a bribe; he did not speak to Kris about

the possibility of demanding an investigation to establish that that contact had occurred; he did not suggest that Kris take a polygraph to 'confirm his veracity' regarding this contact; he did not contact the police; and he did not follow up on the issue in any affirmative way. *Maharaj 3.850 Tr. 231–3, 240.*

7   See Jim DeFede, 'The Great Bistro Brawl: At first Cassis restaurant looked like a South Beach gold mine for its owners. Then the bottom fell out. Now come the investigators and allegations of corruption', *Miami News* (May 25th, 1994), http://www.miaminewtimes.com/content/printVersion/235311.

8   There is an obvious irony in the notion that while Gross was accepting bribes to secure the release of a fake South American drug dealer, he was presiding over the trial of Krishna Maharaj for two murders that may well have been committed by a real South American drug dealer.

9   Swickle's downfall was particularly sad, as his career had included various interesting criminal defence cases, including one that went to the Supreme Court, albeit ultimately without success. See *Murphy v. Florida*, 421 US 794 (1975) (juror exposure to information about a state defendant's prior convictions or to news accounts of the crime with which he is charged do not alone presumptively deprive the defendant of due process).

10 *Florida Bar v. Howard Gross*, No. 88-71,375, Report of Referee, at 7.

11 *Florida Bar v. Howard Gross*, 610 So.2d 442, 443 (Fla. 1992).

12 *Florida Bar v. Howard Gross*, No. 88-71,375, Report of Referee, at 10 n.5 (a charge that was not brought against Gross in the light of the other charges).

13 See Jim DeFede, 'The Great Bistro Brawl', *Miami News* (May 25th, 1994), http://www.miaminewtimes.com/content/printVersion/235311.

14 *Maharaj 3.850 Tr. 235.*

15 *Maharaj 3.850 Tr. 242.* Hendon also said he was anticipating 'other witnesses who would be called by the state whose testimony would be … contradicted by the state's earlier witnesses'. He was referring to Prince Ellis, who had already testified. He thought that Ellis' testimony would prove inconsistent with that of Eddie Dames, who had been deposed prior to trial, and he worried that if the case started over, the prosecution would not call Ellis again. It apparently did not occur to him that the prosecution would not call Dames.

16 King Solomon was meant to have been the author of the Book of Solomon, otherwise called the Book of Wisdom. See Chapter IX, Verse 7 ('Thou hast chosen me to be a king of thy people, and a judge of thy sons and daughters …').

17 *Maharaj 1987 Trial Transcript, Volume Tr. XXI(C),* at 4565.

18   See *Exhibits FAZ, FCL to Maharaj 3.850 petition.*

19   *State v. Riechmann,* Brief of Appellee quoting Record of Post-Conviction Hearing at 5490.

20   *State v. Riechmann,* 777 So.2d 342, n.12 (Fla. 2000) ('Section 921.141, Florida Statutes (1985), required the trial judge to independently weigh the aggravating and mitigating circumstances to determine what penalty should be imposed upon the defendant. This section also requires the trial judge to draft the order'), citing *Fla. Stat. Ann.* 921.141(3) (1999).

21   'The court is overwhelmingly compelled to conclude,' the prosecutor had written, that the death penalty was appropriate, that the aggravating circumstances outweighed the mitigating, and so on, discussing at least eleven different issues. *State v. Riechmann,* Record of Trial at 593–600. As time went by, further examples of Judge Solomon's abdication of his role came to light. Rickey Roberts had been sentenced to die in Judge Solomon's courtroom – though the final verdict was again the prosecutor's, rather than the judge's. Like Kris' case, Roberts' had been the narrowest of jury verdicts, seven-to-five for death, and he had come very close to execution. The governor had signed two warrants on him, and the second time, after he had run through one set of appeals, he had been due to die in the electric chair. Roberts' lawyers figured they should make the same requests that we had made, to see whether Solomon ever wrote his own orders. This time, instead of turning the material over, the prosecutor's office refused the request for public records, and it took an order from the Florida Supreme Court to stay Roberts' execution and produce the records. *State v. Roberts,* SC92496, at 6 (Fla. Dec. 5th, 2002) ('During the hearing on the "Motion to Get the Facts," Roberts' counsel also questioned Judge Solomon about who had prepared the original sentencing order in Roberts' trial. When the State objected to this questioning, Judge Bagley permitted limited questioning on the topic. Judge Solomon revealed that the State had drafted the sentencing order and the judge had merely signed it and read it in court').

22   See *Exhibit FBE to Maharaj 3.850 petition.*

23   Stephen B. Bright & Patrick J. Keenan, 'Judges and the Politics of Death: Deciding Between the Bill of Rights and the Next Election in Capital Cases', 73 *Boston University Law Review* 759, at n.87 (May 1995).

24   The states with capital-punishment statutes are Alabama, Arizona, Arkansas, California, Colorado, Connecticut, Delaware, Florida, Georgia, Idaho, Illinois, Indiana, Kansas, Kentucky, Louisiana, Maryland, Mississippi, Missouri, Montana, Nebraska, Nevada, New Hampshire, New Jersey, New Mexico, North Carolina, Ohio, Oklahoma, Oregon, Pennsylvania, South Carolina, South Dakota, Tennessee, Texas, Utah,

Virginia, Washington and Wyoming. New York had it until recently, when the state courts struck the statute down.

25   Bright & Keenan, 'Judges and the Politics of Death', at n.90. Those that do not are Connecticut, Delaware, New Hampshire, New Jersey, South Carolina and Virginia.

26   The impact of elections on judges is fairly obvious, and well illustrated by the figures in Steve Bright's and Patrick Keenan's article on the subject. Only four states – Alabama, Florida, Indiana and Delaware – have permitted a judge to override a jury's sentence of life imprisonment and impose the death penalty in recent years. In these states the judges are equally permitted to override a death sentence and reduce it to life. Alabama judges face partisan elections every six years (i.e., each must run as a member of a party, normally as Republicans or Democrats); Florida judges face election every six years, but do not run on a party ticket; Indiana judges face retention elections every six years (i.e., they must face the electorate, without opposition, to determine whether they keep their jobs); only Delaware does not elect judges. Thus, if politics were playing a part as we might suspect, the judges in Alabama, Florida and Indiana might be expected to pander to a greater or lesser extent to the 'crime' vote, and change more life sentences to death than vice versa; in Delaware one might expect to see judges act more like judges. The results are as follows:

State	Life up to death ('Tough on Crime')	Death down to life ('Soft on Crime')
Alabama	47 (90.4%)	5 (9.6%)
Florida	134 (72.4 ")	51 (27.6 ")
Indiana	8 (66.7 ")	4 (33.3 ")
Delaware	0 (0 ")	7 (100 ")

See Bright & Keenan, 'Judges and the Politics of Death', at nn.175–182. These figures were accurate up to 1995. Since that time, the US Supreme Court has imposed some as yet ill-defined limits on what a judge can do regarding the imposition of the death sentence. See the line of cases following *Apprendi v. New Jersey*, 530 US 466 (2000), holding that a combination of the Sixth and Fourteenth Amendments provide the accused with the right to a jury (rather than a judge) finding on every fact necessary to conviction in a criminal case. The application of this principle to the sentencing phase is still muddy, as judges normally impose sentence, so there are sentencing decisions that remain beyond the scope of the *Apprendi* principles. Indeed, in the fifteen years since *Apprendi*, only Indiana has moved to a jury-sentencing system. *Wall Street Journal* (June 25th, 2002).

27 Bright & Keenan, 'Judges and the Politics of Death', at n.165, citing Bill Poovey, 'Hooper Criticizes Chief Justice for Soliciting from Lawyers', *Tuscaloosa News*, at B8 (July 20th, 1994); Phillip Rawls, 'Justice Race Another Political Brawl', *Columbus Ledger-Enquirer (Ga.)*, at B2 (Dec. 10th, 1994).

28 In *Bracy v. Gramley*, 520 US 899, 117 S.Ct. 1793, 138 L.Ed.2d 97 (1997), the Supreme Court traces the sordid history of Operation Greylord, which exposed corruption in the state judiciary of Chicago. For other cases where judges have been caught accepting bribes, see also, e.g., *Ohio v. McGettrick*, 40 Ohio App. 3d 25, 531 N. E. 2d 755 (1988); *In re Brennan*, 65 N.Y. 2d 564, 483 N. E. 2d 484 (1985). This is not to say that judges cannot be corrupt when they are appointed, are British or both, since power can corrupt anyone. See, for example, BBC, 'Illegal cleaner's "threat to judges"' (Sep. 27th, 2006), http://news.bbc.co.uk/1/hi/uk/5386330.stm (cleaner had affair with immigration judge; stole a video of him having sex with another judge, who was apparently snorting cocaine; then tried to blackmail both). Nonetheless, it is worth noting that only seven US federal judges have been impeached in more than 200 years; they are appointed with life tenure and therefore have far less 'need' to seek out money and favour than their elected state counterparts. Mary L. Volcansek, Maria Elisabetta Defranciscis & Jacqueline Lucienne Lafon, *Judicial Misconduct* (1996), at 9.

29 See generally Geoffrey Hazard & Angelo Dondi, *Legal Ethics – A Comparative Study* (2004), at 82–3.

30 During this time a majority of the court voted to overturn fifty-eight of the sixty-one death sentences (95 per cent). See Patrick K. Brown, 'The Rise and Fall of Rose Bird: A Career Killed by the Death Penalty', at 10, http://cschs.org/02_history/images/CSCHS_2007-Brown.pdf.

31 See generally Online Archive of California, 'Guide to the Californians to Defeat Rose Bird, 1985–86' (California State Library), http://content.cdlib.org/view?docId=tf8f59n9bn&doc.view=entire_text&brand=oac.

32 Maura Dolan, 'State High Court Is Strong Enforcer of Death Penalty', *Los Angeles Times*, at A1 (April 9th, 1995). See generally Stephen B. Bright & Patrick J. Keenan, 'Judges and the Politics of Death'.

33 See generally Bright & Keenan, 'Judges and the Politics of Death', at n.26.

34 Bright & Keenan, 'Judges and the Politics of Death', at n.70, quoting Leslie Phillips, 'Crime Pays as a Political Issue', *USA Today*, at 11A (Oct. 10th, 1994). 'Presidential candidate Bill Clinton demonstrated that he was tough on crime in his 1992 campaign by scheduling the execution

of a brain-damaged man shortly before the New Hampshire primary. Clinton had embraced the death penalty in 1982 after his defeat in a bid for re-election as governor of Arkansas in 1980. In his presidential campaign ten years later, Clinton returned from campaigning in New Hampshire to preside over the execution of Rickey Ray Rector, an African-American who had been sentenced to death by an all-white jury. Rector had destroyed part of his brain when he turned his gun on himself after killing the police officer for whose murder he received the death sentence. Logs at the prison show that in the days leading up to his execution, Rector was howling and barking like a dog, dancing, singing, laughing inappropriately, and saying that he was going to vote for Clinton. Clinton denied clemency and allowed the execution to proceed, thereby protecting himself from being labeled as "soft on crime" and helping the Democrats to take back the crime issue. Clinton's first three television advertisements in his bid for re-election – already begun a year and a half before the 1996 presidential election – all focused on crime and Clinton's support to expand the death penalty.' Bright & Keenan, 'Judges and the Politics of Death', at nn.65–9.

35 US CONST. Art. II, Section II, Clause 2. The Constitution only defines the selection of Supreme Court Justices, but Congress has applied the same rules for lower-court federal judges.

36 Sometimes both Senators in a state will be from the opposing party. Nevertheless, during the tenure of President Franklin Roosevelt, for example, more than 90 per cent of the nominees were Democrats. See http://www.dsusd.k12.ca.us/users/scottsh/Govt/Nomination%20Process%20For%20Federal%20Judges.htm.

37 The death penalty continues to play a significant role in the confirmation hearings of Supreme Court Justices, with any hint of opposition to the death penalty being cause for concern in some quarters. Julie Davis, 'Sotomayor's Confirmation Hearings to begin July 13', Associated Press (June 8th, 2009), at http://judicialnetwork.com/news/soto mayors-confirmation-hearings-begin-july-13 (accessed Dec. 10th, 2010) (' "The purpose of this sideshow is to avoid facts in Sotomayor's actual record that indicate a soft-on-crime judge who twists the law, particularly law at the intersection of race and crime issues, and who avoids binding precedent as a lower court judge in ways that unnecessarily favor criminals and hinder law enforcement," Wendy E. Long, counsel of the conservative Judicial Confirmation Network, said in a memo. Among the evidence Long cited to back up her claim was a position paper that Sotomayor signed in 1981 on behalf of a task force she chaired for the Puerto Rican Legal Defense and Education Fund. The paper equated the death penalty with racism'); Benjamin

Weiser, 'In '98, Hints from Sotomayor on Death Penalty', *New York Times* (June 24th, 2009), at http://www.nytimes.com/2009/06/25/us/politics/25death.html?_r=1&hp (accessed Dec. 10th, 2010).

38   Justice Sotomayor did precisely this when she was a district court judge, refusing to strike the death penalty down on precisely the grounds she had argued, years before, that it should be held unconstitutional. Benjamin Weiser, 'In '98, Hints from Sotomayor on Death Penalty' (noting how she had argued as a lawyer that the death penalty was overwhelmingly racist, but as a judge refused to accept very strong evidence of racial disparities as a reason to declare the penalty unconstitutional).

39   While it deserves more comment than this brief footnote, the US process has many benefits. The distinction between the executive (the presidency), the legislative (the Senate and House of Representatives) and the judiciary (the Supreme Court and the lower courts) is an exceptionally clear and sensible construction of government, even if it does not always operate as the Founders intended. Compare this to the hotch-potch of the British system, where the Blair 'presidency' essentially co-opted the legislative and executive into one branch, where the House of Lords is relatively toothless, and where the judiciary remains unable truly to enforce the rights set out in the European Convention on Human Rights.

40   See, e.g., Frank Belloni, 'The Labour Community and the British Judiciary', 13 *International Political Science Review* 269 (1992) (discussing a belief in the working class that the judiciary is biased in favour of the wealthy).

41   Nick Cohen, 'Shock! City Slickers are Arrested', *The Observer* (March 28th, 2010), at http://www.guardian.co.uk/commentisfree/2010/mar/28/nick-cohen-finance-fraud (accessed Dec. 11th, 2010).

42   Albie Sachs & Joan Hoff Wilson, *Sexism and the Law: A Study of Male Beliefs and Legal Bias in Britain and the United States* (1979).

43   The US Supreme Court has never had more than two women (two of nine, or 22 per cent) and the current make-up of the federal bench is similarly unrepresentative. Carl Tobias, 'Diversity on the Federal Bench', *National Law Journal* (Oct. 12th, 2009), at http://www.law.com/jsp/nlj/PubArticleNLJ.jsp?id=1202434429480&slreturn=1&hbxlogin=1 (accessed Dec. 11th, 2010) ('Eighty-four percent of federal judges are white. Female jurists comprise 20%. African-Americans constitute 8%. Out of the almost 1,300 sitting federal judges, a mere 11 are Asian-American and only one is a Native American. A significant percentage of the 94 federal districts has never had a jurist who is a woman or a person of color'). In the states, where judges are often elected, the inevitability of race-based voting means that the dis-

parities are often worse. See Ciara Torres-Spelliscy, Monique Chase & Emma Greenman, 'Improving Judicial Diversity', Brennan Center for Justice (2010), at http://brennan.3cdn.net/31e6c0fa3c2e920910_ppm6ibehe.pdf (accessed on Dec. 11th, 2010) (noting that four of ten state Supreme Courts studied in 2008 were all-white; by 2010, the number had risen to six of ten).

44   Sarah Westergren, 'Gender Effects in the Courts of Appeals Revisited; The Data since 1994', 92 *Georgia Law Review* 689 (2004) (noting how, in the US, 'the realist school of legal theory emerged in the 1930s, [and] scholars for the first time began to examine the influence of judges' personal identities on their decisionmaking'; only 14.4 per cent of votes were cast by female judges, and their decisions had more to do with the political leanings of the president who appointed them than with their own gender).

45   Sylvia Lazos Vargas, 'Does a Diverse Judiciary attain a rule of law that is Inclusive?', 10 *Michigan Journal of Race & Law* 101 (2004) (noting how Justice Clarence Thomas, the 'token' black person on the US Supreme Court, has helped to refashion areas of constitutional law of great importance to minorities, in ways that clearly harm their interests; in order to achieve diversity, tokenism is insufficient, and there must be 'a critical mass of minority judges'). Interestingly, Justice Hugo Black (on the court from 1937 to 1971) was a Klansman in his youth, and yet became a champion of the rights of African Americans on the court. See 'Hugo Black and the KKK', at http://www.nisk.k12.ny.us/fdr/ideas/portfolio/vandersee/vandersee.html (accessed Dec. 11th, 2010). His was certainly a far more favourable voting record than that of Clarence Thomas.

46   Kathleen E. Mahoney, 'The Myth of Judicial Neutrality: The Role of Judicial Education in the Fair Administration of Justice', 32 *Willamette Law Review* 785, 791 (1996) (in Canada, '[u]nquestionably, the judiciary is demographically imbalanced. The vast majority of judges are white, well educated, middle-class, middle-aged, male, able-bodied, Christian, of European ancestry, married, apparently heterosexual, and most married to women with less demanding careers or with no careers outside the home', and noting that only two of the first fifty Canadian Supreme Court justices were born into working-class families).

47   The relative insensitivity of British people to issues of race and gender continues to astound me. I say this not because I am a paragon of race and gender sensitivity, but simply because I spent my developmental years in the US, where such matters are constantly on the table. For example, in a recent meeting concerning the so-called Gibson 'Detainee Inquiry', I was struck by the fact that of the nine members not one was a Muslim, even though 100 per cent of those who had

been 'detainees' were Muslim. In the US such lack of representation would be met with howls of derision; in the UK, the subject was simply not broached.

48 The 'Supreme Court' was only created by the Constitutional Reform Act (2005), at http://www.statutelaw.gov.uk/content. aspx?activeTextDocId=1974190 (accessed Dec. 11th, 2010). However, before that time the Law Lords played a similar role.

49 See Adam Wagner, 'Baroness Hale still "embarrassed" to be only diversity Supreme Court Justice', UK Human Rights Blog (Sep. 16th, 2010), at http://ukhumanrightsblog.com/2010/09/16/lady-hale-still-embarrassed-to-be-only-diversity-supreme-court-judge/(accessed Dec. 11th, 2010) (in 2004 Brenda Hale became the first person in the highest court in Britain who was not a white male; there have since been no other 'diversity' appointments among the eleven members). To further illustrate the 'diversity' (as of this writing), of the eleven members six went to Cambridge, four went to Oxford and one went to Queen's University, Belfast.

50 See Schedule 8 of the Constitutional Reform Act (2005), at http://www. statutelaw.gov.uk/content.aspx?activeTextDocId=1974190 (accessed Dec. 11th, 2010).

51 At the time of writing, the commission for England and Wales, for example, had one solicitor and one barrister. There were seven judges of various stripes, and five 'lay' members – one a professor of law, with two of the other four being Oxbridge graduates. One person – a presiding magistrate referred to as a 'lay justice' – was black. (The chair was vacant.) See Judicial Appointments Commission, at http:// www.judicialappointments.gov.uk/about-jac/157.htm (accessed Dec. 11th, 2010).

52 In *Bracy v. Gramley*, 520 US 899 (1997), a corrupt judge's compensatory bias was the precise issue. Bracy had not bribed a judge himself, but claimed that the judge would have imposed harsher penalties on all others, to cover for the fact that he periodically let someone off who paid him money. While the Supreme Court viewed this as a difficult burden of proof for him to carry, the court held that he had a right to discovery on the issue to have a chance to make his case. This is precisely the discovery that we demanded on Kris' behalf, citing *Bracy*, but no court was willing to order it. There has never been a hearing of any kind on the question of Judge Gross' attempt to solicit a bribe from Kris.

14

The Road to Nowhere

1   See *Maharaj v. State*, 684 So.2d 726, 728 (Fla. 1996) ('It does appear that a substantial number of Maharaj's claims may properly be denied without an evidentiary hearing because they were either raised or could have been raised on direct appeal and, consequently, cannot be relitigated in a postconviction relief proceeding').

2   Sykes had, the court said, 'advanced no explanation whatever for his failure to object at trial …' *Wainwright v. Sykes*, 433 US 72, 91 (1977). There is a good reason for this: it was not his job to object, but his lawyer's. Indeed, in a particularly illogical concurrence, Chief Justice Burger explained:

> Once counsel is appointed, the day-to-day conduct of the defense rests with the attorney. He, not the client, has the immediate – and ultimate – responsibility of deciding if and when to object, which witnesses, if any, to call, and what defenses to develop. Not only do these decisions rest with the attorney, but such decisions must as a practical matter, be made without consulting the client. The trial process simply does not permit the type of frequent and protracted interruptions which would be necessary if it were required that clients give knowing and intelligent approval to each of the myriad tactical decisions as a trial proceeds.

Wainwright v. Sykes, 433 US 72, 93 (1977) (Burger, C.J., concurring). Given this, it makes no sense to impute the 'decisions' (or, more likely, omissions) of the lawyer to the person on trial.

3   See Stephen B. Bright, 'Counsel for the Poor: The Death Sentence Not for the Worst Crime but for the Worst Lawyer', *Yale Law Journal* (May 1994).

4   See Austin Sarat, *When the State Kills*, at 61, via Google Books. After a flood of coverage highlighted the horror of this event, Butterworth retreated and announced that he favoured a change in method of execution to lethal injection.

5   *Maharaj 3.850 Transcript*, at 651.

6   *Maharaj v. State*, 778 So.2d 944 (Fla. 2000).

7   *Maharaj v. State*, 778 So.2d 944, 948 (Fla. 2000).

8   *Maharaj v. State*, 778 So.2d 944, 952–3 (Fla. 2000).

9   *Maharaj v. State*, 778 So.2d 944, 952 (Fla. 2000).

10 *Maharaj v. State*, 778 So.2d 944, 950 (Fla. 2000).

11 When the prosecution seeks to *prevent* prisoners from waiving issues

(such as a lawyer trying to represent more than one defendant in an alleged drug conspiracy), the Supreme Court has refused to accept the waiver:

> Petitioner insists that the provision of waivers by all affected defendants cures any problems created by the multiple representation. But no such flat rule can be deduced from the Sixth Amendment presumption in favor of counsel of choice. Federal courts have an *independent interest* in ensuring that criminal trials are conducted within the ethical standards of the profession and that legal proceedings appear fair to all who observe them. [...] Not only the interest of a criminal defendant but the institutional interest in the rendition of just verdicts in criminal cases may be jeopardized by unregulated multiple representation.

Wheat v. United States, 486 US 153, 160 (1988) (emphasis supplied). In other words, there is an institutional interest in ensuring that the trial seems fair, regardless of the wishes of the person on trial to waive a particular right.

12   We did everything we could to stop this, but were unsuccessful. We asked the state court not to waste money but to allow us to challenge the convictions first. Judge Bagley refused. We asked the federal court to proceed with the habeas challenge anyway; all the way up the chain the federal judges refused as well. *Maharaj v. Moore*, 2001 US Dist. LEXIS 24614 (Nov. 28th, 2001) (magistrate's recommendation), *adopted*, 2001 US Dist. LEXIS 24613 (Dec. 27th, 2001), *aff'd*, 394 F.3d 1345 (11th Cir. 2002). The federal Court of Appeals ruled that respect for the state court compelled the federal courts to allow the state proceedings to putter on to a conclusion before the federal courts could intervene.

13   See Death Penalty Information Center, 'Exonerations by State' (Florida leads the nation, with twenty-three Death Row exonerations), http://www.deathpenaltyinfo.org/innocence-and-death penalty#innst.

14   William Geimer & Jonathan Amsterdam, 'Why Jurors Vote Life or Death: Operative Factors in Ten Florida Death Penalty Cases', 15 *American Journal of Criminal Law* 1, 28 (1988). See also Arnold Barnett, 'Some Distribution Patterns for the Georgia Death Sentence', 18 *UC Davis Law Review* 1327, 1338–45 (1985); Michael Mello & Ruthann Robson, 'Judge Over Jury: Florida's Practice of Imposing Death Over Life in Capital Cases', 13 *Florida State University Law Review* 31, 59–60 (1985); Lawrence T. White, 'Juror Decision-Making in the Capital Trial', 11 *Law & Human Behavior* 113, 123–6 (1987). 'The term [lingering doubt] as used in this context of juror responses includes: (a)

reasonable doubt that defendant was guilty of any crime, doubt that normally should have resulted in a vote for a verdict of not guilty; (b) reasonable doubt only that defendant was guilty of first degree murder, a doubt that normally should have resulted in a vote for a verdict of guilty of a lesser included offense; and (c) a lingering doubt about either of the first two matters, sufficient in the mind of the juror to counsel against voting for the irrevocable penalty of death.' Geimer & Amsterdam, at 28. Some states recognise that 'residual doubt' should be an acceptable consideration at a resentencing trial. See, e.g., *State v. Watson*, 572 N.E.2d 97 (Ohio 1991) (error to preclude argument on residual doubt; death sentence disproportionate due to residual doubt). Even the Supreme Court has ruled that certain evidence of innocence must be admitted at the penalty phase. *Green v. Georgia*, 442 US 95 (1979) (exclusion of evidence at sentencing phase based upon Georgia's hearsay rule held unconstitutional). However, more recently, the Supreme Court has gone backwards on the issue. See *Franklin v. Lynaugh*, 487 US 164, 174 (1988) (plurality opinion) ('Our edict that, in a capital case, "the sentencer … [may] not be precluded from considering, as a mitigating factor, any aspect of a defendant's character or record and any of the circumstances of the offense," in no way mandates reconsideration by capital juries, in the sentencing phase, of their "residual doubts" over a defendant's guilt … This Court's prior decisions, as we understand them, fail to recognize a constitutional right to have such doubts considered as a mitigating factor').

15 See *Darling v. State*, 808 So.2d 145, 162 (Fla. 2002) ('We have repeatedly observed that residual doubt is not an appropriate mitigating circumstance').

16 See, e.g., *Brief of Appellee* (the State of Florida), *Merck v. Florida*, No. 91,581 (filed Sep. 1999) (it is inappropriate to 'turn a penalty phase proceeding into a guilt phase proceeding … or … permit evidence to confuse or mislead the jury, in the performance of its responsibility of returning a sentencing recommendation, or … subvert a long line of precedents of this Court that residual or lingering doubt is not a nonstatutory mitigating factor'). Troy Merck's case was reversed because of the failure to consider mitigating evidence of intoxication, but it was okay, apparently, to exclude evidence that he did not commit the crime. *State v. Merck*, 763 So.2d 295 (Fla. 2000) (rejecting the claim that 'the trial court erred in excluding from the resentencing proceedings evidence as to another suspect in the instant crime'; it is worth noting that this was the third trial of the case and, in the first, the jury had been unable to agree as to conviction, let alone death). At a fourth trial Merck was sentenced to death again, and remains on Death Row.

State v. Merck, 975 So.2d 1054 (Fla. 2007).

17 *Fla. Stat. § 921.141(6)(a)* ('has no significant history of prior criminal activity').

18 *Fla. Stat. § 921.141(6)(c)* ('[t]he victim was a participant in the … conduct leading to the murder').

19 While it may generally be aggravating that the prisoner is likely to pose a danger in the future, *Jurek v. Texas*, 428 US 262, 96 S.Ct. 2950, 49 L.Ed.2d 929 (1976), it is, equally, mitigating to prove that this is not the case. *Eddings v. Oklahoma*, 455 US 104, 108, 102 S. Ct. 869, 71 L.Ed. 2d 1 (1982) (in mitigation, '[t]he psychiatrist suggested that, if treated, Eddings would no longer pose a serious threat to society').

20 *Tyler v. Kemp*, 755 F.2d 741, 745 (11th Cir. 1985) (recognising as a mitigating circumstance that the defendant's 'character and reputation … were good').

21 The Florida Supreme Court has held that '*any* emotional disturbance relevant to the crime must be considered and weighed', *Cheshire v. State*, 586 So.2d 908, 912 (Fla. 1990). The federal courts have held the same thing. 'Mental illness is a condition that should militate in favor of a lesser penalty.' *Mathis v. Kemp*, 704 F. Supp. 1062 (N.D.Ga. 1989), citing *Zant v. Stephens*, 462 US 862, 885, 103 S. Ct. 2733, 77 L.Ed. 2d 235 (1983).

22 Mr Washington's able and extremely dedicated lawyer, Jerry Zerkin, continued to fight for his client, and ultimately new DNA tests proved him conclusively to be innocent and he was released from prison.

23 Bagley had made enough mistakes that we would have got the death penalty reversed independently. The only disadvantage of a death sentence would be the requirement that we appeal again to the Florida Supreme Court and go through years more of state appeals, before they would let us go to federal court to challenge his conviction. Indeed, if the state courts sent it back for a third sentencing trial, we could be on the merry-go-round for another twenty years before getting out of state court for the first time. For this reason, life would be preferable to death, but only marginally so.

15

The Appeal Court

1 Judge Bagley had ultimate authority over the sentence but, with such a clear majority in our favour, there was little chance under prevailing legal standards that he would refuse to follow the jury's recommendation.

2   *Maharaj v. Moore, Order on Report and Recommendation*, at 9 Civ. No. 02-22240 (S.D. Fla. August 30th, 2004).

3   *Id.*

4   *Id.*, at 13 n.6.

5   *Id.*, at 13.

6   *Murray v. Giarratano*, 492 US 1 (1989) (states are not required to provide counsel to indigent Death Row prisoners seeking state post-conviction relief in order to have 'meaningful access' to the courts).

7   The district court and the notoriously conservative Fourth Circuit Court of Appeals had sided with Giarratano, ruling that Death Row prisoners could not be expected to represent themselves in capital appeals. However, this did not stop a majority of the Supreme Court from deciding otherwise, with Chief Justice Rehnquist writing another opinion that belied common sense.

8   It was not until sixteen years after *Murray v. Giarratano* that the Supreme Court finally determined that executing juveniles was unconstitutional. See *Roper v. Simmons*, 543 US 551 (2005). Now, only someone who had just reached his eighteenth birthday could be required to represent himself in a capital case. However, children as young as thirteen may still have to fight their appeals against a sentence of life without parole. See Equal Justice Initiative, 'Children in Adult Prison', http://eji.org/eji/childrenprison.

9   Paradoxically, Chief Justice Rehnquist argued that the fact that a minority of states provided legal assistance to Death Row prisoners was proof positive that no such right existed. *Murray v. Giarratano*, 492 US 1, 10 (1989). Surely, to the contrary, this was proof of the need.

10   *Murray v. Giarratano*, 492 US 1, 14–15 (1989) (Kennedy & O'Connor, JJ., concurring) ('While Virginia has not adopted procedures for securing representation that are as far-reaching and effective as those available in other States, no prisoner on Death Row in Virginia has been unable to obtain counsel to represent him in postconviction proceedings').

11   *Id.*, at 49, quoting *Herrera v. Collins*, 506 US 390, 400 (1993).

12   *Id.*, at 50, quoting *Herrera*.

13   *Herrera v. Collins*, 506 US 390 (1993) (refusing to recognise that 'actual innocence' would render the execution of a defendant unconstitutional).

14   *Herrera v. Collins*, 506 US 390 (1993).

15   *Herrera v. Collins*, 506 US 390, 400 (1993).

16   *Herrera v. Collins*, 506 US 390, 410 (1993) (only nine states out of fifty allow newly discovered evidence of innocence to be presented at any time; forty-one have time limits, with seventeen allowing only sixty days after trial).

17   *Herrera v. Collins*, 506 US 390, 400 (1993).

18   *Herrera v. Collins*, 506 US 390, 405 (1993).

19   *Herrera v. Collins*, 506 US 390, 402–3 (1993).

20   The total between 1986 and the end of 2011 was 1,227, but that number rises all the time. See Death Penalty Information Center, 'Executions by Year', at http://www.deathpenaltyinfo.org/executions-year (accessed Dec. 11th, 2003).

21   *Maharaj v. Moore*, No. 02-22240-Huck/Turnoff, *Order of August 30, 2004*, at 54–6 (S.D. Fla.).

22   Professor James S. Liebman, Professor Jeffrey Fagin & Valerie West, 'A Broken System: Error Rates in Capital Cases, 1973–1995' (2000), http://www2.law.columbia.edu/instructionalservices/liebman/liebman_final.pdf.

23   Professor Liebman did not question whether the rules of the game were inadequate. Thus he did not take into account the fact that no prisoner could prevail in his case on the issue of innocence. In other words, his analysis accepted some aspects of the system that most people would disavow. In this sense, his conclusions almost certainly underestimated the scope of the problem.

24   Liebman *et al.*, 'A Broken System', at 1 (emphasis in original).

25   The Act also provided that if the states gave the defendant greater rights, then the federal review process would be expedited still further (the so-called 'Opt-in' provision). However, this would merely have sped the system up even more and has not been used in any meaningful way.

26   This has been going on for quite some time. For example, in *Mann v. Lynaugh*, 840 F.2d 1194 (5th Cir. 1988), the lawyer for the petitioner was one day late filing his notice of appeal in a capital case, so the court simply did not reach the merits of his appeal. See also *William Davis v. Gary Johnson, Director*, No. 98-20507 (5th Cir. 1998); *Thomas James Fisher v. Gary Johnson, Director*, No. 98-50566 (5th Cir. 1998).

27   *Maharaj v. Moore*, No. 02-22240-Huck/Turnoff, *Order of August 30, 2004*, at 7 n.2 (S.D. Fla.) ('even if this Court believes that a state court ruling … is an erroneous application of [federal law], this Court may not overrule the state court unless that application was unreasonable').

28   *Id.*, at 18.

29   *Id.*, at 27.

30   *Id.*, at 21.

31   *Id.*, at 23 n.19.

32   With the Human Rights Act and the European Charter of Human Rights, the UK has taken steps towards the US model of jurisprudence, but they have been tentative ones, and are vitriolically opposed by those who believe Britain has been exporting her national sovereignty to the continent.

33   I do not pretend that this was the kind of study that would pass the
     Ben Goldacre test. See Ben Goldacre, *Bad Science* (2008). For example,
     there is no clear-cut definition of what is 'left' and what is 'right' in
     the sense of some individual votes – e.g., there were no Anglo-Ameri-
     can wars going on in 1990, and while one would expect that a socialist
     would be more pacifist, nationalism sometimes overrides other politi-
     cal tendencies. And a particular bill can contain elements that veer
     from one side to the other.

34   There are some broad exceptions to this. For example, as previously
     discussed, the US has been much more active in its discussions of
     discrimination, whether it be racial or gender. American law has been
     more keenly debated on these subjects, generally for longer than it has
     in the UK.

35   When people speak of the US as a rapidly changing society, or one
     where opportunities are everywhere, they generally mean economic
     changes. Even here, the myth of the American dream is not supported
     by most of the data, but it cannot obscure the fact that the US remains
     wedded to views that have long since been abandoned by the social
     democrats in Europe – notwithstanding periodic oscillations even
     there away from human rights.

36   All nine went to Ivy League law schools (sometimes more than
     one): Roberts, Scalia, Ginsburg, Breyer and Kagan went to Harvard;
     Thomas, Alito and Sotomayor to Yale; and Kennedy to Stanford. Most
     followed a well-beaten path – clerking for judges, before taking jobs
     in government and academia, followed by appointment to a lower
     court – before nomination. See 'Biographies of Current Justices of the
     Supreme Court', http://www.supremecourt.gov/about/biographies.
     aspx (accessed Jan. 3rd, 2011). The only blip in an otherwise wholly
     corporate-academic profile of the court comes in the shape of Ruth
     Bader Ginsburg, who worked for the American Civil Liberties Union
     in their women's rights section. Yet even she walked most of the same
     path: law school at Harvard, LLB at Columbia Law School, clerking
     with a judge, teaching, and thirteen years as an appellate judge.

37   The vigorous right wing of the court has no compunction in over-
     ruling earlier decisions with which they disagree. Justice Scalia has
     written, 'I do not myself believe in rigid adherence to *stare decisis* in
     constitutional cases …' *Lawrence v. Texas*, 539 US 558, 587 (2003) (Sca-
     lia, J., joined by Rehnquist C.J., and Thomas, J., dissenting). While I
     disagree on the outcome most times that Scalia writes, on this point
     he must surely be correct.

38   In *Furman v. Georgia*, 408 US 238 (1972), five justices declared the death-
     penalty statutes then in existence to be unconstitutional. Four years
     later, under heavy political pressure, the court reversed itself. *Gregg v.*

Georgia, 428 US 153 (1976). By then, only Justices Brennan and Marshall dissented, finding the punishment *per se* illegal. Since that time there have never been more than two justices – generally as they verged on retirement – who have decided that they would no longer 'tinker with the machinery of death'. *Callins v. Collins*, 114 S.Ct. 1127, 1130 (1994) (Blackmun, J., dissenting from denial of *certiorari*) ('From this day forward, I no longer shall tinker with the machinery of death. For more than 20 years I have endeavored – indeed, I have struggled – along with a majority of this Court, to develop procedural and substantive rules that would lend more than the mere appearance of fairness to the death penalty endeavor. Rather than continue to coddle the Court's delusion that the desired level of fairness has been achieved and the need for regulation eviscerated, I feel morally and intellectually obligated simply to concede that the death penalty experiment has failed. It is virtually self-evident to me now that no combination of procedural rules or substantive regulations ever can save the death penalty from its inherent constitutional deficiencies. The basic question – does the system accurately and consistently determine which defendants "deserve" to die? – cannot be answered in the affirmative'); *Baze v. Rees*, 170 L.Ed.2d 420, 454 (2008) (Stevens, J., concurring) ('the imposition of the death penalty represents the pointless and needless extinction of life with only marginal contributions to any discernible social or public purposes. A penalty with such negligible returns to the State [is] patently excessive and cruel and unusual punishment violative of the Eighth Amendment'). At the time he had his Road to Damascus experience, Justice Harry Blackmun was eighty-six years old, and had been on the court for twenty-four years; he retired five months later. In his turn, Justice John Paul Stevens was four days shy of eighty-eight years old, had been on the court holding the opposite opinion for thirty-three years at this point, and retired two years later. Their change of heart came too late for many prisoners; both were part of the majority that upheld the death penalty in 1976.

39 *Lawrence v. Texas*, 539 US 558 (2003). The liberal wing also proposed a discussion on whether innocence might act as a bar to execution. *In re Troy Davis*, 130 S.Ct. 1 (2009). However, when the lower court declined to settle on such a standard, the Supreme Court denied review without a dissenting voice. *In re Troy Davis*, No. 08-1443 (March 28th, 2011).

40 'The conclusion that I have reached with regard to the constitutionality of the death penalty itself makes my decision in this case particularly difficult,' Stevens concluded. 'It does not, however, justify a refusal to respect precedents that remain a part of our law. This Court has held that the death penalty is constitutional, and has established a framework for evaluating the constitutionality of particular methods

of execution.' *Baze v. Rees*, 170 L.Ed.2d 420, 455 (2008) (Stevens, J., concurring).

41 Of course we pursued Kris' case to the Eleventh Circuit Court of Appeals in Atlanta, and on to the US Supreme Court in Washington. See *Maharaj v. Secretary for the Department of Corrections*, 432 F.3d 1292, 1312 (11th Cir. 2005), *cert. denied*, 549 US 819 (2006) ('As for the finding that the defence had knowledge of the polygraph results, the district court noted that there was substantial evidence in the post-conviction record to indicate that the defence was not aware of the fact that Butler's answer to one of the questions was indicative of deception. But, the district court observed that even if it were to disagree with the Florida Supreme Court's conclusion, the state high court's finding was not an unreasonable one'). If the Florida Supreme Court said that the polygraph results were not withheld from the defence, and this was patently false, how could their conclusion that the prosecution did not withhold evidence be 'reasonable'? The Supreme Court refused to hear the case, *Maharaj v. McDonough*, No. 05-1555, 127 S.Ct. 348 (Oct. 2nd, 2006), effectively ending Kris Maharaj's campaign for justice in the US courts two weeks before his twentieth anniversary in prison.

42 *Herrera v. Collins*, 506 US 390, 416 (1992) ('In Texas, the Governor has the power, upon the recommendation of a majority of the Board of Pardons and Paroles, to grant clemency').

43 The governor was then Ann Richards, who was not a vocal supporter of the death penalty. The chances of any such thing happening soon dipped even more alarmingly, as George W. Bush defeated Richards in the 1994 election. While he allowed 152 prisoners to be executed on his watch, he granted clemency to one person – confessed serial killer Henry Lee Lucas who, though he was thought to have killed as many as 350 people, had apparently not done the crime for which he was on Death Row. Lucas died of natural causes three years later, while other states lined up to execute him. Lucas became the *only* person to receive clemency in Texas in the two decades since the reintroduction of the death penalty in 1977.

44 http://en.wikipedia.org/wiki/Leonel_Torres_Herrera.

45 http://en.wikipedia.org/wiki/Shaka_Sankofa.

46 Austin Sarat, 'Governor Perry, Governor Ryan, and the Disappearance of Executive Clemency in Capital Cases: What Has Happened to Mercy in America?' (Dec. 29th, 2004), http://writ.news.findlaw.com/commentary/20041229_sarat.html.

47 *Id.* In the thirty-two years since 1976, only six Florida Death Row prisoners had been successful in their applications, all between 1979 and 1983. See Death Penalty Information Center, 'Clemency', http://www.deathpenaltyinfo.org/article.php?did=126&scid=13.

16

The Victims

1   'A Walk Through the System', Texas Department of Criminal Justice, Victim Services Division (undated). The statute upon which this is based reads as follows:

Art. 56.02. CRIME VICTIMS' RIGHTS. (a) A victim, guardian of a victim, or close relative of a deceased victim is entitled to the following rights within the criminal justice system:

(1) the right to receive from law enforcement agencies adequate protection from harm and threats of harm arising from cooperation with prosecution efforts;

(2) the right to have the magistrate take the safety of the victim or his family into consideration as an element in fixing the amount of bail for the accused;

(3) the right, if requested, to be informed:

(A) by the attorney representing the state of relevant court proceedings, including appellate proceedings, and to be informed if those proceedings have been canceled or rescheduled prior to the event; and

(B) by an appellate court of decisions of the court, after the decisions are entered but before the decisions are made public;

(4) the right to be informed, when requested, by a peace officer concerning the defendant's right to bail and the procedures in criminal investigations and by the district attorney's office concerning the general procedures in the criminal justice system, including general procedures in guilty plea negotiations and arrangements, restitution, and the appeals and parole process;

(5) the right to provide pertinent information to a probation department conducting a presentencing investigation concerning the impact of the offense on the victim and his family by testimony, written statement, or any other manner prior to any sentencing of the offender;

(6) the right to receive information regarding compensation to victims of crime as provided by Subchapter B, including information related to the costs that may be compensated under that subchapter and the amount of compensation, eligibility for compensation, and procedures for application for compensation under that subchapter, the payment for a medical examination under Article 56.06 for a victim of a sexual

assault, and when requested, to referral to available social service agencies that may offer additional assistance;

(7) the right to be informed, upon request, of parole procedures, to participate in the parole process, to be notified, if requested, of parole proceedings concerning a defendant in the victim's case, to provide to the Board of Pardons and Paroles for inclusion in the defendant's file information to be considered by the board prior to the parole of any defendant convicted of any crime subject to this subchapter, and to be notified, if requested, of the defendant's release;

(8) the right to be provided with a waiting area, separate or secure from other witnesses, including the offender and relatives of the offender, before testifying in any proceeding concerning the offender; if a separate waiting area is not available, other safeguards should be taken to minimize the victim's contact with the offender and the offender's relatives and witnesses, before and during court proceedings;

(9) the right to prompt return of any property of the victim that is held by a law enforcement agency or the attorney for the state as evidence when the property is no longer required for that purpose;

(10) the right to have the attorney for the state notify the employer of the victim, if requested, of the necessity of the victim's cooperation and testimony in a proceeding that may necessitate the absence of the victim from work for good cause;

(11) the right to counseling, on request, regarding acquired immune deficiency syndrome (AIDS) and human immunodeficiency virus (HIV) infection and testing for acquired immune deficiency syndrome (AIDS), human immunodeficiency virus (HIV) infection, antibodies to HIV, or infection with any other probable causative agent of AIDS, if the offense is an offense under Section 21.02, 21.11(a)(1), 22.011, or 22.021, Penal Code;

(12) the right to request victim–offender mediation coordinated by the victim services division of the Texas Department of Criminal Justice;

(13) the right to be informed of the uses of a victim impact statement and the statement's purpose in the criminal justice system, to complete the victim impact statement, and to have the victim impact statement considered:

(A) by the attorney representing the state and the judge before sentencing or before a plea bargain agreement is accepted; and

(B) by the Board of Pardons and Paroles before an inmate is released on parole;

(14) to the extent provided by Articles 56.06 and 56.065, for a victim of a sexual assault, the right to a forensic medical examination if, within 96 hours of the sexual assault, the assault is reported to a law enforcement agency or a forensic medical examination is otherwise conducted at a health care facility; and

(15) for a victim of an assault or sexual assault who is younger than 17 years of age or whose case involves family violence, as defined by Section 71.004, Family Code, the right to have the court consider the impact on the victim of a continuance requested by the defendant; if requested by the attorney representing the state or by counsel for the defendant, the court shall state on the record the reason for granting or denying the continuance.

Tex. Code Crim. Proc. 56.02(a) (emphasis supplied).

2   'A Walk Through the System', Texas Department of Criminal Justice, (offering support in 'Victim witness screening and preparation prior to viewing an execution').

3   See, e.g., Richard Burr, 'Expanding the Horizons of Capital Defense: Why Defense Teams Should Be Concerned About Victims and Survivors', *The Champion*, Dec. 2006, at 44, 45 ('[A murder] puts the killer in the position of having information that the survivors need to know to be able to live without continually imagining what happened, why, and how death came to their loved one. The act of taking another's life also creates an obligation to the survivors. The killer has taken something of irreplaceable value from the survivors, and he is obliged to make up for that somehow – to restore in some way that is meaningful the loss that has been inflicted'); Jody Lynee Madeira, 'Ties Out of Bloodshed: Collective Memory, Cultural Trauma, and the Prosecution and Execution of Timothy McVeigh', (Indiana University School of Law, Bloomington, Research Paper No. 91 (Oct. 2007), available at http://papers.ssrn.com/sol3/papers. cfm?abstract_id=1005271 (describing the connections fostered between Timothy McVeigh and the families of those who died in the 1995 Oklahoma City bombing); Pamela B. Leonard, 'All but Death can be Adjusted: Recognizing Victims' Needs in Death Penalty Litigation', *The Champion* (Dec. 2006) ('Restorative justice, like the victims' rights movement, gained prominence in the 1970s. However, its historical roots are at least as old as recorded conflict. Advocates of restorative justice view crime as a "fundamental disruption of individual and community relationships that is best addressed by focusing on the needs of the victim and by probing the moral, social, economic and political aspects of the offense." Crime is a violation of people and relationships that creates obligations to make things right. In order to

move toward making things right, victims must have the opportunity to identify and speak their needs and the offender must do what she or he can to address those needs').

4   I am painfully aware that the publication of this book may only add to the Moo Young family's grief. It is not my place to speak for them, and indeed I cannot even attempt to do justice to the story of their suffering, as I have been told by the Assistant States Attorney that any approach I might make to them to hear their views, or share information that we have developed, would be considered harassment. All I can say is that if the courts had ever given Kris Maharaj a full hearing, this book would not need to have been written.

5   *Statement of A to the Clemency Board*, Jan. 4th, 2007. (044_137794) (statements made anonymous by author).

6   *Statement of B to the Clemency Board* (044_137778).

7   *Statement of D to the Clemency Board*, Jan. 3rd, 2007. (044_139690); see also *Statement of D to the Clemency Board*, Jan. 3rd, 2007. (044_139692) ('I pray for Chris that he will accept the punishment he earned and so gain God's mercy').

8   *Statement of D to the Clemency Board*, Jan. 3rd, 2007. (044_139690); see also *Letter of E to ASA Sally Weintraub*, Jan. 4th, 2007. (044_139684) ('My family has endured so much emotionally that people on the outside cannot see what we have gone through. We are all emotionally scarred, one of my sisters is very paranoid, and we have become a dysfunctional family in my eyes').

9   *Statement of F to the Clemency Board* (044_139686).

10   Reprieve investigators interviewed Ms Kurland on July 16th, 2011, as part of the work on a Texas case. Ms Kurland is one of the only victims in Texas who has been able to meet the person who killed her loved one.

11   See Ken Camp, 'Two Mothers fund grace to forgive the men who killed their daughters', Texas Baptist Communications (April 21st, 1999), http://www.baptiststandard.com/1999/4_21/pages/mothers.html.

12   Texas law provides for the training of mediation facilitators. *Tex. Code Crim. Pro. Art. 56.13* ('The victim services division of the Texas Department of Criminal Justice shall: (1) train volunteers to act as mediators between victims, guardians of victims, and close relatives of deceased victims and offenders whose criminal conduct caused bodily injury or death to victims; and (2) provide mediation services through referral of a trained volunteer, if requested by a victim, guardian of a victim, or close relative of a deceased victim').

13   See Victim Offender Mediation/Dialogue, 'Frequently Asked Questions', at http://www.tdcj.state.tx.us/faq/faq-victim-vomd.htm (accessed Sep. 10th, 2011).

14   http://www.mvfr.org/.

15   I later came to know Rais well, because our charity helped to represent Mark Ströman, the person who tried to kill him.

16   Timothy Williams, 'The Hated and the Hater: Both Touched by Crime', *New York Times* (July 18th, 2011), at http://www.nytimes.com/2011/07/19/us/19questions.html?pagewanted=all (accessed Sep. 11, 2001).

17   Williams, *The Hated and the Hater*.

18   Paradoxically this racism could have saved Mark Ströman's life. Under Texas law he could not have been executed for murder alone: in this case, the crime had to be committed in the course of another felony – an armed robbery – yet this was not the reason for the offence. The prosecution went to trial first on the Patel murder, as it was the one where the racial motive was least clear, even though no money was taken from the store.

19   *Defendants' Answer, Affirmative Defenses and Motion to Dismiss*, at 11, *Bhuiyan v. Perry*, Travis County Civil District Court No. 1:11-CV-00603 (July 18th, 2011) ('The convicting court entered an order which prohibited Stroman from having any contact with Plaintiff. In essence, Plaintiff – the victim – is making a collateral attack on the validity of the convicting court's order prohibiting visitation contact by Stroman with him').

20   Reprieve worked closely with Lydia Brandt on Mark Ströman's final appeal. Reprieve had become involved in the case at a late date when his links with Germany emerged.

21   Williams, *The Hated and the Hater*.

22   Three weeks before the scheduled execution, on June 29th, 2011, Rais Bhuiyan made a specific request to appear in person before the Clemency Board:

> (a) that the Board set this matter for a full hearing at a time and a location convenient to the Board, pursuant to Rule 143.43(f)(3) of the Board's rules of procedure; and,
>
> (b) that the Board allow Rais Bhuiyan to appear before it to state his position and the position of other victims with respect to commutation ...

Clemency Petition on behalf of Mark Ströman, at 23 (June 29th, 2011).

23   See http://articles.sfgate.com/2002-11-26/news/17570762_1_crime-incidents-crime-victims-african-americans (FBI statistics).

24   Qur'an 5:32.

25   Qur'an 42:40. See also Qur'an 5:45 ('And we prescribed for them therein: The life for the life, and the eye for the eye, and the nose for

the nose, and the ear for the ear, and the tooth for the tooth, and for wounds retaliation. But whoso forgoeth it in the way of charity it shall be expiation for him').

26   'A crime victim has the following rights: (1) the right to be treated with fairness and with respect for the victim's dignity and privacy throughout the criminal justice process.' Tex. Const. Art. 1, §30(a)(1).

27   See http://www.texansforequaljustice.org/docs/cvrw11.pdf.

28   On April 9th, 2009, Governor Perry issued a statement concerning his perspective on the federal courts:

> Gov. Rick Perry today joined state Rep. Brandon Creighton and spon-sors of House Concurrent Resolution (HCR) 50 in support of states' rights under the 10th Amendment to the U.S. Constitution. 'I believe that our federal government has become oppressive in its size, its intru-sion into the lives of our citizens, and its interference with the affairs of our state'.

See http://governor.state.tx.us/news/press-release/12227/. In advocat-ing his states' rights stance, on the same day Gov. Perry went on:

> I believe the Constitution does not empower the federal to override state laws without restraint. I agree with Texas' 7th governor, Sam Houston, who once said, 'Texas has yet to learn submission to any oppression, come from what source it may.' We didn't like oppression then and we certainly don't like it now. I believe the federal government has become oppressive in its size, its intrusion into the lives of our citizens, and its interference with the affairs of our state. Texans need to ask themselves a question: do they side with those in Washington who are pursuing this unprecedented expansion of power? Or do they believe in the individual rights and responsibilities laid out in our foundational documents? Tex-ans need to stand up and be heard, because this state of affairs cannot continue indefinitely.

'Gov. Perry Speaks in Support of States' Rights', Austin, Texas (April 9th, 2009), http://governor.state.tx.us/news/speech/12228/; see also Kathleen McKinley, 'Texas Sparkle: Will Governor Perry Run for President?' (July 2011), http://blog.chron.com/texassparkle/2011/07/will-governor-perry-run-for-president/ ('Perry is also a staunch advo-cate of states' rights, and of a limited role for the federal government. These two things are rallying cries of the Tea Party').

29   *Defendants' Supplemental Memorandum Of Law In Support Of Defendants' Motion To Dismiss*, at 8–9, filed in *Bhuiyan v. Perry* et al., Civil Action No. 1:11-CV-00603 (W.D.Tex. July 19th, 2011), citing *Martinez v. Texas Dept. of Criminal Justice*, 300 F.3d 567, 575 (5th Cir.

2002) (claiming Gov. Perry had 'immunity [against being] sued in federal court for state-law claims. The State of Texas did not waive its Eleventh Amendment Immunity to suit in federal court for this type of claim').

30   See *Defendants' Answer, Affirmative Defenses and Motion to Dismiss*, at 12, *Bhuiyan v. Perry*, Travis County Civil District Court No. 1:11-CV-00603 (July 18th, 2011) ('Even though Art. 56.13 suggests that TDCJ "shall … provide mediation services" as described in Art. 56.02, it is undeniable that a crime victim such as Plaintiff has a right to *request* victim–offender mediation; he does not have a right to *have* victim–offender mediation. In any case, the "right" is essentially symbolic where Art. 56.02(d) effectively eliminates any recourse in the event the "right" is denied').

31   Williams, *The Hated and the Hater*.

17

Getting Closer

1   *Fla. Stat. § 837.02(2)* defines perjury in a capital case as a second-degree felony, which is punishable by at least fifteen years in prison or, with certain enhancements, thirty years. See *Fla. Stat. § 775.083, 083, 084*.

2   *Fla. Stat. § 914.22(2)(e)* provides that witness tampering in a capital case is punishable by *life in prison*.

3   In 1974, the Jamaican government introduced some draconian laws in an effort to stamp out violence with firearms. Under the Firearms Act, for importing ammunition into Jamaica illegally, Geddes 'on conviction before a Circuit Court [was liable] to imprisonment for life with or without hard labour.' Firearms Act of Jamaica, §4(2)(b)(2), available at http://www.moj.gov.jm/laws/statutes/The%20Firearms%20Act.pdf (accessed Sep. 5th, 2010). Furthermore, his case could have been heard before one of the so-called Gun Courts, which severely restricted his legal rights, and his right to appeal. See Gun Court Act of Jamaica, available at http://www.moj.gov.jm/laws/statutes/The%20Gun%20Court%20Act.pdf (accessed Sep. 5th, 2010).

4   Geddes also admitted in his interviews with British journalists that shortly before he testified at Kris' trial he was arrested for drunk driving in Miami. The prosecutors had arranged for him simply to pay a fine, he said. When we search the driving records we found that he received his Florida license on June 12th, 1986, and the record was

totally clean: so whatever happened seems to have been expunged altogether from his record.

5   These are not the real names of the Shower Posse members. I have rendered them anonymous because the investigation continues, and I do not want to burn our limited entrée into the Jamaican underworld. I hope that further information will be forthcoming. These names are not atypical, though: in a recent wanted notice, the nicknames of gang members included Dutch, Winter Fresh, Popcorn and Cornflakes. See *St James Police releases most wanted list*, RJR News (Jan. 3rd, 2010), http://rjrnewsonline.com/local/st-james-police-releases-most-wanted-list.

18
Getting Even Closer

1   For a good discussion of all the issues surrounding the law enforcement crisis of the early 1980s in Miami, see Kim Michelle Lersch, *Drug Related Police Corruption: The Miami Experience*, Article 10, in Michael J. Palmiotto, *Police Misconduct: A Reader for the 21st Century* (Prentice Hall, 2001). I have drawn many of the facts in the subsequent pages from this article.

2   This comes from a 'source close to the investigation' of the River Cop Scandal, *Miami Herald*, May 15th, 1987.

3   *The Christian Science Monitor*, May 7th, 1987.

4   Others included Robert Gonzalez (a Division Chief), who apparently used to obtain search warrants in order to facilitate drugs rip-offs from rival gangs; Raymond Casamayor (Key West Deputy Police Chief), who was arrested on drugs charges in 1987; Walter Martinez (Deputy Chief), who was appointed to his role despite investigations into bribery and misconduct; and Rudy Arias, Officer of the Month and slated to be named Officer of the Year. See Larry Sherman, *New York Times*, Aug. 3rd, 1986; *Los Angeles Times*, Oct. 6th, 1986; *Miami Herald*, Dec. 17th, 1987; *Miami Herald*, Nov. 28th, 1988; *Miami Herald*, Sep. 10th, 1989; *Miami Herald*, Jan. 26th, 1990; K.M. Lersch, p.141.

5   K.M. Lersch, *supra*, p.141.

6   Captain Judith Bennett, Miami Police, *Los Angeles Times*, Oct. 6th, 1986.

7   For example, in the 'Hot Suits Case', Assistant State Attorney John

Hogan was involved in turning over stolen brand-name clothes.

8   To mention just a few who made it into the newspapers, in 1985, Dan Mitrione, an FBI Agent based in Miami, was charged with drug dealing and other associated offences, *Associated Press*, Oct. 19th, 1985; Raul Puig, a member of the SIS, destroyed evidence to help protect drug dealers and traffickers and would later play an active role in Oscar Cantu's drugs conspiracy, *Miami Herald*, Nov. 28th, 1988; Roger Schow, a DEA Agent based in Miami, cooperated with drugs traffickers and dealers in accepting bribes to provide copies of secret reports about suspected drugs traffickers, *Associated Press*, Oct. 19th, 1985; and Jorge Manresa and Jorge Lopez, both former narcotics detectives, who were convicted of 'shooting up' the house of drug dealer Carlos Quesada and of destroying evidence to protect other criminals. *Miami Herald*, Dec. 4th, 1989.

9   *Miami Herald*, Nov. 17th, 1987. See generally Byron York, *Alcee Hastings, Bribery, and the House Intelligence Committee* (National Review Online, Nov. 17th, 2006), http://www.nationalreview.com/articles/219278/alcee-hastings-bribery-and-house-intelligence-committee/byron-york#. In an example of rehabilitation that is atypical, Hastings later ran for, and won, a US Congressional seat.

10   No charges have been brought against Prado and there seems to have been no official investigation into the journalist's shocking assertions. See Evan Wright, *How to Get Away with Murder in America* (Byliner, 2012).

11   For the Pardo story, see *Miami Herald*, Jan. 22nd, 1985; *Miami Herald*, Feb. 28th, 1985; *Miami Herald*, Jun. 12th, 1986; *Miami Herald*, Mar. 31st, 1988. In a final, written statement prior to his execution, he denied the charges involving three women, but accepted that he had murdered the six men. 'I don't want this hanging over my head,' he wrote, 'especially in these last few minutes of life, because my war was against men who were trafficking in narcotics, and no one else.' He said he had done the world a favour by killing them. At his trial, he had gone even further. Over the objection of his defence attorney, who deemed him insane, Pardo insisted on testifying, telling jurors that he enjoyed killing people and wished he could have murdered more. 'They're parasites and they're leeches, and they have no right to be alive,' he said in court. 'Somebody had to kill these people.' In addition to his mental problems, his lawyer argued that he was a product of the lawless, cocaine cowboys-fuelled zeitgeist of 1980s Miami.

12   Years later, I did have a moment's satisfaction when I read that the federal government had finally taken action and entered a consent decree effectively taking over the New Orleans Police Department.

The US Justice Department announced: 'On May 15, 2010, we opened an investigation of the New Orleans Police Department (NOPD) pursuant to the Violent Crime Control and Law Enforcement Act of 1994, the Omnibus Crime Control and Safe Streets Act of 1968 and Title VI of the Civil Rights Act of 1964. Following a comprehensive investigation, on March 17, 2011, we announced our findings. We found that the NOPD has engaged in patterns of misconduct that violate the Constitution and federal law, including a pattern or practice of excessive force, and of illegal stops, searches, and arrests. We found also a pattern or practice of gender discrimination in the Department's under-enforcement and under-investigation of violence against women. We further found strong indications of discriminatory policing based on racial, ethnic, and LGBT bias, as well as a failure to provide critical police services to language minority communities. On July 24, 2012, we reached a settlement resolving our investigation and asked the Court to make our settlement an order enforceable by the Court. The documents on this page provide more information about the investigation, the Justice Department's findings, settlement, and next steps.' See http://www. justice.gov/crt/about/spl/nopd.php. Despite this, though, the Feds were not addressing the worst sins of the NOPD – framing innocent people for capital crimes.

13   In case anyone has the urge to commit crimes against my witnesses, I should make clear that their testimony has already been reduced to evidentiary formats in order to neutralise such offences.

14   Cuni had a long history in the drug world. He had been convicted on one federal drug charge in the 1980s. See *United States v. Cuni*, 11 Fed. R. Evid. Serv. 1524 (11th Cir, 1982). Some details of Cuni's broader conspiracy – and some of his Miami police confederates – appear in *United States v. Novaton et al.*, No. 95-4445 (11th Cir. Oct. 30th, 2001). Three officers were indicted alongside Cuni in this case, including one Luis Sarmiento, who would keep him apprised of any police investigations in exchange for a periodic 'comma' – narco-speak for $1,000. See *Three Miami Officers Assisted Drug Ring, DEA Says, LA Times* (Dec. 14th, 1993). In line with local practice at the time, Sarmiento may well have been one of the 'local relatives' of Jose Sarmiento, who was convicted alongside F. Nigel Bowe, the Bahamian lawyer who worked with Adam Hosein and the Moo Youngs.

15   *Tragic Pasts Converge In Cafeteria Killings*, Joan Fleischman, *Miami Herald* Final Edition, Local News Section, Nov. 10th, 1988.

16   Another lawyer involved in the investigation had contacted the office of the Miami Dade State Attorney, asking whether they were

interested in investigating a score of unsolved murders in their city. She called twice and was told, each time, to leave a message outlining what she had to say. She was promised a prompt reply. She never received a return call.

Index

www.vintage-books.co.uk